D1383323

The Necessary Peace

The Necessary Peace

Nuclear Weapons and
Superpower Relations

Donald M. Snow
University of Alabama

Lexington Books
D.C. Heath and Company/Lexington, Massachusetts/Toronto

Library of Congress Cataloging-in-Publication Data

Snow, Donald M., 1943–
  The necessary peace.

  Bibliography: p.
  Includes index.
  1. United States—Foreign relations—Soviet Union.
  2. Soviet Union—Foreign relations—United States.
  3. Nuclear disarmament—Soviet Union.   4. Nuclear
disarmament—United States.   I. Title.
JX1428.S65S56   1987   327.73047   86–46293
ISBN 0–669–15332–X (alk. paper)

Published simultaneously in Canada
Printed in the United States of America
Casebound International Standard Book Number: 0–669–15332–X
Library of Congress Catalog Card Number 86–46293

The paper used in this publication meets the minimum requirements of
American National Standard for Information Sciences—Permanence of
Paper for Printed Library Materials, ANSI Z39.48–1984. ∞™

87 88 89 90 91 8 7 6 5 4 3 2 1

Contents

Preface and Acknowledgments

The fundamental purpose of this book is to assert and defend the proposition that the truly revolutionary impact of nuclear weapons on international relations and, more specifically, U.S.–Soviet relationships has been their stabilizing and tranquilizing effect. Both dreadfully fearful of the outcome of a nuclear war between them, the superpowers have treated one another with an extreme caution which has made war between them far less likely than would have been the case in the absence of nuclear weapons.

The result of this phenomenon is the "necessary peace," which has become more enduring and stable as time has gone by and weapons have become more lethal. But with the accompanying weapons balance, the world has indeed become simultaneously more deadly and less dangerous, a situation considerably more satisfactory than many doomsayers would admit. Given this situation, those who would propose basic change have the burden of demonstrating that the changes they propose would not undermine the stabilizing components of the necessary peace.

The organization of the book follows from this construction. Part I consists of two chapters that describe the current situation. Chapter 1 lays out how nuclear weapons have altered world politics, and chapter 2 describes the dynamics of U.S.–Soviet relationships and the stability they have achieved. Part II looks at what the author views as those trends currently on the horizon that are most likely to have an impact on the dynamics of a stable system. In each case, the basic question is whether proposed changes will improve or detract from the ongoing situation. Thus, chapter 3 looks at President Reagan's vision of a defense-dominant world, while chapter 4 examines Mikhail Gorbachev's apparent interest in a nuclear-disarmed world. Chapter 5 explores how these goals might be compromised to reinforce the necessary peace. Part III concludes the book with a single chapter that seeks to integrate the conclusions from the preceding and to show how the stabilizing dynamics of the necessary peace can be applied to the future.

The research and writing of this book occurred while I was Secretary of the Navy (SECNAV) Senior Research Fellow at the U.S. Naval War College, Newport, Rhode Island. While neither the Naval War College nor the Department of the Navy bear responsibility or provide sanction for the opinions expressed in these pages, I am grateful for the generous support provided by the SECNAV program. More specifically, I wish to thank Mrs. Barbara E. Atkins for her superb typing and administrative support and Mrs. Mary Guimond for her help in battling the Navy bureaucracy. Final manuscript preparation and production occurred upon my return to the University of Alabama, and I wish to thank the Department of Political Science, its chairman, Harvey F. Kline, and staff members Mrs. Mary L. Carlson and Mrs. Phyllis M. Barnes for their assistance. Finally, I want to thank my editor, Ms. Jaime Welch-Donahue, for her support and encouragement.

Part I
The Current Balance

1
Nuclear Weapons and International Relations

The "nuclear age" has now spanned slightly over forty years. Since the first test firing at the Trinity site in New Mexico in July 1945, the world's arsenal of fission and fusion munitions has grown from one to around 50,000. The world has known nuclear disarmament for only a brief period after August 9, 1945, when the U.S. detonation of a nuclear device over Nagasaki temporarily depleted the arsenal. In the ensuing years, the number of admitted nuclear-weapons–possessing states has grown from one (the United States) to five (due to the addition of the Soviet Union, Britain, France, and the People's Republic of China). Others such as Israel and India are widely suspected of possessing the capability, and a rogues gallery of other states (South Africa, Iran, Iraq, and Libya, for example) seem poised on the verge of eligibility for membership in the nuclear weapons "club."

Have nuclear weapons made a difference in the international relations of the second half of the twentieth century? If they have had an impact, what has it been? There is remarkable agreement that they have made a difference, and the descriptions typically are expansive; we talk of things such as "nuclear revolution" that has produced a "balance of terror" in which we survive. At the same time, there is far less agreement about *what* difference nuclear weapons have made.

Do nuclear weapons make the world a better or a worse place? At one level, it is a bad question or at least a loaded one, because it is hard to imagine weapons capable of indiscriminately incinerating sizable proportions of mankind being "good" and thus producing a "better" world than would be the case in their absence. The problem is in defining "better," and it is a definitional tangle enlivening the entire debate over nuclear weaponry.

The question suggests a hierarchy of values that are neither necessarily sequential nor mutually consistent. Certainly a primary notion of a better world is one where those weapons are not used in anger. In that regard, Thomas Schelling points out that "we have what ought to be an important source of reassurance, a 'confidence-building' experience: 40 years of nuclear weapons without nuclear war."[1] The further question that this minimum value raises is whether the sheer absence of nuclear war is comfort enough or whether a "better" world requires more. In turn, a judgment on this score requires assessing both whether the current situation is stable (defined as a low, and hopefully lowering, probability of nuclear war) or unstable (a delicate balance where nuclear war is less improbable or even probable) and what the world would be like were nuclear weapons removed from international relations.

There are two basic positions on these questions, each of which, of course, has variations. At one extreme are those who believe that a world of nuclear weapons is an insidious, malevolent place and that "nuclear weapons radically alter our existence. . . . The threat they pose has become the context of our lives."[2] The result, in Robert Jay Lifton and Richard Falk's terms, is something called nuclearism, where the existence of nuclear weapons creates a dependency forcing all sorts of political, economic, and social problems to be conditioned by their relationship to these weapons. Moreover, "the reality that the delicate balance of terror cannot endure forever"[3] assumes an unstable world order. In quite elegant terms, the result is an increasing likelihood of nuclear war: "Nothing prepares this country for apocalypse, yet it tends toward it, drawn steadily 'forward' by the seductive virulence of a nuclear destiny."[4]

The image created by this depiction is one where nuclear war, which would be catastrophic in all senses of the word,[5] is just a matter of time, because the nuclear balance is inherently unstable. A world of nuclear weapons thus cannot be a "better" world by definition, and *denuclearization,* to use Lifton and Falk's term, is the mandate. The ultimate goal is to rid the world of all nuclear weapons, but it will not be an easy task. In the most extreme formulation, no less than the transformation of the international system is required, because the current system's values are beyond reform. As Falk and Lifton put it, "Complete nuclear disarmament is not really plausible so long as leaders hold a Machiavellian world picture. . . . [W]ar, in general, not nuclear weapons in isolation, must become the inevitable focus for any serious effort to overcome *nuclearism.* . . . To get rid of war, however, requires a new type of world order."[6] Even if the argument is not carried to this extreme conclusion, the view of nuclear weapons as a dangerous, destabilizing influence leads to the judgment that a better world necessarily involves moving toward their elimination.

This is not, of course, the only conclusion that can be drawn about the role of nuclear weapons on the international system. Rather, the central thesis developed in the pages that follow is that because nuclear weapons have made the world such a potentially deadly place, the superpowers have been forced to exercise considerable and growing restraint in their relations to ensure that they do not slide into a nuclear exchange both consider unthinkable. As Robert Jervis states it, "Nuclear weapons create an unprecedented common interest between the two adversaries. Their fates are linked together—for the fate of each is in the hands of the other—in a way that was never true in the past."[7] The result is a common interest—avoiding mutual incineration—that would not otherwise dilute whatever antagonisms exist between them. While it is true that "it would be difficult to think of two great powers with less to fight about,"[8] historically, there have nevertheless been ample points of conflict that could have brought the two countries to blows. Fear that coming to blows could lead to nuclear holocaust leavens the relationship, and that leavening has acted progressively to ameliorate differences. Put another way, as the world has become more lethal (i.e., the deadly consequences of nuclear war have increased), the superpowers have been forced to act to make the world less dangerous (i.e., to lower the likelihood that war will occur).

What has evolved is an increasingly stable nuclear balance where the very weight of the balance creates and reinforces stability. In that balance, "U.S. and Soviet strategic forces are not in delicate balance over a sharp fulcrum. Instead they are counterpoised on a broad base,"[9] with the result that "the nuclear equilibrium has successfully deterred World War III."[10] The resulting relationship has a number of characteristics at odds with the more apocalyptic world view of nuclear weapons, which is not without virtue: "The superpowers have not engaged one another's forces in combat; they have not threatened each other's vital interests; and they have not used nuclear weapons against anyone. These rules represent a restraint of antagonism that should be recognized, enhanced, and extended."[11]

The nuclear world that has evolved more or less consciously has become one of increasing stability in the central relationship between the two superpowers. It is a relationship born of fear of the consequences of direct confrontation, not of trust. Neither side knows or can know with certainty what the result of their coming to blows would be. The possibility that a confrontation could devolve to nuclear war that both believe would have unacceptable consequences adds caution to the relationship, while limiting and defining the competition in ways that might well not adhere if the weapons did not exist. The deadliness of nuclear weapons demands that superpower relations be more controlled (less dangerous) and that the conflicts of interest that inevitably arise between the world's two most ideologically opposed powers be channeled in ways that minimize the prospects of direct clash, a necessary peace. As Robbin Laird and Dale Herspring describe this phenomenon,

> By avoiding direct conflict with the United States the Soviet Union clearly isolates Third World military actions from questions of general U.S.–Soviet military and especially nuclear confrontation." . . . [This situation] has increased the significance of the effort to create usable military power, i.e., military below the strategic threshold.[12]

The result is an arms competition carried on virtually for its own sake and quite apart from any intention to use military power against the other. As Laurence Martin says, "In the zones stabilized by nuclear deterrence, the military balance remains for that very reason a more continually absorbing preoccupation than in most if not all previous historical periods."[13]

The idea that nuclear weapons stabilize rather than destabilize that part of international relations affecting and affected by the superpowers and their affiliates seems initially paradoxical. The anomaly of the assertion is captured in the notion of the *security dilemma,* the idea that security is the result of maintaining weapons that, if ever used, absolutely threaten that security, and, indeed, survival itself. Yet, that is the way it is. The very deadliness of the weapons lessens the likelihood they will be used, at least as long as people recognize those consequences. Conversely, lowering that deadliness—ultimately to zero through nuclear disarmament—could lower inhibitions to fight and thereby decrease security, if reducing somewhat the physical characteristics of the insecurity it creates.

That the balance is stable and becoming more so is not universally accepted, especially by those who adhere to the belief that nuclear disarmament is necessary. A. Krass, for instance, points to "the deep contradictions inherent in the notion of a stable nuclear balance. The essence of the contradiction is this: to the extent that a nuclear balance is truly necessary it must be unstable, and to the extent the balance is genuinely stable it is unnecessary."[14] The basis of this assertion is the mutual existence of political conflict that creates the basis for instability and nuclear weapons. This argument posits a causal relationship between the two: conflict justifies the weaponry, which only becomes unneeded if there is no conflict. This hypothesis ignores the possibility that the weaponry might exist quite apart from conflict or, as argued here, that the weaponry mutes the conflict. Krass concludes, however, "either we will have nuclear disarmament or we will have continued preparations for nuclear war. The preparations may go on for a long time without the war actually occurring, but history has shown that preparation for war almost invariably ends in war."[15] Arms lead to war, in other words, except when they don't.

Nuclear weapons balance has not always had a stabilizing influence. Rather, the relationship has evolved over time, so that describing that evolution is the initial task. Since the principal dynamic of this stabilization is fear of the consequences of nuclear war, then examining what causes and maintains that fear is necessary. Finally, since this is a less than orthodox interpretation of the role nuclear weapons play, some attempt will be made to demonstrate that the dynamic is recognized and activates the operation of the nuclear relationship.

The Evolving Role

The basic ideas about how nuclear weapons should be treated were established very early in the nuclear age, although those formulations were not clearly incorporated at the operational levels of strategy until the 1950s and 1960s, when technology reshaped arsenals and the ways in which they had to be viewed. The basic ideas and concerns, however, were outlined in two remarkable books published in 1946, a year after the first successful atomic bomb explosion.

Both books dealt with interrelated problems that have formed the core of the debate over deterrence and declaratory nuclear strategy ever since. At the heart of that debate have been the questions of how nuclear war might be fought and, thus, what kinds of targets one should aim at with nuclear weapons. Answers to those questions in turn define the horror of a nuclear war and, thus, the importance of avoiding such a war (*deterrence*).

In 1946, of course, the deterrence question was a simple matter of U.S. self-restraint in the use of the nuclear arsenal only it possessed. The arsenal was quite small anyway (about thirty bombs), a fact that may help explain why the two books had no more impact at the time than they did. The more famous of the two was a series of essays, symbolically titled *The Absolute Weapon,* and edited by Bernard Brodie. In his own considerable contribution, Brodie argued that a future war would be disastrous because of the qualitative difference introduced by these new weapons and, thus, deterrence must be the primary value of the future. The book is best known for his entreaty that while the purpose of military force in the past had been to fight wars, in the future that purpose must be to deter them.[16] Brodie's ideas were revived in the late 1950s, when deterrence became an important concern because of Soviet development of the intercontinental ballistic missile (ICBM). Implicit in the horror to be avoided was the notion that a nuclear war would involve attacks on urban targets (what became known as *countervalue targeting*), a logical extension of the World War II experience with strategic bombardment.

The far less well known book (also published in 1946) took a different tack. Because William Borden's *There Will Be No Time* has until recently escaped public notice, it is worth discussing here. First, Borden felt that the enormous destructive power of nuclear weapons would reorient targeting and the purposes of war away from the World War II pattern. "Victory in another conflict will not depend on destruction of civilians but on quick elimination of the opponent's forces and stockpiles in being," he argued in a premonition of what became known as *counterforce targeting*. This would reorient the nature of war as well: "The trend is toward a return to eighteenth century warfare and the classical principles of Karl von Clausewitz, because once again the key to victory lies in defeating hostile military forces."[17] He argued that war, including nuclear war, might be limited in its conduct, but he also foresaw another development that would play a pivotal role in the nuclear evolution. "The bomb has attracted the lion's share of publicity but . . . [t]he future of air power must inevitably merge with the future of V-2s, those wingless, bullet-shaped missiles which hurtle through the upper air at ten times the speed of a Superfortress."[18] Borden was, of course, predicting the decisive role of the ICBM, even if he underestimated its performance characteristics.

Borden and Brodie in tandem framed the nuclear debate as it has existed ever since in the United States. Reading the two books is humbling for anyone who believes new ideas are plentiful in the world. From Brodie, one can trace much of the argument that underlies thought on assured destruction; much of the underpinning for philosophies on limited nuclear options can be extracted from Borden. Their impact, however, is more fully felt in thinking about nuclear weapons and the international order now than it was at the time these books first appeared.

Early thinking about nuclear weapons in government and at operational levels did not reflect these ideas closely. Partly this was the result of the availability of the weapons and delivery abilities of the time. In 1946, for instance, the arsenal consisted of only a handful of weapons which were very difficult to construct[19] and for which the United States had a very questionable delivery capability against any Soviet resistance[20] (a problem made more difficult by the lack of good maps of Soviet targets, some of these maps dating back to Tsarist Russia). This situation began to improve in 1948, when the SANDSTONE tests demonstrated "that it [the Atomic Energy Commission] could mass-produce atomic weapons by using the 'levitation technique.'"[21]

The great problem that U.S. foreign policy faced in the immediate postwar period was deterring a Soviet Union with whom it was increasingly obvious the wartime collaboration would not continue. The major military threat was a Soviet attack against a Western Europe weakened by the war to the point of being incapable of self-defense. This risk was heightened by the rapid demobilization after the war that was typical of the United States. The only "hole card" available was nuclear weapons. As Krass explains, "The atomic bomb seemed to most U.S. policymakers to fit the needs of U.S. national and military strategy perfectly. The unprecedented power of this weapon . . . allowed the USA to make threats . . . against the USSR for which the Soviets had no comparable reply."[22] Although in retrospect it seems clear any such threats were at least partially hollow, Communist sources appear to have taken them quite seriously: "Atomic bombs were designated not only and not so much to intimidate Japan. They were tested in order to target them later on socialism."[23]

The absence of a parallel Soviet capability obviated the need for developing a nuclear strategy. Monopoly meant that U.S. superiority defined the nuclear component of U.S.–Soviet relations. The circumstance was shattered by the dual hammer blows of the "fall" of mainland China to the Communists and the first successful Soviet atomic bomb test in 1949. These events helped President Truman to decide in favor of going forward with the controversial plan to develop the hydrogen (fusion) bomb[24] and to look at the future of

Soviet–U.S. relations.[25] One result was the famous NSC-68 policy document that provided the first comprehensive assessment of the Soviet threat; a series of operational plans was also developed:

As early as August 1950 and certainly by 1952, the Joint Chiefs of Staff had approved an emergency war plan for the Strategic Air Command (SAC) which had three basic objectives, noted by code names:

BRAVO: the blunting of Soviet capability to deliver an atomic offensive against the United States and its allies;

DELTA: the disruption of vital elements of the Soviet war-making capacity;

ROMEO: the slowing of Soviet advances into Western Eurasia.[26]

As a matter of reference for future discussions, it should be noted that these targeting directions concentrated on military (counterforce) rather than urban-industrial (countervalue) targets. They were also not unambiguously retaliatory plans.

The 1950s witnessed considerable evolution in views about the role of nuclear weapons. In the early 1950s, the Eisenhower "massive retaliation" strategy assigned paramount responsibility for deterring Soviet provocations across the spectrum of threat to nuclear weapons by threatening to strike "at times and in places of our choosing" should the Soviets commit acts of aggression. As long as the U.S. bomber-based ability to deliver nuclear weapons against the Soviet homeland was unmatched by a comparable Soviet capability, the threat was arguably credible.[27]

As presaged by Borden's book, the ICBM upset this assessment. Because there was no practical defense against ballistically delivered nuclear-armed missiles, Soviet demonstration of ICBM capability in 1957 and subsequent deployment of intercontinental range missiles left U.S. soil at direct risk. The inability to deflect a nuclear attack meant that the only way to avoid the devastation of the American homeland was to avoid nuclear war altogether. A "golden age" of thinking and writing about nuclear deterrence followed over the next decade or so, mostly centering on the evolution of declaratory strategy toward the idea of assured destruction as first suggested by Brodie (while targeting strategy remained largely along the path of counterforce strategy Borden had considered). As Schelling recently summarized the question, "Since 1964 the correct name of the strategy is not 'assured mutual destruction' but assured *capability* for mutual destruction" (emphasis in original).[28]

What evolved was a situation of mutual vulnerability of the two superpowers to attacks by the other. The deadly balance was tilted heavily toward the United States during most of the 1960s until the Soviets' strategic program began to narrow and eventually erase the U.S. advantage. Although this was not the original intent of the program, the fielding of the multiple independently targetable reentry vehicle (MIRV)—first by the United States (1970) and subsequently by the Soviets—raised the deadly odds to something like their present levels.[29]

In this period prior to the early 1970s, two observations relevant to the relationship between nuclear weapons and superpower relations can be made. First, there were clearly periods either when nuclear weapons were viewed as usable weapons or when the threat of nuclear usage could confer advantage to the threatener. In other words, nuclear weapons were seen to have utility beyond deterrence. This attitude was especially evident during the period of U.S. nuclear weapons monopoly and sole possession of effective delivery capability. This perception faded as the Soviet Union achieved the ability to attack the United States with ICBM-delivered bombs; it became especially pronounced when the Soviets achieved "essential equivalence" in deadly abilities around 1970.

The other observation has to do with the pattern of superpower relations prior to and after the 1970s. The first quarter-century of superpower relations was conflictual and confrontational, with a series of direct conflicts between the two with escalatory potential. In all cases, of course, crises were deflected short of shooting war, but on numerous occasions, tensions were allowed to mount to nerve-wracking proportions, such as in the various Berlin crises and the Cuban missile crisis. Barry Blechman and Stephen Kaplan, for instance, surveyed the period between 1948 and 1978 for instances of crises with some escalatory potential.[30] They identified fifteen cases meeting their criteria; the most recent was the Yom Kippur (October) War of 1973 when the U.S. armed forces went on alert in response to Soviet threats to drop paratroopers into Sinai to prevent the destruction in detail of the Third Egyptian Army by the Israelis.

This change in the tone of superpower interactions has continued to the present. Since 1973, there has not been a single instance where an incident with the serious potential to escalate to a confrontation that might result in nuclear exchange has not been avoided altogether or defused at the lowest possible level of intensity. In places such as Europe (e.g., Berlin) where superpower vital interests are most clearly at stake, crises are simply not allowed to occur if there is any danger of confrontation. The Polish Solidarity crisis of 1981 is as close to an exception as one can find; but the precedents of Hungary and Czechoslovakia suggested the United States would not physically oppose application of the Brezhnev Doctrine—which asserts the Soviet "right" to assist Socialist states threatened by capitalist overthrow—there (any more than the Soviets physically opposed U.S. action in Grenada). Poland's crisis was resolved short of the imposition of potentially destabilizing Soviet military force there. In the potentially volatile 1979 Persian Gulf situation (as analysts were intoning gravely the prospects of World War III in light of the fall of the Shah of Iran), the 1979 Soviet invasion of Afghanistan, and the onset of the Iran–Iraq War in 1980,[31] the pattern of superpower actions has shown considerably more restraint than had been expected. Indeed, in 1986 Soviet leader Mikhail Gorbachev was hinting his desire to ameliorate the most provocative element in the area by announcing his intention to begin removing Soviet troops from Afghanistan, although the sincerity of his announcement has been viewed with some suspicion.

Why did the pattern of superpower relations change in the early 1970s? In the absence of direct observational knowledge of either Soviet or American decisionmakers and their motivations, one can only speculate and hypothesize. The hypothesis asserted here is that somewhere around the time the Soviets achieved parity in deadly effects in nuclear weaponry with the United States at very high levels of destruction, they determined conclusively that nuclear war must be avoided. Possibly stimulated by perceptions of the escalatory potential of the Yom Kippur confrontation (the one instance of a superpower conflict with sufficient political importance potentially to justify escalation), "In the fifth phase (1971–1984), the Soviets recognized that assured destruction of Soviet society would result from fighting an all-out nuclear war."[32] The time frame of this apparent judgment is the general period of the flowering of detente between the United States and the Soviet Union. As James Schlesinger points out, the effect of the Soviet conceptualization of detente is compatible with this determination: "For the Soviets, detente represented simply an updated variant of Leninist peaceful coexistence: an absence of direct military conflict between the major powers."[33]

As noted earlier, this formulation is not an orthodox interpretation of the role nuclear weapons play in superpower relations, but it is closer to standard interpretations in substance if not in emphasis than initially meets the eye. Except at the extremes, after all, virtually all serious observers agree that the prospect of there being a nuclear war volitionally begun by either superpower is remote and that the condition of mutual vulnerability has something to do with that low probability. Where there is some divergence is in the implications of that observation. The case being made here is that the condition of fear of nuclear war arising from the unacceptability of the consequences has in the past and continues progressively to stabilize superpower relations. Other interpretations have tended to emphasize the possibility that the system could fail, in which case it may be necessary and prudent to seek alterations in the dynamics to lessen the ensuing disaster. Unfortunately, as will be argued here, such "hedges" against the failure of deterrence may weaken the fabric of what deters and thus make failure more likely in a manner resembling a self-fulfilling prophecy.

Who is correct in all this? The perversity of deductive logic is such that the question cannot be answered conclusively short of reducing the argument to a tautology. In that circumstance, the best one can do is to proceed inductively, citing evidence supporting the proposition and attempting to invalidate contrary arguments. The remainder of this chapter will deal with the first task, looking at U.S. and Soviet support about the effects of nuclear balance on superpower relations.

U.S. Support

The notions of mutual societal vulnerability and the security dilemma that nuclear weapons create have always been difficult concepts to embrace. The use of a genocidal threat to underpin U.S. security[34] and the morality of basing conscious U.S. strategy on maintaining and reinforcing a system whose failure would maximize the suffering of otherwise innocent Americans and Russians have been sources of unease well captured in the Bishops' Pastoral Letter.[35] The incongruity and consequences of deterrence failure have formed a staple argument for those advocating a ballistic missile defense system such as President Reagan's Strategic Defense Initiative (SDI).[36]

Despite the problems associated with embracing vulnerability in the form of advocating assured destruction as a policy, the results are recognized. As Robert Jervis, possibly the leading advocate of this school of thought, asserts, "The ultimate threat that deters each from infringing on the other's vital interests is the fear that the result of the conflict will be the destruction of both societies," and this effect "exists as a fact, irrespective of policy."[37] The consequence of assured destruction thus emerges as a fact of strategic life should deterrence fail—a fact of which both sides are aware. As Klaus Knorr states the case, "Even though the superpowers do not follow deterrent strategies of Mutual Assured Destruction, mutual destruction is very likely to be the consequence of substantial nuclear hostilities between them."[38]

The condition of factual vulnerability is not only descriptive of the past quarter-century, it is likely to continue into the future: "This condition exists today and is likely to persist for the foreseeable future."[39] To those who find this condition frustrating, dangerous, or both and who would thus like to change that circumstance, there is a further admonition: "In short, whether we like it or not and with or without the most ambitious strategic defense Mutual Assured Destruction is here to stay, even if 'assured' has to be written with a lower-case 'a'. MAD is not in fact a doctrine at all. Rather, it is a fact of life."[40]

The determinism and even fatalism that these kinds of statements suggest are profoundly upsetting to many repulsed by vulnerability. The point, which is in basic agreement with the argument here, is that strategies can be devised on the basis of the very healthy fears that assured destruction as fact creates *without* ghoulishly devising plans to incinerate a maximum number of civilians. What is difficult for some is to distinguish between those who say vulnerability is a fact and those who say it is a virtue. The failure to do so results in distorted discussions. "Some who advocate this [assured destruction] policy like to think of it not as a policy, but a 'fact.' There is a . . . mountain of confusion in this assertion . . . The mountain is the conclusion that this is the way we *should* design and plan the use of nuclear weapons" (emphasis in original).[41] To some, this creates inconsistencies between U.S. war-fighting commitments and a suicidal nuclear strategy should it have to be carried out, as in a European conflict. As Keith Payne states this case, "There has been a clear schizophrenia in U.S. strategic thought and policy—it has accepted deterrence responsibilities that are incompatible with wholesale vulnerability and yet endorsed mutual vulnerability as stabilizing."[42]

This latter criticism misses the mark. Referring to U.S. NATO commitments, Payne implies that vulnerability compromises the will of the United States to carry out its responsibilities. That is not the point for two reasons. First, it suggests an "endorsement" of vulnerability as a matter of preference. It is no such endorsement. It *is* a statement of condition about which nothing can be done now or in the short-term future. Vulnerability *is*. Second, the quote (which is from an article whose purpose is to defend SDI) distorts the nature of the responsibility involved. If that purpose is to maximize deterrence (as the statement says), then that which deters most thoroughly—the fear of mutual destruction—is the most appropriate point of emphasis. If the responsibility is war fighting (which Payne does not say and which might actually be made more likely by alleviating vulnerability), then the statement may have merit. In other words, deterrence and vulnerability are compatible; war fighting and vulnerability are incompatible.

The result of mutual vulnerability is self-deterrence by the superpowers or, put another way, "The unprecedented damage nuclear weapons can do has produced an unprecedented prudence—what we have called the crystal ball effect."[43] McGeorge Bundy has called this same phenomenon "existential deterrence."[44] Its salutary and hopeful effects are captured with particular eloquence and force in a February 28, 1986 *Economist* (London) editorial: "The past 41 years suggest that nuclear weapons are not only a deterrent against other nuclear weapons, they are also a way of discouraging any sort of war from starting. . . . The invention of nuclear weapons has given man a historic opportunity to broaden the bounds of peace, as well as posing a fearful threat."[45]

The Soviet View

If it requires some intellectual gymnastics to accept vulnerability-driven fear as the prime factor underlying U.S. perceptions of the consequences of nuclear balance, it is far more difficult to believe that the Soviet Union accepts the same dynamic. This is partly because imputing parallelism runs the risk of resuscitating the ghost of earlier claims that Americans had "educated" the Soviets to acceptance of assured destruction during SALT I, a source of acute embarrassment by those who made the assertion during the 1970s. More forcefully, such an acceptance runs afoul of the "popular" image that the Soviets view nuclear weapons as just another link in the chain of armaments and that they are prepared to "fight, win, survive and recover" from such a conflict, to borrow from Richard Pipes's sensational depiction.[46]

Yet the evidence is that the Soviets also accept the unacceptability of nuclear war and the restrictions on superpower competition that flows from that realization. As one observer recently put it, "The unpredictability and uncontrollability of nuclear war . . . led to the third and present stage, in which the unwinnability of nuclear war, announced by Brezhnev in 1971 and codified in the SALT I agreement, has been the political doctrine."[47]

Soviet political spokesmen have been very forthright and consistent in reiterating this position. The dread of the consequences of a nuclear war partially underlay Nikita Khrushchev's reiteration of the Leninist policy of peaceful coexistence in his famous secret speech before the Twentieth Congress of the Communist Party of the Soviet Union (CPSU) in 1956, and the idea has been resounded by his predecessors. Said Leonid Brezhnev in a forceful statement in *Pravda,* "I will add that only he who has decided to commit suicide can start a nuclear war in the hope of emerging victorious from it."[48] This theme was also articulated by the late Konstantin Chernenko: "In a nuclear war, there can be no victors and no political aims can be achieved by means of it. Any attempt to use nuclear weapons would inevitably lead to a disaster that could endanger the very existence of life on Earth."[49] Similarly, "saving mankind from the threat of nuclear war"[50] was a major part of the rationale advanced by Mikhail Gorbachev in making his nuclear disarmament proposal of January 15, 1986.

These kinds of statements can be dismissed either as political propaganda designed to deceive or lull the American public into complacency or as direct contradictions of the mountainous amount of verbal and physical effort the Soviets have expended on preparing to wage war with nuclear weapons. There is, however, some emerging evidence that the apparent incongruity between political spokesmen and military planners, to the degree it ever existed, is changing in favor of those who find nuclear war unacceptable. Laird and Herspring note, for instance, that "the absence of any serious discussion by Soviet military writers of the positive benefits derived from fighting a nuclear war clearly calls into question the desirability of ever fighting such a war except under the most extreme circumstances."[51] This process of conversion away from the apparent earlier belief in the efficacy of nuclear war fighting has been glacial, but steady and important, according to Albert Weeks:

Ever so slowly, they [the Soviets] are evolving ideas in the direction of excluding nuclear war as a tolerable option. . . . It is significant that such sentiments are being voiced by authentically professional soldiers and military scientists, not by the Chervovs and Milshteins—officers without military academy status who have been chosen by the party to be political-propaganda mouthpieces addressing Western audiences.[52]

The frequency and consistency with which the Soviets declaim nuclear war has not gone entirely unnoticed by American analysts. In his landmark comparative study of U.S. and Soviet strategic thought, Fritz Ermath asserts, "For a generation, the relevant elites of both the United States and the Soviet Union have agreed that an unlimited strategic nuclear war would be a socio-political disaster of immense proportions."[53] The reason the Soviets feel this way is that "Soviet leaders, both civilian and military, recognize the objective reality of assured destruction in an all-out nuclear war."[54] As a result of this assessment, "The Soviets assign the highest priority to the deterrence of nuclear war."[55] This determination, in turn, creates a commonality between the two superpowers: "One of the few goals the West and the Soviets share is avoidance of a nuclear war."[56]

This recognition does not necessarily lead to a blissful state of comity. Charles Burton Marshall, for instance, concludes that the commitment is narrow and bounded: "Like U.S. leaders, Soviet leaders undoubtedly prefer peace in the more immediate sense of actually avoiding warfare."[57] David Holloway adds that the Soviets do not believe the acceptance of war's undesirability rules out its possibility: "Although the Soviet leaders recognize mutual vulnerability . . . as an objective condition, they do not regard nuclear war as impossible."[58] At least part of the reason for that possibility is that "though both countries recognize that they must avoid nuclear war, they are far from agreeing on the nature of the problem, or its solution."[59]

Conclusion

This last statement presents a challenge. The gist of the argument to this point has been that mutual vulnerability has created such fears of the consequences of nuclear war as to make each superpower conclude that such a war must be avoided. It is a coldhearted, bloodless conclusion born from fear, not trust, but it does provide an answer to *why* there has not been nuclear war in the nuclear age.

But that is not enough to know, because avoiding nuclear war in the future is obviously as important as having avoided it in the past. The past, because it has witnessed the absence of nuclear war, is not necessarily a bad model for the future; it is at least something on which one can do more than speculate, since it has happened. To make intelligent choices about the future based on the past requires understanding and agreeing on the nature of the problem. What is needed is a clear understanding of *how* nuclear weapons affect superpower relations in such a way as to prevent nuclear war. In turn, such an understanding may allow us to distinguish ways that reinforce the structure of an otherwise violent peace and to fashion criteria by which to judge the propriety of change. That is the challenge, as summarized by Secretary of State George Shultz: "At the same time, we have a fundamental common interest in the avoidance of war. This common interest impels us to work toward a relationship between our nations that can lead to a safer world for all mankind."[60]

Notes

1. Thomas C. Schelling, "What Went Wrong with Arms Control," *Foreign Affairs* 64, no. 2 (Winter 1985/86), p. 219.

2. Robert Jay Lifton and Richard Falk, *Indefensible Weapons: The Political and Psychological Case against Nuclearism* (New York: Basic Books, 1982), p. 3.

3. Louis Rene Beres, *Mimicking Sisyphus: America's Countervailing Nuclear Strategy* (Lexington, Mass.: Lexington Books, 1983), p. 2.

4. Louis Rene Beres, *Reason and Realpolitik: U.S. Foreign Policy and World Order* (Lexington, Mass.: Lexington Books, 1984), p. 134.

5. For the most elaborate and controversial description, see Jonathan Schell, *The Fate of the Earth* (New York: Alfred A. Knopf, 1982).

6. Lifton and Falk, *Indefensible Weapons,* p. 244–45. See also Richard Falk, *The End of World Order: Essays on Normative International Relations* (New York: Holmes and Meier, 1983).

7. Robert Jervis, *The Illogic of American Nuclear Strategy* (Ithaca, N.Y.: Cornell University Press, 1984), p. 30.

8. Michael M. May, "The U.S.–Soviet Approach to Nuclear Weapons," *International Security* 9, no. 4 (Spring 1985), p. 151.

9. Robert Kennedy, "The Changing Strategic Balance and U.S. Defense Planning," in Robert Kennedy and John M. Weinstein (eds.), *The Defense of the West: Strategic and European Security Issues Reappraised* (Boulder, Colo.: Westview, 1984), p. 22.

10. George Shultz, "A Forward Look at Foreign Policy," *Department of State Bulletin* 84, no. 2093 (December 1984), p. 7.

11. Graham T. Allison, Albert Carnesale, and Joseph S. Nye, Jr., "An Agenda for Action," in Graham T. Allison, Albert Carnesale, and Joseph S. Nye, Jr. (eds.), *Hawks, Doves and Owls: An Agenda for Avoiding Nuclear War* (New York: W.W. Norton, 1985), pp. 236–37.

12. Robbin F. Laird and Dale R. Herspring, *The Soviet Union and Strategic Arms* (Boulder, Colo.: Westview, 1984), pp. 23–24.

13. Laurence Martin, "National Security in an Insecure Age," *Atlantic Community Quarterly* 21, no. 1 (Spring 1983), pp. 45–46.

14. A. Krass, "The Death of Deterrence," in Stockholm International Peace

Research Institute (SIPRI), *Policies for Common Security* (London: Taylor and Francis, 1985), p. 122.

15. Ibid., p. 125.

16. Bernard Brodie (ed.), *The Absolute Weapon: Atomic Power and World Order* (New York: Harcourt, Brace, 1946).

17. William Liscum Borden, *There Will Be No Time: The Revolution in Strategy* (New York: Macmillan, 1946), pp. 218, 72–73.

18. Ibid., pp. 43, 48.

19. For an examination based on recently declassified documents, see David Alan Rosenberg, "The Origins of Overkill: Nuclear Weapons and American Strategy, 1945–1960," *International Security* 7, no. 4 (Spring 1983), pp. 4–71.

20. Harry R. Borowski, *A Hollow Threat: Strategic Air Power and Containment before Korea* (Westport, Conn.: Greenwood, 1982) develops this theme.

21. Steven L. Rearden, *The Evolution of American Strategic Doctrine: Paul H. Nitze and the Soviet Challenge* (Boulder, Colo.: Westview, 1984), p. 10.

22. Krass, "The Death of Deterrence," p. 118. For a detailed discussion, see David Alan Rosenberg, "'A Smoking Radiation Ruin at the End of Two Hours': Documents on American Plans for Nuclear War with the Soviet Union," *International Security* 6, no. 3 (Winter 1981/82), pp. 3–38.

23. Alexander Krivitsky, "Behind a Mask of Decency: An Expose," *World Marxist Review* 28, no. 6 (June 1985), p. 38. In a similar vein, Patrick O'Sullivan asserts, "In 1948 General (Omar) Bradley announced the doctrine of 'massive retaliation.' The containment of Russia within Eastern Europe was to be achieved through the threat of devastation of the Soviet heartland." In "The Geopolitics of Deterrence" in David Pepper and Alan Jenkins (eds.), *The Geography of War and Peace* (New York: Basil Blackwell, 1985), p. 32.

24. See Jonathan Stein, *From H-Bomb to Star Wars: The Politics of Strategic Decision-Making* (Lexington, Mass.: Lexington Books, 1984).

25. Rearden, *The Evolution of American Strategic Doctrine,* p. 8.

26. Michael Nacht, *The Age of Vulnerability: Threats to the Nuclear Stalemate* (Washington, D.C.: Brookings Institution, 1985), p. 86. This same period is described by Desmond Ball in "Targeting for Strategic Deterrence," *Adelphi Papers* 185 (London: International Institute for Strategic Studies, 1983), pp. 3–8.

27. For example, see Donald M. Snow, *Nuclear Strategy in a Dynamic World: American Policy in the 1980s* (Tuscaloosa, Ala.: University of Alabama Press, 1981), pp. 49–57.

28. Schelling, "What Went Wrong with Arms Control," p. 230.

29. For a summary of the motivations underlying the MIRV decision, see Herbert F. York and G. Allen Greb, "MIRV," pp. 407–26 in Bernard Brodie, Michael D. Intriligator, and Roman Kolkowitz (eds.), *National Security and International Stability* (Boston: Oelgeschlager, Gunn & Hain, 1983).

30. Barry M. Blechman and Stephen S. Kaplan, *Force without War: U.S. Armed Forces as a Political Instrument* (Washington, D.C.: Brookings Institution: 1978), pp. 99–100.

31. As an example, John Stoessinger argues: "If World War III should come, it will probably erupt in the Persian Gulf. That region in the early 1980s bears an eerie resemblance to Europe before the outbreak of the First World War." See *Why Nations Go to War,* fourth edition (New York: St. Martin's, 1985), p. 183.

32. Laird and Herspring, *The Soviet Union and Strategic Arms,* p. 9.

33. James Schlesinger, "The Eagle and the Bear: Between an Unfree World and None," *Foreign Affairs* 63, no. 5 (Summer 1985), p. 949.

34. One of the earliest and most forceful statements of this anomaly is Philip Green, *Deadly Logic: The Theory of Nuclear Deterrence* (Columbus, Ohio: Ohio State University Press, 1966).

35. For a fair representation, see three articles in Charles W. Kegley, Jr., and Eugene R. Wittkopf (eds.), *The Nuclear Reader: Strategy, Weapons, War* (New York: St. Martin's, 1985). The articles are National Council of Catholic Bishops, "Nuclear Strategy and the Challenge of Peace: Ethical Principles and Policy Prescriptions," pp. 43–57; Albert Wohlstetter, "Bishops, Statesmen, and Other Strategists on the Bombing of Innocents," pp. 58–76; and Paul M. Kattenburg, "MAD is the Moral Position," pp. 77–84.

36. The leading proponent of this position is Colin S. Gray. For a recent exposition, see "Denting the Shield, Blunting the Sword," *Defense Science 2003 + 4,* no. 6 (December 1985/January 1986), pp. 11–19.

37. Jervis, *The Illogic of American Nuclear Strategy,* pp. 34, 146. Schelling endorses the same idea in "What Went Wrong with Arms Control," p. 233.

38. Klaus Knorr, "Controlling Nuclear War," *International Security* 9, no. 4 (Spring 1985), p. 79.

39. Allison, Carnesale, and Nye, "An Agenda for Action," p. 228.

40. Robert E. Hunter, "SDI: Return to Basics," *Washington Quarterly* 9, no. 1 (Winter 1986), p. 164.

41. Fred S. Hoffman, "The SDI in U.S. Nuclear Strategy," *International Security* 10, no. 1 (Summer 1985), p. 14.

42. Keith B. Payne, "The Deterrence Requirement for Defense," *Washington Quarterly* 9, no. 1 (Winter 1986), p. 141.

43. Graham T. Allison, Albert Carnesale, and Joseph S. Nye, Jr., "Analytical Conclusions: Hawks, Doves and Owls," in Allison, Carnesale, and Nye (eds.), *Hawks, Doves and Owls,* p. 216.

44. McGeorge Bundy, "The Bishops and the Bomb," *New York Review of Books,* June 16, 1983, pp. 3–8.

45. "The Long Nuclear Peace," *Economist* 298, no. 7434 (February 28, 1986), p. 15.

46. Richard Pipes, "Why the Soviet Union Thinks It Could Fight and Win a Nuclear War," *Commentary* 64, no. 1 (July 1977), pp. 21–34.

47. Stan Windass, "Problems of NATO Defense," in Stan Windass (ed.), *Avoiding Nuclear War: Common Strategy for the Defense of the West* (London: Brassey's Defense Publishers, 1985), p. 6.

48. Quoted by Dan L. Strode in "The Soviet Union and Modernization of the U.S. ICBM Force" in Barry R. Schneider, Colin S. Gray, and Keith B. Payne (eds.), *Missiles for the Nineties: ICBMs and Strategic Policy* (Boulder, Colo.: Westview, 1984), p. 146. An almost identical statement, but without attribution, appears in *Whence the Threat to Peace,* third edition (Moscow: Military Publishing House, 1984), p. 13: "Only a person who has decided to commit suicide can start a nuclear war in the hope of winning it."

49. Quoted in *Whence the Threat to Peace,* p. 14.

50. Mikhail Gorbachev, "Nuclear Disarmament by the Year 2000," reprinted as an advertisement in *New York Times,* February 5, 1986, p. A13.

51. Laird and Herspring, *The Soviet Union and Strategic Arms,* p. 67.

52. Albert Weeks, "Soviets May Be Retooling Doctrine," *Defense Science 2003 +* 4, no. 6 (December 1985/January 1986), p. 46.

53. Fritz W. Ermath, "Contrasts in American and Soviet Strategic Thought," reprinted in John F. Reichart and Steven L. Sturm, *American Defense Policy,* fifth edition (Baltimore, Md.: Johns Hopkins University Press, 1982), p. 64.

54. Laird and Herspring, *The Soviet Union and Strategic Arms,* p. 5.

55. Edward L. Warner, III, "Defense Policy of the Soviet Union," in Reichart and Sturm, *American Defense Policy,* p. 53.

56. John G. Keliher, "Discussion," in Richard F. Staar (ed.), *Arms Control: Myth versus Reality* (Stanford, Calif.: Hoover Institution Press, 1984), p. 41.

57. Charles Burton Marshall, "Dinner Address," in Staar, *Arms Control,* p. 183.

58. David Holloway, "The Strategic Defense Initiative and the Soviet Union," *Daedalus* 114, no. 3 (Summer 1985), p. 261.

59. Stephen M. Meyer, "Soviet Perceptions on the Paths to Nuclear War," in Allison, Carnesale, and Nye, *Hawks, Doves and Owls,* p. 167.

60. George Shultz, "U.S.–Soviet Relations in the Context of U.S. Foreign Policy," *Atlantic Community Quarterly* 21, no. 3 (Fall 1983), p. 202.

2
Self-Deterrence, Uncertainty, and Change

The upshot of the argument in the preceding chapter is that the effect nuclear weapons have had on international relations, and especially the superpower relationship, has not been altogether harmful. Rather, nuclear weapons and the common understanding of what nuclear war would be like creates a common bond in the avoidance of war that quite likely would not exist were there no nuclear weapons. As the Harvard Nuclear Study Group puts it, "The shared objective is to keep the nuclear peace; neither superpower wants to fight a nuclear war. . . . [B]ecause of this combination of genuine rivalry and genuine common interest, both superpowers are cautious even when pursuing policies designed to minimize the likelihood of war between them."[1]

This construction has some distinct effects on the way we look at nuclear deterrence, at nuclear weapons' contribution to deterrence, and at proposals to amend the structure of deterrence. There is a high level of agreement within the elite policy communities of both the United States and the Soviet Union and within the American academic community about what the consequences of nuclear war might be. Only a minority (e.g., Colin Gray) would disagree with Jervis's assessment that "MAD as a fact is more important than MAD as policy. The latter is in the realm of choice; the former is not."[2] What is remarkable, however, is the inability or unwillingness to carry the observation through to its logical conclusion in terms of deterrence.

Instead, the debate is marked by confusion and timidity revolving around the familiar if unproductive argument about whether the assured destruction or some form of limited nuclear options best deters Soviet nuclear aggression. Take, for example, a statement from a recent critique of the SDI: "Reliance on mutual deterrence at the price of mutual vulnerability . . . is an uncomfortable posture . . . so long as nuclear weapons exist (even at a fraction of present numbers), deterrence through a clear common awareness of the consequence of initiating nuclear war will be prudent and indispensable."[3] At one level, the statement is unremarkable, a standard defense of the assured-destruction proposition that active defenses of people are destabilizing because they may convince decisionmakers that a nuclear war might be tolerable. What *is* remarkable but apparently not recognized by the authors is that the whole argument is irrelevant.

This may seem a brash, even outlandish statement at direct odds with some well-established ways of examining nuclear dynamics, and in some ways it is. At the heart of understanding and, thus, managing and manipulating nuclear relations is the question of what deters. In the U.S. debate, the question is framed, "What deters the Soviet Union from attacking the United States with nuclear weapons?" Similarly, the Soviets ask the question, "What deters a U.S. attack on the Soviet Union?"

The traditional answers have come in the form of deterrence threats. In the United States, the correct answer alternates between the threat to inflict massive retaliatory fury in response to Soviet aggression (assured destruction) or the threat to take proportionate retaliatory action at any possible level of Soviet nuclear provocation such that the Soviets cannot calculate gain from any nuclear attack they might dream of (limited nuclear options or countervailance).[4] The Soviet Union, on the other hand, maintains it deters U.S. aggression by threatening, and the U.S. accepting, that the Soviet Union would prevail in any nuclear conflagration (the war-winning strategy).

There has always been, in American minds, something slightly unreal about stated Soviet strategy. Despite the evidence of some very real U.S. nuclear-war–making planning in the early years after World War II (see chapter 1), most Americans cannot think of themselves as potential nuclear aggressors who *need* to be deterred from something they would not do in the absence of the threat. That being the case, what does one make of the threat? One can view it as sinister and bellicose by emphasizing the intention to "fight and win" the nuclear war. From this vantage point, the purpose of U.S. counterstrategy is to frustrate the Soviets' calculation that they would certainly win a nuclear encounter. Thus, "Any factor that creates uncertainty in the Soviet warplanner's mind as to the potential effectiveness of a contemplated attack . . . contributes to deterrence, peace and stability."[5] At the extreme, one might even adopt a strategy and force that could convince the Soviets that *they* would lose the war.

There is another way to view the Soviet strategy, of course. Since the United States does not intend to pose an offensive threat to the Soviets, their strategy is beside the point. As Jervis argues, "It is not clear that the Soviet doctrine has any relevance to deterrence at all. Instead, it may only be a discussion of what should be done if deterrence fails."[6]

For anyone interested in listening, the Soviets have been similarly disparaging about U.S. deterrence formulations. Their view of assured destruction as strategy is that it is "second-rate,"[7] a grisly technological oddity of the time when countervalue targeting was the only practicable course of action. The Soviets have also been quite skeptical of the ability to limit a nuclear war, a prime premise of limited options. Pipes admits, "Limited nuclear war, flexible response, escalation, damage limiting, and all the other numerous refinements of U.S. strategic doctrine find no place in its Soviet counterpart."[8]

If U.S. threats are not believed by the Soviets, then what has been deterring their aggression? According to Soviet spokesmen, the question is wrong, because, "in reality, it was a question all these years not of restraining the U.S.S.R. from attacking the United States but, on the contrary, of the U.S.S.R. restraining U.S. imperialism from unleashing a big thermonuclear war."[9] The U.S. debate thus has the problem backwards: "In all the postwar period the military might of the U.S.S.R. has never presented a threat to the security of the United States excluding only one situation—a retaliatory blow in the event of America's attack on the Soviet Union."[10]

What is one to make of such claims? They seem unreal to Americans, but that does not mean the Soviets do not believe what they are saying any less than Americans do when they debate the virtues of assured destruction and limited options. What this discussion raises is the possibility that U.S. nuclear threats are irrelevant to deterring the Soviets, just as Soviet deterrence formulations do not affect U.S. nuclear behavior. Who, then, is deterring whom?

The answer is simple and straightforward: *the Soviet Union and the United States deter themselves.* Deterrence, after all, deals with the presumed hostile intentions of an adversary; the reason one issues the threat is to cause the adversary not to carry out the action one seeks to deter. The act that one seeks to avoid with nuclear weapons is the initiation of nuclear war, and it is at least implicit in this formulation that the intention to start a nuclear war is present and requires deterring. But the heart of the argument to this point has been quite the opposite; rather, the first foreign policy purpose of both states is the avoidance of nuclear war with the other, a proposition for which considerable evidence has already been presented. That being the case, hostile intention (the necessary element in a threat situation) is missing, so that the threats miss a mark that is not there. Self-deterrence, not deterrence, is the dynamic of the nuclear arms balance.

Realistic self-deterrence (RSD),[11] as the concept can be called, should not suggest complacency. It is neither an immutable nor a necessarily permanent dynamic in superpower relations. What has created RSD between the world's two most powerful rivals is not, after all, a sense of kindredness; it is fear. That fear, in turn, is of the unacceptable consequences of nuclear war. To put the matter in terms raised in the previous chapter, as arsenals have become more deadly, fear of their use has made the superpowers act to make the situation less dangerous, and they have done so by self-deterrence.

This situation has not always been the case, and there should be no sense of complacency because of the relative stability that RSD creates. Things can, after all, change, and the situation is not self-regulating. In addition, the fear of using nuclear weapons does not mean that the weapons are not perceived as useful or that circumstances do not exist where one side or the other might not be motivated to take actions that would change the present balance. For instance,

> To argue that Soviet leaders reject nuclear warfare as a "feasible" instrument of policy and consider deterrence of nuclear conflict a paramount political and military objective is not to suggest that they reject the notion that nuclear superiority, or at least the appearance of superiority, may yield tangible political benefits.[12]

As we shall see in the next chapter, the Soviets purport to hold a similar suspicion that nuclear superiority is the real goal of the SDI.

If an RSD-based peace built upon fear is not immutable, it has been enduring and has contributed to a stability in superpower relations that one would hardly have predicted ten or twenty years ago. This has been all the more remarkable in the 1980s given, first, a political regime in the United States that is harshly anti-Soviet consistently in rhetoric and at least occasionally in deed and, second, the destabilizing potential of a long succession process in the Soviet Union culminating in Gorbachev's "coronation" at the Twenty-seventh Congress of the CPSU. Although it is certainly possible to imagine a nuclear balance otherwise configured making as positive a contribution to this milieu as the one I have described, the RSD-driven balance and its impact on overall relations cannot be overlooked. Moreover, casting an understanding of deterrence dynamics in these terms allows a refocusing of the debate about nuclear policy and strategy that may prove beneficial.

If one accepts the premise that deterrence is truly realistic self-deterrence and, further, that the result has been generally stabilizing, the debate over declaratory strategy is refocused. Instead of asking what threats best dissuade the Soviets and, thus, repeating the dreary assured-destruction–limited-options debate, one can focus instead on what conditions have caused both nations to adopt nuclear war avoidance as their first value, what can be done to reinforce that situation, and how change adversely or beneficially affects the balance.

Such a reorientation, of course, assumes that the dynamic underlying self-deterrence is accepted. That dynamic, of course, is fear induced by mutual vulnerability, a notion closely akin to assured destruction as fact. Drawing that analogy automatically raises some level of controversy that muddles the factual existence of vulnerability with its desirability. Focusing on self-deterrence as the organizing concept allows one to focus the discussion by dividing the concern into questions of fact and value.

The factual question has two components: Does vulnerability exist and is there anything that can be done about it? The value question similarly has two parts: Should vulnerability exist and would the world be a better place if it did not?

The current answers to the factual questions are yes and maybe. Given arsenal sizes and the absence of defenses against those arsenals, both sides clearly are vulnerable. At the same time, there are mechanical methods of changing that circumstance. The most obvious of these are either removal of threat (disarmament) or protection against it (movement toward the defense). The first solution is technically possible but, for a variety of reasons explored in chapter 4, has proven politically infeasible. The other solution is politically possible, but its technical feasibility remains an open and, thus, controversial, matter. Whether one wants to move from the current situation of vulnerability to something else is a matter of choices and values conditioned by technical and political realities. Disarmament, in other words, can only occur if the political will to disarm is present, and one can only base a system on defenses if they work (and if, as we shall see, one can agree on a common definition of what *work* means).

If it is possible to move away from vulnerability and, hence, stability based on fear, is it desirable to do so? A disarmed or defended world would be one in which fear of the consequences of nuclear devastation would no longer dampen superpower animosity, and some other dynamic would have to regulate the relationship. What would that be? Would it maintain the nuclear peace or the absence of war between the superpowers better than does the current system? We live in a world of violent peace, but it is also a nuclear-war–free world.

It is very easy to slip into an emotional interpretation. The hideous consequences of deterrence somehow failing in a vulnerable world are reviling and lead one to sympathize with President Reagan's visionary justification of SDI that it is "better to save lives than to avenge them."[13] The problem is how best to save the lives, and the surest way is to make it as unlikely as possible that nuclear weapons are employed in anger.

The simple fact is that the RSD world has worked and that there are no near-term or probably medium-term alternatives to a world based on vulnerability that are both technically and politically possible. Recognizing this is an assertion whose truth cannot be demonstrated without considerably mangling the rules of formal logic, the very least that can be said is that vulnerability-induced RSD and the absence of nuclear war have coexisted for well over a decade and that the chances of nuclear war are more, rather than less, remote than they formerly were.

Is a nuclear peace based on RSD worth maintaining? If it is true that vulnerability has contributed to an increasingly stable nuclear balance and better superpower relations, then one can ask if the future of deterrence is better served by reinforcing the conditions that have produced an RSD world, or whether movement toward an alternative organization is preferable, assuming it is possible. Before that judgment can be made, however, one needs to look at those conditions that have created mutual vulnerability and how they might be reinforced. As we shall see, these conditions contain generous amounts of crisis management, perceptions about nuclear war, and strategic uncertainty.

Conditions for an RSD World

The central argument that mutual vulnerability both creates fear of the outcome of nuclear war and thus removes the intention to start a nuclear war as the basis for RSD also defines the conditions for maintaining deterrence based on self-deterrence. In the absence of volition or intention to initiate nuclear war, nuclear war would only break out inadvertently, probably as the result of the escalation of a crisis directly involving the superpowers or induced by third parties. This suggests that one category of conditions to maintain deterrence involves *crisis management;* either by perfecting means to avoid crises altogether or by terminating them at their lowest possible levels of intensity and danger. The motor of this need to solve crises is fear of the consequences of nuclear war. This suggests the second condition for maintaining self-deterrence, which involves avoiding *perceptual changes* about the unacceptability of nuclear exchange. The twin methods for avoiding such changes are, first, assuring that arsenal imbalances do not reach the proportions that one side or the other can calculate (possibly wrongly) that the consequences of nuclear war would be tolerable and, second, nurturing and reinforcing uncertainty about calculating favorable outcomes.

The intended result of this endeavor is to strengthen a situation akin to what Zbigniew Brzezinski calls "strategically ambiguous equivalence." He describes this situation precisely. "At this stage neither side can be even the least bit confident about the outcome of a surprise attack/second strike by either side or of a military conflict that escalates to a nuclear exchange on the basis of a protracted crisis permitting both sides to fully generate their forces."[14] Even in such an advanced state of crisis, uncertainty about a successful outcome should paralyze a decisionmaker. As I argued a few years ago: "Such problems should be sufficiently sobering to a decision maker conversant with the spotted history of prewar predictions and the potential consequences of guessing wrong."[15] As long as these conditions hold, "The Russians have to ask themselves what the results of an adventure might be, not what American intentions are."[16]

These formulations represent a sort of "worst case" along the spectrum of crisis situations, and what one should aim for are what the Harvard Nuclear Study Group calls "stabilizing measures." These measures, intended as they are to "make their [nuclear weapons] use less likely,"[17] should strive to formulate more stable methods for arresting conflicts. This goal is also espoused in a recent Soviet publication on SDI: "The Soviet Union holds that relations between the nuclear powers should be governed by definite rules. These rules must provide for the prevention of nuclear war."[18]

Crisis Management

The record of Soviet–U.S. tacit or active efforts to avoid or to defuse crises since the early 1970s has been impressive, even if that record has been somewhat neglected in accounts of superpower relations. As stated earlier, the most recent instance of a crisis between the two with real escalatory potential was the Yom Kippur War. At least one observer contends that the outcome of that crisis was to reinforce rather than detract from the accumulating movement toward crisis management: "The one instance sometimes charged to have been a failure of collaboration was, if anything, a success: the defusing of the pseudo-crisis between the two superpowers in October 1973 at the climax of the fourth Arab–Israeli war." Instead, Raymond Garthoff argues, "Too little attention has been paid to the efforts to devise a regime of crisis management and crisis avoidance." He cites as evidence the 1971 accidental war agreement and hot-line–upgrade agreements, the incidents at sea accord of 1972, and the 1973 agreement on the prevention of nuclear war.[19]

The notion that conflict avoidance and conflict termination (management) are important goals is fairly generally accepted.[20] Generally, this opinion is connected at least tacitly to a negative assessment of a planned, volitional initiation of nuclear hostilities. As one analyst summarizes, "Most serious students of Soviet–American relations dismiss the notion that nuclear war would come in the form of a 'bolt out of the blue' sneak attack. . . . This is because such an attack would almost certainly be suicidal for the attacker as well as fatal for the victim."[21] Rather, the assumption is that a war would begin inadvertently. A conflict involving states supported by both sides getting out of hand and dragging the superpowers into confrontation either accidentally or by the conscious act of one or both clients represents one such possible nuclear "horror story." Leon Weiseltier offers another: "If the United States ever fights a nuclear war with the Soviet Union, it will almost certainly not be because the Soviet Union attacked the United States. It will be because the Soviet Union attacked an ally of the United States."[22] A Soviet analyst would probably reverse the attacking state and attacked ally.

The obvious way to avoid the confrontation that could devolve into superpower conflict is crisis avoidance. "It may be best," as one observer says, "to concentrate our energy on *preventing* confrontations, by diplomatic, wise foreign policy and the fostering of a cooperative relationship between the United States and the Soviet Union."[23] The record to date of moving beyond such general statements of desirability, however, has not been especially encouraging, leading Alexander George to the cryptic judgment that "crisis prevention may well be considered the orphan of strategic studies."[24]

It should not be. A crisis that does not occur is clearly less dangerous than one that does, and crisis avoidance should be a conscious, as well as implicit, goal of superpower relations. Such efforts do not necessarily mean or require narrowing the considerable political differences between their conflicting world views, although that would certainly not be an undesirable outcome. Rather, such an effort should aim at creating boundaries around the competition to minimize the likelihood that crisis can occur in a broadening set of circumstances.

There are examples, some more meaningful than others, of this phenomenon in action. During the 1960s, the series of treaties banning the nuclear weaponization of places such as outer space, the seabed, Antarctica, and Latin America, while arguably not tremendously important in and of themselves, did remove certain areas from the roster of potential sites for nuclear confrontation and crises, as well as setting a precedent for future negotiations seeking to eliminate other areas of competition as well. A further, albeit narrow, area of future negotiation might be in the formal negotiation of anti-submarine warfare (ASW) "exclusion zones," areas of the ocean off-limits to "hunter-killer" submarines (SSNs) and other ASW forces. The idea is that nuclear missile submarines (SSBNs) could patrol safely in these zones, so that they would not need to worry about a "use-them-or-lose-them" threat from ASW forces during a political crisis. This particular proposal, one might add, violates certain aspects of the U.S. "forward maritime strategy" and is thus opposed by the Reagan administration, a position that will be examined for its consistency with nuclear stability in chapter 6.[25]

Tacit understandings and agreements to avoid crises can exist as well. Where spheres of influence are established, as in the Soviet zone in Eastern Europe or the U.S. zone in the Western Hemisphere, the power with dominant interest can exert that interest through policies such as the Brezhnev or Monroe Doctrines without the serious worry of escalation by the party with more limited interests. The overt U.S. attempt to dislodge the Marxist Sandanista regime in Nicaragua may test the durability of that understanding, but it may also reinforce it as the Yom Kippur War did. Similarly, it may be possible to expand the "exclusion zone" concept to other geographic areas or, where that is not possible, to agree in advance to early consultation and discussions whenever conflicts erupt elsewhere in the world. It would, for instance, be advantageous to the cause of crisis avoidance if the United States and Soviet Union have agreed in advance that their first action in the event that either Iraq or Iran gains decisive advantage in their war would be mutual consultation on how to contain and resolve that situation.

If crisis cannot be avoided altogether, then it is in the interests of both the United States and the Soviet Union to develop methods to defuse those circumstances that have led to crisis at as low a level of intensity as possible. The two reasons for this are that there is general agreement that a downward spiralling crisis is most likely to trigger nuclear war and, concomitantly, the dynamics of perception and behavior can be altered by the existence of the crisis itself.

There is agreement on both sides that crisis breakdown and control are the "twin towers" of deterrence. Of the Soviets, Stephen Meyers states, "Today, it appears that the broad sweep of Soviet force planning is guided by the belief that a nuclear war between the United States and the Soviet Union would most likely occur in the context of crisis or conflict rather than arise spontaneously."[26] Discussing the criteria for successful arms control agreements, U.S. arms negotiator Max Kampelman in effect agrees: "Stability, under the current pattern of deterrence, requires that the Soviets do not misread the intentions and capabilities of the West, particularly in times of crisis."[27]

If and when crises, or situations that could become crises, occur, the interests of deterrence are served by resolving the issues as quickly as possible, for the simple reason that "deterrence must work under terrible stress as well as in ordinary circumstances. . . . *[D]eterrence is harder in a crisis"* (emphasis added).[28] What makes for greater difficulty is that in a crisis, the possibility increases of "psychological stress that [leads] to a misreading of signals."[29] In such circumstances, perceptions can change, and decisions can be altered:

> What starts out as rational is likely to become less so over time. And accidents that would not matter much in normal times or early in a crisis might create "crazy" situations in which choice is so constrained that "rational" decisions about the least bad alternatives lead to outcomes that would appear insane under normal circumstances.[30]

To reiterate an old and familiar example, it would appear totally irrational to march a troop across a minefield in peacetime just because the shortest route is across the field; if one is being hotly pursued by a superior hostile force, the rationality of the decision might be quite different.

Were a superpower crisis to devolve to desperate straits, national commanders could find themselves facing the minefield on one side and the hostile army on the other. For instance, "In a sufficiently severe crisis, fear might be forgotten, prudence set aside, and drastic actions taken. Nuclear war could begin through accident, misunderstanding, or miscalculation in ways that fear could not negate."[31] It could also occur because within a crisis, one side or the other was unwilling to allow the other to escape the situation with its pride intact. Says Dean Rusk, "It's just possible, however, that you might have a nuclear war if a man or group of men find themselves driven into a corner and elect to play the role of Samson and pull the temple down."[32]

Clearly, these are circumstances to be avoided or diluted. The most dangerous set of circumstances to be avoided is, to borrow Rusk's analogy, the "Samson syndrome": the belief that the situation is so dire that the consequences of starting nuclear war are no worse than the consequences of not starting the war. There are both political/psychological and mechanical/technical methods to deal with this problem.

At the political and psychological levels, it is important that there be clear and well-established means of communication available to allow leaders to interact, that negotiations using those channels be explicitly aimed at resolving differences, and that other actions reinforce rather than work at cross-purposes with negotiating aims. A conciliatory negotiating position should not, for instance, be accompanied by mobilization or the movement of forces into combat-ready positions if one is trying to terminate a crisis. This seems so obvious as not to require stating, yet it is an integral part of the forward maritime strategy to steam naval forces past the Greenland-Iceland-United Kingdom (GIUK) gap in a crisis before shooting begins. Mechanically and technically, building and maintaining secure and survivable retaliatory forces as well as command, control, communication, and intelligence (C^3I) assets and not building forces that threaten adversary offensive forces and C^3I assets help lessen the likelihood that either side will panic and order an escalation out of fear that the failure to do so would prove militarily disastrous.

Perceptual Changes

Under present circumstances, neither superpower will start a nuclear war purposely because it fears the consequences to itself (and by extension the rest of the world as well, if we accept the nuclear winter hypothesis discussed in chapter 6). This fear removes volition from the probable reasons a nuclear war might start; the obverse, however, suggests how intentional decisions to initiate nuclear war might occur. If one or another of the nuclear powers ceases to fear the personal costs of a nuclear war, it may cease to be self-deterred.

Under what circumstances might such a change in perception occur? Laird and Herspring provide an answer: "Victory remains a meaningful concept in a nuclear war to the extent to which one can destroy the adversary's military forces and his military potential at acceptable cost."[33] The key element in perceptual change is captured in the last phrase, "at acceptable cost," and suggests that perceptual change is largely a matter of quantitative and qualitative weapons balance. In the current deadly balance of mutual vulnerability, the calculation is that losses would be unacceptable. What could make that change?

Quantitatively, an overwhelming imbalance in favor of one side or the other that could allow the possessor to contemplate attacking and disarming the opponent and still retaining enough residual force to engage in postattack coercive bargaining would seem to present the most extreme case. As the Harvard Nuclear Study Group warns in this regard, "It is undesirable and possibly disastrous for American nuclear forces to be significantly weaker than Soviet forces; it is unnecessary and probably impossible for them to be significantly stronger than Soviet forces."[34] This question of balance translates into an operational requisite for secure second-strike forces that deny the adversary the ability to calculate the damage limitation that can erode self-deterrence: "The most obvious requirement for American nuclear forces is that they provide the unquestioned ability to destroy the Soviet Union even if the Soviets stage a skillful first strike."[35] Qualitatively, the individual or mutual possession of weapons with offensive or defensive characteristics that appear to create a significant damage-limiting capability for one or both sides might ease inhibitions, especially if such capabilities were accompanied by significant reductions in arsenal sizes.

The difficulty with damage-limitation calculations is that they can prove wrong in the real event. The acquisition of high delivery accuracies that allow the targeting of adversary offensive forces or sophisticated missile defenses apparently endows the possessor with the ability to limit damage and, hence, lower costs to "acceptable" levels. These capabilities, however, are untested in combat and might or might not perform up to expectations. This realization is sobering, because "an *attacker* will want high confidence of achieving decisive results before deciding on so dangerous a course as the use of nuclear weapons."[36] Given the novel aspects of nuclear warheads and, especially, delivery systems, self-deterrence may not be corroded as long as the rejoinder is recognized. "A nation is more likely to be deterred from nuclear attack if it is uncertain of the results. This principle of uncertainty is central to the prevailing doctrine."[37]

Strategic Uncertainty

The paralyzing effects of uncertainty on the decision to initiate nuclear war has, in the past several years, enjoyed great and increasing popularity. Stanley Sienkiewicz was a pioneer in pointing to the operational uncertainties inherent in talking about nuclear planning.[38] When I suggested in 1983 that nuclear strategy be reoriented to reflect and even amplify uncertainty, there was less than a chorus of agreement.[39] Today, uncertainty is extolled widely as a prime ingredient in deterrence and even as the justification for weapons systems whose emergence raised the concern in the first place.

The uncertainty thesis can be stated fairly succinctly. In contemplating the possibility of initiating nuclear war, planners must have high levels of confidence in their ability both to accomplish their offensive purposes and to limit retaliatory fury. They must, in other words, be quite certain that they can engage in a very significant degree—approaching 100 percent—of success because even a slight miscalculation could have absolutely disastrous consequences. Now entering arsenals are weapons that, if they perform up to their promise, allow one to calculate things such as disarming first strikes and airtight defenses. The rub is that these are novel, highly complicated weapons that have not been proven in war and that cannot be tested in a fully realistic manner. As a result, there is considerable uncertainty about whether they can accomplish the tasks that potentially make their employment attractive.

This uncertainty, if recognized and reinforced, can help maintain the fear that results in self-deterrence. Advanced capabilities appear to reduce the vulnerability that fuels fear; uncertainty restores the fear. As John Weinstein explains:

> The vulnerabilities and uncertainties confronting Soviet leaders and military planners will continue to provide powerful incentives to the Soviet Union to avoid war with the West. Rather, the best interests of the Soviet Union would be to maintain an atmosphere of peaceful (albeit politically competitive) coexistence with its political and military rivals.[40]

The merit ascribed to uncertainty is multifaceted. It appeals, for instance, to conservative military planners, because "professional soldiers usually feel the risks and uncertainties associated with first-strike are too great to be willingly undertaken by a responsible government."[41] Moreover, the general concept is applicable in a considerably subtle manner: "In fact, deterrence does not require your enemy to believe you will strike back; it requires only that he not believe you will not. Deterrence does not, in other words, require certainty. Doubt is quite enough."[42]

Somewhat ironically, the uncertainty factor has also been appropriated by those championing weapons systems that gave rise to emphasizing the concept in the first place. Examples of this phenomenon include the problem of ICBM vulnerability and ballistic missile defense.

The ICBM vulnerability problem is the theoretical ability of highly accurate Soviet multiple-warhead missile systems to attack and destroy a very high percentage of U.S. fixed-site, land-based ICBMs in a preemptive launch. Termed the "window of vulnerability," this Soviet achievement of "hard-target kill capability" was used to justify the procurement of the MX or Peacekeeper missile (as a way to compensate for the advantage in hard-target kill capability the Soviets enjoyed) and for new, more invulnerable basing modes for MX (to "close" the window of vulnerability). These advocacies, in turn, have created an "MX-basing mode muddle"[43] of charges and countercharges.

One of the strong objections to the ICBM vulnerability was based on uncertainty. Because of a variety of sources of uncertainty, this argument ran, neither the Soviets nor anyone else could calculate with any degree of confidence what portion of the force it could destroy. Sources of uncertainty included bias (the distance from a target that a missile actually lands), which can be caused by changes in gravitational fields, fluctuations in magnetic fields along the polar flight path of missiles, and the like.[44] Moreover, full-scale testing of these systems never has and never will be possible, and such tests are not entirely realistic anyway, since they generally involve east–west flight trajectories rather than the north–south flight necessary in a real attack.

The reason for making this argument forcefully is to counter the implication of the vulnerability thesis that a state possessing comprehensive hard-target kill capability could drastically reduce its own vulnerability to a retaliatory attack, possibly to the point of making the consequences tolerable. Due to uncertainty, a very high level of success cannot be predicted confidently, and since the survival of even a modest proportion of the attacked force could result in a devastating retaliation, mutual vulnerability is left intact. Deterrence stability is not compromised unless leaders are unaware of the operational uncertainty of their offensive capability.

Unable to find a basing mode that convincingly reduces MX vulnerability, proponents have adopted uncertainty to demonstrate that the ICBM vulnerability problem does not really exist and that placing the missiles in silos formerly described as vulnerable does not matter after all:

> After analyzing the uncertainties facing Soviet warplanners . . . a set of basic conclusions emerge:
> (1) U.S. ICBMs may be far less vulnerable . . . than is commonly supposed.
> (2) The uncertainties faced by warplanners about whether or not a surprise attack against ICBMs will succeed are massive.
> (3) [The] Soviet Union . . . ought to be deterred from attack given the massive penalties for even a slight failure.[45]

What the argument fails to or avoids pointing out is that if uncertainty means that ICBMs are not vulnerable, then MX is unnecessary, since its mission—compensating for Soviet counterforce—does not exist. Instead, the argument cheerfully concludes that MX deployment is now possible and that "any factor that creates uncertainty in the Soviet warplanner's mind as to the potential effectiveness of a contemplated attack against U.S. ICBMs in their silos contributes to deterrence, peace, and stability."[46]

The same kind of convolution has occurred in advocacies of missile defense technologies surrounding the SDI. Long before President Reagan's March 23, 1983 "Star Wars" speech, the potential of these weapons was being lavishly described: "If successfully deployed, beam weapons can end the long reign of nuclear terror introduced by the ballistic missile and the thermonuclear warhead."[47] This dramatic effect would be the result of an impenetrable population defense, an "astrodome," through which offensive warheads could not penetrate.

The problem, once again, is uncertainty. If such a capability were indeed attainable, it would remarkably alter the conditions of deterrence. The possessor would no longer be subject to attack, and the inhibitions created by vulnerability would evaporate. The difficulty, of course, is that there is essentially no margin for error in the performance of a defense intended to protect people; even a small degree of "leakage" would result in levels of death and suffering that only the ghoulish would find "tolerable." Uncertainty enters the picture because, akin to hard-target kill probability, attainment of leak-proof defenses will always be theoretical rather than demonstrated. Full-scale testing will never be possible, so that we cannot know in advance how well the system will perform. Uncertainty rears its head once again to challenge the escape from mutual vulnerability.

There is growing agreement that the astrodome defense is impractical or impossible against anything other than a reduced offensive threat, and so a fallback justification of SDI-created defenses less extravagant than Reagan's is necessary. That defense of the defense, of course, is grounded in uncertainty, and it has found its way into both official and private-sector justifications. General James Abrahamson (head of the SDI Organization), for instance, argues that "a potential aggressor will be far less likely to launch an attack if he harbors grave uncertainties about the outcome of such an attack,"[48] because the attacker would not know either how many *or* which of his warheads got through to target and thus how many *and* which retaliatory systems would survive. Former National Security Advisor Robert McFarlane agrees: "Even defenses that are imperfect strengthen deterrence because they create enormous headaches and uncertainties for anyone contemplating an attack."[49]

Uncertainty thus makes what are often called "less than perfect" defenses more attractive than they might otherwise appear. As one of the leading non-government proponents of defenses, Colin S. Gray, argues, "terminal non-nuclear defenses could provide a very attractive and effective way of strengthening strategic stability. Such defenses would have to promote massive new uncertainties in Soviet attack calculations—calculations that already are beset with major technical, tactical, strategic and political uncertainties."[50] If both sides were to field such a system, the calculation of outcomes becomes even more complicated. "If both superpowers deployed defenses, an attacker would face greater uncertainty about both the effectiveness of his attack *and* the effectiveness of the adversary's retaliation. The net effect of defenses is . . . indeterminate."[51] In addition to demonstrating the versatility of uncertainty as a concept, this suggests that inherent uncertainties in strategic calculations make it difficult to demonstrate the escape from vulnerability and, hence, RSD.

Conclusion: RSD and Change

Mutual vulnerability and the self-deterrence that results from it have produced a stability in superpower relations far greater than earlier formulations about nuclear balance predicted and considerably more durable, flexible, and reliable than current or past doomsayers have admitted. Deterrence has been transformed into self-deterrence, and the system works. The reason is clear: "Because the catastrophic and uncontrollable character of nuclear war is more or less clearly recognized by responsible leaders on both sides, preventing nuclear war and shaping the strategic balance to that end . . . has been accepted as one of the few clear areas of mutual interest."[52]

It is not very important whether this assessment of what nuclear war would be like—"catastrophic and uncontrollable" or not—is correct; at any rate, the judgment can only be rendered definitively if there is a nuclear war. Moreover, it is not necessary to accept this vision in a deterministic, defeatist manner and, thus, not try to make military contingency plans that would mitigate the disaster. Given that self-deterrence can in fact fail, planning to fight such a war at the lowest level and with termination with the least destruction (and, hopefully, on favorable terms) is the only prudent and responsible course.

What *is* necessary is to realize that the assured destruction outcome *could* occur if nuclear weapons are used and despite any thinking, planning, and force development to the contrary. The only real danger in not accepting assured destruction as *the* outcome in a nuclear war is the self-delusion that it *will not be* the outcome. We may make certain outcomes more or less likely by our prior actions; it would, for instance, probably be more difficult to limit a nuclear war if we had never thought about how to do so than if we have thought about it. The problem is that we are flirting with the maelstrom, and if we are sucked into it, we cannot in advance predict confidently the probability of survival. The reasons, of course, are lack of experience and evidence plus "the role of uncertainty in military planning; the scale of risks and consequences in the use, or the threat of use, of nuclear weapons; the unpredictability of warfare."[53] This last statement was made in the context of what might induce nuclear winter. Freeman Dyson puts the same concern in the form of an even more chilling (to risk the pun) analogy: "The meteorological uncertainties of nuclear war will remain at least as great as the uncertainties of peacetime weather prediction."[54]

Just the possibility that the worst case could be the outcome of nuclear exchange should be enough to maintain RSD. Such a world may not represent the best of all worlds, but it certainly has not been the worst either, which would be a world with nuclear war. We may indeed live in the best of all *possible* worlds or at least the best possible nuclear world we can construct today.

The critics, especially those who would produce a nuclear world constructed differently, bear the burden of proof that their visions would accomplish the continuing absence of nuclear war better than has been done up to now. Until those demonstrations have proven persuasive, fundamental change would be foolhardy and possibly irresponsible. Until we can show that some alternative vision will better maintain deterrence, we are far better off maintaining and improving what we have now.

This suggests the direction to be followed in the remainder of this book. Currently, there are two alternative visions on the public policy table: Ronald Reagan's vision of a defense-dominant world in which nuclear weapons are obsolete and can be eliminated (as discussed in chapter 3) and Mikhail Gorbachev's vision of a negotiated nuclear disarmament before the end of the millennium but without Reagan's "space shield" (the subject of chapter 4). It is also possible to construct a future nuclear world that contains elements of both visions (the focus in chapter 5). Finally, the most likely (or least unlikely) place for nuclear war to occur is through the escalation of a conflict involving NATO and the Warsaw Pact, making an examination of the contribution of "extended deterrence" to overall strategic balance a legitimate concern. This is covered in chapter 6.

The analytical lens through which these problems will be viewed is the one that has produced the current stable balance based on RSD. The disarmament explicit in Gorbachev's vision and implicit in Reagan's would make the world a demonstrably less deadly place, but would it also make it more dangerous? Would a nuclear-disarmed world lessen the inhibitions that have moderated conflict and thus "make the world safe" for conventional East–West war? Is such a world a better or worse place?

Moreover, the current balance works because of the dual dynamics of crisis management and perceptions about the consequences of nuclear war. These, in effect, form criteria against which to measure the beneficial or harmful effects of policies or proposals for change. Do, for instance, the policies imbedded in the NATO strategy of flexible response contribute to crisis avoidance or crisis termination? Does a defense-dominant world involve changes in perception about the acceptability of nuclear war?

These are the kinds of questions and criteria that will be applied to the proposals examined in the next four chapters. It is, of course, possible to argue that the imposition is unfair, because the proposals were not framed to respond to those terms. If, however, these criteria represent a useful way to describe the way the nuclear system operates, then it is not only fair but prudent to assess how proposals for change will affect those dynamics.

Notes

1. Harvard Nuclear Study Group (Albert Carnesale, Paul Doty, Stanley Hoffmann, Samuel P. Huntington, Joseph S. Nye, Jr., and Scott D. Sagan), *Living with Nuclear Weapons* (Cambridge, Mass.: Harvard University Press, 1983), pp. 17–18.

2. Robert Jervis, "MAD Is the Best Possible Deterrence," *Bulletin of the Atomic Scientists* 41, no. 3 (March 1985), p. 43.

3. Sidney D. Drell, Philip J. Farley, and David Holloway, *The Reagan Strategic*

Defense Initiative: A Technical, Political, and Arms Control Assessment (Cambridge, Mass.: Ballinger, 1985), p. 96.

4. My own summary of this debate is in *The Nuclear Future: Toward a Strategy of Uncertainty* (Tuscaloosa, Ala.: University of Alabama Press, 1983), pp. 1–34.

5. Barry R. Schneider, "Soviet Uncertainties in Targeting Peacekeeper," in Barry R. Schneider, Colin S. Gray, and Keith B. Payne (eds.), *Missiles for the Nineties: ICBMs and Strategic Policy* (Boulder, Colo.: Westview, 1984), p. 131.

6. Robert Jervis, *The Illogic of American Nuclear Strategy* (Ithaca, N.Y.: Cornell University Press, 1984), p. 108.

7. Richard Pipes, "Why the Soviet Union Thinks It Could Fight and Win a Nuclear War," *Commentary* 64, no. 1 (July 1977), p. 30.

8. Ibid.

9. Harry Trofimenko, "Political Realism and 'Realistic Deterrence' Strategy," in Robert J. Pranger and Robert P. Labrie (eds.), *Nuclear Strategy and National Security: Points of View* (Washington, D.C.: American Enterprise Institute for Public Policy Research, 1977), p. 46.

10. Georgi Arbatov, "The Dangers of a New Cold War," *Bulletin of the Atomic Scientists* 33, no. 3 (March 1977), p. 35.

11. See also Donald M. Snow, "Realistic Self-Deterrence: An Alternative View of Nuclear Dynamics," *Naval War College Review* 39, no. 2 (March/April 1986), pp. 63–73.

12. Robert Kennedy, "The Changing Strategic Balance and U.S. Defense Planning," in Robert Kennedy and John M. Weinstein (eds.), *The Defense of the West: Strategic and European Security Issues Reappraised* (Boulder, Colo.: Westview, 1984), p. 12.

13. Ronald W. Reagan, "National Security: Address to the Nation, March 23, 1983," *Weekly Compilation of Presidential Documents* 19, no. 12 (1983), p. 447.

14. Zbigniew Brzezinski, "Foreword," in Robin F. Laird and Dale R. Herspring, *The Soviet Union and Strategic Arms* (Boulder, Colo.: Westview, 1984), p. xi.

15. Snow, *The Nuclear Future*, p. 161.

16. Jervis, *The Illogic of American Nuclear Strategy*, p. 148.

17. Harvard Nuclear Study Group, *Living with Nuclear Weapons*, p. 210.

18. *Star Wars: Delusions and Dangers* (Moscow: Military Publishing House, 1985), p. 50.

19. Raymond L. Garthoff, "American–Soviet Relations in Perspective," *Political Science Quarterly* 100, no. 4 (Winter 1985/86), p. 548.

20. See, for example, Klaus Knorr, "Controlling Nuclear War," *International Security* 9, no. 4 (Spring 1985), p. 80.

21. Richard Ned Lebow, "Practical Ways to Avoid Superpower Crises," *Bulletin of the Atomic Scientists* 41, no. 1 (January 1985), p. 22.

22. Leon Weiseltier, *Nuclear War, Nuclear Peace* (New York: Holt, Rinehart and Winston, 1983), p. 63.

23. Paul Bracken, "Accidental Nuclear War," in Graham T. Allison, Albert Carnesale, and Joseph S. Nye, Jr. (eds.), *Hawks, Doves and Owls: An Agenda for Avoiding Nuclear War* (New York: W.W. Norton, 1985), p. 49.

24. Alexander L. George, "Toward a Soviet–American Crisis Prevention Regime", in Bernard Brodie, Michael D. Intriligator, and Roman Kolkowicz (eds.),

National Security and International Stability (Boston: Oelgeschlager, Gunn & Hain, 1983), p. 189.

25. For a summary of the maritime strategy, see James D. Watkins, "The Maritime Strategy," *United States Naval Institute Proceedings* 112, no. 1/995 (January 1986), pp. 3–17; and Robert S. Wood and John T. Hanley, Jr., "The Maritime Role in the North Atlantic," *Naval War College Review* 38, no. 6 (November/December 1985), pp. 5–18.

26. Stephen M. Meyer, "Soviet Perspectives on the Paths to Nuclear War," in Allison, Carnesale, and Nye, *Hawks, Doves and Owls,* p. 178.

27. Max M. Kampelman, "SDI and the Arms Control Process," *Atlantic Community Quarterly* 23, no. 3 (Fall 1985), p. 224.

28. Jervis, *The Illogic of American Nuclear Strategy,* p. 160.

29. Graham T. Allison, Albert Carnesale, and Joseph S. Nye, Jr., "Introduction," in Allison, Carnesale, and Nye, *Hawks, Doves and Owls,* p. 19.

30. Graham T. Allison, Albert Carnesale, and Joseph S. Nye, Jr., "Analytical Conclusions: Hawks, Doves and Owls," ibid., p. 214.

31. Harvard Nuclear Study Group, *Living with Nuclear Weapons,* p. 5.

32. Dean Rusk, "The Threat of Nuclear War," *Vital Speeches of the Day* 52, no. 7 (January 15, 1986), p. 204.

33. Laird and Herspring, *The Soviet Union and Strategic Arms,* p. 66.

34. Harvard Nuclear Study Group, *Living with Nuclear Weapons,* p. 159.

35. Jervis, *The Illogic of American Nuclear Strategy,* p. 168.

36. Fred S. Hoffman, "The SDI in U.S. Nuclear Strategy," *International Security* 10, no. 1 (Summer 1985), p. 19.

37. Robert E. Hunter, "SDI: Return to Basics:" *Washington Quarterly* 9, no. 1 (Winter 1986), p. 160.

38. Stanley Sienkiewicz, "Observations on the Impact of Uncertainty in Strategic Analysis," *World Politics* 32, no. 1 (October 1979), pp. 90–110.

39. Snow, *The Nuclear Future.*

40. John M. Weinstein, "All Features Grate and Small: Soviet Strategic Vulnerabilities and the Future of Deterrence," in Kennedy and Weinstein, *The Defense of the West,* pp. 42–43.

41. Dmitri Simes, "Are the Soviets Interested in Arms Control?" *Washington Quarterly* 8, no. 2 (Spring 1985), p. 153.

42. Weiseltier, *Nuclear War, Nuclear Peace,* p. 61.

43. Donald M. Snow, "The MX-Basing Mode Muddle: Issues and Alternatives," *Air University Review* 31, no. 5 (July/August 1980), pp. 11–25.

44. J. Edward Anderson, "First Strike: Myth or Reality," *Bulletin of the Atomic Scientists* 37, no. 9 (November 1981), pp. 6–11. See also Snow, *The Nuclear Future,* chap. 2.

45. Schneider, "Soviet Uncertainties in Targeting Peacekeeper," pp. 110–11.

46. Ibid., p. 131.

47. Robert Hotz, "Editorial: The Beam Weapons Race," *Aviation Week and Space Technology* 109, no. 14 (October 2, 1978), p. 9.

48. Lt. Gen. James A. Abrahamson, "Statement on the Strategic Defense Initiative, Statement to the Committee on Armed Services," United States Senate, 99th Congress, first session, February 21, 1985, p. 1.

49. Robert C. McFarlane, "Strategic Defense Initiative," *Department of State Bulletin* 85, no. 2099 (June 1985), p. 58.

50. Colin S. Gray, "Strategic Defences: A Case for Strategic Defence," *Survival* 27, no. 2 (March/April 1985), p. 52. See also Keith Payne and Colin S. Gray, "Nuclear Policy and the Defensive Transition," *Foreign Affairs* 62, no. 4 (Spring 1984), p. 824.

51. Charles L. Glaser, "Do We Want the Missile Defenses We Can Build?" *International Security* 10, no. 1 (Summer 1985), p. 35.

52. Drell, Farley, and Holloway, *The Reagan Strategic Defense Initiative*, p. 97.

53. Theodore A. Postol, "Strategic Confusion—With or Without Nuclear Winter," *Bulletin of the Atomic Scientists* 41, no. 2 (February 1985), p. 14.

54. Freeman J. Dyson, *Weapons and Hope* (New York: Harper & Row, 1984), p. 21.

Part II
Challenges to the Balance

3
Reagan's Vision:
A Defense-Dominant World

On March 23, 1983, President Ronald W. Reagan announced his vision of a preferred future nuclear world.[1] Apparently culminating a growing interest and commitment germinating since shortly after he became governor of California in 1967,[2] Reagan's proposed reorientation of the strategic nuclear relationship involved a gradual movement away from mutual vulnerability and the absolute dominance of offensive weapons toward strategic defenses that could protect the population rather than simply promise to avenge them. That, he hoped, would ultimately "give us the means of rendering these nuclear weapons impotent and obsolete."[3]

His initiative, part of a broader address to the nation, caught almost everyone off guard. As James Schlesinger captured the initial reaction,

> Even the Department of Defense was unprepared. The president had been moved not by the advice of the technical experts within his Administration, but by some elderly outside advisors [an apparent reference to Dr. Edward Teller]. Until the President's address, the Department of Defense had steadily been expressing skepticism (to put it mildly) regarding space-based defenses.[4]

The president himself as well as his supporters and detractors have been expansive on the prospects he raised. In the original speech, he entreated the scientific community to engage in a research program the equivalent of the Manhattan Project or the space program to explore the various possibilities for defense, an effort christened the Strategic Defense Initiative, with the formal establishment within the Department of Defense of an SDI Organization under the leadership of Air Force Lt. General James A. Abrahamson in 1984. The SDI research program, which was raised to the level of the single largest weapon project in the fiscal year (FY) 1987 budget proposal,[5] is exploring a number of technologies ranging from more or less conventional antiballistic missile (ABM) systems to rail guns to exotic applications of directed energy transfer to the defense. Perhaps the most dramatic, and certainly the most controversial, elements have focused on potential defenses using various forms of laser propagation, especially ones stationed in space (the prospect that earned the project the sobriquet "Star Wars").

Reagan has been steadfast in his defense both of the program and its character. To his critics, he has consistently reflected what he believes to be the benign, stabilizing effect of SDI. "Some say it will bring war to the heavens, but its purpose is to deter war in the heavens and on Earth," he said in his 1985 State of the Union address.[6] Reflecting on the beneficial effects that a strategic defense could provide, arms negotiator Max Kampelman adds, "I believe we would all agree that it would be better to base deterrence on an increased ability to deny the aggressor his objectives than to rely solely on our ability to punish him for his aggression. . . . It is this prospect for a more effective deterrence that research on strategic defense offers."[7]

In one sense, it is difficult to discuss the SDI for two reasons. The first, which the Reagan administration frequently emphasizes, is that SDI is indeed a research rather than a weapons program. As such, what weapons (if any) will emerge from SDI is indeterminate. Although the stated intent is to produce a benign defense, it is literally impossible to predict the outcomes at this juncture. SDI could produce more or less impregnable defenses, weapons with strategic offensive characteristics, weapons with characteristics and applications in quite remote and unforeseen areas such as antisubmarine warfare, or no weapons at all. Although much of the debate over SDI has been about the character of SDI weapons, it is literally a debate about nothing concrete at this point.

A second problem is that the arguments about SDI tend to get enmeshed in quasi-theological debates about the desirability of missile defense that derive from positions on nuclear strategy described in chapter 2. To adherents of the "faith" of assured destruction, missile defense has always been viewed with doctrinal suspicion. Population defense is discouraged because it reduces the perception of personal vulnerability. Defense of retaliatory forces is accepted grudgingly; it adds to the might available for retaliation, but is eyed cautiously as the Trojan Horse presaging population defenses. Champions of limited options, on the other hand, are sympathetic to either form of defense, since part of their doctrine is based on the hope of mitigating the disaster should deterrence fail.[8]

Although its dimensions are amorphous, its intended directions and the controversy they are producing are not, leading the authors of a critical *Foreign Affairs* article to describe SDI as "the most important question of nuclear arms competition and arms control on the national agenda since 1972."[9] Whether this judgment is justified requires looking at what the SDI is, first through the lens of its champions in the form of the New Strategic Concept, and then through the strident public Soviet rejection of the concept and U.S. official reaction to Soviet objections. Since much of the controversy about SDI concerns whether it will work, the discussion will move to whether SDI is a viable concept. Finally, the desirability of strategic defense based on the president's vision will be assessed, using the RSD criteria as the organizational device for the discussion.

The New Strategic Concept

The most elaborate and articulate statement of the end state the president envisages and the steps to its attainment is found in something called the *New Strategic Concept*.[10] This idea was first announced by State Department official Kenneth W. Dam in early 1985,[11] although it has been stated and defended, and hence tends to be more closely associated, with Paul H. Nitze, senior advisor to the president on arms control matters.

The New Strategic Concept consists of two related aspects. The first aspect consists of two criteria for erecting a defense: survivability and cost-effectiveness. Survivability means that a defensive system must be capable of survival against attacks against it by offensive weapons or by similar systems with offensive capabilities. An example of an offensive attack is the so-called "space mine," whereby an explosive is launched into space near the defensive system and detonated, destroying itself and the defensive system. If the defenses consist of space-based lasers, on the other hand, U.S. systems must be impervious to attacks by Soviet laser stations and vice versa.

The failure to achieve survivability is vulnerability and, hence, destabilization, since either or both sides could have the incentive to strike first and destroy the other's defenses in a crisis (a variant of the familiar "use-them-or-lose-them" problem). This survivability, however, need not be absolute, as Teller explains: "Defense must be designed so that destroying is more expensive than deploying it. Defense in itself does not mean progress toward stability. Such progress is only accomplished if defense has a sufficiently low price."[12] For future reference, the problem of survivability is most often raised in the context of space-based systems (e.g., laser battle stations) or components (e.g., satellites used for target acquisition and tracking).

Cost-effectiveness, on the other hand, has to do with the relative expense of a defense and the means to overcome it (offensive countermeasures). In discussing traditional ABM defenses, for instance, there has always been the allegation that such a system could be defeated simply by overwhelming it with so many offensive warheads that it could not cope. The alleged advantage of this approach is that the additional offensive capability could be purchased at a fraction of the unit cost of defense; hence, an offense–defense competition is ultimately a futile and economically ruinous exercise for the defender.

A cost-effective defense must reverse the ratio between offensive and defensive costs such that the marginal costs of defense are less than those of the offense. If that can be achieved, then the builder of offenses will be discouraged because competition will be economically unfavorable to him. Accomplishing that end, however, is no small task, because "a defensive system must not only work, it must maintain its effectiveness, at a favorable cost-ratio, against an opponent who attempts to defeat it."[13] A number of scientists critical of SDI focus on this latter point in suggesting that the president's comparison of SDI to the Manhattan Project or the Apollo program is faulty; the atom put up no countermeasures against being split nor did the moon seek to defeat astronauts Armstrong and Aldrin.

These two criteria create minimum performance criteria for the defense, as described by Assistant Secretary of Defense Richard Perle:

> Defensive technologies . . . must, at a minimum, be able to destroy a sufficient portion of an aggressor's attacking forces so as to deny him either confidence in the outcome of his attack or the ability to destroy a credible portion of the targets he wishes to destroy. . . . Any effective defensive system definitely must be both survivable and cost-effective.[14]

According the Paul Nitze, the result is akin to deterrence by uncertainty: "Survivable and cost-effective defenses could so complicate a potential attacker's planning for a first strike that such an attack could not be seriously contemplated and deterrence would thus be significantly enhanced."[15] As we shall see in the next section, such a definition of success is far more modest than the president publicly suggests.

The other aspect of the New Strategic Concept is the process for moving from a condition of offensive weapons dominance to one of defense dominance. In essence, it calls for a three-stage period, the timing depending on the pace of discovery of increasingly effective nonnuclear defense components. In the first phase, probably for the next decade or so, defenses would not be erected, but offensive forces would be reduced. This is compatible with the administration's Strategic Arms Reduction Talks (START) proposals and would result in a more constrained offensive problem that would presumably be more manageable for eventually deployed defenses.

The second phase consists of deploying defensive technologies as they become available. The concept envisages that this transition would likely begin with the erection of terminal point defenses of retaliatory forces and gradually be expanded to encompass territorial defenses of population as well. The transition is conceived of as a long duration that "would continue for some time, perhaps decades."[16] At the end of this process is the third phase of defense dominance, where the defenses render offensive weapons obsolete: "We envisage, if that search is successful, a cooperative effort with the Soviet Union, hopefully leading to an agreed transition toward nonnuclear defenses that might make possible the elimination of nuclear weapons."[17] This latter statement suggests that achieving the ultimate goal requires cooperation between the Soviets and the Americans on SDI. That cooperation has not been forthcoming, and its likelihood and even desirability remain controversial.

Soviet Reaction to SDI

The Soviet Union has voiced uniform and total opposition to SDI. The condemnation extends particularly to those aspects of SDI connected to space and goes back to 1981, when they introduced before the United Nations their first of two draft treaties prohibiting the weaponizing of space.[18] (Their expanded second draft was introduced in 1983.[19])

The heart of the Soviet public position is that the technologies comprising SDI are not defensive at all, and that U.S. depictions of SDI as a benign defense represent "outright deceit" which will not work: "The U.S. attempts to portray its highly dangerous space plans as defensive cannot fool the Soviet Union."[20] Rather, the Soviets allege that the weapons to be developed, so-called "space-strike systems" or "attack space weapons" are really offensive in character.[21] Their development has, according to public Soviet sources, been going on with sinister purpose since the beginning of the Reagan administration. "Since 1981, on personal instructions of President Reagan, these matters have been repeatedly discussed at the highest level in order to select the most promising ways of developing effective weapons *for destroying targets in outer space and targets in the atmosphere and on Earth from space*" (emphasis added).[22]

According to one European Marxist commentator, the goal is clear: "By coupling space militarization, christened Strategic Defense Initiative, with an upgrading of ballistic and medium-range missiles, Reagan hopes to achieve his goal—world domination."[23] While official Soviet assertions are often not as expansive as this, they do consistently stress both the offensive nature of the SDI and its relation to attempts to achieve first-strike capability against the Soviet Union.

This formulation is remarkable for both what it does and does not allege. The sharp rejection of weapons using technologies and employing media that the Soviets have also been exploring for years[24] is surprising in its intensity and consistency, leading one to speculate about why their reaction has been so strong. At the same time, these denunciations do *not* condemn strategic defenses per se, instead being limited to attacks on the alleged offensive character of SDI. These important observations represent concerns that will be discussed later.

Administration Responses to Soviet Pronouncements

The Reagan administration's reactions to Soviet charges about SDI have been as negative as the charges themselves. These reactions can be broken into three distinct parts: specific denials of the Soviet charges, explanations of why the Soviets are making these false accusations, and statements about how they hope to win the Soviets over to a more "reasonable" position—which is to say their view on SDI and the New Strategic Concept.

The administration generally has not confronted Soviet charges directly, preferring to dismiss them as mere propaganda that does not warrant the dignity of direct denial. Occasionally, however, such denials do occur. Former National Security Advisor Robert McFarlane, for instance, has stated that "The first myth is that the United States is attempting to 'militarize space.' This is a Soviet propaganda line."[25] The president himself, pressed by a reporter at a press interview, explicitly denied that SDI aims at producing an offensive capability, saying "That isn't what we are researching on or what we are trying to accomplish."[26] To the charge that SDI is an attempt to gain decisive strategic advantage, Nitze has said flatly: "Let me be clear that SDI is not an attempt to achieve superiority."[27]

Having asserted that the Soviets are in essence lying about why they object to SDI, the administration has felt compelled to demonstrate why this has been so. The explanation is that "The Soviets will, by virtue of their highly competitive nature and past successes with their propaganda campaigns, be tempted to continue to tie their offers to demands that the United States give up research on defensive systems."[28] According to Kenneth Adelman, director of the Arms Control and Disarmament Agency, the reason for this position is to gain unilateral advantage for the Soviet Union:

> The Soviet propaganda line against SDI is as predictable as it is hypocritical. The Soviets hope to foster a situation in which the United States is pressured unilaterally to restrain its research effort. . . . This approach would leave the Soviets with a virtual monopoly in advanced strategic defense research; obviously they see this as the most desirable outcome.[29]

The Soviet and U.S. positions are clearly diametrically opposed. The Soviets accuse the Reagan administration of lying about its intentions for the SDI program, and the administration accuses the Soviets of lying about why they object to the program. Asked to reconcile the two positions in a way that would allow realization of the president's dream of a defense-dominant world, Reagan administration spokesmen have argued that this disagreement both is and is not fundamental. Arguing that it is an important problem, for instance, Secretary of State Shultz has maintained that the Soviets "have devoted their greatest effort to propaganda and held everything hostage to getting their way on SDI."[30] This line of argumentation became especially obvious in the wake of the 1986 Reykjavik meeting between Reagan and Gorbachev.

Although this would seem to indicate a seriousness about Soviet objections, the administration's position about overcoming them has been decidedly patronizing. First the Soviets have to realize the United States is serious about the whole SDI. As President Reagan said after the 1985 summit, "I think it's fair to point out that the Soviets' main aim at Geneva was to force us to drop SDI. I think I can also say that after Geneva Mr. Gorbachev understands we have no intention of doing so."[31] Once the Soviets realize they cannot propagandize the United States out of its commitment to SDI, then a process of education and conversion can begin. As Shultz describes it, "As our research proceeds and both nations thus gain a better sense of the future prospects, the Soviets should see the advantages of agreed ground rules to ensure that any phasing in of defensive systems will be orderly, predictable, and stabilizing."[32] This process of conversion will not be quick or easy, "But with persistence, patience, and constructive ideas, we hope the Soviets will come to see the merits of our position."[33]

A recent analysis of Soviet attitudes toward SDI throws cold water on these optimistic projections. "Every authoritative Soviet discussion of military strategy—in both their 'open' and 'closed' literature—makes it clear that strategic defense, in and of itself, cannot be the basis of national military strategy," Meyer asserts. As a result, "Western debates over the nature of a 'transition phase' to a defense-dominated world are of academic interest only, since Soviet actions are likely to ensure that there will be no transition phase."[34]

What Is SDI and What Does It Do?

The preceding discussion has sought to present the very different conceptualizations of SDI by the Soviet Union and the Reagan administration. In their pronouncements, the Soviets portray it either as an offensive weapon per se or as a menacing defensive weapon which, in combination with the modernization of U.S. offensive forces (the MX, B1B bomber, Trident D5 missile, and cruise missiles), represent an attempt to achieve strategic superiority. In either case, the intent is offensive. The Reagan administration, by contrast, argues the benign, defensive nature of the program. The president himself emphasizes the long-range "space shield" that will create an astrodome effect protecting the population from nuclear weapons, while others in the administration highlight SDI as enhancing deterrence by defending retaliatory forces. Still others maintain that the fruits of SDI lie not in strategic offenses and defenses at all, but in other military areas such as antisubmarine warfare, surface ship defense against cruise missiles, or even antitank missions.

What, then, is SDI? The answer is that it may produce an offense, a defense, both, neither, or something else. Specifying which at this time is an exercise in futility and empty rhetoric because, as pointed out, the outcomes of the research are unknown at this point, and so too are the weapons possibilities. At the same time, it is somewhat misleading to talk about weapons as offensive or defensive. Weapons simply are weapons, and to typify them further is to risk reification. Rather, the weapons can be *used* for offensive or defensive purposes, which means that both Reagan and Gorbachev could simultaneously be correct about whatever weapons possibilities emerge from the SDI effort. Moreover, the true nature of SDI is beclouded by a veil of secrecy that means "the best publicized defensive systems are those that are rather primitive or will not work at all" and "whenever a truly effective idea is pursued, that is kept secret."[35] Also, there is public confusion on whether SDI will produce a comprehensive defense or whether "there would remain the difficulty of defense against cruise missiles, against bomber aircraft, and against the clandestine introduction of warheads."[36]

If one cannot specify what defensive forms SDI *will* produce, one can enumerate what defenses *may* come into existence. The basic distinction revolves around the question of system performance or how well an SDI-based defense might work. As discussions on this subject have evolved, two performance possibilities have been discussed: perfect and less-than-perfect (LTP) defenses. In turn, the performance levels that may be attained are affected by whether the offensive forces the defense must try to defeat are constrained or unconstrained. These distinctions are depicted in matrix form in figure 3–1.

The distinctions are reasonably straightforward. A perfect defense would intercept all or essentially all the warheads aimed at it. (There is a considerable debate over what constitutes an acceptable definition of "essentially all" and thus what level of so-called leakage would be tolerable.) A perfect defense provides comprehensive protection—an astrodome effect—and is usually associated with population defense. A less-than-perfect defense, then, is one with lesser capability—the capacity to intercept only some portion of the offensive attack. LTP defenses are most often associated with defending retaliatory forces, since destruction of any incoming warheads means that some higher amount of retaliatory force would remain to inflict vengeance.

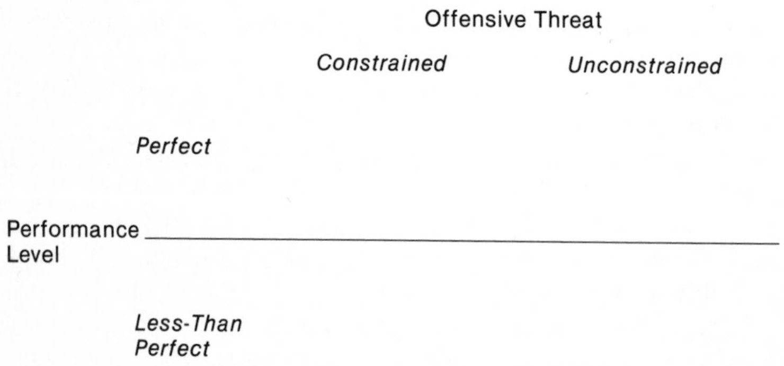

Offensive Threat

Constrained   Unconstrained

Perfect

Performance _____
Level

Less-Than-
Perfect

Figure 3–1

The performance criteria for the two types are fundamentally different. The criterion for a perfect defense is absolute; it must work essentially fault-lessly or it fails, given the enormous death and destruction that would accompany the detonation of even a relatively modest number of penetrating warheads. The criterion for an LTP defense of retaliatory forces, on the other hand, is incremental; any extent to which they perform increases the amount of retaliation available as a dissuasive force; increases in effectiveness simply improve that situation by increments. (The same argument is occasionally made for population; an LTP defense means more people would survive than would in its absence.) These distinctions help to frame the broader concern over the role of defenses, as former Secretary of Defense Harold Brown notes.

> There are now separate debates taking place. . . . The first is whether to replace the threat of retaliation as the basis of U.S. nuclear deterrence strategy with a new strategy based on the defence of the United States. The second is whether and to what extent the United States should deploy active defences with more limited objectives and capabilities.[37]

Reagan's dream of a defense-dominant world in the final phase of the new strategic concept requires a perfect defense: "A research and testing program that may one day provide a peace shield to protect against nuclear attack is a deeply hopeful vision."[38] Only a perfect defense can provide the protection that will render nuclear weapons impotent and obsolete. As former Defense Secretary Schlesinger points out, this strikes a responsive chord with the public: "The American psyche believes that perfect defense *should* be attainable. . . . It is this unique belief that underlines the current hope for the SDI."[39] Walter Slocombe agrees, adding a political dimension to the attractiveness: "The political secret of SDI is that it appeals to an immensely popular idea. That is the idea of getting rid of nuclear weapons. The realism—or lack of it—of an idea as attractive as that has no necessary effect on its popularity."[40] Moreover, at least some analysts believe the capability is attainable. "With technologies already invented or under development, one could build a defense against existing ballistic missiles that would be at least 99.9 percent effective," one study maintains.[41]

The attainability of a perfect defense is hotly contested, with the larger number expressing some reservations. Brown asserts that "American political and military leaders should publicly acknowledge that there is no realistic prospect for a successful population defense, certainly for many decades, and probably never."[42] Schlesinger concurs with the flat statement: "There is no leak-proof defense."[43] Even Edward Teller, who takes credit for spurring and sustaining Reagan's continued commitment to strategic defenses generally, has expressed some reservations about achieving a perfect defense. "A 99.9 percent defense cannot be attained soon. It may never be attained. Even if it is attained, it will not be attained with complete certainty."[44]

Skepticism, or at least uncertainty, about the ability to construct perfect defenses has left many SDI supporters in the administration (other than the president himself) extolling the virtues of less-than-perfect defenses. As pointed out in chapter 2, a major virtue advertised for LTP defenses of retaliatory forces is to raise the Soviets' uncertainty about their ability to succeed in an attempted disarming first strike. Other advocates of LTP defenses point to them as a hedge against the failure of deterrence ("strategic defense would be more likely to prevent an all-out-war—with the added, crucial advantage that if it does not, we are not totally without defense"[45]), as a way to "bring back . . . the McNamara spirit" of limited retaliatory force protection,[46] and even as "a buffering measure against violations of arms control agreements."[47]

Many of the arguments used to support LTP defenses have the clear ring of fallback positions. This is especially true of administration spokesmen trying to defend the SDI but aware that it may never approximate Reagan's hopes for it. Moreover, there have yet to appear any particularly good analyses of how much benefit one gets from LTP defenses of differing levels of efficiency and how these benefits relate to whatever costs (economic and other) may be incurred. One analyst has looked at costs in terms of assault on the ABM Treaty, a likely offensive–defensive countermeasures race, and a general chilling effect on the ability to negotiate future arms control agreements. Using these criteria, he concludes, "Deployment of limited or intermediate ballistic missile defenses would, on balance, reduce U.S. security. . . . [D]eployment of less-than-perfect BMD and the associated evolutionary strategy should be rejected."[48]

A major variable in the attainability of perfect defenses or highly effective LTP defenses is the quantity and quality of the offensive threat that the defenses face. Clearly, an offensive force constrained—frozen or even reduced—by an arms control agreement places limits on the size of the threat and keeps the opponent from expanding his offensive force beyond the size that saturates the defense. Because of the ability simply to build additional warheads, most observers do not believe a cost-effective perfect defense is possible in an unconstrained offensive environment, and there is doubt that a useful LTP defense can be built without offensive force constraints. This creates anomalous situations. On the one hand, building defenses that would test or destroy one arms control agreement (the ABM Treaty) requires an offensive arms control agreement to be attractive. On the other hand, many SDI supporters in the administration (e.g., Richard Perle) have long histories of opposing arms control in general, but are forced to embrace it to get SDI, because there is something close to consensus that "if defensive systems are to contribute to a safer and more stable strategic relationship between the United States and the Soviet Union, they will have to be imbedded in a strict arms-control regime that limits offensive systems."[49]

The relationship between performance levels and the offensive threat thus becomes clear. The president's vision of a defense-dominant world through the SDI clearly calls for a perfect defense against a constrained offensive threat, since each stage of the process envisaged in the New Strategic Concept contains offensive force reductions. Although it is conceivable that these reductions could be made unilaterally by the United States as defenses made offensive stockpiles superfluous, Reagan's vision clearly looks toward bilateral reductions leading to disarmament as the ultimate end. Mutual reductions are desirable not only because they conform to the president's vision, but also because the nature of the threat affects the ability to attain perfect defenses, because "the feasibility of a near-perfect strategic defense depends heavily on the nature of Soviet efforts to counter it."[50]

Perfect defenses, in other words, may require Soviet cooperation in the form of offensive constraints presumably negotiated through arms control agreements, and such cooperation may be not only unlikely but also impossible—a set of problems discussed in chapter 4. If Soviet cooperation in constraining quantitative or qualitative offensive forces cannot be achieved or if long-range research outputs prove inadequate to produce perfect defenses, then the remaining possibilities are LTP defenses which, by definition, fall short of Reagan's vision. Clearly, a less-than-perfect defense also would perform better against a constrained than an unconstrained force. Qualitatively, a smaller attack force creates fewer problems for a defense at any level of efficiency than does a larger force. Quantitatively, regardless of the percentage of warheads a LTP defense can destroy, an attack by a smaller force will result in less getting through than a larger attack.

If a perfect or near-perfect defense is attainable, its likely "architecture" (to borrow the current jargon) will be a "layered defense" design. The proposed shape of such a defense has been described at length elsewhere[51] and need not be elaborated here. A summary description is useful to show the places and technologies a layered defense would likely operate in, what forms of defense must closely resemble designs for a perfect or LTP defense, and how the layered defense concept is compatible with movement toward defense dominance through the New Strategic Concept.

Most conceptions of a layered defense talk about interception of enemy warheads in four phases of their flight using two different kinds of interception technologies. The phases of flight are boost, postboost, midcourse, and terminal. (Colin S. Gray has further subdivided terminal interception into two subphases to create a five-layered design.[52]) Interception technologies generally encompass antiballistic missile and directed energy transfer, notably some form of laser propagation. Interception at each phase with each technology contributes differently to perfect or LTP defenses.

Boost-phase interception involves attacking enemy missiles as they rise through the atmosphere with the booster engines and the postboost vehicle holding the warheads attached. The advantages of interception at this stage are that the missile is most vulnerable during this phase and that killing one rocket destroys several warheads if the missile has multiple warheads (which most missiles do). The technology for this kind of interception involves the use of directed energy weapons, with laser stations in an Earth orbit a common futuristic model. This form of weaponry, however, most clearly approximates the space-strike weapons about which the Soviets are most adamant.

Following the detachment of the booster engines, the missile enters postboost phase. At the beginning of this phase, the postboost vehicle (PBV) is intact, containing all the warheads, dummy warheads, and chaff, and is a high-value target for attack by directed energy transfer weapons. The PBV rapidly loses its value, however, because individual warheads are released during this phase. As the PBV maneuvers to release its payload, it emits heat which can be picked up by sensors to allow attacks.

The longest phase is midcourse. Lasting fifteen to twenty minutes, the warheads, decoys, and chaff drift through space on predetermined courses toward their destinations. Tracking is most difficult during this phase for two reasons. First, the attacking weapons are in space where there is no friction and, thus, little if any heat "signature" produced to guide defensive sensors to target. Second, the weightlessness of space makes it difficult to discriminate between actual warheads and accompanying decoys and chaff which are generally much lighter than the real warheads. Attempts to intercept during this phase are generally associated with large exoatmospheric ABM explosions in the general areas through which the warheads must fly (areas known as "windows"). Historically, this has meant the explosion of megaton-range nuclear warheads in the space above Canada; the SDI is investigating nonnuclear alternatives to such detonations.

The final phase is terminal, when the warheads reenter the atmosphere. Interception during this phase is made easier because the decoys and chaff generally burn up during reentry—thereby allowing discrimination—and because friction heats the reentry vehicle's (RVs) surface, thereby allowing tracking. The problem is that this phase lasts a short time—thirty to one hundred seconds depending on the missile's trajectory. A variety of terminal ABM and ground-based beam weapons are being developed for this form of defense.

A LTP defense that emphasizes protection of retaliatory forces is generally conceptualized as entailing terminal and late-midcourse interception by ground-based ABM and possibly directed energy weapons. These are the most mature missile defense technologies and the ones envisaged in the second stage of the New Strategic Concept. Critics of the prospects of perfect defenses generally say these are the only attainable forms; SDI supporters who argue the value of LTP defenses are implicitly admitting that this may be the case.

A perfect defense—if attainable at all—probably requires a layered defense including space-basing of directed energy weapons. This is the kind of system to which Secretary of Defense Caspar Weinberger refers when he talks about "a thoroughly reliable, layered defense that would destroy Soviet missiles outside the earth's atmosphere and *at all phases of flight*" (emphasis added).[53] General Abrahamson agrees "that a layered defense offers the best chance of achieving the required effectiveness against a broad range of existing and potential future threats and attacks."[54]

As Gray explains, the strength of a layered defense is the reinforcing synergism of the various layers.

> A layered defense would function by cumulative attrition. If each layer of a five-tiered defense architecture could impose 50 percent attrition on a Soviet attack of 10,000 nuclear warheads, 312 should survive to detonate. The important point from the perspective of deterrence is that Soviet defense planners could not possibly know which.[55]

The uncertainty so engendered would, according to this argument, enhance deterrence by making it impossible to determine in advance if an attack achieved its purposes. This, in turn, would allow movement to the last stage of the New Strategic Concept and allow accomplishment of SDI's purposes: "Once Phase Four defenses ('astrodome') are in place, the situation favors improved crisis stability and a more credible extended deterrence pledge."[56]

The erection of a perfect defense is thus a difficult task which may or may not prove attainable and which, at any rate, may require Soviet cooperation in the form of constraints on offensive arms. This does not make the task impossible. Partly the possibility cannot be ruled out because of the pace of technology: "Primarily because of incredible advances in electronics and computing, layered ballistic missile defense may become a reality within the next 20 years."[57] Moreover, it may be that the nay-sayers lack historical perspective about the ebb and flow of weapons developments: "For the strategic defense to achieve a very marked superiority over the offense over the next several decades would be an extraordinary trend in the light of the last 30 years, but not of the last hundred or thousand years."[58]

Is the Reagan Vision Desirable?

The attainability of Ronald Reagan's vision of a defense-dominant world is an open question, but the possibility cannot be ruled out. That being the case, one must further ask if the resulting strategic world is a better or worse place.

The touchstone is the effect of change on stability defined as the increased or decreased likelihood that either side could or would reach the decision to initiate nuclear war. In proposing and supporting the SDI, administration spokesmen maintain that this is also their major concern: "If in the future we decide favorably on SDI, deterrence and stability would be the strategic concepts by which we could measure the value of strategic defenses."[59] Moreover, it is program director Abrahamson's belief that this is exactly what SDI offers: "The overriding importance of SDI . . . is that it offers the possibility of . . . moving to a better, more stable basis of deterrence."[60]

Are these claims warranted? A fully successful SDI would alter the mechanical and technical basis of the nuclear balance, but it would not, in and of itself, ameliorate the political divisions that gave rise to the arms competition in the first place, leaving an irony of sorts. "Salvation in the nuclear arms race . . . lies not in yet another technical fix, but rather in the politics of the relationship. Indeed, if that relationship could be developed to the point where a full-blown Strategic Defense Initiative could be safely implemented, then it would not be needed at all."[61] One can argue that SDI will actually make political relations worse between the superpowers if Soviet opposition remains adamant and the United States continues to insist on pursuing the program.[62] Despite concerted Reagan administration efforts to imbed the program so deeply into the national defense agenda that a successor administration cannot abandon it, the continuation of SDI to fruition is no political certainty. Politically, "at least four administrations and eight congresses must give strong support to the SDI for it to realize its ambitious aims."[63]

The effect of a movement toward a defense-dominant world is to erode the condition of mutual vulnerability on which self-deterrence has been based. A partial movement based on less-than-perfect defenses of retaliatory forces would not have this effect and would, if anything, reinforce vulnerability. This is so both because protection of retaliatory forces means more retributive power would be available after aggression (the standard assured destruction line on defenses) and because such protection would reduce the target set largely to countervalue targets (since counterforce targets would be protected).

Movement to defense-dominance through perfect defenses changes that situation drastically, and "the more comprehensive a U.S. BMD system appeared to be, the more it would undermine previously articulated U.S. declaratory policies."[64] SDI supporters acknowledge and applaud that mechanical change but admit that SDI cannot solve underlying political differences. "The SDI and a defensive transition can change the terms of deterrence, away from retaliatory nuclear threat (which would be no small accomplishment) but in and of itself, it cannot arrest the arms competition."[65]

Whether such a change is indeed an accomplishment depends both on what replaces vulnerability and how both sides feel about the substitution. In one sense, a movement toward defenses is intuitively appealing; defense is, after all, a traditional military function, and attempting to mitigate the potential disaster of nuclear war is obviously prudent—if one does not make that war more likely. Moreover, a movement toward defense and away from vulnerability is congruent with Soviet defense objectives. As Fred Charles Iklé puts it, "There is a fundamental reason why we should not expect the Soviet leadership to settle for the strategic order of consensual vulnerability. . . . [T]he accord on a stable equilibrium of mutual restraint is psychologically incompatible with the constant threat of reciprocal annihilations."[66] Stephen Meyer agrees with this assessment, adding a note of historical context: *"Soviet history and domestic politics prevents any Soviet leader from advocating a military doctrine whose guiding principle is accepting the enemy's . . . blow*—a repeat of the disaster of 22 June 1941" (emphasis in original).[67] A strategic world in which defenses play a part should not be objectionable to the Soviets if the United States can convince them that the SDI will produce such a world.

The dynamics of a strategic world where defense dominates offense so that those offenses are anachronistic and, thus, can be eliminated are clearly very different from the current situation of mutual vulnerability and fear. In describing his vision, Reagan frequently draws an analogy with a 1925 chemical weapons agreement whereby those weapons were banned and stockpiles were destroyed—the equivalent of nuclear disarmament. In his analogy, however, Reagan points out the participants hedged their bets on compliance by keeping their gas masks—the equivalent of strategic defenses in a nuclear-disarmed world. Such a world is clearly less deadly, but is it more or less dangerous? Measuring this condition against the criteria of RSD will help clarify the issue.

Crisis Management

Whether the transition to defensive dominance would reinforce or strain the crisis management system would seem to depend on three considerations. The first is whether the effort is cooperative on the part of the superpowers, the second is whether the system is comprehensive or less-than-perfect, and the third is whether one is talking about the transition to defense or a completed system. Clearly, these concerns are related.

Although a few SDI proponents argue that it does not matter,[68] it seems clear that a cooperative deployment of defenses would create fewer strains that could devolve into crises than if one or another opposes the change. Mutual, symmetrical, and staged deployment would ease the transition period[69] and could result in comparable completed systems. If the Soviets cannot be convinced that SDI is what it is advertised to be, and if they fear the eventual nature of a deployed SDI (both of which are possible given their public positions on SDI), they could be expected to do everything in their power to disrupt deployment. A deployed SDI might well be a fait accompli that stabilizes exactly as the president suggests it might, but it is hard to see how to create that situation in the face of determined Soviet opposition. At the same time, the experience gained in a cooperative deployment could itself provide useful lessons for future crisis avoidance and termination.

The kind of capability being deployed affects stability as well, if in a perverse manner. During the transition period, deployment of LTP defense (and the less perfect the better!) would be less destabilizing than deployment of perfect defenses. On the one hand, less perfect defenses change things less and, thus, cause less upset than more perfect systems. On the other hand, such defenses are probably more within the grasp of the Soviet technological system, thereby avoiding the possibility of serious asymmetry—a U.S. perfect defense versus a Soviet LTP defense—or of sharing technology to bridge the gap. Perfect or near-perfect defenses accentuate these problems and could lead to a situation where "very effective U.S. or Soviet BMD may not be compatible with more stable deterrence because of the dilution of crisis stability during the interim period until complete deployment by both sides is achieved."[70]

As this quote suggests, the situation is reversed when one talks about completed, operational systems. Assuming that the chemical warfare analogy is correct, a nuclear-disarmed world where breaches of disarmament are offset by defenses offers the prospect of being both less deadly and no more dangerous than the current situation. Nuclear disarmament, quite obviously, lowers deadliness, and defenses make breaches of the nuclear peace futile, thereby keeping danger low. In that circumstance, nuclear fear is removed, and the major remaining problem is whether the effect might be to "make the world safe for conventional war"—a problem addressed in chapter 6.

This suggests the dilemma that advocates of SDI must face—the pathway to their utopia. If the route is cooperative and leads toward similar capabilities, then neither the transitional period nor the operational period need produce particular strain or crisis. Under current circumstances, however, this is not the case. Unless Soviet opposition can be overcome by convincing them that Reagan's vision rather than their fear is what composes the final shape of an SDI-dominated world, the road could be rocky indeed.

Perceptual Change

Responding to Fred S. Hoffman's entreaty that the "point of departure ought to be reflection on the motives that might induce Soviet leaders and military planners to contemplate actually using nuclear weapons,"[71] the next question is how a movement toward a defense-dominant world would affect superpower perceptions about the acceptability of war and, especially, clash that might escalate to nuclear confrontation. It is in this area that defensive dominance based on perfect defenses clearly makes the greatest potential change from the current situation. Whether it is a change for better or worse largely is a matter of the relationship between the weapons and the political purposes for which they were developed and for which they are maintained.

This may be a chicken-and-egg dilemma. Nuclear weapons were not developed for the primary purpose of confronting the Soviet Union—although Soviet sources occasionally suggest that they were—but have been applied to Soviet–U.S. competition. Congruent with the general argument developed here, however, the role is both of effect and cause. On the one hand, the cause of the development of a nuclear weapons arsenal was Soviet–U.S. competition—in the U.S. case, largely because they are cheaper than conventional armaments. On the other hand, those arsenals create the vulnerability, fear, and restraint that provide the limits on how that competition is regulated. Political competition is, thus, the first causal link to understanding why the arsenals exist, and the consequences of their size and destructive capability explain why the competition has been and must be restrained short of war.

From this viewpoint, a movement toward Reagan's dream potentially breaks the wrong link in the chain. That chain is depicted with three causal links in figure 3–2. The effect of a perfect SDI is to break the middle link by canceling the effect of the nuclear arsenals. With that link broken, so is the restraint in superpower relations that fear of nuclear war creates. The fundamental problem, however, is that the underlying political competition is unaffected except that whatever restraints nuclear weapons placed on that competition are removed. In removing the harmful consequences of nuclear weapons—their deadliness—one may create a more dangerous world. In fact, if the Soviets continue to resist movement toward an SDI world, as certainly seems possible, both political relations could be further strained and the weapons race could be escalated, because "the more capable that U.S. systems are assumed to be, the more they motivate responsive Soviet deployments that may leave us worse off."[72]

If the political causes of nuclear armament are not removed before the arsenals are negated, the competition will simply shift to the conventional level, with no better effects and probably worse ones. Almost all observers would agree that the shadow cast by strategic nuclear arsenals has also chilled the prospects of conventional war in Europe and has compensated for perceived deficiencies in NATO conventional capabilities. Removing the danger

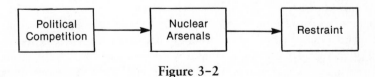

Figure 3–2

of nuclear escalation removes whatever restraint that danger had on conventional war. The likely result is the need to beef up conventional forces at considerable expense to recreate the dynamics of figure 3–2 at the conventional level. In the end, it is difficult to see how eliminating nuclear weapons helps much. Nuclear weapons do create defense at a comparatively low cost and a great deal of expense is incurred both in eliminating them (whatever SDI costs) and in substituting for their beneficial restraining effects by creating additional nonnuclear forces. Given that nonnuclear war could be fought with weapons some of which are virtually indistinguishable from nuclear weapons (some high-powered chemical explosives) and others which are equally nasty or even nastier in effect than nuclear weapons (certain chemical and biological agents), it is difficult to find the gain.

The key to solving this dilemma is prior or simultaneous resolution of the bases of political competition that gave rise to the nuclear arsenals in the first place. Such an outcome, however desirable, is hardly likely in the short run, and, if attainable, creates the irony that the negation of nuclear arsenals would be unnecessary. In other words, the nuclear problem is political at base and is solvable only by removing its political causes. Reagan's vision provides a mechanical solution that treats a symptom of the political problem but not the problem itself. In and of itself, a comprehensive SDI cannot make Soviet–U.S. political relations better and probably makes them worse.

None of this problem exists for an SDI conceived in terms of less-than-perfect defenses, especially defenses of retaliatory forces. The reason, of course, is that such defenses do not negate the vulnerability and restraint caused by nuclear arsenals. Rather than traumatizing or transforming the current basis of the nuclear-weapons–imposed order on superpower relations, such defenses strengthen that order by further guaranteeing the safety of retaliatory forces. Moreover, LTP defenses are congruent with continued political competition; if cooperatively erected by both sides—which is much more likely to occur than in the case of perfect defenses—they could even contribute to reducing that competition. Also, such defenses minimize the ability of the Soviet Union to calculate gain through nuclear weapons use: "Development of strategic defenses . . . is important for the U.S. . . . because it cancels an advantage—the current superiority of Moscow in heavy land-based missiles—that could encourage the Kremlin to take risks leading to conflict with the U.S."[73]

Uncertainty

The notion of uncertainty enters the evaluation of Reagan's vision in two ways, one mechanical and one conceptual. Mechanically, there is uncertainty about what the SDI will produce and what effect it will have, leading one critic to argue, "All one can say with confidence is that a new world of uncertainty and unforseen consequences is taking shape."[74] If this seems a less-than-ideal condition, SDI advocate Gray cheerily dismisses it, saying "the SDI-*technical uncertainties and novel strategic problems admitted*—offers the only path that may be available to lead toward our living in much greater safety" (emphasis added).[75] That path itself is uncertain, and "it should not be assumed that such research will lead to an effective defense of cities."[76]

The conceptual effects of uncertainty are similar to those regarding perceptual changes. The development and deployment of perfect defenses would also reduce uncertainty; if nuclear weapons were rendered absolutely ineffectual, one could calculate with great certainty that a nuclear attack would fail—assuming such a calculation were even possible with a system never fully tested. Whether that absence of uncertainty about the possibility of escalation to nuclear exchange would loosen inhibitions to engage in nonnuclear conflict, of course, would depend on the restraints built into the conventional balance. Perfect defenses would reduce whatever restraints escalatory uncertainty contributed to that restraint.

Less-than-perfect defenses, on the other hand, increase the uncertainty of Soviet attack, and this uncertainty enhancement is a major selling point for supporters both within and outside the administration. Thus, Richard Perle argues that "by destroying the bulk of an attacker's ballistic missile warheads, an effective defense can undermine a potential aggressor's confidence in his ability to predict the likely outcome of an attack on an opponent's military forces."[77] Defense thus breeds "uncertainties about the prospects for successfully executing Soviet strategy"[78] which, in turn, "would enhance deterrence by making it more difficult to calculate the advantages of a first strike."[79]

Conclusion

Whether one concludes that SDI is a good thing depends on two related judgments: whether the current balance requires radical alteration and whether one is advocating a comprehensive SDI in line with the president's vision or a more limited SDI based on LTP defenses.

The Reagan vision is clearly the more radical; its goal of nuclear disarmament through nuclear obsolescence ties him in effect with Gorbachev's January 15, 1986 disarmament proposals and "denuclearization" proposals of people such as Richard Falk (see chapter 1). As such, this goal at least implicitly suggests the ongoing situation to be in need of radical transformation. The call for more limited defenses, on the other hand, is compatible with maintenance and strengthening of the current deterrence system, since LTP defense of retaliatory forces reinforces the dynamics of the system.

Whether or not Reagan's vision is desirable boils down, in the end, to a judgment about whether nuclear weapons are the cause or the effect of the world's ills. If they are the cause, then rendering them "impotent and obsolete" is clearly the right thing to do; if a defense-dominant world through SDI will accomplish that goal, it should be pursued. The other side of the argument, though, sees nuclear weapons as an effect, in which case their elimination does not respond to the real problem, which is political and military division. In that view, a comprehensive SDI would create a situation where "at best, the world would be no better off than it is today, after a colossal effort to build weapons systems of unprecedented magnitude and cost."[80]

Notes

1. Ronald Reagan, "National Security: Address to the Nation, March 23, 1983," *Weekly Compilation of Presidential Documents* 19, no. 12 (March 28, 1983), pp. 442–48.

2. Edward Teller, "Better a Shield than a Sword," *Defense Science 2003 + 4*, no. 5 (October/November 1985), p. 12.

3. Reagan, "National Security," p. 448.

4. James Schlesinger, "The Eagle and the Bear: Between an Unfree World and None," *Foreign Affairs* 63, no. 5 (Summer 1985), p. 959.

5. Bill Keller, "No. 1 Weapons in 1987 Budget Is Missile Shield," *New York Times* (February 5, 1986), pp. A1, A22.

6. Ronald W. Reagan, "State of the Union Address," *Department of State Bulletin* 85, no. 2097 (April 1985), p. 9.

7. Max M. Kampelman, "SDI and the Arms Control Process," *Atlantic Community Quarterly* 23, no. 3 (Fall 1985), p. 224.

8. For a more detailed discussion, see Gary L. Guertner and Donald M. Snow, *The Last Frontier: An Analysis of the Strategic Defense Initiative* (Lexington, Mass.: Lexington Books, 1986), pp. 9–12.

9. McGeorge Bundy, George F. Kennan, Robert S. McNamara, and Gerard Smith, "The President's Choice: Star Wars or Arms Control," *Foreign Affairs* 63, no. 2 (Fall 1984), p. 264.

10. For a description, see Guertner and Snow, *The Last Frontier,* pp. 103–5, 132–33.

11. Kenneth W. Dam, "Geneva and Beyond: New Arms Control Negotiations," *Current Policy,* no. 647, U.S. Department of State, Bureau of Public Affairs, January 14, 1985.

12. Teller, "Better a Shield than a Sword," p. 20.

13. Gerald Yonas, "The Strategic Defense Initiative," *Daedalus* 114, no. 2 (Spring 1985), p. 87.

14. Richard N. Perle, "The Strategic Defense Initiative: Addressing Some Misconceptions," *Journal of International Affairs* 30, no. 1 (Summer 1985), pp. 23–24.

15. Paul H. Nitze, "SDI: Its Nature and Rationale," *Atlantic Community Quarterly* 23, no. 3 (Fall 1985), p. 265.

16. Paul H. Nitze, "Statement before Foreign Relations Committee," United States Senate, 99th Congress, first session, February 26, 1985.

17. Paul H. Nitze, "On the Road to a More Stable Peace," *Department of State Bulletin* 85, no. 2097 (April 1985), p. 27.

18. "Soviet Proposal for a Draft Treaty on the Prohibition of the Stationing of Weapons of Any Kind in Outer Space," in Bhupendra Jasani (ed.), *Outer Space—A New Dimension of the Arms Race* (London: Taylor and Francis, 1982), pp. 401–3.

19. Reported in *World Armaments and Disarmament: SIPRI Yearbook 1984* (London: Taylor and Francis, 1984), pp. 614–15.

20. *Star Wars: Delusions and Dangers* (Moscow: Military Publishing House, 1985), pp. 7, 34.

21. Mikhail Gorbachev, "Outer Space Should Serve Peace," *Information Bulletin* 23, no. 18 (1985), p. 4 (reprinted from *Pravda,* July 6, 1985); *Pravda* editorial, "Geneva: What Has the First Round of Talks Shown?" *Information Bulletin* (Moscow) 23, no. 14 (1985), p. 44.

22. *Whence the Threat to Peace,* third edition (Moscow: Military Publishing House, 1984), p. 37.

23. Louis Baillot, "Not One Step Forward in the Escalation of the Star Wars," *Information Bulletin* (Moscow) 23, no. 20 (1985), p. 57.

24. For a recent review from the West German perspective, see Hans Ruhle, "Gorbachev's Star Wars," *Atlantic Community Quarterly* 23, no. 4 (Winter 1985/86), pp. 5–13.

25. Robert C. McFarlane, "Strategic Defense Initiative," *Department of State Bulletin* 85, no. 2099 (June 1985), p. 59.

26. Ronald W. Reagan, "The President's News Conference of September 17, 1985," *Weekly Compilation of Presidential Documents* 21, no. 38 (September 23, 1985), p. 1106.

27. Paul H. Nitze, "The Objectives of Arms Control," *Department of State Bulletin* 85, no. 2098 (May 1985), p. 62.

28. Edward L. Rowny, "Gorbachev's Next 100 Days," *Department of State Bulletin* 85, no. 2103 (October 1985), p. 18.

29. Kenneth L. Adelman, "Making Arms Control Work," *Department of State Bulletin* 86, no. 2106 (January 1986), p. 41.

30. George Shultz, "Arms Control, Strategic Stability, and Global Security," *Department of State Bulletin* 85, no. 2015 (December 1985), p. 23.

31. Ronald W. Reagan, "United States–Soviet Relations," *Weekly Compilation of Presidential Documents* 21, no. 48 (December 2, 1985), p. 1435. In the same vein, Secretary of Defense Weinberger has stated: "We took a course radically different from that of the Soviet Union—we actually told the world what we were doing, and we invited the world to help us achieve such a defense. We have even briefed the Soviet Union on the Strategic Defense Initiative in Geneva." See Caspar Weinberger, "Strategic Defense in Perspective," *Defense 86* (January/February 1986), p. 5.

32. George Shultz, "Arms Control: Objectives and Prospects," *Department of State Bulletin* 85, no. 2098 (May 1985), pp. 26–27.

33. Nitze, "On the Road to a More Stable Peace," p. 29.

34. Stephen M. Meyer, "Soviet Strategic Programmes and the US SDI," *Survival* 27, no. 6 (November/December 1985), pp. 285, 290.

35. Edward Teller, "Defense: Retaliation or Protection," in Richard F. Staar (ed.), *Arms Control: Myth versus Reality* (Stanford, Calif.: Hoover Institution Press,

1984), p. 106; and Edward Teller, "Science and Technology in SDI," *Defense Science 2003 + 4*, no. 2 (April/May 1985), p. 17.

36. Bundy, Kennan, McNamara, and Smith, "The President's Choice," p. 268. The same point is made in Alvin M. Weinberg and Jack N. Barkenbus, "Stabilizing Star Wars," *Foreign Policy,* no. 54 (Spring 1984), p. 165.

37. Harold Brown, "The Strategic Defense Initiative: Defensive Systems and the Strategic Debate," *Survival* 27, no. 2 (March/April 1985), p. 55.

38. Ronald W. Reagan, "U.S.–Soviet Relations," *Department of State Bulletin* 86, no. 2107 (February 1986), p. 23 (taken from his November 23, 1985 radio address to the nation).

39. James R. Schlesinger, "Rhetoric and Realities in the Star Wars Debate," *International Security* 10, no. 1 (Summer 1985), p. 6.

40. Walter Slocombe, "An Immediate Agenda for Arms Control," *Survival* 27, no. 5 (September/October 1985), p. 208.

41. George F. Chapline, "In Defense of SDI," *Defense Science 2003 + 4*, no. 4 (August/September 1985), p. 14.

42. Brown, "The Strategic Defense Initiative," p. 63.

43. Schlesinger, "Rhetoric and Realities in the Star Wars Debate," p. 5.

44. Teller, "Better a Shield than a Sword," p. 17.

45. Daniel O. Graham and Gregory A. Fossedal, *A Defense that Defends: Blocking Nuclear Attack* (Old Greenwich, Conn.: Devin-Adair, 1983), p. 113.

46. Thomas C. Schelling, "What Went Wrong with Arms Control," *Foreign Affairs* 64, no. 2 (Winter 1985/86), p. 232.

47. Robert H. Kupperman, "Using SDI to Reshape Soviet Strategic Behavior," *Washington Quarterly* 8, no. 3 (Summer 1985), p. 83.

48. Charles L. Glaser, "Do We Want the Missile Defenses We Can Build?" *International Security* 10, no. 1 (Summer 1985), pp. 27–28.

49. David Holloway, "The Strategic Defense Initiative and the Soviet Union," *Daedalus* 114, no. 3 (Summer 1985), p. 277.

50. Meyer, "Soviet Strategic Programmes and the US SDI," p. 274.

51. Guertner and Snow, *The Last Frontier,* pp. 69–75; Donald M. Snow, *The Nuclear Future: Toward a Strategy of Uncertainty* (Tuscaloosa, Ala.: University of Alabama Press, 1983), pp. 107–111.

52. Colin Gray, "Strategic Defense, Deterrence, and the Prospects for Peace," in Russell Hardin, John J. Mearsheimer, Gerald Dworkin, and Richard E. Goodwin (eds.), *Nuclear Deterrence: Ethics and Strategy* (Chicago, Ill.: University of Chicago Press, 1985), pp. 285–98.

53. Weinberger, "Strategic Defense in Perspective," p. 6.

54. James A. Abrahamson, "Statement on the Strategic Defense Initiative, Statement to the Committee on Armed Services," United States Senate, 99th Congress, first session, February 21, 1985, p. 7.

55. Gray, "Strategic Defense, Deterrence, and the Prospects for Peace," pp. 287–88.

56. Barry R. Schneider, "U.S. Military Space Policy in 2110," *Defense Science 2003 + 4*, no. 4 (August/September 1985), p. 28.

57. Kupperman, "Using SDI to Reshape Soviet Strategic Behavior," p. 77.

58. Keith Payne and Colin S. Gray, "Nuclear Policy and the Defensive Transition," *Foreign Affairs* 62, no. 4 (Spring 1984), p. 826.

59. Kampelman, "SDI and the Arms Control Process," p. 226.

60. Abrahamson, "Statement on the Strategic Defense Initiative," p. 5.

61. Robert E. Hunter, "SDI: Return to Basics," *Washington Quarterly* 9, no. 1 (Winter 1986), p. 165.

62. This is a central conclusion of Meyer in "Soviet Strategic Programmes and the US SDI."

63. John W. Kiser, "How the Arms Race Really Helps Moscow," *Foreign Policy,* no. 60 (Fall 1985), p. 50.

64. Stephen J. Cimbala, "The Strategic Defense Initiative: Political Risks," *Air University Review* 37, no. 1 (November/December 1985), p. 29.

65. Colin S. Gray, "Strategic Defences: A Case for Strategic Defence," *Survival* 27, no. 2 (March/April 1985), p. 51.

66. Fred Charles Iklé, "Nuclear Strategy: Can There Be a Happy Ending?" *Foreign Affairs* 63, no. 4 (Spring 1985), p. 817. In advocating his "live-and-let-live" defense-dominant world, Freeman J. Dyson makes much the same point. See *Weapons and Hope* (New York: Harper & Row, 1984).

67. Meyer, "Soviet Strategic Programmes and the US SDI," p. 278.

68. Graham and Fossedal make this argument in *A Defense That Defends.*

69. See, for instance, Donald M. Snow, "BMD, SDI and Future Policy: Issues and Prospects," *Air University Review* 36, no. 5 (July/August 1985), pp. 9–10.

70. Cimbala, "The Strategic Defense Initiative," p. 31.

71. Fred S. Hoffman, "The SDI in U.S. Nuclear Strategy," *International Security* 10, no. 1 (Summer 1985), p. 18.

72. Cimbala, "The Strategic Defense Initiative," p. 35.

73. Carnes Lord, "The U.S.–Soviet Strategic Nuclear Relationship," in W. Bruce Weinrod (ed.), *Confronting Moscow: An Agenda for the Post-Detente Era* (Washington, D.C.: Heritage Foundation, 1985), p. 6.

74. Kiser, "How the Arms Race Really Helps Moscow," p. 51.

75. Colin S. Gray, "Space Arms Control: A Skeptical View," *Air University Review* 37, no. 1 (November/December 1985), p. 78.

76. Graham T. Allison, Albert Carnesale, and Joseph S. Nye, Jr., "An Agenda for Action," in Graham T. Allison, Albert Carnesale, and Joseph S. Nye (eds.), *Hawks, Doves and Owls: An Agenda for Avoiding Nuclear War* (New York: W.W. Norton, 1985), p. 228.

77. Perle, "The Strategic Defense Initiative," p. 25.

78. Lord, "The U.S.–Soviet Strategic Nuclear Relationship," p. 6.

79. Zbigniew Brzezinksi, "East–West Relations," *Atlantic Community Quarterly* 22, no. 4 (Winter 1984/85), p. 297.

80. Hunter, "SDI: Back to Basics," p. 163.

4
Gorbachev's Vision:
A Disarmed World

One man's dream can be another man's nightmare, and that is exactly the way the Soviet Union and its political leader Mikhail Gorbachev depict Reagan's vision of a defense-dominant nuclear world where nuclear disarmament occurs behind the protection of SDI-based defenses. To counter the U.S. program, the General Secretary made his own proposal on January 15, 1986, and it was as radical in potential effect as the New Strategic Concept. Both documents propose a common end, the elimination of all nuclear weapons from the earth, and each suggests a timetable to achieve that end. Where they differ is on the SDI—it is the heart of the transition to and enforcement of Reagan's nuclear-disarmed world; it is entirely absent from Gorbachev's vision and acts as the principal barrier to moving to the desired goal.

Although the individual components of Gorbachev's plan have been derided as unoriginal, imbalanced, and warmed-over, the cumulative effect of implementing it are truly radical and would transform the nature of international politics fundamentally. I will not take any particular position on the sincerity of the offer, but it does place the Soviet Union in a public position of advocating a program that, if called on to carry out, they could only back out of with some considerable embarrassment. Because of this radicalism and the proximity of its announcement to the SDI, it deserves elaboration, including a comparison with the New Strategic Concept. The conjunction of the Gorbachev proposal and SDI requires detailed attention, partly because the Soviet proposal may have been partially motivated by their repellence with SDI and partly because the Gorbachev disarmament proposal offers an alternative strategic world. Such an examination requires looking at possible Soviet motives for rejecting SDI that go beyond what have become standard Soviet "space-strike weapons" charges and U.S. administration counter-charges of duplicitous Soviet propaganda. This discussion includes the distinction between Soviet attitudes toward ballistic missile defense generically and SDI specifically. Finally, the effect of Gorbachev's vision on the strategic balance will be assessed.

Gorbachev's Plan for Disarmament by 2000 A.D.

The Soviet leader proposed a three-stage process akin to the New Strategic Concept. It would lead to universal nuclear disarmament by the year 2000, so that "we should enter the third millennium without nuclear weapons, on the basis of mutually acceptable and strictly verifiable agreements."[1] The complete proposal extends beyond a direct concern with strategic arsenals, calling for the elimination of all chemical weapons and a concomitant reduction in conventional force levels in those regions of most direct Soviet concern, Europe and Asia. The core of the proposal, however, deals with the three-step plan for worldwide nuclear disarmament.

Stage One. According to the proposal, the first stage is to begin in 1986 and extend for five to eight years. Its major goal is to reduce by one-half the total U.S. and Soviet weaponry "that can reach each other's territory" so that each side would be left with no more than six thousand "nuclear charges" apiece. The qualification means both U.S. weapons designated strategic and theater weapons capable of attacking targets in the Soviet Union would be affected; Soviet strategic weapons would be affected, but not those theater forces aimed at Western Europe but incapable of reaching U.S. soil. This has been the subject of some controversy, arousing objections of asymmetrical sacrifices favoring the Soviets.

During this first stage, three additional actions are called for. The first, aimed at the SDI, is a renunciation of testing, development, and deployment of space-strike weapons. The March 21, 1986 summary of the Soviet proposal emphasizes the importance of this action, saying "this pledge is a MUST." In his January 15, 1986 message, Gorbachev repeated the consistent Soviet position: "The development of space strike weapons will dash the hopes for a reduction of nuclear weapons on earth." The second additional action calls for both sides to eliminate all of their "ballistic and medium-range cruise missiles in Europe," for the United States not to provide any of these missiles to others, and for Britain and France not to expand their nuclear arsenals. Third, the United States and Soviet Union should enter a moratorium on all nuclear testing and issue a joint call for others to join the test ban. At the time they were issued, objections were raised in some quarters to these proposals as well: the space-strike ban was viewed as a way to give the Soviets a monopoly on BMD; the European proposal would force the United States to move forces back to North America while the Soviets could simply move theirs east of the Ural mountains; and the test ban was opposed on the grounds that the Soviets have an advantage due to past testing that the United States must match.

Stage Two. The second stage is to begin no later than 1990 and is conceived to be five to seven years in duration. (The proposal contains provision for overlaps in the various stages.) During this stage, at least one additional initiative is undertaken, while four processes begun in stage one are expanded. First, other nuclear weapons states would join the disarmament process, initially by freezing their arsenals and agreeing not to transfer nuclear weapons to other countries. Second, the Soviet Union and the United States freeze their tactical arsenals (those systems with a range of one thousand kilometers or less) and move to eliminate remaining medium-range forces, while all others freeze their tactical arsenals. Third, the ban on nuclear testing is expanded to encompass all countries. Fourth, the ban on space-strike weapons is extended to all "leading industrial nations."

The second stage contains one final initiative. Both the January and March 1986 drafts propose without additional explanation or example a ban on nonnuclear weapons "based on new physical principles whose destructive power is close to that of nuclear weapons or other weapons of mass destruction." Presumably, the target technologies implied are those associated with the various forms of directed energy weapons in applications other than those under development under the SDI guise.

Stage Three. The third stage begins no later than 1995 and is concluded by 1999. It consists of three activities. The first epic action is the destruction of all remaining nuclear weapons, such that "By 1999 there are no nuclear weapons on Earth, and an agreement is concluded to prevent their return." In order to implement this accord, the second action is taken: "Special procedures are worked out and agreed upon in detail for the destruction of nuclear warheads and for dismantling, conversion, or destruction of the delivery vehicles." The third action is the negotiation of verification procedures to insure both compliance with actual disarming and with continued compliance. As part of this portion of the proposal, "the Soviet Union has no objection to any verification procedures, including the use of national technical facilities, on-site inspection, etc."

To pass judgment on the sincerity of the offer or the willingness of the Soviet government in fact to engage in total nuclear disarmament is, at this point, idle speculation, and the only methods to reach a definitive judgment are too outlandish to suggest seriously. One might, for instance, propose hooking Gorbachev to a polygraph and asking him pointed questions about his proposal (just as Gorbachev would probably like to do to Reagan on offensive aspects of SDI). Alternatively, the U.S. government might simply accept the proposal at Geneva, figuratively roll up its sleeves, say "let's get on with it," and see what the Soviets do in response.

These kinds of solutions are, of course, simplistic and not put forward seriously. Governments — and individuals within governments — do things for a variety of reasons including public posturing, propagandist advantage, and sincere attempts to ameliorate differences. Regardless of which of these is the major source of Soviet motivation, at least two aspects of the Gorbachev proposal stand out.

The first is the radical nature of the future world it proposes. If taken literally, what the Soviet leader has proposed is no less than the dismantling of the main basis of the Soviet claim to superpower status, its military power, the pinnacle of which is its thermonuclear arsenal. It may well be that the Soviet leadership would be the first to impede movement to the goal it has articulated, but that leadership must know that there is a chance, however faint, of their offer being accepted, in which case they could be forced down the road to disarmament. No amount of objection that the proposal is framed in such a lopsided manner as to preclude U.S. acceptance can entirely remove that risk.

The vision portrayed by Gorbachev's proposal is not, after all, entirely incompatible with the vision held by President Reagan. Leslie Gelb reports that, "fundamental issues aside, Administration officials admit that the new Gorbachev proposal is an innovative package."[2] If one displays the two proposals side-by-side, as table 4–1 does, one is struck by both the structural similarities and the common end results they seek. The Gorbachev proposal contains a more rigid implementation timetable that would presumably be accomplished sooner than envisaged under the New Strategic Concept, and it is more elaborate and extensive than the Reagan call, but the end of both is nuclear disarmament. If the goal is indeed honestly held by both sides, is it

Table 4–1
Comparison of Gorbachev's and Reagan's Proposals

	Phase			
	1	*2*	*3*	*Vision*
	1986–94	1990–97	1995–99	2000–
Gorbachev	Reduce offensive forces by one-half Renounce space-strike	Further reduce offensive forces Extend space-strike ban	Complete nuclear disarmament	
	1985–95	1990–95	1995–2015	2015–
Reagan	Reduce offensive arms	Point defenses (LTP SDI)	Population defense (perfect SDI)	Offensive forces unneeded

unreasonable to assume that accommodation could not be reached on the details of transition within the three-stage framework that both Reagan and Gorbachev have put forward?

There is, of course, one major point of difference which is also the second major aspect of the Gorbachev proposal—its adamant position on space-strike weapons. The Soviet–U.S. debate on this issue is at best oblique. The Soviets insist that these weapons must be banned as a *sine qua non* for progress in arms control, and the United States does not publicly admit that the weapons exist or may exist. Instead, the administration argues that "Soviet criticism of SDI is more than a little hypocritical" and part of an attempt "intent on undermining the U.S. SDI program, while minimizing any constraints on their ongoing strategic defense activities"[3] that is basically a program of "disinformation and misinformation."[4] For their part, the Soviets have only very recently begun to admit that SDI might possibly be something more than a Strategic Offensive Initiative, and even that admission is grudging and tempered: "No matter how much it is sought to present the Star Wars program as having a defensive nature, it can, at the minimum, double as a nuclear force."[5]

The consistency of Soviet efforts to undercut SDI is clearly fundamental, and offering an arms control proposal as far-reaching as the Gorbachev plan indicates just how important it is to them. Bialer and Afferica offer this assessment of their motivations:

> The new Soviet leadership makes manifest their genuine interest in a comprehensive agreement to reduce offensive strategic weapons. . . . Soviet security concerns . . . include the widening American technological preponderance, the accelerating American offensive nuclear arms program, and the tension and danger inherent in a new arms race. Even more important than the fear of the known is the fear of the unknown, the terrible uncertainty concealed in America's grandiose Strategic Defense Initiative.[6]

The SDI issue is so important in Soviet–U.S. strategic relations that its basis must be understood before one can possibly assess the impact of either dream—in the present case Gorbachev's—on the strategic system.

The Soviets and SDI

As indicated in the previous chapter, the Soviets are unwavering in their opposition to SDI, and the Reagan administration is equally adamant in not taking those objections seriously. Also as indicated, the tone of that dismissal is often decidedly patronizing, as shown in a statement by Paul Nitze regarding the interchange between Gorbachev and Reagan on the subject at the November 1985 summit:

> One of the less encouraging aspects of the summit was Gorbachev's unwavering opposition to SDI. . . . It is also noteworthy that the President seems to have made some progress in convincing Gorbachev that he is sincere in his stated intent for SDI, even though the Soviet leader vigorously disputed the President's conclusions about its consequences.[7]

Dialogue of that sort is clearly not going to overcome any real objections the Soviets have to SDI, since it implies either that the Soviets are simply lying or are not bright enough to understand SDI. Neither implication seems likely to produce the kinds of constructive compromises on which negotiating success must be based, and avoiding arms control progress may indeed be the whole purpose of the exercise. (Certainly, there are among the administration's leadership several officials such as Fred C. Iklé and Richard Perle whose attachment to arms control as a concept is suspect.)

While it is possible that those who dismiss Soviet fears of SDI out of hand are correct, it is also possible they are wrong. Expert opinion on whether they should be very concerned is mixed. Michael MccGwire contends that they should be frightened, because "Were the United States to be successful in developing its space-based defence system, it would have regained the position of relative military advantage that it enjoyed for twenty years after the Second World War. Experience suggests the Soviet Union will make every effort to prevent this."[8] William Kincade agrees with this conclusion: "Too much is involved for the Soviets to do anything but reject and try to counter the threat."[9] Jerry Hough, on the other hand, dismisses the problem, at least in the short run: "As for nuclear balance, no foreseeable weapons program on either side can really upset it. The real problem has become how to structure nuclear forces so as to reduce the anxiety on both sides."[10] He admits, however, that SDI does "pose an ill-defined yet potentially enormous danger over the long run."[11]

It is this matter of long-term potential — what SDI might someday become or produce — that is at the heart of Soviet objections. If one looks at the potential of SDI, it is possible to glean five possible reasons for that objection:

1. The Soviets believe what they have been saying.
2. Their objections represent their own hopes for the technologies surrounding SDI but which they fear the United States will be able to produce sooner.
3. The major promise of SDI is control of access to space.
4. It is the weapons potential of SDI in areas unrelated or tangentially related to defense that they really fear.

5.   They worry that SDI is stimulating a U.S. technological base in ways that are unpredictable but potentially disastrous to Soviet security.

Clearly, these possibilities are neither mutually exclusive nor exhaustive; and all, some, or none of them may indeed activate the concerted Soviet campaign against SDI. All of them, however, are plausible and important enough if true to warrant consideration.

1. Space-strike weapons are, or are a part of, a U.S. plan to gain strategic superiority. This has been the consistent Soviet position at least since Reagan's 1983 speech. Presumably honing in on space-based laser systems, the 1984 edition of *Whence the Threat to Peace* (Moscow's equivalent to the Department of Defense's *Soviet Military Power*[12]) states U.S. purposes: "Washington is pursuing two objectives. The first is to create a comprehensive (total) land- and space-based ABM system. . . . The second goal is to simultaneously build up strategic offensive armaments clearly aimed at acquiring a first-strike capability."[13]

Although the United States portrays SDI as a benign, passive shield, the Soviets view it as a major component of the strategic offensive force modernization program announced in October 1981—a five-pronged initiative that included "improvement in strategic defenses including civil defense to help deter nuclear attack, and *to degrade its effectiveness if it is attempted*" (emphasis added).[14] This latter characteristic—degrading Soviet forces—reveals what the Soviets believe is the real purpose underlying U.S. purported defenses. As Gorbachev maintains, "There is every indication that the U.S. antimissile space system is not at all conceived as a 'shield,' but as a part of an integral offensive complex." The effect would be quite the opposite of the stabilizing role advertised for SDI: "No one's security would be strengthened by the start of an arms race in space, or even the deployment in near-earth space of antimissile systems alone. Covered with a space 'shield,' nuclear means of attack will become even more dangerous."[15] At worst, this weaponization of space "would dramatically increase the threat of a truly global, all-destructive military conflict."[16]

The Soviets have been most evocative in their depictions of the SDI weapons they envision and in U.S. duplicity in describing intents for them. A quasi-official Soviet publication summarizes their public belief about U.S. intentions:

> Named 'defenses' to deceive the public it is really designed to create space-strike weapons, a whole new family of weapons with a number of wholly unique properties. To begin with, their range would be global. . . . [T]hey can appear over the territory of any state at practically any time and create a tangible threat to its security. . . . [conjuring the image of the "death star" from the movie "The Empire Strikes Back"] the space strike weapons . . .

can . . . serve as a most effective offensive weapon. They may be used not only to knock out ballistic missiles after the latter are launched, but also to deliver a strike from outer space at earth, air, and sea targets.[17]

Because of these malevolent potential characteristics, the Soviet Union maintains that it is forced to block progress in arms control until the United States abandons the SDI program: "Washington is certainly aware that, pursuing a course aimed at sapping the ABM Treaty and developing space-strike weapons, the USA eliminates thereby at the Geneva talks the very basis for a possible agreement on reducing strategic offensive armaments."[18] This expresses the Soviet view of "linkage" between the three sets (offensive, space, and intermediate) of arms talks at Geneva—the idea being that progress in one forum requires progress in all three, a position reiterated at the Reykjavik summit. The U.S. government has rejected the linkage idea repeatedly.

2. Soviet depictions represent their own aspirations which they fear the United States will realize first. Research into the military potentials of SDI technologies is not exactly a U.S. monopoly. Equivalent or larger Soviet programs exploring weapons potential of areas such as lasers and charged particle beams have been going on at least as long as U.S. efforts. Soviet-stated fears may be no more than mirror images of Soviet hopes and desires, as Secretary of State Shultz hints: "Rather than asking what will be the Soviet response to SDI, critics ought to be asking: given the Soviet Union's major strategic defense effort and its huge offensive forces, what are the consequences for deterrence, stability and Western security if we do not pursue an adequate research effort?"[19] To provide at least indirect evidence that SDI may represent Soviet dreams turned to nightmares by the prospect of greater U.S. success, he later states, "some of the Soviet scientists most active in signing declarations against our SDI are themselves the men leading the Soviet military research in the same technologies."[20]

Moreover, it may well be that concerned Soviet developmental programs have spurred U.S. counterparts that threaten to create a self-fulfilling prophecy of the problem that the Soviets were seeking to obviate in the first place. Thus, the Soviets begin from the problem that "[d]eterring the enemy from having a . . . possible surprise strategic success is the preeminent challenge for Soviet strategic forces."[21] To solve this problem, the Soviets attempted to devise a defensive system with the additional advantage of a possible offensive role. Unfortunately, the result was to help spawn a U.S. capability that poses that very problem. Thus, "[t]he worst fear of all is that a major American antiballistic missile system could give the United States a possible first-strike capability for perhaps a few years until the Soviet Union succeeded in deploying a comparably effective ABM system of its own."[22] That the Soviets fear they may have created the monster they hoped to cage may help explain the richness and detail of their descriptions of U.S. intentions—intentions Americans from the president down deny they hold at all.

3. Space-strike weapons will provide control of the access to space for military and nonmilitary purposes. One of the major elements of a layered, comprehensive missile defense is boost-phase interception of rising Soviet ICBMs by laser battle stations orbiting the Earth and in position over or near Soviet territory. This has been among the most widely publicized aspects of SDI. It is also the most futurist element of "Star Wars" and evokes vivid science fiction images. At the same time, strategic enamour with the prospect of destroying multiple warheads with a single attack has been balanced by doubts about feasibility, vulnerability, and arms race potential.

Weaponizing space has been the most prominent aspect of Soviet attacks on SDI. Presaging the Gorbachev proposal by over a year, the late Konstantin Chernenko framed the Soviet concern in December 1984:

> If the militarization of outer space is not reliably blocked, it will erase everything that has been achieved in the area of arms limitation . . . and dramatically increase the danger of nuclear war. The Soviet Union is prepared for the most radical agreements that would make it possible to advance along a route to cessation of the arms race, and prohibition and eventual and complete scrapping of nuclear weapons.[23]

In a similar vein, then Foreign Minister Andrei Gromyko stated emphatically, "Any use of force in outer space, from space against Earth and from Earth against targets in space should be banned without delay. There is no other choice."[24]

These are strong and arguably excessive accusations to make about a system whose sole stated purpose is to help dilute an offensive missile launch against the United States. It is not so clearly excessive if one believes that "[s]pace has become a major issue in the arms race, and it is necessary to emphasize that its exploitation is only just beginning . . . what is at stake is nothing less than the future of the human race."[25] While one can argue about the hyperbole of that statement, it is not sheer fantasy to project more ambitious and threatening potentials to space-strike weapons.

An obvious potential of a laser station capable of destroying ICBMs rising into space is that it could also be used to shoot down anything else that the Soviets were attempting to project into space. Laser battle stations, if effective enough to combat swarms of ICBMs, could also effectively regulate the access to space for other military and nonmilitary purposes—such as launching reconnaissance, weather, or communications satellites into orbit. Those stations could thus serve in effect as "permissive action links" on who would be allowed to do what in space. Given the dependence of earthbound communication on satellites, for instance, this would provide considerable advantage. Moreover, satellites with that much capability might have additional offensive utility as well. As Marshall Shulman describes it, "A Soviet concern is that the priority emphasis in the SDI program on directed-energy research in space, whether or not it succeeds in creating a defensive system in orbit over the Soviet Union, will lead to space weapons capable of offensive use and a new stage of military competition in space."[26]

A perceived threat of this nature makes Soviet denunciations of space-strike weapons not excessive at all, particularly if they believe the United States could achieve the operational capability first—thereby possessing the ability to prevent the Soviet Union from deploying a counterpart. Indeed, the colorful imagery of death stars lurking over the horizon, popping up, and menacing the earth below is entirely consistent with this interpretation. The United States categorically denies any intent of this nature, and it is immaterial whether this denial is true or not if the Soviets believe this will be the outcome of the SDI. This position and belief are not necessarily incompatible over the long run, after all; the United States could end up with a weapon with death star capabilities whether or not that is the current intention. The stridency of Soviet objection to SDI makes sense if they believe this scenario; offering disarmament does not make sense to avert the "space shield."

4. What the Soviets fear is not SDI itself, but the other weapons its research will produce. As discussed in the previous chapter, the ability to build a BMD system that meets Reagan's criterion of rendering nuclear weapons impotent and obsolete—a leak-proof, perfect layered defense—is problematical. Such a system would have to be dizzyingly complex. Public discussions have tended to focus on the kill mechanisms that might be employed—lasers versus nonnuclear explosives, for example—but these represent no more than the tip of the technological iceberg that surrounds the SDI. As Meyer explains, "the keys to the success or failure of SDI are the technologies of target acquisition, tracking and pointing, and command and control. Sensors, computers, and highly engineered electro-mechanical subsystems—products of electronics and miniaturization—are the linchpins of SDI."[27] As some notion of the complexity involved, it is estimated that the computer program necessary for an eventual SDI will, according to a recent estimate, require *ten to thirty million lines*.[28]

Soviet scientists working on their counterpart programs are aware of this and certainly must have told Soviet political leaders that SDI may never reach fruition because it is simply too difficult a task. Space defense is not, as the Soviets know equally well, the only purpose of the research effort. As the Congressional Office of Technology Assessment (OTA) has stated, "other goals . . . include . . . developing new technologies which may or may not be applied ultimately to BMD, but which could have other military and civilian applications."[29] No less an authority than General Secretary Gorbachev has himself opined on the sophisticated hardware that SDI may produce: "A situation would be created in which fundamentally important decisions, irreversible in their possible consequences, would essentially be taken by electronic machines, without the participation of human reason and political will, and without regards for the criteria of ethics and morality."[30]

Regardless of what one thinks of that assessment, it does admit a grudging admiration for the sophistication of U.S. military technology. SDI may never produce an astrodome defense, but sensor technology may improve the next generation of antitank weapons, laser optics may produce new breakthroughs in antisubmarine warfare, or miniaturization could heighten the capabilities of the next generation of cruise missiles. Any spinoff from SDI can be troubling, and it makes matters worse that these breakthroughs are often unpredictable.

5. SDI will stimulate the U.S. technological base and thereby accentuate the gap between U.S. and Soviet technological bases. One important impact of SDI is that it is creating jobs for a large number of American scientists and engineers. Whether this large group will produce a workable SDI is debatable; that the collective efforts of this group of bright people will produce a great deal of new discoveries—some with military applications—is not. The likely result is to sharpen and accentuate already invidious comparisons between the U.S. and Soviet technological bases.

The SDI research program is at the cutting edge of scientific research, and this creates a problem for the Soviets. "The gravity of the technological challenge of the 'new arms race' is far broader than is often realized in Western discussions of Soviet reactions to SDI. SDI, then, comes to be seen as a fundamental challenge to Soviet military-economic and military-technical policy."[31] It is a challenge that the highly rigid, incremental nature of the Soviet technological structure, which has always been weakest in innovative aspects of technology,[32] may be ill-equipped to meet. Although a great deal has been written about how the Soviets have been closing the technological gap, such appearances may prove deceiving. "Despite the Soviet Union's many achievements, it is difficult to find any of them that is not less than it seems."[33]

The gap is particularly evident in the SDI areas, because "the United States remains ahead of the Soviet Union in key areas required for advanced BMD systems, including sensors, signal processing, optics, microelectronics, computers, and software."[34] SDI is stimulating U.S. efforts in all these areas, and Soviet backwardness feeds upon itself to widen the difference. As Louis Lavoie explains,

Part of the Soviet technical failure can be attributed to a Catch-22. Almost every Soviet technical project has been seriously limited because it lacked good instrumentation, whether for monitoring civilian production or assessing scientific results. And there is little good instrumentation because of the limited ability of the Soviet industrial base to produce it.[35]

This situation creates a number of severe potential problems for the Soviets. For instance, "the Soviet Union has fallen further behind the West in the computer age. . . . [This gap] threatens to erode the Soviet military position further as the world's armies begin the transition to computerized conventional weapons."[36] Computerization and the semiconductor industry go hand in glove, and this is an area of particular Soviet disadvantage: "The Soviets lag far behind the West in all technologies based on semiconductors, and this gap may well create profound problems for them in the decades ahead."[37]

Gorbachev has acknowledged that SDI creates this challenge to the Soviet scientific and technological community. "Venturing on its own arms race in space, [the United States] is now hoping to outstrip us in electronics and computers."[38] Moreover, past experience may predispose the Soviets to overestimate the nature of the difficulty. The ability of the United States to surge past them in areas such as the ballistic missile and space programs "is likely to bias internal military and scientific assessments of the U.S. SDI toward an assumption of feasibility."[39] An obvious way to avoid the unpleasant results of an all-out technological competition is to dampen and slow the U.S. effort by killing its major stimulant, the SDI.

Is the Gorbachev Vision Desirable?

The proposals made by Reagan and Gorbachev are similar in that they both offer radical solutions to the problem created by the existence of large thermonuclear arsenals. Although they differ in important ways, they share the ultimate dream of a world where nuclear weapons no longer exist. They differ in terms of the motivation that gave rise to them, the physical capability to realize them, and the sincerity of their issuance.

In the case of Reagan's proposal, its motivation was clear in his initial statement: he finds a world organized around the concept of mutual vulnerability undesirable and unacceptable. He believes that disarmament triggered by the obsolescence of the weapons is the only acceptable solution. He has been steadfast and consistent in his vision, although the Soviets doubt that SDI will produce what he says it is intended to. There is little reason to doubt his personal commitment and sincere belief in his vision. Where there is ample doubt is in its attainability, doubt shared by Americans and Soviets alike. Many Americans in and out of government do not believe a perfect defense is possible; their support for SDI is for a defense (or offense) quite dissimilar to that which enlivens Reagan's vision. The Soviets profess to a disbelief in the ability to produce a perfect defense—at least one they cannot overcome—but they say that is not the problem. Their argument may not be with Reagan himself, but with those who implement his programs but dream different dreams. And their fears may have substance.

Gorbachev's motivation is not so easy to assess, partly because we are automatically suspicious of anything the Soviets say, partly because their actions—a vigorous nuclear buildup over the past two decades—seem inconsistent with their proposal, and partly because the result of implementing the proposal would be to rob them of their most visible symbol of superpower status, their nuclear arsenal. The Soviets, of course, could and would use the same first two arguments to question the veracity of Reagan's proposal. Unlike the SDI road to nuclear disarmament, however, there are no mechanical or technical roadblocks to implementing the Soviet plan except at the margins—such as the verifiability of continuing compliance. At heart, the problem is not whether one could physically get to Gorbachev's vision; it is whether it is sincerely offered.

Whether he means it is largely a matter of why he offered it. The Soviet's public explanation is not at all unlike Reagan's: "The U.S.S.R. is a confirmed opponent of nuclear war in any of its variants"[40] and "the elimination of nuclear weapons is the goal all nuclear powers should strive for."[41] In the Soviet view, this need is made pressing because SDI destabilizes relations: "The introduction of strike weapons in outer space . . . would necessarily diminish the stability of the strategic situation and would increase the risk of the outbreak of nuclear war."[42]

Americans who dismiss such statements and the proposals such as Gorbachev's that are associated with them miss an important point. That point arises from the fact that, at this time, there is not *an* SDI; there are as many SDI designs and ends as there are designers and analysts. There is no reason not to believe that the Soviets—for one or more of the reasons suggested—are sincerely frightened by the SDI they envisage and that they may feel the need to take drastic action to avoid its consequences. Nuclear disarmament is one such radical action. Most of those who dismiss Soviet pronouncements as mere propaganda do so because the Soviet SDI is not *their* SDI, just as the Soviets dismiss Reagan's version of SDI because it does not match theirs. It is not easy to establish a dialogue if the subject is not common.

Because the net results of the Reagan and Gorbachev proposals are similar, the Gorbachev proposal is open to the same criticisms as the Reagan plan. The major difference between the two plans lies in how enforcement would occur. In Reagan's vision, the space shield guarantees the continuing sanctity of a nuclear-disarmed world, because not enough weapons could be assembled clandestinely to challenge it. The defenses remove any incentive to cheat and act, in terms of Reagan's own analogy, as the gas mask enforcing a chemical weapons ban. There is no direct parallel to the defense in Gorbachev's world; rather, the enforcement of nuclear disarmament would be entrusted to negotiated verification mechanisms, potentially including on-site inspection.

The major criticism common to both proposals is that they solve the wrong problem. As argued in the previous chapter, the causal sequence begins with political disagreement and competition, which causes nations to arm, not the other way around. Thus, a solution to the physical effect (nuclear arsenals) leaves the cause (political competition) intact, but removes whatever restraints resulted from the weapons, as figure 4–1 shows.

The real problem here is the political competition, and it must be solved if the nuclear problem is to be overcome. Disarmament is a solution only if one assumes the underlying causes are rearranged, as in figure 4–2. In this depiction, nuclear weapons create the problem of competition, which in turn results in instability. If this is the correct causal ordering of the relationship between nuclear weapons and conflict, then disarmament solves the real problem.

Unfortunately, the first ordering not the second, is correct. Curiously — given his own proposal — Reagan states the relationship most clearly and succinctly: "Countries don't mistrust each other because they're armed. They're armed because they mistrust each other."[43] The first step to overcoming the problem has to be to bounding or overcoming the political bases of competition — and nuclear weapons themselves help create some bounds which their

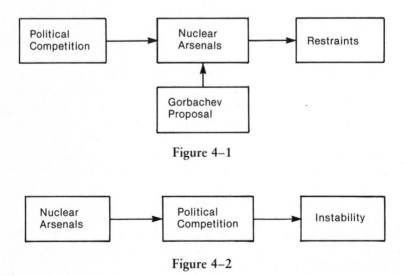

Figure 4–1

Figure 4–2

disappearance would likely erase. Solving the problems out of sequence, which disarmament without prior solution to underlying political problems would do, is thus potentially disastrous: "Ironically, while complete disarmament may be a worthy long-term goal, trying to achieve it before the requisite political conditions exist could actually increase the prospects of war. If the political pre-conditions of trust and consensus are missing, complete disarmament is inherently unstable."[44]

If one assumes that disagreements deeply enough held to produce the armed competition between the superpowers will not simply disappear or be subject to simple solution, then attacking the causes of political disagreement must be gradual and incremental. One way is by lessening sources of tension by perfecting means of crisis avoidance and termination. As MccGwire explains this consequence, "it is world war, however it starts, not Soviet aggression, that poses the greatest threat to all our people. We should therefore pay less attention to the military means to deter the onset of war, and concentrate more on developing the political means of averting those situations that make war more likely."[45]

Without prior removal of political tensions, disarmament adversely affects all the factors that enforce deterrence. In a crisis, cheating and assembling weapons clandestinely—assuming no verification scheme is airtight—may make sense, either to gain advantage or to keep the other side from gaining advantage. In either case, escalating incentives that can deepen the sense of crisis may well be stimulated, rather than dynamics leading to averting or terminating conflict. In this regard, the Gorbachev solution is inferior to Reagan's, because the Reagan defenses do provide a kind of safety net that inhibits cheating.

The effect on perceptions about the consequences of war are similar for the two plans. Whatever useful inhibitions the realization of mutual vulnerability to nuclear attack creates are removed, and competition is refocused on the conventional level. The Gorbachev proposal does suggest simultaneous attention to conventional balance, but it is not clear how one could remove all arms from a relationship that caused the perceived need for the arms in the first place and is not otherwise reformed. Danger, after all, has political roots that deadliness has restrained. The Gorbachev proposal does not solve that problem. Its sole advantage is that it is probably cheaper than building the defenses that Reagan's plan demands.

Conclusion

After analyzing schemes that would result in nuclear disarmament from the leaders of the world's two most powerful nations, one is left with a dilemma. Both sides pose physical methods to rid the world of the menace and pros-spect of nuclear annihilation, yet neither speaks directly to the divisions that created this potential horror in the first place. Recognizing that one can over-do the rationality and order of how threat perception is translated into weapons arsenals, it is equally clear that, for instance, the United States would hardly maintain an arsenal of ten thousand strategic nuclear warheads if Canada were our sole concern.

The Reagan and Gorbachev proposals address the deadliness of Soviet–U.S. strategic relations, but not their danger. If deadliness has reduced the danger of clash and that deadliness is moderated, does the danger—in this case of conventional clash—rise? Before one embarks on as radical a course as either proposal would have us do, some satisfactory answer to that question needs to be provided. Advocates of either future have yet to provide a satisfactory answer.

The other thing that comparison of the two proposals reveals is the central importance of that amorphous beast, the SDI. It is the cornerstone of the Reagan vision of the strategic future; it is the monster that must be slain before one can begin to move toward Gorbachev's vision. What is clear is that the disagreement about SDI stands as a major—possibly *the* major—impediment to improving the political and strategic relationship between the superpowers.

Notes

1. Mikhail Gorbachev, "Nuclear Disarmament by the Year 2000, Statement by Mikhail Gorbachev, General Secretary of the CPSU Central Committee, January 15, 1986," printed as an advertisement in *New York Times,* February 5, 1986, p. A13. The substance of the proposal is printed as "Soviet Program for Total Abolition of Nuclear Weapons in the World," once again as an advertisement in *New York Times,* March 21, 1986, p. A18. Unless otherwise noted, descriptions of the actual proposal are taken from these sources.

2. Leslie H. Gelb, "Weighing the Soviet Plan," *New York Times,* January 17, 1986, p. A1.

3. Ronald W. Reagan, "Interview with J.N. Parimoo," *Weekly Compilation of Presidential Documents* 21, no. 43 (October 28, 1985), pp. 1285–86.

4. Kenneth L. Adelman, "SDI: Setting the Record Straight," *Department of State Bulletin,* 85, no. 2103 (October 1985), p. 42.

5. Eduard Shevardnadze, "A Nuclear-Free World: Excerpts from a Speech at the 27th CPSU Congress," reprinted as an advertisement in *New York Times,* March 21, 1986, p. A19.

6. Seweryn Bialer and Joan Afferica, "The Genesis of Gorbachev's World," *Foreign Affairs (America and the World)* 64, no. 3 (1986), pp. 642–43.

7. Paul H. Nitze, "The Nuclear and Space Arms Talks: Where We Are after the Summit," *Department of State Bulletin* 86, no. 2107 (February 1986), p. 60.

8. Michael MccGwire, "Deterrence: the problem—not the solution," *International Affairs* (London) 62, no. 1 (Winter 1985/86), p. 64.

9. William H. Kincade, "Arms Control or Arms Coercion," *Foreign Policy,* no. 62 (Spring 1986), p. 44.

10. Jerry F. Hough, *The Struggle for the Third World: Soviet Debates and American Options* (Washington, D.C.: Brookings Institution, 1986), p. 2.

11. Jerry F. Hough, "Gorbachev's Strategy," *Foreign Affairs* 64, no. 1 (Fall 1985), p. 48.

12. See, for instance, *Soviet Military Power, 1985* (Washington, D.C.: U.S. Government Printing Office, 1985).

13. *Whence the Threat to Peace,* third edition (Moscow: Military Publishing House, 1984), p. 40.

14. Caspar W. Weinberger, *Annual Report to the Congress, Fiscal Year 1983* (Washington, D.C.: U.S. Government Printing Office, 1982), pp. I–40.

15. Mikhail Gorbachev, "Our Policy Is Clear: It Is a Policy of Peace and Cooperation," *Information Bulletin* 24, no. 2 (1986), pp. 17, 13 (text of speech to Supreme Soviet on November 27, 1985).

16. Mikhail Gorbachev, "Speech Welcoming Willy Brandt," *Information Bulletin* 23, no. 15 (1985), p. 16.

17. *Star Wars: Dangers and Delusions* (Moscow: Military Publishing House, 1985), pp. 9, 27.

18. G. Stakh, "Curbing the Arms Race as a Crucial Problem of Today," *International Affairs* (Moscow), no. 2 (1986), p. 7.

19. George Shultz, "Arms Control: Objectives and Prospects," *Department of State Bulletin* 85, no. 2098 (May 1985), p. 27.

20. George Shultz, "Arms Control, Strategic Stability, and Global Security," *Department of State Bulletin* 85, no. 2015 (December 1985), p. 24.

21. Robbin F. Laird and Dale R. Herspring, *The Soviet Union and Strategic Arms* (Boulder, Colo.: Westview, 1984), p. 69.

22. Bialer and Afferica, "The Genesis of Gorbachev's World," p. 643.

23. Konstantin Chernenko, "Reply to an Appeal from the Fourth World Congress of 'International Physicians for the Prevention of a Nuclear War'," *Information Bulletin* 23, no. 3 (1985), p. 4.

24. Andrey Gromyko, "Along a Leninist Course in Foreign Policy," *World Marxist Review* 28, no. 4 (April 1985), p. 16.

25. M. Felden, "Recent Advances in the Use of Space for Military Purposes and on Second Generation Nuclear Weapons," in Bhupendra Jasani (ed.), *Outer Space: A New Dimension for the Arms Race* (London: Taylor and Francis, 1982), p. 263.

26. Marshall D. Shulman, "The Future of U.S.–Soviet Relations," *Arms Control Today* 15, no. 9 (November/December 1985), p. 5.

27. Stephen M. Meyer, "Soviet Strategic Programs and the US SDI," *Survival* 27, no. 6 (November/December 1985), p. 276.

28. Ware Myers, "The Star Wars Software Debate," *Bulletin of the Atomic Scientists* 42, no. 2 (February 1986), p. 32.

29. Office of Technology Assessment, *Ballistic Missile Defense Technologies: Summary* (Washington, D.C.: Office of Technology Assessment, 1985), pp. 8–9.

30. Gorbachev, "Our Policy Is Clear," p. 10.

31. Meyer, "Soviet Strategic Programs and the US SDI," p. 276.

32. This argument is made especially forcefully in Harley D. Balzer, "Is More Less? Soviet Science in the Gorbachev Era," *Issues in Science and Technology* 1, no. 4 (Summer 1985), pp. 29–46.

33. Louis Lavoie, "The Limits of Soviet Technology," *Technology Review* 88, no. 8 (November/December 1985), p. 71.

34. Office of Technology Assessment, *Ballistic Missile Defense Technologies,* pp. 17–18. The same basic assessment is attributed to Undersecretary of Defense Donald Hicks in R. Jeffrey Smith, "U.S. Tops Soviets in Key Weapons Technology," *Science* 231, no. 4742 (March 7, 1986), p. 1063.

35. Lavoie, "The Limits of Soviet Technology," p. 72.

36. Hough, *The Struggle for the Third World,* p. 284.

37. Lavoie, "The Limits of Soviet Technology," p. 74.

38. Gorbachev, "Our Policy Is Clear," p. 18.

39. Meyer, "Soviet Strategic Programs and the US SDI," p. 274.

40. "The Central Direction of Soviet Foreign Policy: From the Resolution of the 27th Congress of the Communist Party of the Soviet Union," printed as an advertisement in *New York Times,* March 21, 1986, p. A19.

41. Mikhail Gorbachev, "The Soviet Communist Party Congress on the International Situation and Soviet Foreign Policy," printed as an advertisement in *New York Times,* March 21, 1986, p. A18.

42. Stakh, "Curbing the Arms Race as a Crucial Problem of Today," p. 4.

43. Ronald W. Reagan, "President's News Conference on Foreign and Domestic Issues," *New York Times,* April 10, 1986, p. A22.

44. Harvard Nuclear Study Group (Albert Carnesale, Paul Doty, Stanley Hoffman, Samuel P. Huntington, Joseph S. Nye, Jr., and Scott D. Sagan), *Living with Nuclear Weapons* (Cambridge, Mass.: Harvard University Press, 1983), p. 190.

45. MccGwire, "Deterrence," p. 69.

5
Between the Poles:
A Compromise for Arms Control

A s the two prior chapters have attempted to show, the public agenda on nuclear matters is dominated by the publicly stated visions of the two superpower leaders. Each leader professes a horror over the continuing existence of and reliance upon offensive nuclear weapons as the commanding feature of superpower relations, and each proposes the radical solution of nuclear disarmament as the means to solve the current dilemma. Their visions, however, are incompatible, and the principal source of disagreement is the Strategic Defense Initiative.

Arms control is also a central part of the equation in two ways. The first is the existence and prominence of the Geneva arms control negotiations. This three-tiered negotiating forum provides the focal point for proposals and counterproposals. Progress (or its absence) will likely be recorded there. A second aspect of arms control's place is that the realization of either vision requires an ambitious arms control accord that provides the mechanism and timetable for moving toward one kind of nuclear-disarmed world or the other. Probably less ambitious designs require some features made most attainable within an arms control context as well.

Implementation of either vision would replace the current system of nuclear deterrence which has seen a dynamic interplay and growth in nuclear arsenals. As William Lewis describes it,

> The United States and the Soviet Union continue to be locked into a cycle of open-ended weapons competition in both the nuclear and conventional armaments fields. They do so in the belief that, given the absence of confidence in one another's pledges and stated intentions, security can only be vouchsafed through a balance of nuclear forces.[1]

The result of this dynamic growth has been an unambiguous condition of mutual vulnerability which creates such fear of the possible consequences of crossing the nuclear threshold that self-deterrence is induced. The consequence has been an enduring and increasing sense of stability in superpower relations despite considerable continuing political disagreement. As Christoph Bertram says, "A remarkable military—as opposed to a political—stability between East and West characterizes international security today. . . . This rather relaxed view of military balance depends, of course, on a belief in the continuing relevance of nuclear deterrence."[2]

Not everyone, by any means, finds this situation satisfactory. The sheer growth of arsenal sizes measured in terms of warhead numbers and lethality (if not in gross megatonnage) leaves many uneasy, because, as a consequence of unforeseen change, "the West may begin to feel trembling beneath its feet the strategic ground made familiar, if far from comfortable, over forty years of Soviet–American competition."[3] Mutual vulnerability is not, after all, a very comfortable position, especially when one realizes that deterrence could in fact fail. The consequences of that failure would be no less than catastrophic, thereby fueling "a crude but understandable impulse to remove once-and-for-all the sense of vulnerability to nuclear destruction."[4] That very instinct, however, is a prime mover of official U.S. policy as described by Defense Secretary Weinberger: "The knowledge that any conflict between the United States and the Soviet Union might escalate to nuclear catastrophe is certainly part of deterrence today. . . . [B]ecause it poses dangers, we must seek better alternatives for the future. The President and I believe that the answer lies in the Strategic Defense Initiative."[5]

The Central Role of Arms Control

The arms control process languished visibly during Reagan's first term. Obvious reasons for this diminished place included the administration's general dismay with a decade of arms control activity which had produced what it described as a "fatally flawed" SALT II Agreement (to which it nonetheless strictly adhered until 1986), its perceived need to rebuild strategic forces to provide a Soviet incentive to take negotiations seriously, and the difficulty of dealing with a series of infirm Soviet leaders who would not be in office long.

By 1986, those conditions had changed. SALT II remained in informal force until late in that year, and the administration decided to scrap two Polaris submarines as the seventh *Ohio*-class (Trident) submarine came on line—the failure to do so would have put submarine and MIRV levels above those allowed by the treaty and thus have given the Soviets an excuse to break out of the strictures as well. Late in the year, the conversion of the 131st B-52 to carry cruise missiles did exceed SALT II limits. The force modernization program was well underway, and the administration believed that growing U.S. strength had induced a Soviet return to the negotiating table. At the same time, the Soviet succession process ended, so the United States had an authoritative, if formidable, Soviet leader with whom to interact.

Moreover, arms control is central to realizing any fundamental change in the nuclear system. Certainly, it is a *sine qua non* for the Gorbachev disarmament proposal, which—beyond whatever propagandist purposes it was intended to serve—was clearly tailormade for the negotiating table at Geneva and Reykjavik. In fact, the three-step proposal is a framework and set of substantive issues for organizing those talks, if the proposal is taken literally and seriously.

A movement toward disarmament through defense-dominance—Reagan's pure vision for the SDI—equally relies on arms control agreements because of the relationship between offensive and defensive forces, as Weinberger himself admitted in his first force posture statement after the birth of SDI: "For the longer term, offensive force reductions and defensive technologies can be mutually reinforcing. Effective defenses that reduce the utility of ballistic missiles and other offensive forces have the potential for increasing the likelihood of negotiated reductions of those offensive forces."[6]

This particular statement, of course, could be applied equally well to less-than-perfect defenses, which are less reliant on prior offensive force limitations. Since the performance requirement for LTP defenses is incremental, offensive actions that degrade that performance (buildups) or enhance it (builddowns) affect the system's attractiveness at the margins unless an unconstrained growth can render the LTP defense totally ineffective.

A general defense as reflected in the Reagan version of the SDI has a much more demanding set of performance standards; it must work essentially perfectly to have any substantial attraction. The problem is that there is virtual unanimity in the expert community that a perfect defense is unattainable against an unconstrained offensive force, a problem recognized early on within the Reagan administration. "Richard De Lauer, the Undersecretary of Defense for Research and Engineering, pointed out about six weeks after the Star Wars speech that the proposed defensive system could be overcome by Soviet offensive weapons unless it was to be coupled with an offensive-arms–control agreement."[7] There is disagreement about how much limitation is necessary to allow effectiveness—if perfection is attainable under any circumstances. Clearly, however, the extent to which the quantitative and qualitative problems facing defenses are simplified enhances the probability that the defense will suffice. This need is made explicit in the New Strategic Concept's emphasis on offensive force reductions during the first stage of transition to an SDI world.[8]

This brings together the conjunction of arms control and the possibility of moving toward an altered strategic environment. On the one hand, it is clear that missile defenses are most attractive—because they would be most effective—if combined with offensive force reductions. It is conceivable (if hardly practicable) that a movement to defense could be taken unilaterally; for instance, as defenses are erected and protect offensive forces, higher survival rates would mean smaller offensive forces would be needed. More likely, however, mutual, negotiated, and agreed upon phasing in of defenses and winding down of offenses within an arms control framework is necessary for success, as most schemes to date have advocated.[9]

If restraint is necessary to make perfect defenses conceivable, then some form of offensive arms control—either a freeze or, more likely, substantial reduction—is the only obvious means to accomplish the purpose. The analysis to this point, however, has shown that the principal obstacle to moving toward either a defenseless or defense-protected nuclear disarmament—or any other form of arms control regime—is the SDI. The positions of the two sides are fundamentally opposed on this issue. Until it is resolved, the SDI is simultaneously the goal of the Reagan administration and the major impediment to its realization.

The Status of Arms Control Negotiations

After a roughly two-year hiatus, arms control negotiations between the United States and the Soviet Union resumed in 1985 in Geneva. The actual negotiations were broken into three distinct forums, each with its own agenda and negotiating teams. Separate talks were conducted on intermediate nuclear forces (INF) primarily stationed in Europe, strategic offensive forces (the legacy of SALT and START), and on space weapons. As talks commenced, Secretary of State Shultz proclaimed them "the most comprehensive and complex of any in history."[10]

After a year of sporadic discussions, as of this writing, they are also among the least productive. Much of the negotiation, if that is the proper term, has come in the form of so-called public diplomacy, where negotiating positions are announced in the media at the same time or even before they are presented formally at the talks; the purpose is clearly to gain popular support more than to further agreement. As U.S. negotiator Edward Rowny described the situation in April 1986, "The Russians' proposals—and this is particularly true with respect to the Geneva negotiations—are presented primarily for their public impact, not as serious negotiating positions."[11]

That is an extraordinary public position for a senior official whose supposed mission is to evaluate and negotiate differences between the positions of the two countries, but it is consistent with the somewhat condescending tone of U.S. official reaction to Soviet objections to SDI, as reported in chapter 3. Much of the public diplomacy has indeed focused on the contrasting visions of the SDI. The Soviets have mounted an extensive campaign against space-strike weapons, and the United States has responded generally with derision. For instance, Robert Hunter asserts that "assuming the Soviet Union fails in its U.S.-beating campaign on SDI, the two superpowers might someday agree to permit limited defensive systems."[12] As long as the two sides remain apart and publicize their differences—thereby making compromise impossible—progress toward successful arms control, which Michael Nacht argues "will succeed only if each side sees that the process of arms control reduces security threats in ways that no other method or strategy can,"[13] seems unlikely.

Arms control negotiations are rather clearly at an impasse, despite a flurry of well-publicized proposals in late 1986. Looking at the situation, three possible explanations for this seem most likely, either individually or in some combination. One explanation is that the current situation is just the way both sides want it—the semblance of arms control negotiations to satisfy political demands that they be conducted, but with effective roadblocks to ensure that no formal agreements can be reached. The second is that the task at hand is simply too extensive and difficult ever to reach agreement, so that the talks are bogged down by their own weight. The third is that differences are so fundamental that they cannot be reconciled. An obvious example in that third explanation, of course, is the SDI. But, regardless of whichever of these explanations—individually or in combination—is the true basis of the problem, it is hard to argue with Arnold Kanter's assessment of the current situation: "This combination of circumstances is more likely to lead to political jockeying and propaganda exercises in Geneva than to arms control agreements."[14] Since that absence of agreement also forecloses meaningful change in nuclear relationships—most notably movement toward each leader's stated objective—the possible causes deserve examination.

Possible Bases of Impasse

As suggested, one explanation of why there is no progress at Geneva is that this is exactly what the negotiating parties want. In this view, arms control negotiations are politically necessary in the United States, at least, for both domestic and international reasons. Domestically, appearing to engage in arms control softens charges of bellicosity and comports with the public's generalized—if not specific—belief in the attraction of controlling nuclear arms. Internationally, negotiations calm global criticisms of the perceived nuclear arms race. Both the Soviet Union and the United States would like to soothe such criticism.

If appearing to pursue arms control is politically unavoidable, reaching agreements may be viewed as not in the best interests of the United States. Many, including numerous members of the Reagan administration, believe that past arms control efforts have actually harmed the United States, either by allowing or codifying Soviet advantage or by creating circumstances encouraging Soviet cheating. From this vantage point, a "number of key officials in the new Administration believed that arms control had been in their phrase, 'bad medicine.' . . . If forced to keep up the appearance of playing the old arms-control game, they believed, the U.S. would do best with gambits at the negotiating table that would lead to diplomatic stalemate."[15] At the same time, arms control activity has coincided with the buildup of U.S. strategic arms (partially justified as returning the United States to a position of strength from which to negotiate). Until that position of strength has indeed been established, "Perhaps an administration with no genuine interest in arms limitation finds in arms control the best pulpit from which to preach arms competition."[16] One of the aspects of the strategic modernization program potentially subject to limitation, of course, is the SDI.

This is an admittedly somewhat cynical description of Reagan administration motivations, and the group that makes it is generally critical of the administration more broadly. Nonetheless, they do provide some evidence supporting their contention.

One such assertion is that relevant policymakers have established public positions opposing arms control. As Walter Slocombe puts it,

> Paradoxically, the upswing in the general popularity of reaching arms-control agreements with the Soviet Union comes in the midst of the ascendancy in the United States of people who have been throughout their political careers strong critics not just of the details, but of the very concept of arms-control agreements with the Soviet Union.[17]

This opposition is generally depicted as doctrinaire and intransigent: "The executive branch is heavily populated, at high levels of the departments and agencies primarily concerned, by hard-line ideologues with a clear record of hostility to past agreements and deep-seated suspicion of any compromise with Moscow."[18] The official most frequently identified as an example of this type of individual is Assistant Secretary of Defense for International Security Policy, Richard Perle.[19] Even President Reagan is not exempted from questions about the sincerity of arms control motives: "In almost two years, he has not shown any serious concern at any time for the negotiability of his proposals. . . . The apparent absence of such intent is a matter of great importance in assessing the prospects for new agreements."[20]

Part of the problem may be inconsistency in the positions taken by various administration actors. At the top of the pinnacle sits President Reagan with his grand — if possibly impractical — vision of a negotiated movement toward nuclear disarmament. At the other extreme are the hard-liners who use the president's vision to block all progress toward arms control: "Most refuse to contemplate negotiating restraints on 'Star Wars' with Moscow, some in the hope that this will kill prospects for an arms control process that they believe harms American interests."[21] Somewhere between the extremes lies a middle ground represented by former Assistant Secretary of State for Politico-Military Affairs, Richard Burt, who, in an article published in 1982, argued that, "at SALT III, the United States should not seek severe quantitative reductions or tighter qualitative constraints. An accord that would provide both sides with some flexibility . . . [might be] more conducive to overall stability."[22]

One cause of this lack of consensus may well be bureaucratic in origin. This is certainly the charge leveled by Klaus Knorr, who argues,

> The presence of competitive priorities and incompatible bureaucratic behavior . . . explain why the governments of the superpowers have done very little by way of arms control to improve the prospects of war avoidance, and have done so much by way of deploying nuclear arms that are both vulnerable and dangerous to an opponent . . . to detract from the prospects.[23]

At least three competing bureaucracies are at work with conflicting interests: the Arms Control and Disarmament Agency, which needs ongoing arms control negotiations to justify its existence; the State Department, which uses negotiations as a way to assert some control over defense policy; and the Department of Defense, which often views arms control negotiations as a threat to weapons systems and control over defense matters. The bureaucratic and political infighting that result are a major element in Strobe Talbott's examination of strategic arms control in the first Reagan administration,[24] while Burt observes that "in a bureaucratic sense, the establishment of an arms control process is in some ways more important than whether the process produces an agreement."[25]

A second possible reason for the absence of arms control progress at Geneva is that the talks have been so extensive and complex that they simply defy human solution. Brzezinski believes so: "One should not expect again a comprehensive agreement on the mode of SALT I or on the mode of the even more ambitious SALT II agreement. More likely are segmented, narrow agreements focused on specific aspects of the problem."[26]

There are several ways in which the structure and nature of the Geneva enterprise could work to reduce the likelihood of reaching broad agreement. One is the sheer size and variety of the agenda, which is much more ambitious than any past negotiation. In addition to a focus on strategic offensive arms similar to SALT, there are separate agendas on both space weapons and INF. The latter agenda adds enormous complication to the entire enterprise by creating a whole new category of weaponry (whose definitions are in disagreement) and new weapons possessors (the British, French, *and* Chinese forces) whose interests and arsenals must be taken into account. Suddenly, a bilateral negotiation over one category of weapons (SALT/START) which was quite complicated enough as it was becomes potentially a multilateral, multitiered set of discussion.

If agenda and participant proliferation do not add enough complication, all three levels are interconnected. To make matters worse, a fourth agenda, the conventional balance in Europe, must be addressed. The interconnections are shown in figure 5–1. Beginning in the upper left corner, an agreement on overall forces, as both sides have proposed, means aggregating strategic and intermediate nuclear forces somehow, such that "It is virtually certain that there will be no START agreement unless the INF deadlock is broken."[27] START also relates to what is or is not done in regulating space (the SDI), and vast reductions in START would increase greatly the value of conventional forces and thus the forum in which they are considered—mutual and balanced force reductions (MBFR). The erection of a comprehensive defense in space would similarly affect the value of INF and, hence, conventional balance. Finally, of course, the disposition of INF affects the conventional balance by making disparities more or less acceptable.

This murky situation is made all the more difficult by two associated complications. On the one hand, reaching trade-offs both within negotiation fora and between negotiations are complicated "because the forces on the two sides differ so much that reductions in broad categories may affect one side quite differently from the other."[28] At that, each arena of discussion is not of equal importance, and the two nations disagree about which arena is most important. Thus, according to David Holloway, "the Soviet Union has made it clear that it regards space weapons, and especially space-based BMD, as the most pressing issue for arms control. The United States, on the other hand, regards the reduction of offensive forces—especially the Soviet ICBM force—as a more urgent matter."[29]

Holloway's comment suggests something of a transition between the second and third possible cause of stagnation. That basis, of course, is that in addition to an incredibly broad and complex agenda, there are fundamental points of disagreement between the two sides. Most obvious is the issue of space-based SDI. The fundamental nature of this is such that Gorbachev has

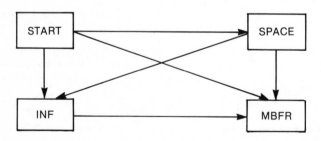

Figure 5–1.

stated firmly and repeatedly, "The stand taken by the U.S. side on the Star Wars issue is the main obstacle in the way of an agreement on the control of armaments."[30] A recent *New York Times* article reported that this impasse covers the range of Geneva discussions,[31] and the depth of disagreement was clearly evident at Reykjavik.

As discussed earlier, the basis of difference is over which SDI one is talking about, a disagreement made all the more problematic because there is no SDI weapons system, and any of the alternatives are feasible. Reagan and Weinberger talk about a layered comprehensive defense leaving nuclear weapons obsolete and involving space-based systems. Other Americans talk more modestly about LTP defenses of retaliatory forces. The Soviets, meanwhile, remain adamant that SDI is intent on producing offensive space-strike weapons that "could also be used to strike from outer space at ground, air, and naval targets, including missiles on launching pads, and control and communications centers. Such weapons could at any moment appear over any region or state posing a threat to its security."[32]

The common theme and point of division is the weaponization of space. One quasi-official Soviet document, for instance, warns, "In actual fact, the United States wants to initiate an arms race in yet another sphere and to secure military superiority there. . . . Allocations for the development of attack weapon systems designed primarily to destroy spacecraft account for an ever-growing share of the U.S. military space budget."[33] Quoting the Soviet journal *Voyennaya Mysl (Military Thought)*, Stewart Menaul suggests that concern for space has been long-standing in the Soviet Union: "As far back as 1965, the USSR defined its doctrine for space. . . . The doctrine was said to 'envisage active hostilities in space and regarding the mastery of space as a prerequisite for achieving victory in war.' "[34] This statement may well be more dramatic than what the Soviets actually believe. Indeed, their objections, though no less fundamental, may be more pragmatically based, as David Rivkin suggests: "The USSR's opposition to the SDI reflects simply a conviction that deploying the kinds of defenses envisioned by the SDI would not serve its interests in the strategic environment Moscow sees existing today and continuing for the future."[35]

These sources of impediment need not be viewed as mutually exclusive or exhaustive. It is quite possible, for instance, that a terribly complicated agenda and a sticking point on SDI are tactical solutions to engaging in arms control negotiations without running the risk of reaching agreements. Similarly, unwillingness to acknowledge that Soviet objections to SDI may have potential validity and to negotiate in the recognition of that possibility may also be a way to insure that unwanted agreements are avoided.

Getting a handle on why there has been no arms control progress is inherently difficult. As of 1986, for instance, the West has not truly had an opportunity to assess adequately Mikhail Gorbachev as an opponent or as a negotiating partner. His style in dealing with the West was clearly more sophisticated and apparently more open than that of his aged, stolid predecessors, and he has already done some things (such as allowing President Reagan to appear live on Moscow television, permitting limited coverage of the nuclear reactor accident at Chernobyl, and publicizing arms control initiatives through advertisements in the *New York Times* and on Moscow television) that simply would have been inconceivable by his predecessors. What is not known is whether beneath the cloak of style and Madison Avenue urbanity is a man of different substance than his predecessors. More specifically, it is difficult to know whether the aggressive arms control posture of Mikhail Gorbachev represents an honest change in Soviet policy or whether the protege of Yuri Andropov, creator of the Office of Disinformation within the Committee on State Security (KGB), is simply perfecting his mentor's art.

It is likewise difficult to assess the Reagan administration's position. The problem here, however, derives from the multiple voices and tunes of the administration on arms-control–related matters, especially long-term goals. This is especially true regarding the SDI issue. When Reagan speaks of his vision, he is clear that his vision is of an astrodome defense and nuclear obsolescence, and there is no reason to doubt *his* sincerity. Other administration figures, such as Defense Secretary Weinberger, talk more vaguely about the long-term and more about the shorter-term prospects of LTP defenses; others at lower levels barely mention perfect defenses at all and even privately admit they are probably unattainable. Given that each version of a defensive world has different impacts on the structure of the nuclear balance and hence the contribution of arms control to structuring and regulating that relationship, it is critical to know to which voice one should listen.

The SDI issue thus sits at the heart of contention between the two superpowers and their contrasting views of the future. It is central for two reasons. The first, to repeat, is that the existence of absence of an SDI-based perfect defense is the primary, fundamental difference in the strategic visions publicly espoused by Reagan and Gorbachev. The two positions, as currently articulated, are irreconcilable, and to the degree they are seriously advanced, they require reconciliation and resolution. Second, the SDI is the single most important substantive point of disagreement on the arms control agenda, and it is difficult, if not impossible, to imagine meaningful progress in arms control as long as the two sides remain at loggerheads on this issue. Since both visions require a vital arms control process and substantive agreements, the two aspects are inextricably intertwined.

Possible Arms Control Outcomes

If there is to be movement toward the radically altered world of nuclear disarmament or some more modest alterations in the strategic condition in which arms control plays a part, then one must look at the alternative outcomes of the SDI issue. In essence, there are three possibilities: that both sides will maintain their positions unchanged; that one side or another will repudiate its position; or that some compromise will be reached. Each possible outcome has different strategic consequences and different attractions and liabilities.

1. Neither side relinquishes its position. Given that both sides are strongly committed on the public record to the antithetical positions that they hold, this is the easiest and most natural outcome to imagine. From the U.S. viewpoint, it has the major advantage of leaving the SDI research program unfettered, so that is can blossom into whatever promise it may have, including realization of the president's hope for it. Given the level of personal commitment that Reagan has invested in the SDI—to say nothing of the actual and projected financial and human investment—it is hard to imagine that he could do anything but continue.

In the short and even medium term, the Soviets too are unlikely to change their position on SDI. Partly, this predilection shows their judgment about the program, which Meyer summarizes: "On the purely military side, it is clear that the Soviet military and political leaders do not see the US SDI as an opportunity to improve mutual security, nor are they ever likely to see it as such."[36]

Continued opposition may well make sense for tactical political reasons as well. The chief supporter of SDI, after all, leaves office in January 1989, and a successor—especially if it is a Democrat—may prove a far less erstwhile patron. Despite efforts to ensconce SDI so securely in the budget that it will be difficult to dislodge, the program will become more controversial as its costs increase and as developmental actions tax the limits of permissibility under the ABM Treaty. Moreover, since major decisions with strategic implications lie somewhere in the future, the Soviets have some time to see if the effort collapses of its own weight. As Kincade argues, "The Soviets can afford to wait him out, pursuing economic reforms and rejuvenation while postponing a deeper commitment to their own strategic defense research program until after 1989, when the risks and difficulties of such a venture will be more evident and when a deal might be cut with Reagan's successor."[37]

Inertia and inactivity may be attractive in the short run but look quite different in the long run when strategic consequences begin to take shape. If both sides remain adamant, SDI research will continue—unless killed for political reasons—possibly to the point of producing one of the possible SDIs. Whether that is desirable depends upon where one sits, which SDI is produced, and, thus, what costs attach to the relatively passive strategy of verbal opposition.

The most unacceptable outcome would be if the space-strike weapons outcome is allowed to occur under a deadlocked situation. This would be an extraordinary failure for the Soviets given their stated perception. Although it is not entirely clear that everyone connected to SDI would be entirely dismayed by such an outcome, it would be particularly traumatic in terms of the traditional structure of deterrence (as will be discussed below). A space shield likely requires both a layered defense — the space-based aspect of which the Soviets will not tolerate — and constrained offensive forces through arms control — which the Soviets will only entertain if SDI is abandoned. There is clearly a paradox involved here. Unless the United States relents on SDI, the Soviets will not allow the condition for its success — constrained offensive forces. If the United States does relent, however, it will likely have to give up parts of its space-based layered defense, which is probably necessary to maintain the astrodome. Something has to give.

The only group that benefits from continued deadlock are those who either favor or believe the attainable defense is less-than-perfect defense of retaliatory forces. The absence of restrictive agreements avoids restrictions on missile defense research concerning realizable defenses that individuals of this strategic persuasion argue reinforce deterrence by maximizing Soviet uncertainty about how much and which elements of an attacking force would penetrate those defenses. This position is clearly less radical in its effect than the plan put forward by either national leader. It is less than coincidental that this position is held by most of those in the Reagan administration who are generally suspicious of arms control.

2. One side or the other relinquishes its position. Given the public investment that both superpowers have made in their stated postures on SDI and the absence of incentives to change, this is clearly the least likely outcome. For either leader to drop his objection to the other's view would be tantamount to admitting his previous position was duplicitous. Gorbachev would, in essence, have to admit that he was just kidding about the U.S. intention to produce space-strike weapons aimed at gaining decisive strategic superiority or else Reagan would have to admit that SDI is not really intended to produce a defense after all but, yes indeed, is an effort to produce the death star. Since SDI is now neither a defense nor an offense but could become either, neither, or both, depending on what the research produces and how the technologies are applied, the incentives for public recanting are meager indeed.

Yet it is the policy of U.S. government that this is exactly how the current conceptual logjam over SDI will be resolved. When asked about Soviet objectives and how SDI can be implemented in the face of Soviet noncooperation, the consistent response questions the sincerity of Soviet pronouncements and speaks confidently of "negotiating such a cooperative transition with the Soviet Union."[38] As noted earlier, it was a prime personal purpose of Reagan at the Geneva summit in late 1985 to convince Gorbachev that SDI was indeed intended to produce a benign defense that the United States will share with the Soviets. Gorbachev has publicly replied that if the United States will not share oil extracting technology, it is unlikely to share SDI.

Even if the administration is correct about Soviet motives regarding SDI—which is a dubious proposition—the prospect that Gorbachev will become a "born-again Reaganite" on SDI borders on the nonexistent. If there is any chance that either side will change its basic position, it is that the president who succeeds Reagain—especially if that individual is a Democrat—will dump the SDI concept. This could be done on the basis that the ultimate vision is a fantasy—for which a great deal of expert support could be derived—or for budgetary reasons. Moreover, such an abandonment could be done without admitting that the Soviet assessment was correct and without abandoning some of the potentially useful research programs now included under the SDI umbrella.

3. They reach a compromise. The prospects for surmounting the current impasse are not necessarily as bleak as they may appear. There are, indeed, both political and technical bases for compromise, because the positions of the two sides are not in fact as diametrically opposed as is often portrayed. The problem is that the SDI debate portrays the Soviets as being opposed to missile defenses when that is not the case at all. What the Soviets are opposed to is the prospect of space-based weapons systems aimed at their territory. The solution is the conscious reorientation of SDI so that it does not pose a threat to the Soviet Union itself. The key concept is to root SDI as an *unambiguously defensive defense*.

There is no reason to maintain that the Soviets are hostile to active defenses. Gray forcefully states their congeniality to the idea: "The Soviet Union is not unfriendly to the idea of homeland defence, only to the idea of American homeland defence."[39] Holloway maintains the Soviet intellectual rejection of the consequences of defenselessness. "Soviet BMD policy in the early 1960s was rooted in an unwillingness to regard vulnerability to nuclear attack as an acceptable basis for Soviet security."[40] Based on that assessment of a strong Soviet penchant for homeland defense,[41] the Soviet Union has, after all, developed one of the world's most extensive civil defense networks, an air defense system second to none, and the world's only missile defense system.[42]

What the Soviets are opposed to are SDI weapons prospects that could be offensive as well as defensive in their applications. As Paul Barrett points out, space-based weapons fit this definition: "Unlike old-fashioned, ground-based missile defense systems, which had no potential for making a first strike more feasible, space-based beam weapons could easily be transformed from shield to arrow."[43] The Soviets, in other words, object to ambiguous defenses— weapons and weapons configurations that could be employed either offensively or defensively. Unambiguous defenses—weapons configured so that they can only be employed for defensive purposes—are another matter.

Because most weapons are inherently neither offensive nor defensive but are so designated by the ways they are used, the key element is how weapons are deployed. This is so because deployment affects the potential range of employment opportunities. The example of a cannon may clarify the point.

The cannon is neither intrinsically offensive nor defensive, but becomes one sort of weapon or the other by the method of its employment. If one bolts a cannon to the ground inside a fortification guarding access to home territory, the cannon is an unambiguously defensive weapon. If, on the other hand, one takes that same cannon, places it on a motorized chassis with a turret and armor, and still calls it a defensive weapon, the designation is no longer unambiguous.

The extrapolation to missile defenses is obvious and straightforward. The obvious analogy to the emplaced artillery piece is ground-based point defenses—whether traditional ABMs or some form of ground-based lasers or particle beams. It is also possible that other forms of unambiguous defense could be developed. For instance, a space-based system in orbit over the United States which, by virtue of range or the physical curvature of the earth, could never approach Soviet territory with its weapons, might provide a possibility. On the other hand, laser battle stations over or near Soviet territory for boost-phase interception whose weapons could reach Soviet territory represent the kind of offensive as well as defensive prospect to which the Soviets object.

Looking toward a negotiation for unambiguous defenses could well be in the interests of both sides. As Gray points out, it could provide a way for the Soviets to short-circuit U.S. ambiguous defenses: "If Moscow really is concerned that the U.S. might choose to deploy a terrestial-bombardment 'space sword' in the guise of a 'space shield,' it could suggest discussions or negotiations for the suitable restriction of the capabilities of defensive weapons."[44] The attraction for Americans could well be to avoid the unpredictable and potentially destabilizing spiral of measures and countermeasures that could accompany continued U.S. development and deployment of a system the Soviets genuinely fear. Rather, "our expectations of Soviet reactions might lead us to deploy a less threatening but therefore less capable system."[45] If such negotiations proved successful, the way opens to a cooperative transition to a strategic nuclear world in which defenses play a part, because "Soviet leaders will have an attractive alternative both to suicide today and inferiority tomorrow—and that is a defensive competition managed by arms control."[46]

What are the potential costs and benefits of pursuing the kind of compromise solution suggested here? If the Soviets have been honest in their objections and about the basis of the future world Gorbachev envisions, they have little reason to object. A negotiation aimed at agreement on unambiguous defenses does not force them to relent on space-strike weapons, since these would be obvious candidates for elimination in a world organized around unambiguous defenses. Such negotiations could break the negotiation impasse that is blocking the path of arms reduction toward their stated goal of nuclear disarmament by the year 2000. Moreover, if unambiguous defenses exclude space-strike systems, then there is nothing in the Soviet proposals that is compromised; the Soviet proposal makes no mention of missile defenses one way or the other.

The Soviets, in other words, could only really object to negotiations aimed at unambiguous defenses if their objections to SDI, their nuclear disarmament proposal, or both are disingenuous. If, for instance, they really fear SDI because of its stimulation of the U.S. technological base, then they would likely oppose anything that does not greatly restrict U.S. missile defense research in general. The call for negotiations on unambiguous defense thus effectively forces them to show their hands.

The cost/benefit calculation for the United States is somewhat more mixed. Positively, the offer meets and overcomes Soviet objections head-on and affirms Reagan's oft-repeated insistence about the defensive character of the SDI. Depending on whether unambiguous defenses were limited to ground-based systems or whether some limited forms of space basing were included, the breadth of SDI research might not even be restricted. At the same time, breaking the SDI logjam opens the possibility of negotiating the restraints or reductions on offensive arsenal size that it is agreed are necessary for an effective defense.

The major cost is the probable abandonment of boost-phase interception of Soviet ICBMs by space-based laser systems, since such systems would almost inevitably have to be located near enough to Soviet soil when on duty status to pose a potential offensive threat to the Soviet Union. Since virtually all projections of a perfect or near-perfect defense are based on a layered defense design incorporating boost-phase interception as an integral element, this sacrifice would compromise the attainability of an astrodome defense to some significant extent that cannot be accurately measured at this point. Whether there is much cost involved in this sacrifice depends on one's assessment of the likelihood of achieving perfect defenses under any circumstances. Also, space-basing systems that could not physically reach adversary territory might partially compensate for the loss of boost-phase intercept.

The need to eliminate space-based boost-phase interception as a way to make possible meaningful arms control negotiations that include constraint, reduction, or even elimination points to a fundamental dilemma for those advocating perfect defenses. That dilemma, of course, is that even a theoretically impenetrable defense is impossible without a limitation on offensive arms, but the most promising technological solution to the problem of defending against missile attacks precludes reaching the agreements that would limit offenses to manageable proportions. The result is two unsatisfactory outcomes. On the one hand, one can pursue the most capable physical system, including boost-phase interceptors, but knowing one would face an unconstrained and probably unmanageable threat. On the other hand, one can compromise the physical capability of the defensive system in exchange for a constrained offensive problem, thereby placing in confrontation a less-than-perfect defensive capability and an offensive force manageable by the defense whose capability has been forfeited.

Is a Compromise Desirable?

If one starts from the premise that the current nuclear balance is essentially stable and does not require such radical alteration as the obsolescence of nuclear weapons or nuclear disarmament, then unambiguous defenses may be appealing. Their appeal is partly because of the practical and conceptual unattractiveness and self-contradiction of the more radical proposals and partly because the kind of capability that they would likely produce is fundamentally compatible with the dynamics that produce self-deterrence.

The Reagan vision is conceptually flawed in two ways. The first, as discussed in chapter 3, is that it attacks the wrong problem, the existence and lethality of nuclear arsenals, rather than the underlying political competition and distrust which gave rise to their development. If that competition is not overcome before SDI is implemented or simultaneously with such action, the competition will simply move to a different arena, such as the conventional balance in Europe. Conversely—and perversely—if the political distrust and competition is overcome, the United States would need a perfect missile defense against the Soviet Union about as badly as it currently needs one against Canada.

The second flaw is related. If a perfect SDI is only attainable through a constrained offensive threat regulated by arms control agreements, two difficulties arise. One is that the offensive constraint to make the defense effective would, in effect, amount to requiring the Soviets to configure and deploy their forces to be compatible with and destructible by U.S. defenses. This would require an enormous degree of cooperation between the two superpowers. If they could cooperate to that extent, one would wonder if they had sufficient enmity to arm against one another. Moreover, it is virtually self-contradictory to design a weapons capability so that it will be impotent against the adversary for which it was designed.

The second difficulty is the requirement for arms control to create and monitor offensive constraints as a prerequisite or corequisite for defenses to perform perfectly. A perfect defense apparently requires boost-phase interception by space-based systems — what the Soviets call space-strike weapons. Since they say they will negotiate no agreement that does not ban those weapons, it is clearly an either–or situation: one can have *either* a comprehensive defense system *or* arms control constraint — but not both.

The administration either does not understand these dilemmas, rejects them, or ignores them. The extent to which it fails to address or acknowledge these contradictions is captured in a speech by Paul H. Nitze:

> The United States cannot accept the self-serving Soviet definition of "space-strike arms." . . . This definition calls for a subjective judgment as to the purpose for which a system has been designed. The Soviets have made it clear that they reserve to themselves alone the right to make such judgments. *The U.S. position is that an agreement must address specific systems and that limits must be based on evident capabilities,* not on subjective judgments of intentions. The work in Geneva on defense and space issues cannot move forward until the Soviet definition is abandoned. Furthermore, the work on START . . . cannot progress until the Soviets abandon the linkage they have imposed between progress in the START talks and prior U.S. agreement to a ban on "space-strike weapons." (emphasis added)[47]

This statement is remarkable. It asserts first that the Soviets must abandon — not compromise — the position they have systematically taken on SDI. It then asserts that limits can only be negotiated after weapons are developed enough so that their capabilities are known and can be judged; in other words, no limits on SDI weapons can be negotiated for the next ten to twenty years. Finally, the United States refuses to negotiate the START constraints on offensive forces that are the necessary preconditions for an effective defense *as long as the Soviets insist that offenses and defenses are related to one another.* The flights of logic entailed are nothing less than breathtaking.

Each assertion is incredible. The clear implication of this statement by President Reagan's chief advisor on arms control is to harpoon arms control. Possibly that is the intent. Certainly, many in the administration would agree with Burt's summary dismissal that, "arms control, in the final analysis, is mostly useful only in defining military problems."[48] Yet, the necessity of arms control remains, because "The only prospect of an effective strategic defense depends on tightly constraining the offenses technically and numerically."[49] As Kruzel carefully explains, constraints require that the space and START negotiations be linked together, not separated:

> Limiting defensive forces should theoretically make offensive forces less attractive, but limiting offensive forces will make defensive forces more attractive. . . . [T]he only way strategic defense will ever be a good investment is against a constrained offensive force. . . . SDI does not make sense without a START agreement.[50]

Somewhat reflecting the fuzzy thinking that underlies the advocacy of movement toward perfect defense, Robert Art has even created an uncomplimentary acronym to describe it, "the BAD world (Both Assured of Defense)."[51]

These problems do not exist for unambiguous defense that abandons boost-phase interception and which, as a consequence, adopts a more modest mission for the defenses—probably limited to selected point targets such as retaliatory forces; command, control, communications, and intelligence (C^3I) assets; or political leadership. Such defenses fall back into the less demanding and, hence, more attainable performance criteria of less-than-perfect defenses, whose contribution is measured in increments of additional assets that are saved by the defenses. Moreover, LTP defenses can reinforce, rather than detract from, the dynamics of an RSD world.

Crisis Management

Defenses devoted to protecting retaliatory forces and other counterforce targets are perfectly compatible with deterrence based on mutual vulnerability and fear, because they assure that some greater proportion of retaliatory might would be available for retribution than would be the case in their absence. The effect is to make the sense of self-deterrence more complete by further assuring the unacceptable consequences of initiating nuclear war. This effect reflects a rather conventional assured-destruction analysis. From that conceptual base, for instance, Alton Frye describes these kinds of defense as "deterrence-enhancing" as opposed to "deterrence-escaping" population defenses of the type forming the core of perfect SDI.[52] Moreover, even quite effective LTP defenses are compatible with Soviet as well as U.S. conceptualizations of the role of defenses—as long as they stop short of the appearance of space-strike weapons. As Rivkin points out, "the Soviets . . . have never claimed that a situation in which each superpower's territory is largely invulnerable to strategic attack necessarily upsets deterrence."[53]

LTP defenses can also contribute to the two prime aspects of crisis management: crisis avoidance and crisis termination at the lowest possible level. The knowledge that those defenses would insure the survival of more retaliatory forces (even if one could not specify with much confidence how much more) adds to the incentives to avoid crises in the first place. At the same time, LTP defenses do not exacerbate tensions in a crisis, because they dampen any "use them or lose them" fears that may evolve as a crisis unfolds and perspectives on options may change. Defenses may not make it easier to terminate crises, but they do at least reduce some of the dynamics that could make crisis escalation occur.

Perceptual Changes

The major burden of Soviet objections to SDI is the assertion, in effect, that U.S programs are designed to upset the current balance in weaponry to the point that the United States might be able to calculate gain from the offensive use of its nuclear arsenal. Thus, "a steep enhancement of the U.S. offensive nuclear capability"[54] has ominous portent: "What we are dealing with in reality are measures that are part of an overall offensive plan directed at upsetting strategic parity . . . and [creating] preparations for delivering a first nuclear strike."[55] Given the indeterminancy of what final shape the current SDI program might take and the ambiguous characteristics of boost-phase interceptors, this objection cannot be dismissed out of hand.

The same problem does not attach to more limited, unambiguous defenses. A defense limited to protecting counterforce targets leaves population at risk and even enhances countervalue targeting, since weapons aimed at those unprotected targets are more likely to penetrate to those targets than are weapons designated for protected objects. If the effect of removing the boost-phase layer of an SDI is to remove the ability to calculate perfection and, thus, to realize that even a relatively modest proportion of adversary weapons will penetrate to target, that should be enough to dampen any perception of decisive advantage that the possessor of such a defense might be able to calculate.

Uncertainty

As pointed out earlier, much of the justification of less-than-perfect defenses is couched in terms of their uncertainty-enhancing characteristics. According to this argument, even an LTP defense assures a potential attacker that some of his force will be intercepted. While neither attacker nor defender can predict with absolute confidence how much or what elements of an attacking force will be destroyed, the uncertainty of which weapons will or will not proceed to and destroy their designated targets means a potential aggressor cannot confidently predict accomplishing whatever objectives were in mind. That uncertainty, in turn, is self-deterring.

Advocacy of the compromise solution amounts to arguing that a less capable defense is better than a more capable one, because it entails less change in an essentially satisfactory situation. The contribution of LTP defenses is at the margins—some enhancement of crisis stability, less ability to calculate advantage from the use of nuclear weapons, and additional uncertainty. A compromise that allows LTP defenses fine-tunes the existing system; it does not revolutionize it.

Since a major focus of this chapter has been the relevance of arms control to various strategic visions, the role of arms control in a movement toward a compromise on SDI requires attention. Naturally, experts disagree on the subject. Colin Gray, who would certainly not be regarded as reflexively pro-arms control, believes the role is crucial: "What one can and should do today is to outline, broadly, a strategy for arms control assistance for a strategic condition characterized by major defensive advantage."[56] Others, however, believe the role of arms control is more peripheral: "The principal constraint on the further strengthening of Soviet offensive forces is likely to be supplied by a serious U.S. commitment to strategic defense rather than by arms control as such."[57]

Regardless of the centrality of arms control processes in the change to a defense-participatory nuclear balance, arms control can be useful in aiding that change in at least two regards. First, the erection of anything resembling meaningful LTP defenses will require, at a minimum, substantial revisions in the regime created by the ABM Treaty. That document is of sufficient symbolic and political importance that the violence a movement toward defense would do it cannot be ignored. Some negotiations aimed at modifying the regime are dictated by the existence and longevity of the treaty.

Second, the movement toward defenses entails change in the structural conditions of the system, some of which are bound to be unsettling. An arms control regime, possibly modelled on the Standing Consultative Commission created under the ABM Treaty, could prove invaluable in minimizing any instability that might arise in the process of change. Gray maintains both this value and the tendency of SDI supporters to underplay it: "Where SDI supporters tend to err is in neglecting to talk directly to the anxieties of the allies and of the Soviet Union. . . . The latter must be recognized, if not necessarily treated, if the United States is at all serious about pursuing a (partially) cooperative defensive transition."[58]

The virtue of the compromise solution is that it does not change much, which is valuable if one believes the current situation is essentially satisfactory. Another way of stating that is to say LTP defenses do not do much, which raises the question of whether they are worth the investment. That is ultimately the most difficult question to answer, but it is also the bottom line of a policy decision either to build or not to build defenses.

Notes

1. William H. Lewis, *The Prevention of Nuclear War: A United States Approach* (Boston: Oelgeschlager, Gunn & Hain, 1986), p. 25.

2. Christoph Bertram, "Security without Order: Nuclear Deterrence and Crisis Management in the 1980s," in Roman Kolkowicz and Neil Joeck (eds.), *Arms Control and International Security* (Boulder, Colo.: Westview Press, 1984), p. 3.

3. Walter Slocombe, "An Immediate Agenda for Arms Control," *Survival* 27, no. 5 (September/October 1985), p. 206.

4. Laurence Freedman, "Strategic Arms Control," in Josephine O'Connor Howe (ed.), *Armed Peace: The Search for World Security* (New York: St. Martin's, 1984), p. 42.

5. Caspar W. Weinberger, "U.S. Defense Strategy," *Foreign Affairs* 64, no. 4 (Spring 1986), p. 681.

6. Caspar W. Weinberger, *Annual Report to the Congress, Fiscal Year 1985* (Washington, D.C.: U.S. Government Printing Office, 1984), p. 58.

7. Strobe Talbott, *Deadly Gambits: The Reagan Administration and the Stalemate in Nuclear Arms Control* (New York: Alfred A. Knopf, 1984), p. 318.

8. Gary L. Guertner and Donald M. Snow, *The Last Frontier: An Analysis of the Strategic Defense Initiative* (Lexington, Mass.: Lexington Books, 1986), pp. 103–5.

9. See, for example, Alvin M. Weinberg and Jack N. Barkenbus, "Stabilizing Star Wars," *Foreign Policy,* no. 54 (Spring 1984), pp. 164–170; and Alton Frye, "Strategic Build-Down: A Context for Restraint," *Foreign Affairs* 62, no. 2 (Winter 1983/84), pp. 293–317.

10. George Shultz, "Arms Control: Objectives and Prospects," *Department of State Bulletin* 85, no. 2098 (May 1985), p. 24.

11. Edward Rowny, "Enough Diplomacy in Public; Now, Quiet Talks at Geneva," *New York Times,* April 16, 1986, p. A27.

12. Robert E. Hunter, "SDI: Return to Basics," *Washington Quarterly* 9, no. 1 (Winter 1986), p. 158.

13. Michael Nacht, *The Age of Vulnerability: Threats to the Nuclear Stalemate* (Washington, D.C.: Brookings Institution, 1985), p. 119.

14. Arnold Kanter, "Thinking about the Strategic Defense Initiative: An Alliance Perspective," *International Affairs* (London: Royal Institute of International Affairs) 61, no. 3 (Summer 1985), p. 460.

15. Talbott, *Deadly Gambits,* p. xii.

16. Thomas C. Schelling, "What Went Wrong with Arms Control," *Foreign Affairs* (64, no. 2 (Winter 1985/86), p. 229.

17. Slocombe, "An Immediate Agenda for Arms Control," p. 206.

18. McGeorge Bundy, "Some Thoughts about Unilateral Moderation," in Kolkowicz and Joeck, *Arms Control and International Security,* p. 16. Michael Krepon also makes the charge that "key executive positions are held by ideologues opposed to arms control with the Soviet Union." See "Dormant Threat to the ABM Treaty," *Bulletin of the Atomic Scientists* 42, no. 1 (January 1986), p. 31.

19. Perle denies animosity to arms control per se. In his early career, in fact, his position was quite unexceptional. He generally accepted the assured destruction position. See, for instance, his *Criteria for the Evaluation of Arms Control Options,* ASG Monograph no. 3 (Waltham, Mass.: Westinghouse Electric Corporation Advanced Study Group, April 1970).

20. Bundy, "Some Thoughts about Unilateral Moderation," p. 16.

21. Leslie Gelb, "Star Wars Advances: The Plan vs. the Reality," *New York Times,* December 15, 1985, p. 34.

22. Richard Burt, "Defense Policy and Arms Control: Defining the Problem," in Richard Burt (ed.), *Arms Control and Defense Postures in the 1980s* (Boulder, Colo.: Westview, 1982), p. 13.

23. Klaus Knorr, "Controlling Nuclear War," *International Security* 9, no. 4 (Spring 1985), p. 82.

24. Talbott, *Deadly Gambits.*

25. Burt, "Defense Policy and Arms Control," p. 10.

26. Zbigniew Brzezinski, "East–West Relations," *Atlantic Community Quarterly* 22, no. 4 (Winter 1984/85), p. 297.

27. Alton Frye, "Strategic Synthesis," *Foreign Policy,* no. 58 (Spring 1985), p. 20.

28. Harvard Nuclear Study Group (Albert Carnesale, Paul Doty, Stanley Hoffman, Samuel P. Huntington, Joseph S. Nye, Jr., and Scott D. Sagan), *Living with Nuclear Weapons* (Cambridge, Mass.: Harvard University Press, 1983), p. 205.

29. David Holloway, "The Strategic Defense Initiative and the Soviet Union," *Daedalus* 114, no. 3 (Summer 1985), p. 276.

30. Mikhail Gorbachev, "Our Policy Is Clear: It Is a Policy of Peace and Cooperation," *Information Bulletin* 24, no. 2 (1986), p. 15.

31. Michael R. Gordon, "U.S. Not Sure If Soviet Links Missile Accord to 'Star Wars,' " *New York Times,* February 6, 1986, p. A10.

32. M. Somov, " 'Star Peace,' not 'Star Wars'," *International Affairs (Moscow),* no. 3 (March 1986), p. 57. For similar treatments, see, for example, R. Ovinnikov, " 'Star Wars' Programme: A New Phase in Washington's Militaristic Policy," *International Affairs (Moscow),* no. 8 (August 1985), pp. 13–22; and Yu Tomilin, "To Stop the Arms Race: Imperative Task of Our Day," *International Affairs (Moscow),* no. 10 (October 1985), pp. 88–97, 117.

33. *Whence the Threat to Peace,* third edition (Moscow: Military Publishing House, 1984), pp. 40, 37. See also Michael Setton, "The Pentagon: Pushing Its Way into Space," *World Marxist Review* 28, no. 9 (September 1985), p. 124.

34. Stewart Menaul, "Military Uses of Space—Ballistic Missile Defense," *Space Policy* 1, no. 2 (May 1985), p. 122.

35. David B. Rivkin, "What Does Moscow Think?" *Foreign Policy,* no. 59 (Summer 1985), p. 86.

36. Stephen M. Meyer, "Soviet Strategic Programmes and the US SDI," *Survival* 27, no. 6 (November/December 1985), p. 290.

37. William H. Kincade, "Arms Control or Arms Coercion," *Foreign Policy,* no. 62 (Spring 1986), p. 45.

38. Paul H. Nitze, "The Alastair Buchan Memorial Lecture: The Objectives of Arms Control," *Survival* 27, no. 3 (May/June 1985), p. 106.

39. Colin S. Gray, "Space Arms Control: A Skeptical View," *Air University Review* 37, no. 1 (November/December 1985), p. 85.

40. David Holloway, "The Strategic Defense Initiative and the Soviet Union," *Daedalus* 114, no. 3 (Summer 1985), p. 258.

41. See, for instance, John M. Collins, "What Have We Got for $1 Trillion?" *Washington Quarterly* 9, no. 2 (Spring 1986), pp. 50–51.

42. *Soviet Military Power, 1985* (Washington, D.C.: U.S. Government Printing Office, 1985), pp. 43–59.

43. Paul Barrett, "Star Wars: Revenge of the Nerds," *Washington Monthly* 17, no. 12 (January 1986), p. 51.

44. Colin S. Gray, "Denting the Shield, Blunting the Sword," *Defense Science 2003+* 4, no. 6 (December 1985/January 1986), p. 19.

45. Stephen J. Cimbala, "The Strategic Defense Initiative: Political Risks," *Air University Review* 37, no. 1 (November/December 1985), p. 28.

46. Colin S. Gray, "Strategic Defenses: A Case for Strategic Defense," *Survival* 27, no. 2 (March/April 1985), p. 53.

47. Paul H. Nitze, "The Promise of SDI," *Current Policy,* no. 810 (Washington, D.C.: U.S. State Department, Bureau of Public Affairs, April 1986), p. 2.

48. Burt, "Defense Policy and Arms Control," p. 19.

49. Sidney D. Drell, Philip J. Farley, and David Holloway, *The Reagan Strategic Defense Initiative: A Technical, Political, and Arms Control Assessment* (Cambridge, Mass.: Ballinger, 1985), p. 95.

50. Joseph Kruzel, "What's Wrong with the Traditional Approach?" *Washington Quarterly* 8, no. 2 (Spring 1985), p. 130.

51. Robert J. Art, "Between Assured Destruction and Nuclear Victory: The Case for a 'MAD-Plus' Posture," in Russell Hardin, John J. Mearscheimer, Gerald Dworkin, and Robert E. Goodin (eds.), *Nuclear Deterrence: Ethics and Strategy* (Chicago, Ill.: University of Chicago Press, 1985), p. 139.

52. Frye, "Strategic Synthesis," p. 9.

53. Rivkin, "What Does Moscow Think?" p. 89.

54. *Star Wars: Delusions and Dangers* (Moscow: Military Publishing House, 1985), p. 23.

55. *Pravda* editorial from May 23, 1985, reprinted as "Geneva: What Has the First Round of Talks Shown?" *Information Bulletin* 23, no. 14 (1985), p. 46.

56. Gray, "Space Arms Control," p. 84.

57. Carnes Lord, "The U.S.–Soviet Strategic Nuclear Relationship," in W. Bruce Weinrod (ed.), *Confronting Moscow: An Agenda for the Post-Detente Era* (Washington, D.C.: Heritage Foundation, 1985), p. 9.

58. Gray, "Denting the Shield, Blunting the Sword," p. 13.

Part III
The Future

6
Stability in a Changing World

T
he nuclear doomsayers, who have argued since the dawn of the nuclear age that the cascading deadliness of everexpanding nuclear arsenals is sending the world careening toward the increased likelihood of nuclear holocaust, have been wrong. Their warnings ring shrill and hollow. Intones one prominent critic:

> Not only is the danger growing of a deliberate attack by one side or the other, because of progress toward a first-strike capability but, perhaps more seriously, there is an increasing danger of nuclear war by accident, miscalculation or madness. Even if political leaders wanted to maintain their old policy of nuclear deterrence by mutual assured destruction they would be prevented from doing so by the characteristics of the new nuclear weapons developed by military scientists. Military science, it can be argued, is no longer under political control.[1]

It can also be argued that the moon is made of green cheese, but the assertion makes it no more so. This statement of the unstable deterrence argument first presented in chapter 4 asserts, in effect, that nuclear arsenals create political conditions resulting in instability that leads to war. It is an incorrect construction of the problem; rather, the stable deterrence model maintains that political distrust and competition cause nations to arm but that the awesome destructive capacity of nuclear arsenals has seriously constrained the competition between the superpowers. It is this model that has been argued and reinforced in the preceding pages.

From this construction, two related observations that form the core of the argument, follow. The first is that the condition of mutual vulnerability, fear of the consequences of nuclear war, and the resultant self-deterrence have been remarkably durable and increasingly stabilizing, and there is little reason for this condition to change as long as the proper steps are taken to maintain and reinforce the system. Because of this, proposals to change the dynamics of nuclear balance bear the burden of demonstrating that they improve matters, and such proposals should be submitted to increasingly microscopic examination as their consequences are more radical. The second observation relates to the condition for change. Since political differences are the root cause and sustaining dynamic of the nuclear arms balance, prior or simultaneous improvement in political relations is the precondition to meaningful, stabilizing change in the nuclear relationship. Each of these observations is of sufficient import to require additional reiteration and elaboration.

Current and Prospective Nuclear Dynamics

Has the nuclear balance served us well, or is change required? One can argue, as Marshall Shulman has recently, that "the time has come to open a new debate on whether our own security interests require that this [nuclear] competition be managed in a more rational way than is now the case."[2] The results of that examination, however, would not be to suggest radical change. Indeed, the system of self-deterring, stable balance has evolved and is increasingly recognized by serious observers, although many are somewhat surprised at their own conclusions.

Former Secretary of State Dean Rusk summarizes this position: "To me the most important single thing one can say about this post-war world is that in this year of 1985 we have put behind us forty years without the firing of a nuclear weapon in anger, despite a considerable number of serious and even dangerous crises."[3] Bertram agrees, taking the assertion a step further: "The experience of the past thirty-seven years suggests that the existence of nuclear weapons has prevented, not promoted war."[4] This beneficial effect, moreover, has occurred despite or even possibly because of the anomaly and moral ambiguity of possessing these awesome weapons of mass destruction: "Although deterrence rests today, as it rested yesterday, on the threat and intent to do evil, the prospects that evil will one day be done have not increased. If anything, they appear to have modestly diminished."[5]

The reason for this is the fear of nuclear war that creates self-deterrence and the absence of intent to initiate nuclear war—indeed the absolute repellence at the prospects. Collins, in typical fashion, makes this point dramatically with regard to the Soviet Union: "The probability that the Soviets are going to launch a nuclear attack against the United States as a deliberate act of national policy is somewhere between zero and about minus eight million."[6] Moreover, there are those who believe that stabilization has achieved a momentum such that it is essentially self-sustaining: "Trends in the strategic balance would, if left to themselves, have sustained a stable balance. They do not require concerted corrective action. Indeed I would argue that the situation remains stable."[7]

One need not adopt a laissez faire attitude toward system dynamics to appreciate how they have operated to contribute to stability. According to the Harvard Nuclear Study Group, the movement toward a stable nuclear relationship was not a conscious, purposive process, but rather an incremental movement based in experience and the increasing realization that nuclear war must be avoided. As the group put it, "Through trial and error the superpowers have developed some prudent practices for handling crises. Both sides continue to avoid direct clashes of forces; each has avoided the use of nuclear weapons, and observes some restraint in the other side's sphere of dominant influence."[8] This latter comment suggests the point that nuclear weapons restrain the behavior of the superpowers in ways where restraint might dissipate in their absence.

It also suggests a more subtle and sophisticated understanding of how nuclear weapons affect human behavior toward them than simplistic, mechanistic notions that weapons characteristics make nuclear weapons use more or less likely. One recognition is the subtle way in which vulnerability dissuades nuclear weapons use and leaves notions of victory as not frightening but merely banal brave talk. As Art says, "It is not necessary to win a nuclear war in order to deter it; one has only to ensure that both are likely to lose it."[9] Moreover, there is a more sophisticated understanding of the immense relationship between the deadliness of the weapons arsenal and the likelihood (danger) that there will be a spiral to nuclear war. What has been argued here is that the deadlier the arsenals have become, the more the consequences of their use inhibits contemplation of weapons use, and, thus, the danger of the decision to initiate war declines. Collins agrees: "The most dangerous capability that you can possibly imagine is not necessarily a dangerous threat."[10]

A further evidence of the broad-ranging impact of nuclear weapons is that their existence not only restrains the use of other nuclear weapons—itself an accomplishment of more than trifling proportions—but that fear-induced "effects extend far beyond simply dissuading initial nuclear use."[11] Bernard Brodie, generally regarded as the preeminent theorist and the individual credited with identifying the critical role of deterrence in nuclear matters, agrees and expands the point: "Nuclear weapons do act critically to deter wars between the major powers, and not nuclear wars alone but any wars. That is really a very great gain."[12] Not all analysts, of course, are quite so expansive. Catudal, for instance, acknowledges some restraint upon nuclear matters but not much else. "Apparently," he argues, "the possession of nuclear weapons by the superpowers has made the leaders of these states more cautious over the years. But otherwise, the existence of these weapons of mass destruction does not appear to have radically changed the behavior of the United States and the Soviet Union."[13]

There is also expert support for the notion that this condition of stability and nuclear war avoidance can continue into the future. Tucker writes:

> There is reason to believe that prudent behavior can be maintained by both sides. For both sides have already behaved quite prudently for nearly three decades. This is no guarantee of the future. . . . But it is at least a substantial reason for believing that deterrence may be a manageable arrangement for an indefinite period ahead.[14]

Regarding the central dynamic of the balance, Senator Nancy Kasselbaum of Kansas further argues that the continuing existence of that vulnerability be acknowledged and accepted, despite the potentially gruesome consequences of deterrence failing. As she puts it, "Although this is an unfortunate state of affairs, it is important at this point that we acknowledge this reality and handle it responsibly. By calling our current policy 'immoral,' we are only sowing the seeds of disillusionment with what will probably be our longstanding deterrence strategy."[15]

The winds of change, as represented by proposals reviewed in the three previous chapters, are blowing with increasing vigor, and one needs to ask whether adaptation is possible within a framework of mutual vulnerability. In support of his preferred strategy of "live-and-let-live," Dyson believes that a fairly fundamental movement away from holding Soviet society at risk would actually strengthen deterrence by reducing Soviet anxieties: "The confidence of the Russian people in their ability to survive the worst that we can do to them is a stabilizing influence which it is to our advantage to preserve. The demand for survival is the main driving force on the Soviet side of the arms race."[16]

Any major change—or even many lesser changes—in the current regime require or are certainly facilitated by an orderly, vital arms control process. One of the burdens of the analysis in the three previous chapters, however, has been that the prospects for future arms control agreements—and especially sweeping agreements—are made less optimistic by both the complexity of the issues and basic disagreements on key matters such as boost-phase intercept missile defense. If this is indeed a reasonable analysis, does the absence of negotiated arms control agreements mean the system will thereby be compromised unacceptably? The failure to reach major agreements since 1979 has not seemed to upset the system in any noticeable manner. The late Brodie, in one of his last articles published in 1976, effectively predicted this outcome. Regarding the notion that arms control results would not save much money, he stated, "This conclusion must include among other things, either a high confidence that the probability of war between the superpowers will continue to be extremely low, or the conviction that we cannot do much about the problem through arms control. . . . I subscribe to both propositions."[17]

The Conditions for Change

As long as nuclear arsenals menace human society, the desire to remove them or vastly reduce their influence in world affairs will be present. No matter how unlikely the failure of deterrence is and how skillfully the balance is managed, the heart of the security dilemma remains. Deterrence can, in fact, fail, and the consequence could be that those weapons we have kept to protect us would ultimately destroy us. The only way nuclear devastation is impossible is if there no longer are nuclear weapons.

The problem of doing away with nuclear weapons, however, requires considerably more than bumper stickers saying, "no more nukes" or city councils proclaiming their jurisdictions nuclear-free zones. If one is to alter the basic relationship in a manner that demonstrably improves the current security dilemma, one needs to start with a clear understanding of what caused the problem in the first place and continues to provide the basic dynamic of nuclear and nonnuclear armament.

The root of the problem, of course, lies in the political relationship between the two superpowers. Political distrust caused the United States and the Soviet Union to arm against one another, not the other way around. Thus, overcoming distrust must precede fundamental change. As MccGwire states the proposition, "the danger of war stems from the adversarial nature of the Soviet–American relationship, not from their nuclear arsenals. . . . The problem is primarily political—and so must be our solutions."[18] Such a change is necessary in both the long and short terms: "If there is to be a real step away from nuclear danger in the next four years, it will have to begin at the level of high politics, with a kind of communication between Moscow and Washington that we have not seen for more than a decade."[19]

Movement away from a world based on mutual vulnerability to one that is simultaneously less deadly *and* less dangerous—or at least no more dangerous—is the goal. To arrive at that goal, however, "requires the establishment of a structure of political understanding and formalized restraint"[20] quite unlike that which exists currently. When such a structure is mentioned, arms control processes are invariably identified as the mechanism for change. Whether arms control processes are robust enough or even relevant to such change, however, requires understanding the preconditions for successful arms control and what such negotiations realistically can and cannot be expected to accomplish.

In the early 1970s, when arms control was extolled as the harbinger of happier times to come, excessive expectations emerged. In fact, as we have learned, arms control processes are merely a reflection of political tensions or moderation, not the cause of improved relations. As a result, "an improvement in East–West political relationships is the absolute precondition for breaking the logjam (in arms control)."[21] This revelation is hardly revolutionary, since it reflects that the conditions for the success of arms control processes are the same conditions as those necessary to achieve the ends for which those means might be used. William Lewis is one of a relative few to identify this connection: "The accumulation of nuclear arms is not a cause of international tensions but is one of its direct consequences. It follows, therefore, that disarmament negotiations, if they are to be successful, must be preceded or accompanied by progress in the resolution of global and superpower issues."[22] Burt (the State Department official most closely responsible for strategic nuclear matters when he wrote this passage) concurs, if in a somewhat more guarded manner: "U.S.–Soviet tensions are responsible, in part, for the controversy that surrounds arms control."[23]

What one can and cannot expect from arms control is thus a direct product of the state of superpower relations rather than a force that affects those relations or a force that operates *deus ex machina* apart from the political context. As Gray states it simply, "Progress in arms control reflects the quality of political relationships."[24] If those political relationships are not so cordial as to create an atmosphere wherein broad accord could sweep away decades of animosity, then one should neither expect great change orchestrated by arms control nor be surprised when progress does not occur. Rather, "arms control is unlikely to produce either miracles or calamities. Kept in that perspective, formal arms control has a modest but useful role to play in an overall strategy of avoiding nuclear war."[25]

It should be evident that change in the circumstances marking superpower relations is the key both to changing the rules—including thermonuclear rules—governing those relationships and to activate mechanisms to make those changes. Unfortunately, a part of the debate, especially that surrounding the SDI, proceeds as if the relationship between politics and weaponry does not exist.

Two examples from opposite sides of the political debate illustrate this point. At one point in a generally excellent report, the Office of Technology Assessment warns that "an extremely unstable situation would arise if each side's space-based BMD system were vulnerable to attack, but only from the other's BMD system."[26] Doubtless such an arrangement would be undesirable in a crisis management situation, since it contains the ability to reap gain by starting hostilities. The OTA suggests an arms control solution, but the point is not the weaponry or its mechanical effect on the balance. Rather, the real issue is why, politically, one or both sides would elect to expend scarce resources to build such a capability. If the perceived political need is there, the solution is to alter that perception—clearly a political task.

In a recent article, Payne makes an even more astounding assertion—essentially arguing that progress toward an SDI arms control agreement does not require political cooperation at all. "The key to removing Soviet opposition to a defense-reliant arms control regime," he argues, "is to convince the Soviet leadership that the United States is prepared to pursue the SDI with or without Soviet arms control cooperation."[27] Political cooperation can, in other words, be replaced by coercion, bullying, and fear as the basis for negotiating arms control regimes. Even if this is true—a proposition that requires more than simple assertion before it is accepted—the result would surely be to make political relationships worse rather than better. Thus, Payne's suggestion not only would solve the wrong problem—negating nuclear arsenals through SDI rather than attacking the underlying political animosities that gave rise to the armaments—it would also make the real problem worse by inflaming existing Soviet animosity.

Certainly, this analysis applies to both Reagan and Gorbachev proposals detailed in chapters 3 and 4. A movement toward the kinds of defenses that would make nuclear weapons "impotent and obsolete"—a perfect defense— has three related requirements, if it is possible at all. The first of these is boost-phase interception of rising Soviet rockets by space-based systems deployed in some proximity to the Soviet Union. The unclassified literature is mute on exactly how critical boost-phase interception is, but this author has been unable to find any technical expert who believes a perfect defense is attainable without the early attrition boost-phase interception would impose.

The second requirement is a constrained offensive threat. Without such constraint, the problem of perfect defense may simply be too difficult; if the Soviets proliferate offensive forces in the face of U.S. defense—something they have threatened to do—the defense cannot succeed unless the doubtful New Strategic Concept criterion of cost-effectiveness at the margins can be met. The third requirement (a related one) is a successful arms control regime both to constrain offenses and to monitor erection of defenses. Ultimately, of course, these negotiations must produce an agreement whereby each side deploys offensive forces designed and configured so they can be destroyed by the other's offensive forces. This is obviously an utterly fantastic idea in the absence of quite substantial political accord between the superpowers, possibly to a level of unity wherein the proposed defenses would be quite unnecessary.

These requirements are both sequential and inconsistent. Clearly, an arms control regime is necessary to produce constrained offensive forces, orderly deployments of defenses, and assurances that offensive and defensive agreements are being complied with. At the same time, if those defenses require boost-phase interception, a snag appears. This aspect of the defense is exactly what the Soviets mean when they express their strong opposition to space-strike weapons; they have said consistently that if these weapons are not abandoned, there can be neither arms control nor constrained offensive forces. Given the necessity of all three criteria to the Reagan vision, some more serious consideration of the Soviet position than has been publicly forthcoming would seem necessary.

Some of the same objections can be raised about the Gorbachev proposal for nuclear disarmament by the year 2000. If Soviet–U.S. political relations do not improve markedly prior to or simultaneously with implementing such a plan, there is the risk of solving the symptom while leaving its cause unattended. Thus, the political antagonisms that produced the nuclear arms competition could be transferred to scarcely less deadly areas such as the so-called "conventional" balance in Europe. Solution of political differences is, thus, the *sine qua non* for the Gorbachev plan to make much sense, just as it is with the Reagan vision.

But is political agreement and goodwill between the United States and the Soviet Union about to break out? Hardly. As has been argued here, competition is unlikely to disappear, but it is remarkably stable competition because of fear-induced realistic self-deterrence (RSD). Until it becomes possible to resolve deep-seated political differences, a regime based on mutual vulnerability and fear is probably the best that can be done; certainly the burden of proof regarding improvement lies with those who would propose change in the absence of political accord. In that circumstance, reiterating how an RSD world appears to work, how it can be made to work better, and how its criteria can be applied is a worthwhile exercise.

Operating an RSD World

There is an initial tendency—similar to that experienced when first confronting the ideas composing assured destruction as a doctrine—to recoil from embracing a politico-military situation premised on mutual vulnerability, fear, and insecurity. In response to this discomfort, two rejoinders must be put forward. The first is that the situation exists and will continue for the foreseeable future quite apart from whether one likes it or not. This fact has been most eloquently and elaborately stated by Robert Jervis[28] and is stated well by Neville Brown: "There is one strict respect in which the situation has, in the judgment of not a few of us, evolved from dynamic instability to profoundly stable equilibrium. That is that each superpower now possesses . . . the capacity to inflict utterly unendurable damage on its chief rival under any conceivable circumstances."[29]

The reference to "stable equilibrium" suggests the second rejoinder: A world based in RSD has worked and increasingly does work to restrain behavior toward one another and progressively to render unacceptable any war—especially nuclear war—between them. As Lawrence Freedman puts it, "The nuclear relationship is stable, in that neither side could enter war conscious of anything other than the most horrific consequences."[30] This knowledge of terrible consequences restrains and provides leaders with a clear and vivid picture of future war that past leaders did not have prior to plunging their nations into the wars of the past. As a result, "nuclear weapons . . . have forced national leaders, every day, to confront the reality of what war is really like, indeed to confront the prospect of their own mortality, and that, for those who seek ways to avoid war, is no bad thing."[31]

If the current situation has produced a tolerable violent peace, then the need for radical change is not manifest; its need and effects require justification. On the other hand, the fact that the system works should not breed complacency. Rather, every effort needs to be made to enhance the dynamics that make RSD vital: crisis management, perceptual change about the acceptability of war, and enhanced uncertainty about the ability to calculate gain from nuclear weapons use.

The key to deterrence is to avoid the initiation of nuclear war. In the current situation, fear of the consequences negates initiation of nuclear war by a hard-headed, political decision aimed at attaining some political goal. Rather, the dangers are two: that a nuclear war might begin by inadvertence apart from conscious volition; and that because someone was able to calculate, rightly or wrongly, that circumstances had changed enough so profit from nuclear war might be possible. The major problem of war by inadvertence is that a crisis begun by one of the superpowers or a third party might get out of hand, and the solution is enhanced crisis management techniques. The second problem could occur if the nuclear balance became quantitatively or qualitatively imbalanced; its solution is to avoid perception of advantageous imbalance, including the enhancement of uncertainties in the calculation of gain through nuclear employment.

Nuclear crisis management shares some of the empirical fragility of other key concepts such as the nuclear threshold and the escalatory process; having never crossed the firebreak nor observed whether escalation occurs after a nuclear war begins, our observational knowledge is nonexistent. Moreover, since empirical knowledge can only be expanded by deterrence failing, the enterprise is committed to avoiding such an expansion of knowledge.[32]

This same problem exists regarding the dynamics of severe superpower crises and how they might degenerate toward the nuclear threshold. Most agree that either the Cuban missile crisis of 1962 or the alerts during the Yom Kippur War of 1973 were as close to being crises that got out of hand as mankind has experienced, but we do not know how close we came to disaster. Moreover, the only way to be sure is to push a crisis to its outward limits in nuclear terms, wherever those may be.

If precise specification of the dynamics is elusive, the general recognition of the problem is not. As Nitze notes, "The greatest strain on deterrence could arise in a crisis, or a series of crises, stemming from a complex of factors difficult to control."[33] The problem is that in crisis situations, perceptions about acceptable behavior can be distorted in unpredictable ways that should be avoided: "Owls worry about deterrence because of the nonrational factors that degrade rationality as stress mounts and time is compressed during a crisis. They think the appropriate policy is to avoid crises and increase controls."[34]

The last part of this quotation from Graham Allison, Albert Carnesale, and Joseph Nye suggests the dual goals of crisis management: crisis avoidance and crisis termination at the lowest level of hostility. A potential crisis situation that is avoided lacks escalatory potential, and earlier discussions suggested that both sides have endeavored to engage in crisis avoidance systematically since the early 1970s. At the same time, crises can occur, creating the need to "structure greater crisis stability with the goal of preventing war in tense crisis situations."[35] This need is great, because such mechanisms do not exist and likely could not be fashioned once a crisis were upon us. "We urgently need to develop East–West structures for the management of major international crises. Today they do not exist. . . . Once a crisis is upon us, it is usually too late to set up the mechanisms for crisis management."[36]

This problem has not gone unnoticed in official circles. In a recent *Foreign Affairs* article, for instance, Defense Secretary Weinberger listed recent administration accomplishments in areas related to crisis management:

> In June 1985, both countries agreed to clarify their obligations under the 1971 "Accidental Measures" agreement to consult in the event of a nuclear accident involving terrorists. In October 1985, technical testing of the upgraded Moscow–Washington hotline was successfully conducted, and operational testing of the new capability to send facsimiles began in January 1986. In November in Geneva, President Reagan and Secretary Gorbachev agreed that both governments will examine the possibility of creating risk-reduction centers.[37]

The risk-reduction center idea refers to a Congressional proposal championed by, among others, Senator Sam Nunn of Georgia to create centers in Moscow and Washington jointly manned by Soviets and Americans with the express purposes of developing crisis management techniques and of defusing crisis situations.

The problem of perceptual change avoidance is to maintain the unambiguous belief that any conceivable use of nuclear weapons is unacceptable; the reinforcement of mutual vulnerability is thus desirable and necessary until there is a change in political relationships that can allow movement of the deadly balance in some other direction.

There are several ways to do this. One is to assure, through deployment programs, arms control, or some combination, that the quantitative or qualitative balance of capabilities does not become so skewed that one side or another can calculate succeeding at nuclear aggression. A second is for both sides to refrain from fielding weapons systems that directly menace one another's retaliatory forces and that could be crisis-destabilizing. The reason for this is explained by Robert McNamara regarding potential U.S. deployments: "Our problem is not to persuade the Soviets not to initiate war today.

It is to cause them to reach the same decision at some future time when, for whatever reason . . . they may be tempted to gamble and try to end what they see as a great threat to their security."[38]

A third way to avoid perceptual change is to reinforce the integrity of the deterrent and, hence, to reinforce the unacceptability of nuclear war through actions such as point defenses, because these produce what Nacht calls "threat control": "Any unilateral step taken to reduce the vulnerability of a retaliatory system that simultaneously reduces the fear of preemption by the potential adversary is an act of threat control."[39] Yet another method is to enhance the uncertainty that political goals could be achieved through nuclear weapons usage. The result of enhancing uncertainty is, according to Art, ironic: "Nuclear weapons have narrowed the range of matters about which statesmen can be certain because they have widened the range of over which uncertainty reigns. *Ironically, miscalculation has decreased because uncertainty has increased*" (emphasis in original).[40]

Clearly, these are examples of ways to enhance RSD rather than definitive statements. They are all measures intended to reinforce the common goal: "We must pay more attention to convincing the Soviets that, even in an extreme crisis, war is not inevitable."[41] That goal is paramount, and the criteria of RSD can be useful for attaining those goals. The utility of the RSD approach can be shown by applying its criteria to other parts of strategy (such as the forward maritime strategy) and phenomena such as nuclear winter.

1. The Maritime Strategy Case

In 1985 and 1986, the U.S. Navy began to publicize the manner in which it plans to contribute to the prosecution of a war involving NATO and the Warsaw Pact. Labeled the maritime component of national military strategy or, more simply, the maritime strategy or forward maritime strategy, it gives a general orientation and blueprint for how the naval aspects can be prosecuted successfully and a rationalization of why this will make a meaningful difference in the overall outcome of hostilities.

Nuclear weapons inventories, of course, reduce the likelihood that the maritime strategy will ever be invoked. Despite the apparent belief on the Soviets' part that the West is plotting aggression and that "the only reason the 'imperialists' have not attempted a surprise attack on them is fear of failure,"[42] the European balance has been and continues to be the strongest testimony to the superpowers' recognition of the unacceptability of war between them. Indeed, "Nuclear weapons have made a general war, either conventional or nuclear, between the superpowers and their clients less likely."[43] The fact of European stability arising from nuclear balance has confounded some early predictions about the future of European peace,[44] but there is a recognition that it is indeed the deadly balance that reduces the danger of European war. As Nitze puts it: "The deterrent effect of nuclear weapons has helped to prevent conventional as well as nuclear conflict. Were we to move to a situation in which nuclear weapons were eliminated, the need for a stable conventional balance would become even more important than today."[45]

Given that the level of interests involved in a NATO–Warsaw Pact conflict would likely cause escalation to some indeterminate level of nuclear exchange (a likelihood the maritime strategy denies), the primary criterion for assessing the maritime strategy is its contribution to deterrence. Hence, the standards for RSD are reasonable criteria for measuring whether the maritime strategy makes a positive contribution to achieving national purposes.

The maritime strategy is an aggressive offensive plan to neutralize and destroy the Soviet Navy before it can enter the world's oceans. As described by Secretary of the Navy John Lehman in Congressional testimony, the strategy consists of three phases: the transition to war, seizure of the initiative, and carrying the fight to the enemy.[46] Each phase is critical to the strategy, and each is controversial.

The first phase occurs during the mounting crisis that leads to war. During this phase, U.S naval vessels, especially nuclear attack submarines (SSNs), will move north of the Greenland-Iceland-United Kingdom (GIUK) gap to bottle up the Soviet North Atlantic fleet, particularly its SSNs and missile-carrying submarines (SSBNs), thus "forcing them north into the Barents Sea and into positions protecting their nuclear missile submarines and their Kola and Murmansk coasts."[47] The purpose of this early action is twofold. By seizing the early initiative, according to Robert Wood and John Hanley, "our taking the high ground early enough increases the Soviets' calculation of the costs of achieving their objectives by force and of the risks of not succeeding at all." In addition,

A revision in maritime strategy to fight at least as far forward as northern Norway was seen as necessary to prevent an increase in Soviet influence in Scandinavia by virtue of their military might, to deter Soviet aggression in the north, and to prevail in war. . . . Control of Norway is essential for Soviet naval operations in the North Atlantic.[48]

Although this thrust forward might make military sense should deterrence fail, one must ask if the action taken in the first phase is not so aggressive and provocative as to worsen the crisis and make the failure of deterrence more likely. Supporters of the strategy, such as Admiral H.C. Mustin, brush such criticism aside: "NATO is a defensive alliance *politically,* but there is no logical, historical, or legal reason to insist on a *military* strategy that is purely defense" (emphasis in original).[49] If the national objective is deterrence, and if crisis termination at the lowest levels of intensity is one of the strategies for achieving that objective, it is difficult to reconcile the *military* actions envisaged in phase one with the *political* purposes of the nation. Lehman has as much as admitted this contradiction himself: "All of our war games, all of our exercises . . . indicate that, in fact we will not make the political decision to move forces early. . . . A matter of a few days may make the difference of the loss of Norway to the Soviet Union."[50] The absence of provocative military activity during those same few days might also make the difference between averting and precipitating the third world war.

Once hostilities begin, the second phase begins. As its name implies, the purpose in this phase is to seize the initiative and to carry out basic objectives. According to Lehman, "The broad war-fighting objectives resulting from this national strategy are, first, to secure the critical sea lanes of communications (SLOCs); next, is to defeat the threat to interdict them, to neutralize the Soviet ability to interdict our SLOCs."[51]

Operationally, this means attacking and sinking the Soviet fleet as quickly and as close to Soviet ports as possible because, as Wood and Hanley explain, "sea control can be established more rapidly by going after the Soviet fleet rather than awaiting their attack."[52] Attacking the Soviet Navy in the Norwegian Sea is advantageous, because if "sea control cannot be established in the Norwegian Sea it follows that sea control will be in dispute in the North Sea."[53]

Once the Soviet fleet—and particularly Soviet SSNs—are dispatched either by sinking them or by driving back to port or under the Arctic ice cap, the second part of phase two begins. Carrier battle groups (CVBGs) can move north of the GIUK gap, where they can be used to provide air cover for landing a marine force in northern Norway, thus denying the Soviets a valuable piece of territory. As Stanley Heginbotham argues, "Few military analysts question that . . . an early Soviet military priority would be the invasion of Norway in order to protect its own facilities on the Kola Peninsula and to establish airbases from which to challenge Atlantic sea lanes of communications."[54]

This aspect of the strategy is also controversial because of its emphasis on antisubmarine warfare (ASW), which "would subject Soviet submarines to attack from the time they leave port."[55] The controversy arises because U.S. SSNs would attack both Soviet SSNs *and missile-carrying submarines (SSBNs).* As Heginbotham explains,

As attention focuses on the antisubmarine aspects of the strategy, European concern is likely to focus on the destabilizing of an American threat to Soviet nuclear missile submarines. . . . As Europeans focus on the possibility that the United States . . . would, in a conventional conflict, threaten significant numbers of Soviet nuclear missile submarines, they are likely to argue vigorously that the Forward Maritime Strategy is highly destabilizing in crises.[56]

The sinking of part of the Soviet strategic arsenal would certainly escalate a heretofore nonnuclear conflict, possibly constituting a breach of the nuclear threshold. If that were the case, the action would violate basic U.S. policy (the avoidance of nuclear war), its own rationale (since "its premise is to plan for a protracted conventional war"), and its warfighting concept ("war termination without the use of nuclear weapons").[57] Admiral Mustin airily dismisses such concerns as essentially effete: "The final issue involves the question of whether our forward strategy . . . would be unduly escalatory. War is not an idle exercise in intellectual polemics. There will always be risks and uncertainties, including the uncertainty of the actions of an adversary."[58]

The third phase, carrying the fight to the enemy, consists of menacing the Soviet homeland by harassing and attacking the Northern Flank, probably by "Kola-bashing" air attacks against Soviet facilities on the Kola Peninsula. Along with sea control, the intents are dual. First, it is hoped that such attacks will force the Soviets to divert valuable resources away from the main land battle in central Europe. Second, sea control means both that resupply of the central front is guaranteed and that, regardless of the continental outcome, victory is denied to the enemy.

All of this is controversial. Direct attacks on Soviet territory could be viewed as escalatory, possibly exceeding the nuclear threshold—if it has not already been crossed. Even if such attacks were to have the desired military effects of relieving pressure on the central front (a controversial proposition in and of itself), actions that could raise the ante by crossing the nuclear threshold and inviting homeland exchange (which direct conventional attacks on Soviet soil would certainly suggest) run at some odds with U.S. political objectives.

What is more controversial is how much difference successful execution of the maritime strategy makes in the overall war. To reiterate, proponents argue three objectives. First, a Soviet Navy on the bottom of the ocean poses little threat to the SLOCs necessary to supply the effort on the central front. While this proposition is self-evident, what is not so obvious is whether the same objective could not be accomplished with a more modest, less potentially escalatory strategy, such as barricading the GIUK gap. The second objective is to relieve pressure on the central front by attacking the flanks and possibly providing carrier-based air support on the central front. The effectiveness of this action is questioned even by supporters of the strategy, who suggest, "To expect that NATO naval forces operating on the flanks can cause Warsaw Pact forces to be drawn from the Central Front may be too optimistic."[59]

The third, and most controversial objective is to prolong the war, insuring that the Soviets cannot achieve unambiguous success and, thus, "increasing uncertainty about the terms of the war."[60] Naval forces, in other words, guarantee that the Soviets face continuing hostile force regardless of the outcome in continental Europe.

This assertion has been greeted with skepticism in some quarters. Robert Komer, a defense official under President Carter, questions the effect that victorious naval forces have:

> This is the basic strategic flaw in the maritime superiority strategy. . . . Sweeping up the Soviet navy, nibbling at the U.S.S.R.'s maritime flanks, even dealing with Soviet surrogates . . . would hardly suffice to prevent a great Eurasian heartland power like the U.S.S.R. from dominating our chief allies, any more than naval superiority was decisive in defeating Germany in two world wars.[61]

John Collins puts the same objection more succinctly: "If we win the naval war and do not have land and air forces strong enough to prevail on the Eurasian land mass, we still lose."[62]

The maritime strategy was only declassified and made available for public debate around the beginning of 1986. Thus, a full and mature interaction between advocates and opponents leading to an improved document has not yet had time to occur. It is in this dialectic spirit that the criteria of RSD as a means of avoiding nuclear war have been applied to it. The major criterion that implementation of the maritime strategy potentially violates is crisis management and termination at the lowest level; indeed, major actions during each of the strategy's three stages (steaming into the Norwegian Sea early in a crisis, sinking SSBNs early during hostilities, and initiating attacks on the Soviet homeland) would appear to be crisis-escalating, and the second and third stages raise the significant prospect of breaching the firebreak. In purely military terms, each action may be justifiable and advisable—although that is not a given. If their execution seriously raises the possibility of exceeding national political objectives, then either the objectives or the military means must be subjected to change.

2. The Nuclear Winter Case

As the result of a number of articles written by prominent scientists beginning in 1982, a potential phenomenon known as the nuclear winter was identified.[63] Briefly put, the nuclear winter hypothesis refers to the collective ecological effects of a nuclear war caused by the injection of various particulants—notably microscopic soot particles from bomb-induced firestorms and dust—into the atmosphere as a consequence of nuclear detonations. With sufficient atmospheric perturbation, the cloud so created could girdle the Northern Hemisphere and possibly part of the Southern Hemisphere as well. The result would be the blockage of the sun's rays and a lowering of surface temperatures to such a degree that plants and animal life would perish and supplies of surface water would freeze. Combined with more familiar ill effects of nuclear war such as residual radiation (fallout), the end effect could be ecological disaster up to and including the extinction of all but the biologically simple organisms.

A major problem with the nuclear winter hypothesis is that it is just that—a hypothesis. The phenomena and dynamics associated with the nuclear winter have never been systematically observed and recorded; when atmospheric testing was going on, nobody thought to look for atmospheric effects. Akin to other key concepts about nuclear weapons, no one wants to gain definitive knowledge on what triggers the winter, since the only reliable way to do so would be to cross the threshold that induces the winter. As a result, "There is little doubt that atmospheric modifications . . . would occur. But their extent and duration—and hence their potential impact on people, food supplies, and other biological systems—are very difficult to determine, and they remain controversial."[64] Although most scientists accept the general nuclear winter scenario—Edward Teller being a notable exception—narrowing disagreement and gaining predictive precision is made more difficult by the absence of reliable observational data. As a very thorough RAND study observes, "While it is important to model this phenomenon, it is naive to expect there will ever be a definitive simulation that settles this controversial issue."[65]

Disagreement on exactly when and how nuclear winter might happen notwithstanding, the agreement that it could happen at some point reinforces the necessity of deterrence and the motivation for self-deterrence because, "The nuclear winter is, as it were, the final impracticality applying to any operational use of nuclear weapons."[66] At the same time that the nuclear winter reinforces an RSD world, however, aspects of it undercut the appeal of deterrence based on assured destruction and limited options.

The effect of nuclear winter on assured destruction is curious. The smoke to induce nuclear winter would be generated most efficiently by attacking cities—thus executing AD's hostages—and seems to fulfill AD's warning: "If the effect does occur, massive attacks on cities would be not only homicidal but also suicidal."[67] That is the danger about which AD proponents have frequently warned. In specifying the disaster, however, the winter leaves the threat hollow and unbelievable. As McFarlane points out: "Those . . . who continue to support the discredited policy of assured destruction must face the following fact: the kind of war that could occur if their policies were adopted is precisely the kind of war most likely to cause nuclear winter."[68]

The fact that nuclear winter makes AD unattractive does not make limited options especially more attractive. By definition, a less than total exchange would be less likely to trigger the winter than a total exchange, but operational uncertainty about exactly when the adverse ecological process would be triggered (presumably, the totally disastrous winter would be preceded by a nasty, but slightly less devastating "nuclear autumn"[69]) makes calibrating limited attacks short of the threshold risky. As Knorr explains:

"Since the level and pattern of immediate and longer-range damage inflicted by nuclear explosions depend on a host of factors and hence remain uncertain before the event, we are unable to bracket with precision the magnitude of limited nuclear exchanges that would preserve a powerful incentive to bring them to a halt."[70] By this same logic, the contemplation of nuclear use by the Soviets should be stunted: "As a result of the possibility that the explosion of large-size warheads would bring the belligerents more rapidly to the edge of the nuclear winter threshold, much of the Soviet nuclear inventory would become less usable and would decline in credibility."[71]

The enormous uncertainties about the ability to limit nuclear war help reinforce self-deterrence and the impulse to avoid nuclear war. As J.J. Gertler argues, "If both the United States and the Soviet Union believe that (a) nuclear winter may occur and (b) it is not survivable, the constraints on both nations' behavior should be similar."[72] Destabilizing phenomena such as "use-them-or-lose-them" first-strike incentives are reduced, because such an attack could be suicidal and, hence, "still more remote than before."[73]

These uncertainties are themselves deterring, despite certain knowledge of winter's potential. "Unlike the classic Doomsday device, nuclear winter is not an inevitable consequence of nuclear war. It is only a possibility, and the triggering mechanism is complex and poorly understood." Moreover, uncertainty will persist, and "some of the key uncertainties will remain unless there is a nuclear war."[74] This uncertainty has the happy effect of making life more difficult for anyone hoping to plan to fight and survive nuclear war—in other words, to change perceptions about the acceptability of nuclear war. "Even after the scientists have done their best to understand the problem, there will continue to be major uncertainties in the global climatic consequences of nuclear war. These uncertainties will make it difficult for strategic planners to take into account the nuclear winter effect."[75] Given the potentially disastrous consequences of finding out how truly mutually vulnerable we all are, erring on the conservative side would appear to make most sense. Nuclear winter thus is just one more very good reason to avoid nuclear war.

Conclusion

The necessary peace has been in place for over a third of a century. Under the reign of nuclear weapons, the major powers have avoided direct confrontation not out of a sense of kindredness or love, but of necessity. The reason is a well-grounded fear of the potential consequences of the failure of deterrence. As John Lewis Gaddis puts it, "the existence of nuclear weapons—and more to the point, the fact that we have direct evidence of what they can do when used against human beings—has given this generation a painfully vivid awareness of war that no previous generation ever had."[76]

The peace of which nuclear weapons are such an integral part has been remarkably durable and stable. As Nacht concludes, "The nuclear stalemate remains in place. It will take a truly revolutionary technogolical innovation or a massive exercise of human stupidity before this stalemate is seriously threatened."[77] Although the peace imposed by nuclear weapons is uncomfortable because of the potential threat it poses, it works. Surely, it can work better. Suggestions about how to make the system more enduring formed a central focus of the preceding pages. At the same time, there is little indication of basic malaise that requires basic alteration. Until there is stronger evidence that the system is failing, it falls upon the reformers to demonstrate that their innovations represent positive change.

Notes

1. Frank Barnaby, "Must the Nuclear Arms Race Lead to War?" in Ron Hazzard and Christopher Meredith (eds.), *World Disarmament: An Idea Whose Time Has Come* (Nottingham, U.K.: Russell Press, 1985), pp. 28–29.

2. Marshall Shulman, "The Future of U.S.–Soviet Relations," *Arms Control Today* 15, no. 9 (November/December 1985), p. 3.

3. Dean Rusk, "The Threat of Nuclear War," *Vital Speeches of the Day* 52, no. 7 (January 15, 1986), p. 203.

4. Christoph Bertram, "Security without Order: Nuclear Deterrence and Crisis Management in the 1980s," in Roman Kolkowicz and Neil Joeck (eds.), *Arms Control and International Security* (Boulder, Colo.: Westview, 1984), p. 4.

5. Robert W. Tucker, "Morality and Deterrence," in Russell Hardin, John J. Mearsheimer, Gerald Dworkin, and Robert E. Goodin (eds.), *Nuclear Deterrence: Ethics and Strategy* (Chicago, Ill.: University of Chicago Press, 1985), p. 69.

6. John M. Collins, "What Have We Got for $1 Trillion?" *Washington Quarterly* 9, no. 2 (Spring 1986), p. 49.

7. Laurence Freedman, "Strategic Arms Control," in Josephine O'Connor Howe (ed.), *Armed Peace: The Search for World Security* (New York: St. Martin's, 1984), p. 38.

8. Harvard Nuclear Study Group (Albert Carnesale, Paul Doty, Stanley Hoffmann, Samuel P. Huntington, Joseph S. Nye, Jr., and Scott D. Sagan), *Living with Nuclear Weapons* (Cambridge, Mass.: Harvard University Press, 1983), pp. 238–39.

9. Robert J. Art, "Between Assured Destruction and Nuclear Victory: The Case for the 'MAD-Plus' Posture," in Hardin et al., *Nuclear Deterrence,* p. 123.

10. Collins, "What Have We Got for $1 Trillion?", p. 50.

11. Art, "Between Assured Destruction and Nuclear Victory," p. 123.

12. Bernard Brodie, *War and Politics* (New York: Macmillan, 1983), p. 430.

13. Honoré M. Catudal, *Nuclear Deterrence: Does It Deter?* (London: Mansell, 1985), pp. 485–86.

14. Tucker, "Morality and Deterrence," -. 59.

15. Nancy Landon Kasselbaum, "Arms Control after the Summit," *Arms Control Today* 15, no. 9 (November/December 1985), p. 8.

16. Freeman J. Dyson, *Weapons and Hope* (New York: Harper & Row, 1984), p. 190.

17. Bernard Brodie, "On the Objectives of Arms Control," *International Security* 1, no. 1 (Summer 1976), p. 19.

18. Michael MccGwire, "Deterrence—The Problem—Not the Solution," *International Affairs* (London) 62, no. 1 (Winter 1985/86), p. 70.

19. McGeorge Bundy, George F. Kennan, Robert S. McNamara, and Gerard Smith, "The President's Choice: Star Wars or Arms Control," *Foreign Affairs* 63, no. 2 (Fall 1984), p. 278.

20. John Steinbruner, "Arms Control: Crisis or Compromise," *Foreign Affaris* 63, no. 5 (Summer 1985), p. 1049.

21. Freedman, "Strategic Arms Control," p. 45.

22. William H. Lewis, *The Prevention of Nuclear War: A United States Approach* (Boston: Oelgeschlager, Gunn & Hain, 1986), pp. 69–70.

23. Richard Burt, "Defense Policy and Arms Control: Defining the Problem," in Richard Burt (ed.), *Arms Control and Defense Postures in the 1980s* (Boulder, Colo.: Westview, 1982), p. 2.

24. Colin D. Gray, "Space Arms Control: A Skeptical View," *Air University Review* 37, no. 1 (November/December 1985), p. 75.

25. Graham T. Allison, Albert Carnesale, and Joseph S. Nye, Jr., "An Agenda for Action," in Graham T. Allison, Albert Carnesale, and Joseph S. Nye, Jr., (eds.), *Hawks, Doves and Owls: An Agenda for Avoiding Nuclear War* (New York: W.W. Norton, 1985), p. 242.

26. Office of Technology Assessment, *Ballistic Missile Defense Technologies: Summary* (Washington, D.C.: Office of Technology Assessment, 1985), p. 31.

27. Keith B. Payne, "The Soviet Union and Strategic Defense: The Failure and Future of Arms Control," *Orbis* 29, no. 4 (Winter 1986), pp. 688–89.

28. Robert Jervis, *The Illogic of American Nuclear Strategy* (Ithaca, N.Y.: Cornell University Press, 1984).

29. Neville Brown, "Limited World War?" *Canberra Papers on Strategy and Defense,* no. 32 (Canberra, Australia: Strategic and Defence Studies Research Centre, Australian National University, 1984), p. 58.

30. Freedman, "Strategic Arms Control," p. 45.

31. John Lewis Gaddis, "The Long Peace: Elements of Stability in the Postwar International System," *International Security* 10, no. 4 (Spring 1986), p. 123.

32. For a more complete discussion, see Donald M. Snow, "Deterrence Theorizing and the Nuclear Debate: The Methodological Dilemma," *International Studies Notes* 6, no. 2 (Summer 1979), pp. 1–5.

33. Paul H. Nitze, "The 1985 Alastair Buchan Memorial Lecture: The Objectives of Arms Control," *Survival* 27, no. 3 (May/June 1985), p. 99.

34. Graham T. Allison, Albert Carnesale, and Joseph S. Nye, Jr., "Analytical Conclusions: Hawks, Doves and Owls," in Allison, Carnesale, and Nye, *Hawks, Doves and Owls,* p. 212.

35. Richard Ned Lebow, "Practical Ways to Avoid Superpower Crises," *Bulletin of the Atomic Scientists* 41, no. 1 (January 1985), p. 22.

36. Bertram, "Security without Order," pp. 12–13.

37. Casper W. Weinberger, "U.S. Defense Strategy," *Foreign Affairs* 64, no. 4 (Spring 1986), p. 694.

38. Robert S. McNamara, "The Military Role of Nuclear Weapons: Perceptions and Misperceptions," *Foreign Affairs* 62, no. 1 (Fall 1983), p. 73.

39. Michael Nacht, *The Age of Vulnerability: Threats to the Nuclear Stalemate* (Washington, D.C.: Brookings Institution, 1985), p. 200.

40. Art, "Between Assured Destruction and Nuclear Victory," p. 125.

41. Jervis, *The Illogic of American Nuclear Strategy,* p. 15.

42. William T. Lee, "Soviet Perceptions of the Threat and Soviet Military Capabilities," in Graham D. Vernon (ed.), *Soviet Perceptions of War and Peace* (Washington, D.C.: National Defense University Press, 1981), p. 70.

43. Art, "Between Assured Destruction and Nuclear Victory," p. 125.

44. Paul Bracken, "Accidental Nuclear War," in Allison, Carnesale, and Nye, *Hawks, Doves and Owls,* p. 28.

45. Nitze, "The 1985 Alastair Buchan Memorial Lecture," p. 106.

46. U.S. Congress, Senate Committee on Armed Services, Subcommittee on Sea Power and Force Projection, *Department of Defense Authorization for Appropriations for Fiscal Year 1985* (Washington, D.C.: U.S. Government Printing Office, March 14, 1984), p. 3864.

47. Stanley J. Heginbotham, "The Forward Maritime Strategy and Nordic Europe," *Naval War College Review* 38, no. 6 (November/December 1985), p. 23.

48. Robert S. Wood and John T. Hanley, Jr., "The Maritime Role in the North Atlantic," *Naval War College Review* 38, no. 6 (November/December 1985), pp. 12, 11.

49. H.C. Mustin, "The Role of the Navy and the Marines in the Norwegian Sea," *Naval War College Review* 39, no. 2 (March/April 1986), p. 2.

50. U.S. Congress, *Department of Defense Authorization,* p. 3860.

51. Ibid., p. 3855.

52. Wood and Hanley, "The Maritime Role in the North Atlantic," p. 18.

53. Hans Garde, "Alliance Navies and the Threat in the Northern Waters," *Atlantic Community Quarterly* 23, no. 1 (Spring 1985), p. 58.

54. Heginbotham, "The Forward Maritime Strategy and Nordic Europe," p. 21.

55. Wood and Hanley, "The Maritime Role in the North Atlantic," p. 14.

56. Heginbotham, "The Forward Martime Strategy and Nordic Europe," pp. 25–26.

57. F.J. West, Jr., "Maritime Strategy and NATO Defense," *Naval War College Review* 38, no. 5 (September/October 1985), pp. 7, 6.

58. Mustin, "The Role of the Navy and the Marines in the Norwegian Sea," p. 5.

59. Wood and Hanley, "The Maritime Role in the North Atlantic," p. 17.

60. West, "Maritime Strategy and Nordic Europe," p. 11.

61. Robert W. Komer, "Maritime Strategy vs. Coalition Defense," *Foreign Affairs* 60, no. 5 (Summer 1982), pp. 1133–34.

62. Collins, "What Have We Got for $1 Trillion?" p. 47.

63. The major works include Paul J. Crutzen and J.W. Birks, "The Atmosphere after a Nuclear War: Twilight at Noon," *Ambio* 11 (1982), pp. 114–25; Paul R. Ehrlich, John Harte, Mark A. Harwell, et al., "Long-Term Biological Consequences of Nuclear War," *Science* 222, no. 4630 (December 23, 1983), pp. 1293–300; James B. Pollack, O.B. Toon, Carl Sagan, et al., "Volcanic Explosions and Climatic Change: A Theoretical Assessment," *Journal of Geophysical Research* 81 (1976), pp. 1071–83;

Carl Sagan, "Nuclear War and Climatic Catastrophe: Some Policy Implications," *Foreign Affairs* 62, no. 2 (Winter 1983/84), pp. 257–92; Richard P. Turco, Owen B. Toon, Thomas P. Ackerman, James F. Pollack, and Carl Sagan, "Nuclear Winter: The Global Consequences of Multiple Nuclear Explosions," *Science* 222, no. 4630 (December 23, 1983), pp. 1283–92; and Richard B. Turco et al., "The Climatic Effects of Nuclear War," *Scientific American* 251, no. 2 (August 1984), pp. 33–34.

64. George F. Carrier, "Nuclear Winter: The State of the Science," *Issues in Science and Technology* 1, no. 2 (Winter 1985), p. 14.

65. Wendell K.H. Hahm, *Nuclear Winter: A Review of the Models,* no. 9-7121-RGI (Santa Monica, Calif.: RAND Graduate Institute, July 1985), p. 6.

66. Stan Windass, "Problems of NATO Defence," in Stan Windass (ed.), *Avoiding Nuclear War: Common Security as a Strategy for the Defence of the West* (London: Brassey's Defence Publishers, 1985), p. 14.

67. Theodore A. Postol, "Strategic Confusions—With or Without Nuclear Winter," *Bulletin of the Atomic Scientists* 41, no. 2 (February 1985), p. 16.

68. Robert C. McFarlane, "Strategic Defense Initiative," *Department of State Bulletin* 85, no. 2099 (June 1985), p. 58.

69. Donald M. Snow, "Strategic Uncertainty and the Nuclear Winter: Implications for Policy," in Paul R. Viotti (ed.), *Conflict and Arms Control: An Uncertain Agenda* (Boulder, Colo.: Westview, 1986), p. 63.

70. Klaus Knorr, "Controlling Nuclear War," *International Security* 9, no. 4 (Spring 1985), p. 86.

71. Dan Horowitz and Robert J. Lieber, "Nuclear Winter and the Future of Deterrence," *Washington Quarterly* 8, no. 3 (Summer 1985), p. 69.

72. J.J. Gertler, *Some Policy Implications of Nuclear Winter,* paper no. P-7045 (Santa Monica, Calif.: RAND Corporation, January 1985), p. 16.

73. Horowitz and Lieber, "Nuclear Winter and the Future of Deterrence," p. 68.

74. Owen Greene, Ian Percival, and Irene Ridge, *Nuclear Winter: The Evidence and the Risks* (Cambridge, U.K.: Polity Press, 1985), pp. 152, 154.

75. Michael M. May, "Nuclear Winter: Strategic Significance," *Issues in Science and Technology* 1, no. 2 (Winter 1985), p. 18.

76. Gaddis, "The Long Peace," p. 122.

77. Nacht, *The Age of Vulnerability,* p. 201.

Bibliography

Books and Articles

Allison, Graham T., Albert Carnesale, and Joseph S. Nye, Jr. (eds.) *Hawks, Doves and Owls: An Agenda for Avoiding Nuclear War*. New York: W.W. Norton, 1985.

Altfield, Michael F. "Uncertainty as a Deterrent Strategy: A Critical Assessment," *Comparative Strategy* 5, no. 1 (1985), pp. 1–26.

Anderson, J. Edward. "First Strike: Myth or Reality." *Bulletin of the Atomic Scientists* 37, no. 9 (November 1981), pp. 6–11.

Arbatov, Georgi. "The Dangers of a New Cold War." *Bulletin of the Atomic Scientists* 33, no. 3 (March 1977), pp. 33–40.

Baillot, Louis. "Not One Step Forward in the Escalation of the Star Wars." *Information Bulletin* (Moscow) 23, no. 20 (1985), pp. 56–62.

Ball, Desmond. "Targeting for Strategic Deterrence." *Adelphi Papers* 185. London: International Institute for Strategic Studies, 1983.

Balzer, Harley D. "Is More Less? Soviet Science in the Gorbachev Era." *Issues in Science and Technology* 1, no. 4 (Summer 1985), pp. 29–46.

Barnaby, Frank. "Must the Nuclear Arms Race Lead to War?" Pp. 17–30 in Ron Hazzard and Christopher Meredith (eds.), *World Disarmament: An Idea Whose Time Has Come*. Nottingham, U.K.: Russell, 1985.

Barrett, Paul. "Star Wars: Revenge of the Nerds." *Washington Monthly* 17, no. 12 (January 1986), pp. 50–52.

Beres, Louis Rene. *Mimicking Sisyphus: America's Countervailing Nuclear Strategy*. Lexington, Mass.: Lexington Books, 1983.

———. *Reason and Realpolitik: U.S. Foreign Policy and World Order*. Lexington, Mass.: Lexington Books, 1984.

Berman, Robert P., and John C. Baker. *Soviet Strategic Forces: Requirements and Responses*. Washington, D.C.: Brookings Institution, 1982.

Bialer, Seweryn, and Joan Afferica. "The Genesis of Gorbachev's World." *Foreign Affairs (America and the World)* 64, no. 3 (1986), pp. 605–44.

Blechman, Barry M., and Stephen S. Kaplan. *Force without War: U.S. Armed Forces as a Political Instrument*. Washington, D.C.: Brookings Institution, 1978.

Borden, William Liscum. *There Will Be No Time: The Revolution in Strategy*. New York: Macmillan, 1946.

Borowski, Harry R. *A Hollow Threat: Strategic Air Power and Containment before Korea.* Westport, Conn.: Greenwood, 1982.

Brodie, Bernard (ed.) *The Absolute Weapon: Atomic Power and World Order.* New York: Harcourt, Brace, 1946.

———. "On the Objectives of Arms Control." *International Security* 1, no. 1 (Summer 1976), pp. 17–36.

Brodie, Bernard (ed.). *War and Politics.* New York: Macmillan, 1973.

———, Michael D. Intriligator, and Roman Kolkowicz (eds.). *National Security and International Stability.* Boston: Oelgeschlager, Gunn & Hain, 1983.

Brown, Harold. "The Strategic Defense Initiative: Defensive Systems and the Strategic Debate." *Survival* 27, no. 2 (March/April 1985), pp. 55–64.

——— and Lynn E. Davis. "Nuclear Arms Control: Where Do We Stand?" *Foreign Affairs* 62, no. 5 (Summer 1984), pp. 1145–60.

Brown, Neville. "Limited Nuclear War?" *Canberra Papers on Strategy and Defence* no. 32. Canberra, Australia: Strategic and Defence Research Centre, Australian National University, 1984.

Brzezinski, Zbigniew. "East–West Relations." *Atlantic Community Quarterly* 22, no. 4 (Winter 1984/85), pp. 295–300.

Bundy, McGeorge, "The Bishops and the Bomb." *New York Review of Books,* June 16, 1983, pp. 3–8.

———, George F. Kennan, Robert S. McNamara, and Gerard Smith. "The President's Choice: Star Wars or Arms Control." *Foreign Affairs* 63, no. 2 (Fall 1984), pp. 264–78.

Burt, Richard. "Defense Policy and Arms Control: Defining the Problem." Pp. 1–20 in Richard Burt (ed.), *Arms Control and Defense Postures in the 1980s.* Boulder, Colo.: Westview, 1982.

Carrier, George F. "Nuclear Winter: The State of the Science." *Issues in Science and Technology* 1, no. 2 (Winter 1985), pp. 14–17.

Carter, Ashton G., and David N. Schwartz (eds.). *Ballistic Missile Defense.* Washington, D.C.: Brookings Institution, 1984.

Catudal, Honoré M. *Nuclear Deterrence: Does It Deter?* London: Mansell, 1985.

"The Central Direction of Soviet Foreign Policy: From the Resolution of the 27th Congress of the Communist Party of the Soviet Union." Advertisement printed in *New York Times,* March 21, 1986, p. A19.

Chapline, George F. "In Defense of SDI." *Defense Science 2003 + 4,* no. 4 (August/ September 1985), pp. 12–23.

Chernenko, Konstantin. "Reply to an Appeal from the Fourth World Congress of 'International Physicians for the Prevention of a Nuclear War'." *Information Bulletin* (Moscow) 23, no. 3 (1985), pp. 3–4.

Cimbala, Stephen J. "The Strategic Defense Initiative: Political Risks." *Air University Review* 37, no. 1 (November/December 1985), pp. 24–37.

Cochran, Thomas B., William M. Arkin, and Milton Hoenig. *Nuclear Weapons Data Book: Volume I, U.S. Nuclear Forces and Capabilities.* Cambridge, Mass.: Ballinger, 1984.

Collins, John M. "What Have We Got for $1 Trillion?" *Washington Quarterly* 9, no. 2 (Spring 1986), pp. 47–54.

Crutzen, Paul J., and J.W. Birks. "The Atmosphere after a Nuclear War: Twilight at Noon." *Ambio* 11 (1982), pp. 114–25.

Douglass, Joseph D., Jr., and Samuel T. Cohen. "SDI: The Hidden Opportunity." *Defense Science 2003* + 4, no. 4 (August/September 1985), pp. 5–11.

Drell, Sidney D., Philip J. Farley, and David Holloway. *The Reagan Strategic Defense Initiative: A Technical, Political, and Arms Control Assessment.* Cambridge, Mass.: Ballinger, 1985.

Dyson, Freeman J. *Weapons and Hope.* New York: Harper & Row, 1984.

Economist editorial. "The Long Nuclear Peace." *Economist* 298, no. 7434 (February 28, 1986), pp. 15–16.

Ehrlich, Paul R., John Harte, Mark A. Harwell, et al. "Long-Term Biological Consequences of Nuclear War." *Science* 222, no. 4630 (December 23, 1983), pp. 1293–1300.

Ermath, Fritz W. "Contrasts in American and Soviet Strategic Thought." *International Security* 3, no. 2 (Fall 1978), pp. 138–55. Reprinted in John F. Reichart and Steven L. Sturm, *American Defense Policy,* fifth edition (Baltimore, Md.: Johns Hopkins University Press, 1982).

Falk, Richard. *The End of World Order: Essays on Normative International Relations.* New York: Holmes and Meier, 1983.

Felden, M. "Recent Advances in the Use of Space for Military Purposes and on Second Generation Nuclear Weapons." Pp. 257–64 in Bhupendra Jasani (ed.), *Outer Space: A New Dimension for the Arms Race.* London: Taylor and Francis, 1982.

Freedman, Laurence. "A New Strategic Revolution?" *Space Policy* 1, no. 2 (May 1985), pp. 131–34.

———. "Strategic Arms Control." Pp. 31–47 in Josephine O'Connor Howe (ed.), *Armed Peace: The Search for World Security.* New York: St. Martin's, 1984.

Frye, Alton. "Strategic Build-Down: A Context for Restraint." *Foreign Affairs* 62, no. 2 (Winter 1983/84), pp. 293–317.

———. "Strategic Synthesis." *Foreign Policy,* no. 58 (Spring 1985), pp. 3–27.

Gaddis, John Lewis. "The Long Peace: Elements of Stability in the Postwar International System." *International Security* 10, no. 4 (Spring 1986), pp. 100–42.

Ganev, Gancho, Yevgeny Kazar, and Sarada Mitra. "The Nuclear Threat and Politics." *World Marxist Review* 27, no. 4 (April 1984), pp. 41–47.

Garde, Hans. "Alliance Navies and the Threat in the Northern Waters." *Atlantic Community Quarterly* 23, no. 1 (Spring 1985), pp. 57–64.

Garthoff, Raymond L. "American–Soviet Relations in Perspective." *Political Science Quarterly* 100, no. 4 (Winter 1985/86), pp. 541–59.

Gelb, Leslie, "Star Wars Advances: The Plan vs. the Reality." *New York Times,* December 15, 1985, pp. 1, 34.

———. "Weighing the Soviet Plan." *New York Times,* January 17, 1986, p. A1, A8.

Gertler, J.J. "Some Policy Implications of Nuclear Winter." RAND Corporation Paper no. P-7045. Santa Monica, Calif.: RAND Corporation, January 1985.

Glaser, Charles L. "Do We Want the Missile Defenses We Can Build?" *International Security* 10, no. 1 (Summer 1985), pp. 25–57.

Gorbachev, Mikhail. "Nuclear Disarmament by the Year 2000." Reprinted as an advertisement in *New York Times,* February 5, 1986, p. A13.

———. "Our Policy Is Clear: It Is a Policy of Peace and Cooperation." *Information Bulletin* (Moscow) 24, no. 2 (1986), pp. 6–28.

———. "Outer Space Should Serve Peace." *Information Bulletin* (Moscow) 23, no. 18 (1985), pp. 3–5.

———. "The Soviet Communist Party Congress on the International Situation and Soviet Foreign Policy." Advertisement printed in *New York Times,* March 21, 1986, p. A18.

———. "Soviet Program for Total Abolition of Nuclear Weapons in the World." Advertisement printed in *New York Times,* March 21, 1986, p. A18.

———. "Speech Welcoming Willy Brandt." *Information Bulletin* (Moscow) 23, no. 15 (1985), pp. 15–18.

Gordon, Michael R. "U.S. Not Sure If Soviet Links Missile Accord to 'Star Wars.'" *New York Times,* February 6, 1986, p. A10.

Graham, Daniel O., and Gregory A. Fossedal. *A Defense That Defends: Blocking Nuclear Attack.* Old Greenwich, Conn.: Devin-Adair, 1983.

Gray, Colin S. *American Military Space Policy: Information Systems, Weapons Systems and Arms Control.* Cambridge, Mass.: Abt Books, 1982.

———. "Denting the Shield, Blunting the Sword." *Defense Science 2003 +* 4, no. 6 (December 1985/January 1986), pp. 11–19.

———. "Space Arms Control: A Skeptical View." *Air University Review* 37, no. 1 (November/December 1985), pp. 73–86.

———. "Strategic Defences: A Case for Strategic Defence." *Survival* 27, no. 2 (March/April 1985), pp. 50–55.

——— and Keith Payne. "Victory Is Possible." *Foreign Policy,* no. 39 (Summer 1980), pp. 14–27.

Green, Philip. *Deadly Logic: The Theory of Nuclear Deterrence.* Columbus, Ohio: Ohio State University Press, 1966.

Greene, Owen, Ian Percival, and Irene Ridge. *Nuclear Winter: The Evidence and the Risks.* Cambridge, U.K.: Polity Press, 1985.

Gromyko, Andrei. "Along a Leninist Course in Foreign Policy." *World Marxist Review* 28, no. 4 (April 1985), pp. 8–18.

Guertner, Gary L., and Donald M. Snow. *The Last Frontier: An Analysis of the Strategic Defense Initiative.* Lexington, Mass.: Lexington Books, 1986.

———. "Offensive Doctrine in a Defense-Dominant World." *Air University Review* 37, no. 1 (November/December 1985), pp. 2–11.

Hahm, Wendell K.H. *Nuclear Winter: A Review of the Models.* No. 9-7121-RGI. Santa Monica, Calif.: RAND Graduate Institute, July 1985.

Hardin, Russell, John J. Mearsheimer, Gerald Dworkin, and Robert E. Goodin (eds.). *Nuclear Deterrence: Ethics and Strategy.* Chicago, Ill.: University of Chicago Press, 1985.

Harvard Nuclear Study Group (Albert Carnesale, Paul Doty, Stanley Hoffmann, Samuel P. Huntington, Joseph S. Nye, Jr., and Scott D. Sagan). *Living with Nuclear Weapons.* Cambridge, Mass.: Harvard University Press, 1983.

Heginbotham, Stanley J. "The Forward Maritime Strategy and Nordic Europe." *Naval War College Review* 38, no. 6 (November/December 1985), pp. 19–27.

Hoffman, Fred S. "The SDI in U.S. Nuclear Strategy." *International Security* 10, no. 1 (Summer 1985), pp. 13–24.

Holloway, David. "The Strategic Defense Initiative and the Soviet Union." *Daedalus* 114, no. 3 (Summer 1985), pp. 257–78.

Horowitz, Dan, and Robert J. Lieber. "Nuclear Winter and the Future of Deterrence." *Washington Quarterly* 8, no. 3 (Summer 1985), pp. 59–70.

Hotz, Robert. "Editorial: The Beam Weapons Race." *Aviation Week and Space Technology* 109, no. 14 (October 2, 1978), p. 9.

Hough, Jerry F. "Gorbachev's Strategy." *Foreign Affairs* 64, no. 1 (Fall 1985), pp. 33–55.

———. *The Struggle for the Third World: Soviet Debates and American Options.* Washington, D.C.: Brookings Institution, 1986.

Hunter, Robert E. "SDI: Return to Basics." *Washington Quarterly* 9, no. 1 (Winter 1986), pp. 155–67.

Iklé, Fred Charles. "Nuclear Strategy: Can There Be a Happy Ending?" *Foreign Affairs* 63, no. 4 (Spring 1985), pp. 810–26.

Jervis, Robert. *The Illogic of American Nuclear Strategy.* Ithaca, N.Y.: Cornell University Press, 1984.

———. "MAD is the Best Possible Deterrence." *Bulletin of the Atomic Scientists* 41, no. 3 (March 1985), pp. 43–45.

Kahn, Herman. *Thinking about the Unthinkable in the 1980s.* New York: Simon and Schuster, 1984.

Kampelman, Max M. "SDI and the Arms Control Process." *Atlantic Community Quarterly* 23, no. 3 (Fall 1985), pp. 223–28.

Kanter, Arnold. "Thinking about the Strategic Defence Initiative: An Alliance Perspective." *International Affairs* (London) 61, no. 3 (Summer 1985), pp. 449–64.

Kasselbaum, Nancy Landon. "Arms Control after the Summit." *Arms Control Today* 15, no. 9 (November/December 1985), pp. 7–9.

Kegley, Charles W., Jr., and Eugene R. Wittkopf (eds.). *The Nuclear Reader: Strategy, Weapons, War.* New York: St. Martin's, 1985.

Keller, Bill. "No. 1 Weapon in 1987 Budget Is Missile Shield." *New York Times,* February 5, 1986, pp. A1, A22.

Kennedy, Robert, and John M. Weinstein (eds.). *The Defense of the West: Strategic and European Security Issues Reappraised.* Boulder, Colo.: Westview, 1984.

Kincade, William H. "Arms Control or Arms Coercion." *Foreign Policy,* no. 62 (Spring 1986), pp. 24–45.

Kiser, John W. "How the Arms Race Really Helps Moscow." *Foreign Policy,* no. 60 (Fall 1985), pp. 40–51.

Kissinger, Henry. "A New Approach to Arms Control." *Time,* March 23, 1983, pp. 24–26.

Knorr, Klaus. "Controlling Nuclear War." *International Security* 9, no. 4 (Spring 1985), pp. 79–98.

Kolkowicz, Roman, and Neil Joeck (eds.). *Arms Control and International Security.* Boulder, Colo.: Westview, 1984.

Komer, Robert W. "Maritime Strategy vs. Coalition Defense." *Foreign Affairs* 60, no. 5 (Summer 1982), pp. 1124–44.

Krass, A. "The Death of Deterrence." Pp. 107–28 in Stockholm International Peace Research Institute (SIPRI), *Policies for Common Security.* London: Taylor and Francis, 1985.

Krepon, Michael. "Dormant Threat to the ABM Treaty." *Bulletin of the Atomic Scientists* 42, no. 1 (January 1986), pp. 31–34.

Krivitsky, Alexander. "Behind a Mask of Decency: An Expose." *World Marxist Review* 28, no. 6 (June 1985), pp. 36–40.

Kruzel, Joseph. "What's Wrong with the Traditional Approach?" *Washington Quarterly* 8, no. 2 (Spring 1985), pp. 121–32.

Kupperman, Robert H. "Using SDI to Reshape Soviet Strategic Behavior." *Washington Quarterly* 8, no. 3 (Summer 1985), pp. 77–83.

Laird, Robbin F., and Dale R. Herspring. *The Soviet Union and Strategic Arms.* Boulder, Colo.: Westview, 1984.

Lavoie, Louis. "The Limits of Soviet Technology." *Technology Review* 88, no. 8 (November/December 1985), pp. 68–75.

Lebow, Richard Ned. "Practical Ways to Avoid Superpower Crises." *Bulletin of the Atomic Scientists* 41, no. 1 (January 1985), pp. 22–28.

Lee, William T. "Soviet Perceptions of the Threat and Soviet Military Capabilities." Pp. 67–95 in Graham D. Vernon (ed.), *Soviet Perceptions of War and Peace.* Washington, D.C.: National Defense University Press, 1981.

Lewis, William H. *The Prevention of Nuclear War: A United States Approach.* Boston: Oelgeschlager, Gunn & Hain, 1986.

Lifton, Robert Jay, and Richard Falk. *Indefensible Weapons: The Political and Psychological Case against Nuclearism.* New York: Basic Books, 1982.

Lord, Carnes. "American Strategic Culture." *Comparative Strategy* 5, no. 3 (1984), pp. 269–94.

———. "The U.S.–Soviet Strategic Nuclear Relationship." Pp. 1–9 in W. Bruce Weinrod (ed.), *Confronting Moscow: An Agenda for the Post-Detente Era.* Washington, D.C.: Heritage Foundation, 1985.

Martin, Laurence. "National Security in an Insecure Age." *Atlantic Community Quarterly* 21, no. 1 (Spring 1983), pp. 44–51.

May, Michael M. "Nuclear Winter: Strategic Significance." *Issues in Science and Technology* 1, no. 2 (Winter 1985), pp. 18–20.

———. "The U.S.–Soviet Approach to Nuclear Weapons." *International Security* 9, no. 4 (Spring 1985), pp. 140–53.

MccGwire, Michael. "Deterrence: The Problem—Not the Solution." *International Affairs* (London) 62, no. 1 (Winter 1985/86), pp. 55–70.

McNamara, Robert S. "The Military Role of Nuclear Weapons: Perceptions and Misperceptions." *Foreign Affairs* 62, no. 1 (Fall 1983), pp. 59–80.

Menaul, Stewart. "Military Uses of Space—Ballistic Missile Defence." *Space Policy* 1, no. 2 (May 1985), pp. 122–30.

Meyer, Stephen M. "Soviet Strategic Programmes and the US SDI." *Survival* 27, no. 6 (November/December 1985), pp. 274–92.

Mustin, H.C. "The Role of the Navy and the Marines in the Norwegian Sea." *Naval War College Review* 39, no. 2 (March/April 1986), pp. 2–6.

Myers, Ware. "The Star Wars Software Debate." *Bulletin of the Atomic Scientists* 42, no. 2 (February 1986), pp. 31–36.

Nacht, Michael. *The Age of Vulnerability: Threats to the Nuclear Stalemate.* Washington, D.C.: Brookings Institution, 1985.

Nitze, Paul. H. "SDI: Its Nature and Rationale." *Atlantic Community Quarterly* 23, no. 3 (Fall 1985), pp. 263–68.

———. "Strategy in the Decade of the 1980s," *Foreign Affairs* 59, no. 1 (Fall 1980), pp. 82–101.

———. "The 1985 Alastair Buchan Memorial Lecture: The Objectives of Arms Control." *Survival* 27, no. 3 (May/June 1985), pp. 98–107.

O'Sullivan, Patrick. "The Geopolitics of Deterrence." Pp. 29–41 in David Pepper and Alan Jenkins (eds.), *The Geography of War and Peace*. New York: Basil Blackwell, 1985.

Ovinnikov, R. "'Star Wars' Programme: A New Phase in Washington's Militaristic Policy." *International Affairs* (Moscow), no. 8 (1985), pp. 13–22.

Payne, Keith B. "The Deterrence Requirement for Defense." *Washington Quarterly* 9, no. 1 (Winter 1986), pp. 139–54.

——— and Colin S. Gray. "Nuclear Policy and the Defensive Transition." *Foreign Affairs* 62, no. 4 (Spring 1984), pp. 820–42.

———. "The Soviet Union and Strategic Defense: The Failure and Future of Arms Control." *Orbis* 29, no. 4 (Winter 1986), pp. 673–88.

Perle, Richard. *Criteria for the Evaluation of Arms Control Options*. ASG Monograph no. 3. Waltham, Mass.: Westinghouse Electric Corporation Advanced Study Group, April 1970.

———. "The Strategic Defense Initiative: Addressing Some Misconceptions." *Journal of International Affairs* 39, no. 1 (Summer 1985), pp. 23–29.

Pipes, Richard. "Why the Soviet Union Thinks It Could Fight and Win a Nuclear War." *Commentary* 64, no. 1 (July 1977), pp. 21–34.

Pollack, James B., O.B. Toon, Carl Sagan, et al. "Volcanic Explosions and Climatic Change: A Theoretical Assessment." *Journal of Geophysical Research* 81 (1976), pp. 1071–83.

Postol, Theodore A. "Strategic Confusion—With or Without Nuclear Winter."*Bulletin of the Atomic Scientists* 41, no. 2 (Feburary 1985), pp. 14–17.

Pranger, Robert J., and Roger P. Labrie. *Nuclear Strategy and National Security: Points of View*. Washington, D.C.: American Enterprise Institute for Public Policy Research, 1977.

Pravda editorial. "Geneva: What Has the First Round of Talks Shown?" *Information Bulletin* (Moscow) 23, no. 14 (1985), pp. 43–50.

Reagan, Ronald W. "President's News Conference on Foreign and Domestic Issues." *New York Times,* April 10, 1986, p. A22.

———. "The U.S.–Soviet Relationship." *Atlantic Community Quarterly* 22, no. 1 (Spring 1984), pp. 4–9.

Rearden, Steven L. *The Evolution of American Strategic Doctrine: Paul H. Nitze and the Soviet Challenge*. Boulder, Colo.: Westview, 1984.

Rivkin, David B. "What Does Moscow Think?" *Foreign Policy,* no. 59 (Summer 1985), pp. 85–105.

Rosenberg, David Alan. "The Origins of Overkill: Nuclear Weapons and American Strategy, 1945–1960." *International Security* 7, no. 4 (Spring 1983), pp. 4–71.

———. "'A Smoking Radiation Ruin at the End of Two Hours': Documents on American Plans for Nuclear War with the Soviet Union." *International Security* 6, no. 3 (Winter 1981/82), pp. 3–38.

Rowny, Edward. "Enough Diplomacy in Public; Now, Quiet Talks at Geneva." *New York Times,* April 16, 1986, p. A27.

Ruhle, Hans. "Gorbachev's Star Wars." *Atlantic Community Quarterly* 23, no. 4 (Winter 1985/86), pp. 5–13.

Rusk, Dean. "The Threat of Nuclear War." *Vital Speeches of the Day* 52, no. 7 (January 15, 1986), pp. 203–4.

Sagan, Carl. "Nuclear War and Climatic Catastrophe: Some Policy Implications." *Foreign Affairs* 62, no. 2 (Winter 1983/84), pp. 257–92.

Schell, Jonathan. *The Fate of the Earth.* New York: Alfred A. Knopf, 1982.

Schelling, Thomas C. "What Went Wrong with Arms Control." *Foreign Affairs* 64, no. 2 (Winter 1985/86), pp. 219–33.

Schlesinger, James. "The Eagle and the Bear: Between an Unfree World and None," *Foreign Affairs* 63, no. 5 (Summer 1985), pp. 937–61.

———. "The International Implications of Third-World Conflict: An American Perspective." *Adelphi Papers* no. 166, London: International Institute for Strategic Studies, Summer 1981.

———. "Rhetoric and Realities in the Star Wars Debate." *International Security* 10, no. 1 (Summer 1985), pp. 3–12.

Schneider, Barry R., Colin S. Gray, and Keith B. Payne (eds.). *Missiles for the Nineties: ICBMs and Strategic Policy.* Boulder, Colo.: Westview, 1984.

———. "US Military Space Policy in 2110." *Defense Science 2003 + 4,* no. 4 (August/September 1985), pp. 24–31.

Scott, Harriet Fast, and William F. Scott (eds.). *The Soviet Art of War: Doctrine, Strategy, and Tactics.* Boulder, Colo.: Westview, 1982.

Setton, Michael. "The Pentagon: Pushing Its Way into Space." *World Marxist Review* 28, no. 9 (September 1985), pp. 124–28.

Shevardnadze, Eduard. "A Nuclear-Free World: Excerpts from a Speech at the 27th CPSU Congress." Advertisement in *New York Times,* March 21, 1986, p. A19.

Shulman, Marshall D. "The Future of U.S.–Soviet Relations." *Arms Control Today* 15, no. 9 (November/December 1985), pp. 3–7.

Shultz, George. "U.S.–Soviet Relations in the Context of U.S. Foreign Policy." *Atlantic Community Quarterly* 21, no. 3 (Fall 1983), pp. 202–15.

Sienkiewicz, Stanley. "Observations on the Impact of Uncertainty in Strategic Analysis." *World Politics* 32, no. 1 (October 1979), pp. 90–110.

Simes, Dmitri. "Are the Soviets Interested in Arms Control?" *Washington Quarterly* 8, no. 2 (Spring 1985), pp. 147–58.

Slocombe, Walter. "An Immediate Agenda for Arms Control." *Survival* 27, no. 5 (September/October 1985), pp. 204–12.

Smith, R. Jeffrey. "U.S. Tops Soviets in Key Weapons Technology." *Science* 231, no. 4742 (March 7, 1986), pp. 1063–64.

Snow, Donald M. "BMD, SDI and Future Policy: Issues and Prospects." *Air University Review* 37, no. 5 (July/August 1985), pp. 4–13.

———. "Deterrence Theorizing and the Nuclear Debate: The Methodological Dilemma." *International Studies Notes* 6, no. 2 (Summer 1979), pp. 1–5.

———. "The MX-Basing Mode Muddle: Issues and Alternatives." *Air University Review* 31, no. 5 (July/August 1980), pp. 11–25.

———. *The Nuclear Future: Toward a Strategy of Uncertainty.* Tuscaloosa, Ala.: University of Alabama Press, 1983.

———. *Nuclear Strategy in a Dynamic World: American Policy in the 1980s.* Tuscaloosa, Ala.: University of Alabama Press, 1981.

———. "Realistic Self-Deterrence: An Alternative View of Nuclear Dynamics," *Naval War College Review* 39, no. 2 (March/April 1986), pp. 63–73.

———. "Strategic Uncertainty and the Nuclear Winter: Implications for Policy."

Pp. 61–75 in Paul R. Viotti (ed.). *Conflict and Arms Control: An Uncertain Agenda.* Boulder, Colo.: Westview, 1986.

Sokolovskii, V.D. *Soviet Military Strategy.* Englewood Cliffs, N.J.: Prentice-Hall, 1963.

Somov, M. "'Star Peace' Not 'Star Wars'." *International Affairs* (Moscow), no. 3 (March 1986), pp. 54–62.

"Soviet Proposal for a Draft Treaty on the Prohibition of the Stationing of Weapons of Any Kind in Outer Space." Pp. 401–3 in Bhupendra Jasani (ed.), *Outer Space—A New Dimension of the Arms Race.* London: Taylor and Francis, 1982.

Staar, Richard F. (ed.). *Arms Control: Myth versus Reality.* Stanford, Calif.: Hoover Institution Press, 1984.

Stakh, G. "Curbing the Arms Race as a Crucial Problem of Today." *International Affairs* (Moscow), no. 2 (1986), pp. 3–11.

Star Wars: Delusions and Dangers. Moscow: Military Publishing House, 1985.

Stein, Jonathan. *From H-Bomb to Star Wars: The Politics of Strategic Decision-Making.* Lexington, Mass.: Lexington Books, 1984.

Steinbruner, John. "Arms Control: Crisis or Compromise." *Foreign Affairs* 63, no. 5 (Summer 1985), pp. 1036–49.

Stockholm International Peace Research Institute (SIPRI). *World Armaments and Disarmaments, SIPRI Yearbook, 1985.* London: Taylor and Francis, 1985.

Stoessinger, John G. *Why Nations Go to War,* fourth edition. New York: St. Martin's, 1985.

Talbott, Strobe. *Deadly Gambits: The Reagan Administration and the Stalemate in Nuclear Arms Control.* New York: Alfred A. Knopf, 1984.

Teller, Edward. "Better a Shield than a Sword." *Defense Science 2003 +* 4, no. 5 (October/November 1985), pp. 12–27.

———. "Science and Technology in SDI." *Defense Science 2003 +* 4, no. 2 (April/May 1985), pp. 16–25.

Tomilin, Yu. "To Stop the Arms Race: Imperative Task of Our Day." *International Affairs* (Moscow), no. 10 (October 1985), pp. 88–97, 117.

Turco, Richard P., et al. "The Climatic Effects of Nuclear War." *Scientific American* 251, no. 2 (August 1984), pp. 33–43.

Turco, Richard P., Owen B. Toon, Thomas P. Ackerman, James B. Pollack, and Carl Sagan. "Nuclear Winter: The Global Consequences of Multiple Nuclear Explosions." *Science* 222, no. 4630 (December 23, 1983), pp. 1283–92.

Turner, John, and Stockholm International Peace Research Institute (SIPRI). *Arms in the 80s: New Developments in the Global Arms Race.* London: Taylor and Francis, 1985.

Warner, Edward L., III. "Defense Policy of the Soviet Union." Pp. 48–59 in John F. Reichart and Steven L. Sturm (eds.), *American Defense Policy,* fifth edition. Baltimore, Md.: Johns Hopkins University Press, 1982.

Watkins, James D. "The Maritime Strategy." *United States Naval Institute Proceedings* 112, no. 1/995 (January 1986), pp. 8–17.

Weeks, Albert. "Soviets May Be Retooling Doctrine." *Defense Science 2003 +* 4, no. 6 (December 1985/January 1986), pp. 41–46.

Weinberg, Alvin M., and Jack N. Barkenbus. "Stabilizing Star Wars." *Foreign Policy,* no. 54 (Spring 1984), pp. 164–70.

Weinberger, Caspar W. "U.S. Defense Strategy." *Foreign Affairs* 64, no. 4 (Spring 1986), pp. 675–97.

West, F.J., Jr. "Maritime Strategy and NATO Defense." *Naval War College Review* 38, no. 5 (September/October 1985), pp. 5–19.

Whence the Threat to Peace, third edition. Moscow: Military Publishing House, 1984.

Weiseltier, Leon. *Nuclear War, Nuclear Peace.* New York: Holt, Reinhart and Winston, 1983.

Windass, Stan (ed.). *Avoiding Nuclear War: Common Security as a Strategy for the Defence of the West.* London: Brassey's Defence Publishers, 1985.

Wood, Robert S., and John T. Hanley, Jr. "The Maritime Role in the North Atlantic." *Naval War College Review* 38, no. 6 (November/December 1985), pp. 5–18.

World Armaments and Disarmament: SIPRI Yearbook 1984. London: Taylor and Francis, 1984.

Zonas, Gerald. "The Strategic Defense Initiative." *Daedalus* 114, no. 2 (Spring 1985), pp. 73–91.

York, Herbert F. "Nuclear Deterrence and the Military Uses of Space." *Daedalus* 114, no. 2 (Spring 1985), pp. 13–32.

Official Government Statements and Publications

Abrahamson, Lt. Gen. James A. "Statement on the Strategic Defense Initiative, Statement to the Committee on Armed Services," United States Senate, 99th Congress, first session, February 21, 1985.

Adelman, Kenneth L. "Making Arms Control Work." *Department of State Bulletin* 86, no. 2106 (January 1986), pp. 39–42.

———. "SDI: Setting the Record Straight." *Department of State Bulletin* 85, no. 2103 (October 1985), pp. 42–46.

Dam, Kenneth W. "Geneva and Beyond: New Arms Control Negotiations." *Current Policy,* no. 647. Washington, D.C.: U.S. Department of State, Bureau of Public Affairs, January 14, 1985.

McFarlane, Robert C. "Strategic Defense Initiative." *Department of State Bulletin* 85, no. 2099 (June 1985), pp. 57–59.

Nitze, Paul H. "The Nuclear and Space Arms Talks: Where We Are after the Summit." *Department of State Bulletin* 86, no. 2107 (February 1986), pp. 58–60.

———. "The Objectives of Arms Control." *Department of State Bulletin* 85, no. 2098 (May 1985), pp. 57–63.

———. "On the Road to a More Stable Peace." *Department of State Bulletin* 85, no. 2097 (April 1985), pp. 27–29.

———. "The Promise of SDI." *Current Policy,* no. 810. Washington, D.C.: U.S. Department of State, Bureau of Public Affairs, April 1986.

———. "Statement before the Foreign Relations Committee," United States Senate, 99th Congress, first session, February 26, 1985.

Office of Technology Assessment. *Ballistic Missile Defense Technologies: Summary.* Washington, D.C.: Office of Technology Assessment, 1985.

Reagan, Ronald W. "Interview with J.N. Parimoo." *Weekly Compilation of Presidential Documents* 21, no. 43 (October 28, 1985), pp. 1281–86.

———. "National Security: Address to the Nation, March 23, 1983." *Weekly Compilation of Presidential Documents* 19, no. 12 (March 28, 1983), pp. 442–48.

———. "The President's News Conference of September 17, 1985." *Weekly Compilation of Presidential Documents* 21, no. 38 (September 23, 1985), pp. 1100–8.

———. "State of the Union Address." *Department of State Bulletin* 85, no. 2097 (April 1985), p. 9.

———. "U.S.–Soviet Relations." *Department of State Bulletin* 86, no. 2107 (February 1986), p. 23.

———. "United States–Soviet Relations." *Weekly Compilation of Presidential Documents* 21, no. 48 (December 2, 1985), pp. 1435–36.

Rowny, Edward L. "Gorbachev's Next 100 Days." *Department of State Bulletin* 85, no. 2103 (October 1985), pp. 17–19.

Shultz, George. "Arms Control: Objectives and Prospects." *Department of State Bulletin* 85, no. 2098 (May 1985), pp. 24–28.

———. "Arms Control, Strategic Stability, and Global Security." *Department of State Bulletin* 85, no. 2105 (December 1985), pp. 20–25.

———. "A Forward Look at Foreign Policy." *Department of State Bulletin* 84, no. 2093 (December 1984), pp. 5–10.

Soviet Military Power, 1985. Washington, D.C.: U.S. Government Printing Office, April 1985.

U.S. Congress, Senate Committee on Armed Services, Subcommittee on Sea Power and Force Projection. *Department of Defense Authorization for Appropriations for Fiscal Year 1985.* Washington, D.C.: U.S. Government Printing Office, March 14, 1984, pp. 3851–900.

Weinberger, Caspar W. *Annual Report to the Congress, Fiscal Year 1983.* Washington, D.C.: U.S. Government Printing Office, 1982.

———. *Annual Report to the Congress, Fiscal Year 1985.* Washington, D.C.: U.S. Government Printing Office, 1984.

———. "Strategic Defense in Perspective." *Defense 86,* January/February 1986, pp. 3–6.

Index

About the Author

Donald M. Snow (B.A., M.A., University of Colorado; Ph.D., Indiana University) is professor of political science and director of international studies at the University of Alabama. During 1985–86, he served as Secretary of the Navy Senior Research Fellow and Professor of Management at the U.S. Naval War College. He has also served as visiting professor of national security affairs at the United States Air Command and Staff College. He has had articles appear in *International Studies Quarterly, Political Science Quarterly, International Studies Notes, Bulletin of the Atomic Scientists, Arms Control Today, U.S. Naval War College Review, Parameters, Air University Review,* and *Christian Science Monitor.* His other books include *Nuclear Strategy in a Dynamic World: American Policy in the 1980s* (Alabama, 1981); *The Nuclear Future: Toward a Strategy of Uncertainty* (Alabama, 1983); with Gary L. Guertner, *The Last Frontier: An Analysis of the Strategic Defense Initiative* (Lexington, 1986); and *National Security: Enduring Problems of U.S. Defense Policy* (St. Martin's, 1986).

the scandal of susan sontag

Gender and Culture

GENDER AND CULTURE
A Series of Columbia University Press
Nancy K. Miller and Victoria Rosner, Series Editors

A complete list of works in this series follows the index.

the scandal of
susan sontag

EDITED BY

Barbara Ching and Jennifer A. Wagner-Lawlor

 Columbia University Press   New York

Columbia University Press
Publishers Since 1893
New York   Chichester, West Sussex
Copyright © 2009 Columbia University Press
All rights reserved

Chapter 12 was originally published in *Artforum* 43, no. 7 (March 2005): 195–97, as "Perspicuous Consumption," by Wayne Koestenbaum, © Artforum, March 2005.

Library of Congress Cataloging-in-Publication Data

The scandal of Susan Sontag / edited by Barbara Ching and
Jennifer A. Wagner-Lawlor.
p. cm. — (Gender and culture)
Includes bibliographical references and index.
ISBN 978-0-231-14916-7 (cloth : alk. paper) — ISBN 978-0-231-14917-4
(pbk. : alk. paper) — ISBN 978-0-231-52045-4 (e-book)
1. Sontag, Susan, 1933–2004—Criticism and interpretation. I. Ching,
Barbara, 1958– II. Wagner-Lawlor, Jennifer A. III. Title. IV. Series.
PS3569.O6547Z878   2009
818'.5409—dc22
2009033601

Contents

Acknowledgments

The editors would like to thank all the contributors for their enthusiasm for this project and for their tremendous cooperation in keeping up with our tight timetable. More importantly, we are grateful for the opportunity to collaborate on the legacy of Susan Sontag, a writer and artist whose range of work exceeds the grasp of any one of us. This project began in Puebla, Mexico, for the American Comparative Literature Conference in 2007, where Terry Castle, Leslie Luebbers, Nancy Miller, Greg Peariso, Julia Walker, and ourselves, spent two days talking and thinking together about the life and work of Susan Sontag. We are grateful to Nancy Miller in particular for her enthusiasm about the idea of compiling a volume including these and other new essays on Sontag. Her support and advice along with that of her Gender and Culture series coeditor, Victoria Rosner, made possible the volume that now exists. Jennifer Crewe and her assistant, Afua Adusei, were wonderfully patient with our many questions. John Nale compiled the index with care and intelligence.

Barbara Ching is grateful to the UCLA libraries for a James and Sylvia Thayer Short-Term Research Fellowship to use the Sontag archive in the Special Collections Department of the Charles E. Young Research

Library at UCLA. The librarians there made my work a pleasure. The College of Arts and Sciences at the University of Memphis made much of my research on Sontag possible through a Dunavant Professorship and a professional-development assignment.

Jennifer Wagner-Lawlor would like to thank the College of the Liberal Arts at the Pennsylvania State University for its generous research support, which has underwritten the permissions cost of several illustrations.

The Ching and Lawlor families provided support of all kinds and deserve many thanks. This collection would never have been completed without them.

We have made every effort to identify the photographers and copyright holders for the images reproduced in this volume. We are especially grateful to photographers Michael Coupon and Mathieu Bourgois for their generosity in granting permission to use their photos of Sontag; also to Lorraine Adams, Jennifer Buonocore, and Paula Mazotta at VAGA (Visual Artists and Galleries Association), for helping with the rights for Joseph Cornell's *The Ellipsian*; Harriet Spurlin, executor of the estate of photographer Victor Thomas; and finally, Stephen Koch, director of the Peter Hujar Archive, LLC.

Abbreviations for Commonly Used Titles

Aids and Its Metaphors (1989)	*AM*
Against Interpretation (1966)	*AI*
Alice in Bed (1993)	*AB*
At the Same Time (2007)	*AST*
Conversations with Susan Sontag (ed. Poague, 1995)	*CSS*
I, Etcetera (1978)	*IE*
Illness as Metaphor (1978)	*IM*
In America (2000)	*IA*
On Photography (1977)	*OP*
Regarding the Pain of Others (2003)	*RP*
Styles of Radical Will (1969)	*SRW*
Swimming in a Sea of Death (Rieff, 2008)	*SSD*
Under the Sign of Saturn (1980)	*USS*
The Volcano Lover (1992)	*VL*
Where the Stress Falls (2001)	*WSF*

Note that citations to *AM* and *IM* are to the collected volume *Illness as Metaphor and Aids and Its Metaphors* (New York: Anchor Books, 1989).

Figures

the scandal of susan sontag

introduction

Unextinguished
Susan Sontag's Work in Progress

BARBARA CHING AND JENNIFER A. WAGNER-LAWLOR

Susan Sontag (1933–2004) holds a unique status in the United States as both a female public intellectual *and* a celebrity, an unlikely combination that garnered her both scorn and adulation. Refusing the shelter and specialization of the academy, she proclaimed an interest "in everything" and demonstrated it by working in theater, literature, and film and by writing about photography, painting, dance, travel, illness, and politics. She earned many professional laurels—the MacArthur Foundation genius grant in 1990 and initiation into l'Ordre des Arts et des Lettres in France, to name only two. At the same time, Sontag's volatile blend of art and activism inflamed many critics, most notably after her response to the September 11, 2001, attacks on Manhattan's World Trade Center and the Pentagon and to the American foreign policies, including war, that followed. Likewise, her penchant for the magisterial statement, combined with her readiness to revise her own ideas, left her open to charges of empty trendiness and attention seeking.

Four years after her death, Sontag retains her power to provoke. The twelve essays that make up this volume not only ask how Sontag kindled, and even created, an aura of awe and scandal during her forty years in the public eye; they also articulate and advance the ongoing debates about Sontag's achievements and legacy. From her first journal pieces to her last, posthumously published essays, she entered into age-old debates about the status of art and what, if anything, art does in the world. Sontag believed in art as a potential and ideally potent encounter with truth and beauty. She supplemented that traditional reverence with a devotion to what she called "seriousness," a quality linking the aesthetic, the ethical, and the political in an attentive person's experience of the world. She explored the role of art not only in essays on a range of subjects but also through her own creative work in various genres.

As a critic her favorite task was to admire. As an artist she borrowed freely and unashamedly from those she admired (and faced plagiarism accusations several times). Several of the essayists in this volume ask what Sontag's devotion to film, theater, and literature contributed to these genres and how her criticism of them advances our understanding of them. Likewise, many of the essays raise the question of Sontag's originality although the emphasis throughout is on what Sontag accomplished through admiration. Moreover, Sontag was a much admired "original" in another sense, a beautiful woman, an artist, and a public intellectual in an era of astonishing social upheaval. What does her public status tell us about the role of women in art and culture? What, if anything, are her contributions to feminism? Sontag's writing and lectures, her public image and the care that she took in being photographed, her reticence about her private life, particularly her bisexuality: all these figure into the debate.

Taking as their purview the full range of Sontag's creative and cultural output, the essays here offer new analyses of Sontag's private and public affairs. They tell us why the sensibility that Sontag embodied and articulated—a way of engaging with the world and with art that was simultaneously aesthetic and ethical—really matters and will continue to matter. As we will argue in this introduction, because Sontag's work was so committed to inspiring engagement, it was never done. It was, and will be, work on and in progress. What Sontag said in praise of Roland Barthes can apply equally to her own work: "Along with the backward look of grief comes the awareness that confers upon his large, chronically mutating body of writing . . . its retroactive completeness" (WSF, 63). The wide-angle perspective on Sontag's work will take a long time to fully come into focus, but certain trajectories and stages already emerge. In this introduction, we want especially to zoom in on

Sontag's status as a woman writer and her activist's commitment to the "seriousness" of art as an offspring of her passionate embrace of the "erotics of art" (*AI*, 14)

Scandalizing and Prizing

The title of our volume, *The Scandal of Susan Sontag*, emulates Sontag's style of provocation. As she asserted in one of her last lectures, literature "incarnates an ideal of plurality, of multiplicity, of promiscuity" (*AST*, 149). In a 2003 lecture, she describes the work of literature similarly: "One task of literature is to formulate questions and construct counterstatements to the reigning pieties. . . . Literature is dialogue; responsiveness" (*AST*, 204). Promiscuity, accumulation, dialogue, collection: all of these are terms in which Sontag described the work that literature does, that art does, that learning does, that writing does. It is important to understand that this promiscuity is not a scandalous spectacle for Sontag's audience but rather a scandalizing activity that involves them: Sontag is talking about what art does *to* us and *for* us. That promiscuity defines Sontag's public role: it's the source of her "erotics of art"; it's the motivation of her lifelong meditation on "a new sensibility," the characteristics of which evolved over her almost five-decade career. It also explains her ongoing arguments with herself. The promiscuity of Sontag's intellectual and artistic endeavors creates the kind of scandal we evoke in our title. Sontag's promiscuity is intentionally transgressive, it risks the embarrassment of a fall, and it is designed implicitly or explicitly to discredit what for her was the greatest sin, laziness in all its manifestations: lack of will, lack of movement, lack of commitment, lack of interest, lack of seriousness, lack of imagination, lack of sympathy, lack of hope for social and political transformation.

Sontag was promiscuously engaged in all sorts of work. But work, for Sontag, need not exclude pleasure. Her promiscuity creates the kind of intellectual *jouissance* characterized by her much admired confrère Roland Barthes: both critics exuded an unbounded curiosity, an "avidity," to borrow one of Sontag's characteristic terms, that was sometimes exhausting to those around her but inexhaustible to her; "only the exhausting," she said, "is truly interesting" (*USS*, 59). Similarly, discussing Godard's late films, she describes the pleasure she takes in them as *work*: "There are so many different kinds of pleasures you can get. . . . let's say, the pleasure of being puzzled or even of being frustrated. I don't understand everything that he's doing now, and it's very interesting also not to understand" (*CSS*, 28).

Sontag's own life offers many examples of "scandalizing" promiscuity, such as her obsessive collecting. Books may have been the primary and most representative prize: "Bookhunting, like the sexual hunt, adds to the geography of pleasure—another reason for strolling about in the world" (*USS*, 121). Reading books created another layer of collectible experience. We could say of Sontag what she says of Benjamin, that "learning was a form of collecting, as in the quotations and excerpts from daily reading which Benjamin accumulated in notebooks. . . . Thinking was also a form of collecting, at least in its preliminary stages" (*USS*, 127). Writing likewise takes the form of collecting. Citing Benjamin, she notes that "the most praiseworthy way of acquiring books is by writing them" (*USS*, 125). Thus writing, too, was an obsession, affording her a vehicle for "mental travel" that taught her how to step over, to transgress, to "travel into the past . . . and to other countries. . . . And literature was criticism of one's own reality, in the light of a better standard" (*AST*, 179).

The multiple and overlapping possibilities of endless writing and endless accumulation encompass not only collecting objects and experiences but also a more abstract pursuit of the new, the life changing, or the mind altering. In other words, promiscuity involves motion and emotion, a literal *and* figurative concept informing Sontag's view of literature and even language itself. She wrote about the etymological truths of "translation" as a form of "ferrying" or "bringing across," a way of traveling through "the geography of our [linguistic] dispersal" and arriving, at least temporarily, at communication. At the same time, the truth she sought in her own work mirrored what she described as "the truth of fiction": that it "depicts that for which one can never be consoled and displaces it with a healing openness to everything" (*AST*, 88). This openness to everything, unsurprisingly, inspired Sontag to work in multiple genres. Whereas her favorite literary genre, the novel, is ruled by the generic imperative to reach "the sense of an ending," Sontag's signature genre, the essay, is ruled by a different imperative: a resistance to the ending. When she chooses in her essays and fiction to call her journeys "trips"—the trips to Hanoi, to China—that choice signals a "mental tripping" that was positive, in the 1960s sense of "mind altering," but the choice also signals, precisely to the degree that these trips turn out to be consciousness and also conscience altering, "scandalous" trips, public stumblings or missteps that dramatically alter Sontag's perspectives, and, ideally, the perspectives of her audience as well. Her 1968 trip to Hanoi in particular initiated a turn in Sontag's thought that shifted her attention to politics, action, and national identity in a way that her earlier aesthetic did not so explicitly articulate.

The Work of Art, the Art of Work

In an early, undated journal entry, Sontag worried that "I'm not sure what purpose my work serves" ("On Self," 55), but as the years passed, the purpose of her life became work. As David Rieff tells us in his pained memoir of his mother, during the last year of her life she never referred to "my work," but to "*the* work" (*SSD*, 76; his emphasis), a telling shift of language as her interests shifted from establishing herself as a writer to exploring the ways in which writing transcends self and becomes work for us *all* to move forward. Indeed, Rieff makes it clear that "the work" fueled his mother's avid search for a cure to her cancer: "when she spoke of remission she was banishing death, at least enough to go back to work, back to planning the books she would write in the future, back to collecting books and prints, back to traveling" (*SSD*, 93). But at the same time she hoped that "the work" would offer a wider cultural and political curative of its own.

As we begin to assess the work, life, and image of Susan Sontag, we should particularly heed her insistence that art's crucial role is "extending the life." In her late essay on Victor Serge, "Unextinguished," she underscores Serge's assertion that writing offers what she would call a "zone of freedom," whose center is the self, but whose horizons are forever expanding outward:

> "Later [she is quoting Serge here], with the enrichment of the personality, one discovers its limits, the poverty and the shackles of the self, one discovers that one has only one life, an individuality forever circumscribed, but which contains many possible destinies. . . . Writing then

5

> becomes a quest of poly-personality, a way of living diverse destinies, of penetrating into others, of communicating with them . . . of escaping from the ordinary limits of the self."
> (*AST*, 77–78)

As Rieff touchingly reveals to us, Sontag approached the threat of mortality and unconsciousness with a terror matched only by her will to stay alive and to continue writing, which for her were the same thing. For writing must "remind us that we can change" (*AST*, 154), and as such it comes to be a particular kind of work: inherently and "preeminently an ethical task, . . . which is to extend our sympathies; to educate the heart and mind; to create inwardness; to secure and deepen the awareness (with all its consequences) that other people, people different from us, really do exist" (*AST*, 177).

Ultimately, this commitment to work led Sontag, at the end of the twentieth century, to address the role of popular culture in her life and thought more openly and more dismissively. In fact, she had never paid popular artists the respect of extended public attention: there is no essay on, say, Jim Morrison to sit beside the many essays on European writers. But then there is no essay on Sontag's favorite writer, Shakespeare. She had nothing useful to say about him, she explained (*CSS*, 198), implying at the same time that Shakespearean scholars and critics already *have* said something useful. But popular culture clearly hasn't attained the same embarrassment of choice, and Sontag, usually brave enough to risk embarrassment, didn't tread here. In "Thirty Years Later . . . ," her late-career postscript to the essays collected in *Against Interpretation*, she proclaims "Certainly, there's hierarchy. If I had to choose between the Doors and Dostoyevsky, then—of course—I'd choose Dostoyevsky. But do I have to choose?" (*WSF*, 270–71).

Of course, she did choose; every time she wrote an essay on Godard or Godot, she made her choice and reinforced the hierarchy. Her untitled prose poem, written as a liner note to Patti Smith's 2002 anthology *Land*, reveals much in this respect. A sort of unintentional burlesque, jarringly yoking high and low diction, the piece condescends to the audience as it offers a pseudoerotics of art. An obscure Latin quotation anchors the poem, which Sontag immediately translates, something she never does in other venues. Without the cachet of the classical language, her description of a Patti Smith concert could come from a high-schooler's diary: "*Hic dissonant ubique, nam enim sic diversis cantilen-sis clamore solent*. Here all voices are at variance, as different songs are being roared out simultaneously. . . . Women were sassier and felt sexier. Because of you, precious friend. The music spread everywhere. In the mouth. In the armpits. In the crotch" (liner notes). In sum, Sontag never saw popular culture as anything but a respite from seriousness, play in contrast to the work of art. As early as her 1969 essay on the Cuban revolution she praises recreational drugs, sex, and "listening to music" precisely because they are "unproductive."[1]

Although Sontag clearly welcomed occasional respite, work had her abiding devotion. In her essay on Artaud, Sontag describes the relation-ship between artists' lives and their work:

> In the view initiated by the romantic sensibility, what is produced by the artist (or the philosopher) contains as a regulating internal struc-ture an account of the labors of subjectivity. Work derives its creden-tials from its place in a singular lived experience; it assumes an inex-haustible personal totality of which "the work" is a by-product, and inadequately expressive of that totality. Art becomes a statement of self-awareness—an awareness that presupposes a disharmony between the self of the artist and the community. . . . any single "work" has a dual status. It is both a unique and specific and already enacted literary gesture, and a meta-literary declaration . . . about the insufficiency of literature with respect to an ideal condition of consciousness and art. Consciousness conceived of as a project creates a standard that inevita-bly condemns the "work" to be incomplete.
> (*USS*, 16)

In retrospect, this passage also describes her own work. The inevitable aim is incompleteness, an ongoing project that will be both "inexhaust-ible" (*USS*, 16) and "unextinguishable." "Incompleteness," she argues, "becomes the reigning modality of art and thought, giving rise to anti-genres—work that is deliberately fragmentary or self-canceling, thought that undoes itself" (*USS*, 17).

Work forever in progress also figures as a way of life in the 1973 short story "Debriefing" (collected in *I, Etcetera*) in which Sontag fic-tionalizes her relationship with Susan Taubes, a friend and fellow writer who committed suicide in 1969.[2] Completing the work of mourning, the narrator simply returns to her work, her writing: "You're the tears in things, I'm not. You weep for me, I'll weep for you. Help me, I don't want to weep for myself. I'm not giving up. Sisyphus, I. I cling to my rock, you don't have to chain me. . . . Nothing, nothing could tear me away from this rock" (*IE*, 52). While Sontag has often alluded to her own melancholy temperament, forged, like Benjamin's, "under the sign of Saturn," work in this passage is a natural object, a tear-stained rock that tethers the writer to this even more intractable rock, earth. As Camus concluded in his essay, which transformed Sisyphus from a victim of the Gods to an existential master of his fate, the struggle "toward the heights" gives Sisyphus' life and work meaning—even as the struggle also includes the downward motion. Moreover, as Sontag's continuation of the Sisyphus theme demonstrates, in choosing life over death, we identify with Sisyphus and take on the work in progress of rolling the rock.

One "scandal" of Susan Sontag that our volume's title refers to is this Sisyphean commitment to *un*doing and redoing, complete with missteps and misstatements but also replete with a utopian commitment to change. An etymological connection between stumbling and standards (whether ethical or artistic) inheres in the very definition of "scandal." In fact, among the first definitions that the *Oxford English Dictionary* offers is "perplexity of conscience occasioned by the conduct of one who is looked up to as an example"; it goes on to compare scandal to travel and downward motion, as in "to trip morally." In Sontag's own vocabulary, the word "scandal" seems to be one of several antonyms of the word "aesthetic"—and also akin in a surprising way to Sontag's concept of the "useful." In other words, in her sense of "scandal" lurked her activist political visions for the work of art. This passage from *Illness as Metaphor*, for example, contrasts the innumerable nineteenth-century associations between tuberculosis and artistic insight with our own attitudes toward cancer: "Cancer is a rare and still scandalous subject for poetry; and it seems unimaginable to aestheticize the disease" (20). In other words, while cancer does lend itself to metaphor, it cannot be easily exempted from moral judgments in the way that artistic creations have traditionally isolated themselves. Cancer, like corruption, violence, and oppression, is a force that Sontag works against. While here Sontag argues that the metaphors used to think about cancer harm cancer's victims, her use of the word "scandalous" is approving, expressing the moralist's relief that some things remain too serious for detached contemplation and so serious that they require action.

In this respect, the work became increasingly uninterested in an *ironical* pursuit of "fragmentary" and "self-canceling" forms of incompletion; that is to say, her writing turns decisively away from the kind of formal experiments that produced her unsatisfactory first novels, *The Benefactor* (1963) and *Death Kit* (1967). These are dead ends, youthful narrative disguises of what Sontag finally allows to emerge from her thought and writing: faith in art, and a commitment to changing the world with art that few could have predicted when Sontag wrote "Notes on Camp" in the 1960s. Furthermore that engagement resonates in our new century in ways that Sontag herself appeared not to have anticipated, though by a 1995 *Paris Review* interview, speaking as both a writer and reader, she proclaims: "I can't care about a book that has nothing to contribute to the wisdom project."[3]

That "project," we argue, is the work in progress that Sontag wills to her readers. In her 1964 "Notes on Camp," the various figures she includes in "the pantheon of high culture" embody intellectual, historical, and spiritual genius: "Socrates, Jesus, St. Francis, Napoleon, Savonarola" (*AI*, 286). But as she imagines future entrants, now in a 1988 interview, she broadens her perspective dramatically: "We are required to continue to make an effort to invite people in who are willing to do the work and to accept the difference in their own lives and their own consciousness that these loyalties will imply. It is a question of recruitment just as you recruit people into a religious order" (*CSS*, 249). Indeed, the language of Western religion pervades her life and work, shaped by her graduate work in theology and comparative religion, her own manner of pilgrimages, an attachment to the parsing of good and evil, an optimistic belief in miracle working, and a reverence for literature that rendered a broad range of texts sacred.

A Woman in Progress

Early in her career, Sontag did little to call attention to her singularity as a woman writing in the male-dominated world of New York intellectuals—perhaps because others did it for her.[4] The trivializing misogyny of this attention is worth noting, however. In his 1967 memoir *Making*

9

It, New York intellectual Norman Podhoretz dubbed her "the dark lady of American letters," a "position," he claimed, that had been filled by Mary McCarthy in earlier decades. This patronizing nickname has been reiterated and varied ever since without much conscious reckoning with the implicit insult even though we all know that Shakespeare preferred the fair-haired boy. Similarly, in 1968, Irving Howe, also writing about the New York intellectuals, coined a backhanded compliment with a metaphor that compared Sontag's work to a kind of womanly handicraft, characterizing her as a "publicist able to make brilliant quilts from grandmother's patches."[5]

While Sontag's gender preoccupied these commentators, until the early 1970s she wrote in the classic humanist mode, using "he" as a universalizing pronoun even in the intimate pages of her journals. One such entry, dated November 19, 1959, is interspersed with talk of her "homosexuality" (her word) and discovery of the orgasm—yet it now startles by its almost self-obliterating inattention to gendered language, as well as by its (unintentionally?) sexualized characterization of her writerly desire: "The only kind of writer I could be is the kind who exposes himself." In her breakthrough essay "Notes on Camp," though, she distances herself from the homosexual tastes she is anatomizing with the use of "one." While nearly all contemporary theorists of camp focus on the essay as an expression of sexual identity,[6] it took Sontag years fully to come out, and whether she was ever open about her woman-centered sexuality is a matter of debate. By 1972, she was writing feminist-themed essays such as "The Double Standard of Aging" in *The Saturday Review*, although the closest she came to airing her own concerns as she neared her fortieth birthday was this wet-blanket pronouncement: "no one escapes a sickening shock upon turning 40."[7] In 1973's "The Third World of Women," published in *The Partisan Review* and based on her responses to a questionnaire created by the editors of the Spanish quarterly *Libre*, she retains her impersonal tone as she argues for nonsexist usage, such as avoiding the universal "he," and dubs English grammar "the ultimate arena of sexist brainwashing" (186). In response to a question about sexual liberation, she remains aloof, almost pedantic: "the question is: *what* sexuality are women to be liberated to enjoy? The only sexual ethic liberating for women is one which challenges the primacy of genital heterosexuality" (188). Subtly disavowing her own challenges to "genital heterosexuality," Sontag states that "I would never describe myself as a liberated woman. . . . But I have always been a feminist" (204).

In the decade immediately following these feminist essays, Sontag took few explicit actions to improve the status of women or to undermine what Adrienne Rich calls "compulsory heterosexuality." The essays themselves never appeared in any of Sontag's subsequent collections, and she went on to publish her groundbreaking books *Illness as Metaphor* and *On Photography* in the late 1970s. In retrospect, her films and fiction of the period suggest a struggle over what form Sontag could give to her work on feminism. While the short stories in *I, Etcetera* offer a mosaic of autobiographical elements, the sexuality on display is tritely normal: a married couple consulting a psychiatrist about their precocious son in "Baby" and a woman enjoying a fling with an appealing waiter on her European travels in "Unguided Tour." *Brother Carl* (1971), her second film, can be seen as a struggle to speak and embody the kind of liberation for which Sontag argued in "Third World of Women," yet like the heroes of her first two novels, Carl, the title character, is male, a former dancer who won't speak. Intriguingly, he is a sort of kindred spirit or brother to Anna, a speechless child whom he finally brings to language. Although the setting is Sweden, Sontag seems to have cast her own silenced childhood into the film; dark-haired Anna and Carl look like a young Susan Sontag cast among Nordic blonds (see fig. 1), and in her preface to the screenplay (published in 1974), Sontag insinuates that the story chimes with a momentous incident in her life. The book is dedicated to one "Carlotta del Pezzo," or "the (female) Carl of the piece" (our translation). Sontag further hints that this is a screenplay à clef when she recounts an exchange between herself and Laurent Terzieff, the actor who played Carl. After he had read the script, he "observed . . . that in the tormented history of Martin and Carl I was evoking the legendary relationship between Diaghilev and Nijinsky. I told him he was right [but] . . . I wasn't telling the truth" (ix). Instead, she says, these two are "emblems of the dramaturgy of silence (or voluntary mutism) that has been a recurrent theme *in my life* and in my novels as well as my films" (x; emphasis added).

Sontag elaborates on the connections between her life and her work when she introduces her interest in working miracles. Discussing the miracles that close the film—Carl's unsuccessful attempt to resuscitate Lena and his success at bringing Anna to words—the filmmaker reveals

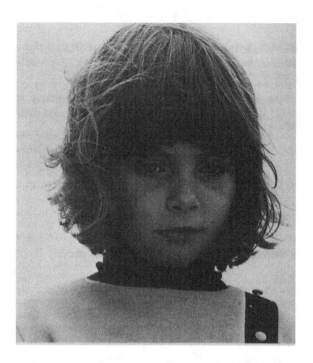

Figure 1 Actress Pernilla Alfeldt as Sontag look-alike in *Brother Carl. Source*: *Bröder Carl*, 1971, distributed by Sandrew Meteronome and used by permission of Sandrew Meteronome.

that she, too, has attempted to work a miracle. She doesn't say what it is, only that after shooting the film, she traveled to Rome to discover that her attempted miracle had failed. She closes her preface to the screenplay by averring that, nevertheless, "failure has not destroyed my belief in miracles" (xvi). The arduous task of speaking out is still underway, and the miracle may still be worked.[8]

In the 1990s, Sontag began to speak out more explicitly. In a preface to her lover Annie Leibovitz's 1999 collection of photographs, entitled *Women*, she notes that women are "a minority . . . by every criterion except the numerical" (*WSF*, 238). In her creative work, she takes angry women as a theme in both the play *Alice in Bed* (1993) and in her novel *The Volcano Lover* (1992). While the novel's title seems to refer to its main character, Sir William Hamilton, and his love for Vesuvius, the epigraph, again in Italian, puts the emphasis on women: "Nel petto un Vesuvio d'avere mi par" ("I have a Vesuvius in my heart"). The quotation comes from Mozart's *Cosi Fan Tutte*, often translated (although Sontag doesn't translate it at all) as *All Women Are Like That* or *Thus Do All Women*. More importantly, using plain English in the novel's last paragraph, she connects the epigraph to her own status as a woman. As she awaits her execution, the Neapolitan revolutionary Eleonora di Fonseca Pimentel recalls:

> I did know about power, I did see how this world was ruled, but I did not accept it. I wanted to set an example. . . . But I was afraid as well as angry, in ways I felt too powerless to admit. So I did not speak of my fears but rather of my hopes. I was afraid my anger would offend others, and they would destroy me. . . . Sometimes I had to forget that I was a woman to accomplish the best of which I was capable. Or I would lie to myself about how complicated it is to be a woman. Thus do all women, including the author of this book.
> (*VL*, 419)

In her afterword to *Alice in Bed*, Sontag characterized it as a play "about the grief and anger of women" and as a culmination of sorts: "I think I have been preparing to write *Alice in Bed* all my life" (117). Her heroine, the invalid Alice James, sister of "the greatest American novelist" (114), achieves an imaginary "triumph" when she takes a mental trip to Rome (that site of miracles, again). But Sontag closes in an exhortatory mode: "the victories of the imagination are not enough" (114). Similarly, in her preface to the Leibovitz collection, Sontag rather cheerfully notes that "men, unlike women, are not a work in progress" since equality, that ongoing work, is a long way off (*WSF*, 239).

This increasing focus on women's victories, whether exceptional or typical, can be linked to Sontag's increased willingness to advocate bisexuality by example rather than precept. Perhaps prompted by the revelations in Carl Rollyson and Lisa Paddock's unauthorized biography, she was discussing it with journalists in mainstream magazines such as the *Guardian* and the *New Yorker*. In 2000, she told her unnamed interviewer in the *Guardian* that she had been in love with "five women. Four men." But the "work in progress" she alludes to in her preface to the Leibowitz photographs involves much more than an exemplary avowal of erotic adventures. As Sontag's earliest writing about feminism makes clear, women also must engage in the work and develop the will to travel a critical distance from popular and high culture notions of "the beautiful."[9]

A Collection of Voices

In the essays that follow, these facets of Sontag's personality and career—her promiscuous intellect, her ambivalent sexuality, her increasingly fervent exploration of the aesthetic as the political and the political as the moral, her peculiar and contradictory impulses toward private reticence and public provocation—come under review. It's fair to say that each of these essays is written in the spirit with which Sontag came to so many of her subjects: admiration. Sontag's own essayistic admirations are hardly noncritical or naïve; rather, they take up their subject in the spirit of wonder and reflection that the word "admiration" originally connoted. And while the essays here range in stance from the personal to the partisan and in tone from the eulogistic to the academic to the elegiac, what underlies each is an appreciation of Sontag's work as a whole, acknowledging the intellectual "promiscuities," the willingness to reside in contradiction that seems at one time her weakness, at another her greatest strength as a critic. What scandalized Sontag in others was a moral or political certainty born of resistance to change, indeed, resistance to thinking; what scandalized others about Sontag was precisely her will to think again, and think forward.

Our collection of responses to Susan Sontag opens with Terry Castle's essay "Some Notes on 'Notes on Camp,'" adapting Sontag's playful, fragmentary form to suggest that Sontag, late in her career, disavowed her interest in camp for several reasons. First, she no longer needed to keep the private scandal, the "wounding secret of her homosexuality," that camp covered up; second, she had come to see herself as a follower not of the epigrammatical wit Oscar Wilde but rather of the novelistic moralist George Eliot. Most intriguingly, Castle suggests that Sontag's sympathy for camp stemmed from a "family romance" in which her early promotion of camp tastes compensated for her estrangement from her parents; camp stands, then, as a form of revenge against the homophobia many parents feel toward their gay children. In later reconciling herself to her sexuality, Sontag can also let go of both the guilt and the defensive strategy; the "sympathy modified by revulsion" that Sontag claimed was necessary to describe camp thus gives way, concludes Castle, to a more complex and far-reaching sympathy and a revulsion focused more on ethical failures than on the wry failures that console the camp sensibility.

Conversely, Wayne Koestenbaum's appreciation of Sontag, "Susan Sontag, Cosmophage," which closes this volume, cites a sentence from *The Benefactor*, her first novel, to praise her for coming out "forcibly" and "repeatedly": "I am a homosexual and a writer." Equally attractive to him are her "hot lexical choices," which allowed Sontag to zero in on "what matters" over the course of her long career, even if what mattered shifted many times.

Dana Heller's "Absolute Seriousness: Sontag and Popular Culture" looks at Sontag's image as a sort of lightning rod for contemporary debates about the role of intellectuals in American public life. While the Absolut Vodka ad featuring Sontag is Heller's prime example, she also looks at Sontag as a reference point in popular films, such as *Bull Durham*. Most hopefully, she finds that new technologies of popular culture such as YouTube have the potential to activate the "seriousness" so important to Sontag's legacy.

Barbara Ching's "'Not Even a New Yorker': Susan Sontag in America" revisits some of the themes of Castle's essay in its attention to an underlying note of shame sounding in Sontag's relatively rare "personal" writing and interviews. The obfuscation is not sexuality this time but rather Sontag's embarrassment over and embrace of her roots in provincial America. Through journeys away from home, however, to the world of the intellect and to Europe, Hanoi, and beyond, Sontag rediscovers a connection between American ideals, the vocation of literature, and her own work. By carefully reading the images and metaphors Sontag uses in her autobiographical writing, Ching shows how Sontag recuperates an admiration for the political and personal freedoms promised by her own country.

In a turn from the life to the work, Jennifer A. Wagner-Lawlor offers one of the first extended analyses of *The Volcano Lover* and *In*

America. Like Heller and Ching, she explores Sontag's legacy of hope by reading her last two novels as utopian narratives that center not on voyages to ideal societies but on provoking the reader's desire for alternative ways to live. This hope for a shared future animates the plots of both novels, as does Sontag's interest in evoking the communal emotion of sympathy. In these last novels, Sontag's ethical and aesthetic sensibilities coalesce around a commitment to working toward a better world.

The struggle between silence and expression finds its way into more than just Sontag's writing: in the only piece on Sontag's film work, E. Ann Kaplan traces the early explication—in Sontag's essays and even more impressively in her films—of an "aesthetics of silence" that is "touched by trauma," historical and, as we've seen, personal as well. Kaplan connects Sontag's resistance to interpretation to her extraordinary role as a female "public intellectual" and, even rarer, a woman filmmaker. The visual medium offered a space to explore "the pure, untranslatable, sensuous immediacy" of life without language. Kaplan thus suggests that film offers Sontag the most direct way of combining "emotions and form" in a way that will both frustrate our willing acceptance of the false images of Hollywood convention and encourage us to attend to the silences that permeate our real lives. In this context Kaplan clearly postulates a connection with Sontag's female perspective (recalling Castle's essay) that was remarked in its time but is only interpretable in retrospect: we can see the same radical insistence on the primacy of affect and sympathy that would form the ethical foundation of Sontag's later politics and inform so much later thought and critical work.

The relationship between form and content undergirds Julia Walker's essay, "Sontag on Theater." Tracing the *metaphor* of theater through much of Sontag's critical work—most notably, the articulation of self as performance in "Notes on Camp" but also through the theatrical pieces she authored—Walker argues that the theatrical "predominates over Sontag, the essayist, the novelist, and even the activist." Together these theoretical as well as theatrical pieces reveal Sontag's "unwavering belief," Walker asserts, "that, at its best, art has a cathartic power to inspire its audience to take moral and political action"—and that drama and performance most effectively satisfy "social, aesthetic, and phenomenological problems" not resolved by other expressive genres, including, contra Kaplan's argument in the previous essay, the medium of film. The figure of "the actor" becomes critical for Sontag, Walker concludes, as a certain kind of "self-authorization" always at work in her life.

Craig J. Peariso's "The 'Counter Culture' in Quotation Marks: Sontag and Marcuse on the Work of Revolution" also looks at Sontag's role in debates about intellectuals and cultural change. He places Sontag's early essays on the new left and the new sensibility in the context of countercultural theory, especially Herbert Marcuse's concerns about the "repressive desublimation" that affluent permissive capitalism enables. By reading Sontag's essays in *Against Interpretation* (1966) with Marcuse, Peariso calls attention to the interplay between these theorists of radicalism in order to restore complexity to the 1960s cultural landscape.

The scandal of the "unsayable" is also what attracted Sontag to some painting—most notably to Howard Hodgkin, whose collaboration with Sontag is explored by Leslie Luebbers in "A Way of Feeling Is a Way of Seeing: Sontag and the Visual Arts." The two artists began a firm and fruitful relationship in the publication of their limited-edition artist's book, *The Way We Live Now* (1991), which, according to Luebbers, is the product of their common advocacy of "a way of feeling" that "is a way of seeing." Hodgkin's ambition to "paint representational pictures of emotional situations" aligns with Sontag's championing of sensory experience in art and also with her conviction that great art touches both the horizon separating expression or representation and also the inexpressible. Both Hodgkin and Sontag therefore share a stance "against interpretation," a refusal to separate form from content any more than body from mind, resisting, too, any easy autobiographical readings of the paintings. So distanced, the work of art is set apart as an "articulate symbol"; as such it is "transparent" not toward any particular "meaning" but precisely the "strangeness" of the work itself. The work of art is an expressive artifact gaining meaning as it is perceived by an observer.

The question of form and content is approached from another direction in Jay Prosser's engagement with Sontag's "Against Interpretation." Beyond explicating that famous manifesto, Prosser draws out its implications for the experience of art. Sontag's rejection of interpretation, he argues, does more than clarify her view that an interpretation is a process of translation that "displaces the material, the thing, or what Sontag calls the world"; Sontag also *redescribes* interpretation as a "hypertrophy" of the intellect "at the expense of energy and sensual capability—like the cancer Sontag didn't yet have." Prosser traces Sontag's remarkable rejection of the displacement of the body by language and interpretation into her later works on metaphor and illness. Her attack on the way metaphors of illness distance one from a "real" experience of illness thus evolves directly out of her earlier position but, like all of Sontag's work, has implications well beyond aesthetics. Indeed, Prosser argues, *Illness as Metaphor* is a defense of life "in itself," on its own terms, not on the terms that language offers instead.

It is fitting that the next two essays in the volume should take up, more explicitly, the "posthumous life" of the iconic Susan Sontag. Nancy K. Miller takes up precisely that iconic stature by exploring the way the final photographs of Sontag, taken by celebrity photographer and lover Annie Leibovitz, complicate the "self-idealizations" that the critic, according to her son, "lightly assent[ed]" to having cultivated. Even accepting, as Miller does, Leibovitz's defense for publishing her "personal" photos ("I don't have two lives"), it is another question entirely, Miller argues, whether "some of kind of new knowledge, or vision," either about Sontag or about Leibovitz or even more abstractly about "celebrity," accompanies this decision. Is Leibovitz's memorial project an act of unseemly predation, as Rieff suggests in his homage to his mother? Or is there a story, an argument, in or through these photographs that we can reconcile to Sontag's own compelling writing about images and the body, about illness, about mortality and the "unextinguished," and about art's role in representing all those conditions of life and death?

And Sohnya Sayres reviews Sontag's essays from the last decade of her life, finding in them a remarkable consistency of perspective and ideas even from her earliest work. Despite the fact that Sontag writes to the occasion, in accessible prose for more popular vehicles, she writes as an aestheticist and social philosopher whose thought takes shape through the venerable concerns about the good, the true, and the beautiful. From those concerns, Sayres draws a portrait of Sontag engaged upon a project to discover "how we live now": that is, to ask how we *do* live morally and aesthetically in a world saturated with glittering, fragmentary pieces of knowledge.

It may seem to some readers that Sontag's final scandal was her turn to some kind of aesthetic piety, but Sontag would likely brush away this last charge as a postmodernist piety of its own. As this introduction has argued, Sontag came to see as impoverished—indeed, scandalous—a view of art work that has no ambition to extend the experience of its audiences; no interest in exposing the hydra-headed perversions, personal and political, of bad faith; and no avowal of art's potential for continuing to drive human(e) progress. Our hope is that these essays, which cover a scandalizing range of topics, begin to highlight myriad possibilities for continuing Sontag's work of art, critique, and public criticism. As the journals continue to appear in the coming years, we will all learn more about the life and the work and about her central project: to keep alive the dialogue with, and the responsiveness to, the promiscuous richness of art and experience.

Notes

1. "Some Thoughts on the Right Way (for Us) to Love the Cuban Revolution," in *Divided We Stand*, ed. the editors of *Ramparts* with Richard H. Dodge (San Francisco: Canfield Press, 1970), 167.
2. For the details about the Taubes-Sontag friendship, see Carl Rollyson and Lisa Paddock, *Susan Sontag: The Making of an Icon* (New York: Norton, 2000), 142–43.
3. Interview, "Susan Sontag: The Art of Fiction CLXIII," *Paris Review* (Winter 1995): 196.
4. The thesis of Liam Kennedy's excellent *Susan Sontag: Mind as Passion* (New York: Palgrave Macmillan, 1997) is that Sontag's early work is shaped by her need to distinguish herself from the New York intellectuals.
5. Cited by Kennedy in *Mind as Passion*, 132–33n. 31.
6. See, for examples, the essays collected by David Bergman in *Camp Grounds: Style and Homosexuality* (Amherst: University of Massachusetts Press, 1993); Pamela Robertson, *Guilty Pleasures: Feminist Camp from Mae West to Madonna* (Durham, N.C.: Duke University Press, 1996), and Fabio Cleto, *Camp: Queer Aesthetics and the Performing Subject* (Ann Arbor: University of Michigan Press, 1999). Sontag herself recognized that "the diffusion

of camp taste in the early '60s should probably be credited with a considerable if inadvertent role in the upsurge of feminist consciousness in the late 1960s" (*CSS*, 70).

7. "The Double Standard of Aging," *Saturday Review*, September 23, 1972, 32.

8. Testimony from others verifies that Sontag's writing did, in fact, provide intercession. Consider, for example, the late Ellen Willis's testimony that Sontag's writing helped her find her "voice" during her college years in the late 1960s: "I was an English major at Barnard around the time that budding critics like Marshall Berman and Morris Dickstein were across the street studying with the likes of Lionel Trilling; but the Columbia English department would not allow Barnard women in its classes." *New York Times* writer Daphne Merkin gives similar witness: "I will never forget the thrill I felt upon coming to the conclusion of her piece 'Fascinating Fascism,' when it first appeared in *The New York Review of Books* in 1975. I was 20, a literature-besotted senior at Barnard, and here was evidence of a woman with the intellectual stamina equal to that of the male critics I studied." Ellen Willis, "Three Elegies for Susan Sontag," *New Politics* 10, no. 3 (2005), http://www.wpunj.edu/~newpol/issue39/Willis39.htm, accessed May 25, 2009; Daphne Merkin, "The Dark Lady of the Intellectuals," *New York Times Book Review*, October 29, 2000.

9. "A Woman's Beauty: Put-Down or Power Source?" *Vogue* (April 1975): 119.

chapter one

Some Notes on "Notes on Camp"

TERRY CASTLE

These notes are for George Eliot.

Rereading my abstract for this essay (composed last year for a conference), I confess to feeling a bit bemused—particularly by the cool, bureaucratic, indeed "abstract" tone I chose to adopt for it:

> Susan Sontag's essay "Notes on Camp" (1964) remains—in the minds of many—her defining work. With good reason: it is an uncanny, bravura accomplishment and helped to set in motion a host of intellectual and cultural transformations that would come to fruition over the next four decades. For reasons worth exploring, Sontag herself came to dislike the essay and in later years took umbrage at anyone who mentioned it or wished to discuss it. I hope to examine both the uncanniness and the umbrage: why "Notes on Camp" remains unforgettable (one still knows sentences from it by "heart") and why it evoked in Sontag such self-distancing and contempt.

What is held at bay in this careful little statement—and the holding at bay, I realize, is both precarious and more than a little Sontagian—is precisely any hint of the personal: any sense of the roiling, arm-flapping, flowing-scarved, silver-maned emotions that Sontag—the writer, the speaker, the *monstre sacrée*, the semi-or-briefly-or-not-quite-friend—automatically evokes in me. True, I mention a certain susceptible reader, an unnamed "one" who supposedly knows lines from "Notes on Camp" by heart—but even there, I see, I've put the word "heart" in campy (if vaguely incriminating) quotation marks. I'm particularly struck by the abstract's oddly fraught vocabulary: the words "uncanny," "dislike," "umbrage," "wish," "hope," "unforgettable," "self-distancing," and "contempt" might suggest something more histrionic than the usual panel-discussion fare. Still, the thing keeps the lid on well enough to qualify as "academic"—i.e., to deaden the reader with charmlessness and official-sounding phrases.

But dispassion be damned: I find I can't talk about "Notes on Camp" without "getting personal" at once. Camp, after all, is itself bound up with the personal—with the freaks of individual taste, with unusual or flamboyant modes of self-presentation. Human beings can be camp, of course; what makes them camp, Sontag argues, are precisely certain exaggerated "personality mannerisms." The film world offers many examples. Among Sontag's icons: the haunting androgynous Garbo; the flamboyantly feminine Jayne Mansfield; the "great stylists of temperament and mannerism," such as "Bette Davis, Barbara Stanwyck, Tallulah Bankhead, Edwige Feuillière." (I'll come back to this interesting little pantheon in a moment.) Though not an actress or performer in the ordinary sense, Sontag herself could no doubt be added to this list of "camp" lady-thespians. In person, she was as eccentric, theatrical, and mesmerizing as any of them.

But "Notes on Camp" is itself an insistently personal piece of writing—more backhanded confession, I would argue, than truly analytic accounting, more flight of self-expression than impersonal treatise. How do I know? The glib answer would be because it elicits a similarly autobiographical urge in me. However veiled, confessional impulses are always contagious, and as soon as the young author, thirty-one at time of the essay's publication, begins to list what things are "camp" and what aren't, I can't help but feel she wants both to reveal herself—the books she has read, the films she's seen, the personalities she has encountered, what she thinks is funny, what she thinks is sexy, what she thinks is dumb, *who she is, in other words*—and to seduce her imaginary reader into some corresponding self-revelation. I'm happy to oblige: rereading "Notes on Camp," even now, all I want to do is to seduce back (however pathetically) by itemizing all the books *I've* read, films *I've* seen, what *I* think is sexy, dumb, beautiful, etc., etc. Part of the essay's allure lies in its cataloguing mania, its strange urge to *specify*—an urge so intense and charged as to become a form of greeting and provocation, a complex hello to an absent yet much-desired unknown. The essay's mock didacticism, I would offer, is only a screening device. Though it may lend the essay a superficial air of intellectual rigor and self-restraint, it also allows its author to gesture—as in a *journal intime*—toward a tumultuous world of feeling. This indirect yet potent insinuation of feeling —especially, I think, of feelings associated with sexuality—may explain in part why Sontag was so uncomfortable with the essay in later years. The cool, analytic, supposedly educative pose was simply a rhetorical gambit; the private content, in retrospect, too obvious, jejune, and exposed.

First, a field sighting: It's 1995 and Sontag has been invited to the Stanford Humanities Center as a Distinguished Visitor. On the first evening after her arrival, the wealthy donors who have subsidized the visit, an elderly physicist and his wife, hold a small and select reception at their bucolic McMansion in Portola Valley. After we perambulate the Japanese garden—a terraced extravaganza with gazing balls, philosopher's stones, and mock-Shinto shrines—and gather sedately for cocktails on the deck, one of the older male guests remarks, by way of gallant icebreaker, on the extraordinary influence of "Notes on Camp" and how much he still admires the essay. Nostrils flaring, Sontag instantly fixes him with a basilisk stare. How can he say such a dumb thing? She has no interest in discussing that essay and never will. He should never have brought it up. He is behind the times, intellectually dead. Hasn't he ever read any of her other works? Doesn't he keep up? As she slips down a dark tunnel of rage—one to become all-too familiar to us over the next two weeks—the rest of us watch, horrified and transfixed.

Now the offending interlocutor is a person of no little eminence himself—the inventor, in fact, of the birth-control pill. He is clearly not used to having women tell him to shut up and feel ashamed of himself. He sits down, somewhat groggily, on a sort of embroidered tuffet-thing and falls into chagrined silence. That the whole scene—the Japanese lanterns hanging in the eucalyptus trees, our pink-tinged cosmopolitans, the convenient tuffet, and Sontag's operatic outburst—could also be described as camp of a fairly high order, seems lost on the party's still-incensed guest of honor. For some time afterward, Sontag simply glowers—magnificently—rather like Maria Callas in the famous film clip from *Tosca* at the Paris Opera, just after she's stabbed Tito Gobbi, the rotund singer playing evil Scarpia. *Muori, muori!*

Coming so soon after Sontag's arrival, the episode was obviously God's way of warning us: *don't ever mention "Notes on Camp" in front of her!* Or if you must, be very, very careful. More by luck than design, sheer sycophancy saved me from similar humiliation: soon after we were introduced I made a quasi-joke about having first read "Notes on Camp" when I was nine. The remark delighted Sontag and to my mingled pride and embarrassment she repeated it later during a seminar on *The Volcano Lover*. (No ban from her on discussing the novels of course; she was ready to expatiate on *them* for hours.) My claim to precocity, I feel obliged to explain, was not entirely obsequious untruth. Certainly I have a vague prepubescent memory of rifling through a stash of magazines at my father's house in the early 1960s and discovering an article that I now think might have been "Notes on Camp." I just can't be sure *what* magazine. It's hard to believe it was *Partisan Review*, the periodical in which "Notes on Camp" first appeared in 1964. For some weird reason I keep thinking it was *Vogue*. But why would my decidedly un-campy father, a cold and morose space engineer, have been reading *Vogue*? Not that he would have been reading *Partisan Review* either. I'm forced to consider the possibility that I may have made this whole Sontagian "scene of reading" up. Still, the thought of having been so "downtown" at an early age—a sort a juvenile Des Esseintes—is too gratifying, I confess, for me to disavow at this late stage.

Back to Sontag and the personal. Out of what kinds of private experience might a love of camp arise? When you reread Sontag's essay it turns out that she is spectacularly vague about the *emotional* dimensions of camp—what psychic determinants may go to produce the camp "sensibility" in any given individual. Instead, she leaps immediately to the sociological and an explication that is sketchy at best. The appreciation of camp, she says, is usually found in "small urban cliques," where it functions like a "private code, a badge of identity even." An ironically cultivated affection for camp phenomena—the bloated films of Cecil B. De Mille, Liberace's sequined outfits, the histrionic dancing of Martha Graham, male figure skaters—can be a way, she suggests, for the socially alienated to feel part of a coterie, a select group of mock cognoscenti. Like the Black Mass of old, camp facilitates Satanic small-group bonding: ordinary aesthetic values are inverted, the bad worshipped in place of the good. You and your fellow warlocks make a heaven out of hell, and the ugly, it turns out, is the new *divine*. Late in the essay, of course, she links this perverse rebel-angel sensibility with male homo-sexuality: gay men use camp, she argues, to create ironic solidarity in the face of social opprobrium. Camp taste, according to Sontag, is simply a late and paradoxical version of "aristocratic" taste—snobbish, witty, amoral, knowing. By treating the shoddy and overblown products of mass culture as "fabulous" or "heavenly," Sontag avers, gay men trans-form themselves—with an irony at once comic, self-conscious, and vo-luptuous—into a new aesthetic vanguard or smart set, a fey cohort of (pseudoaristocratic) patron-connoisseurs.

Now all of this is no doubt true. But it also leaves a lot unsaid—or at least spectacularly undeveloped. Indeed, Sontag's final, seemingly throwaway comments on the "aristocratic" nature of the camp sensi-bility, in particular, seem to obscure certain crucial underlying psycho-logical questions. What impulses—conscious or unconscious—make someone fantasize about being an aristocrat? Blue-bloodedness is hardly something you can choose, and besides, in most Western democratic societies the aristocratic premise itself has long been officially discred-ited. Yet as Freud once famously suggested, the wish for such high sta-tion is a common one and in some individuals neurotic in the extreme. For Freud the wish is linked, of course, to what he called—in the fa-mous 1908 essay of the same name—the "family romance": the child-hood fantasy that one is of royal birth and one's humdrum, dreary, or fallible parents merely vulgar, low-status impostors. Through some mysterious accident—some dire mix-up in the cradle perhaps—one has ended up stuck with them, but it's obvious (at least to the child) that everyone is living a lie. How could such a dull, talentless, badly dressed, and inconsequential pair have produced such a superior being as *one-self*? No doubt one's real parents are a glamorous king and queen who will one day reappear, identify themselves as such, and take one back with them to that fairy-tale place one should have rightfully occupied since birth. One's changeling status will be revealed; one's exalted des-tiny, confirmed.

Freud explained the family romance as part of the process—always difficult, often excruciating—by which the young child seeks to liber-ate himself or herself from parental authority. This separation typically begins in wounding and disappointment: the child's feeling—Freud writes—that he or she has been cruelly "slighted" by the parents. The birth of a sibling, classically, can elicit this narcissistic sense of injury: one feels displaced, neglected, abandoned. Injury in turn produces rage, and, at least in daydream, a wish to retaliate. On the unconscious level the assertion of royal birth is a striking act of symbolic vengeance: an indirect yet psychologically gratifying way of "doing away with"—or at least nullifying—one's thoughtless, inept, selfish, and no doubt malevolent progenitors. In the most extreme cases it is the functional equivalent of patricide or matricide.

Now, if Sontag were alive and kicking today, I would hesitate, I'm sure, to offer the theory I'm about to float: a fear of defenestration would no doubt inhibit me. But I do think—have always thought—that "Notes on Camp" hints, fairly flagrantly, at something that might be called the Sontagian *family romance*. My theory is entirely speculative and subjective—some will say absurdly subjective. But at the essay's emotional core I can't help but infer authorial feelings of pain and anger—an undercurrent of indignation if not, indeed, a desire for revenge. Revenge on whom or what? I have no special knowledge about Sontag's childhood—she seldom discussed it—but given the singular eminence she achieved, it's very hard indeed not to be struck by the oddity and unexpectedness of her early years. Like Swift's Gulliver, she's always seemed a sort of *lusus naturae*—a biographical goof or non sequitur. How did she ever get from Point A to Point B? Born in New York, okay . . . — but raised in Tucson, Arizona, followed by *Los Angeles*? Father a fur trader in China (!) who died when Sontag was five? The mysterious navy-captain stepfather whose name she adopted in place of Rosenblatt? Three years at North Hollywood High? "Sue Sontag's" yearbook picture is beyond discombobulating. (People usually giggle when they see it.) And where, in all of this, was Sontag's *mother*? No doubt because I myself hail from San Diego, the Southern Californian connection particularly confounds me: I find it difficult to associate the stunted cultural ambiance of my own smog-enhanced childhood—a pageant of Taco Bells, Mobil gas stations, and Midas Muffler shops—with anyone as epicene as the author of *Against Interpretation*.

Sontag once wrote, very charmingly, in the *New Yorker* about an extraordinary high-school visit she and a geeky male friend paid to Thomas Mann, then living out his later years in exile in Los Angeles.

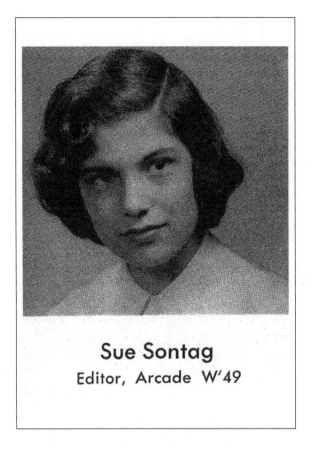

Sue Sontag
Editor, Arcade W'49

Figure 2 Susan Sontag's high-school yearbook photo. *Source*: Courtesy of Kevin Killian.

What I remember most about the essay was Sontag's account of Mann's Old World courtliness and hospitality but also the sense she conveyed, obliquely yet ferociously, of the barrenness of her early life—the intellectual, aesthetic, and emotional impoverishment of her family situation and West Coast milieu, and her extraordinary yearning, even then, to be *somewhere else*, to helicopter herself up and out and into a world intellectually, artistically, and emotionally refined enough to satisfy her complex needs for beauty, love, seriousness, and permanence.

The sensitivity to camp, I think, is intimately related to childhood disappointment—to the feeling of being misplaced, misunderstood, *fine* but unappreciated, "wasted" on those around one. As a child, you can't help blaming the dullness of existence on your parents, it would seem: they are the ones, after all, who seem responsible for the unglamorous setting in which you find yourself. They seem to have arranged, if not created, the whole banal *mise-en-scène*. How easy for an intellectually precocious child to begin thinking of her parents as vulgar and stupid. Such resentment—often exfoliating wildly in adolescence—may cast back in turn to even earlier pains, losses, and "slightings," the archaic, mostly suppressed traumas of infancy.

In this fraught psychic context the love of camp mediates, one might venture, between childhood outrage and a more sophisticated "adult" self. From one angle, camp objects summon up the detested paraphernalia of the *past*—they are emblems of that world of ugliness, dishonesty, and emotional bathos one prides oneself on having escaped or transcended. Camp is indeed *heimlich*—excruciatingly bound up with "home" in its negative aspect, the seemingly trashy, dreary, or love-starved parental milieu. Yet camp objects are also *unheimlich*—precisely because of the way, like mortifying phantoms, they can stand *in* for the parental.

The camp sensibility grows out of revulsion and disgust: you cringe at the thought of a fridge magnet in the shape of Michaelangelo's *David*; you recoil, listening to *Tristan*, when the onstage Isolde—fat and freaky—reminds you of your morbidly obese stepsister who lives in Van Nuys. At the same time, however, your repugnance elicits guilt. Some transvaluation of the negative emotion is necessary: some psychological revision. Hence what Sontag, in one of her essay's more saccharine asides, calls the affection, even "tenderness" with which camp objects or experiences are rehabilitated. ("Camp taste is a kind of love, love for human nature. It relishes, rather than judges, the little triumphs and awkward intensities of 'character.'") One purports to "adore" the very thing that at one time depressed, disgusted, mortified, frightened, etc., etc. "Fabulous" as she may be onscreen, who would *really* want Joan Crawford for his or her own "Mommie Dearest"? The appropriate real-world response to such a vile and selfish person—especially if she were in charge of looking after you—would be hatred or fear.

The homosexual theme in "Notes on Camp" is profoundly linked, I would argue, with the Sontagian "family romance" and helps, in turn, to explain the antipathy the essay evoked in its author later in life. Again, I intuit—but again, out of a kind of fellow feeling. Viewed in hindsight, the emphasis on homosexuality in "Notes on Camp" strikes me as spectacularly overdetermined—as part of a coy yet now-unmissable "coming out." Not that many readers would have absorbed it as such in 1964: though Sontag seems regularly to have referred to her "homosexuality" in her diaries of the 1950s and early 1960s—some astonishing portions of which recently appeared in the *New York Times* magazine—she refused, as everyone knows, to speak publicly about her lesbian relationships until late in life. There is nothing in the way of *explicit* autobiography in "Notes on Camp." The interested reader might still speculate, of course: reading and rereading the essay in the 1970s, in the first flushes of undergraduate sapphism, I inevitably lingered on what its author called the "mostly unacknowledged truth of taste"—that "the most refined form of sexual attractiveness (as well as the most refined form of sexual pleasure) consists in going against the grain of one's sex. What is most beautiful in virile men is something feminine; what is most beautiful in feminine women is something masculine." Breathtaking— especially for an impressionable twenty-two-year-old in Tacoma, Washington. *How does she know all this stuff?*

Considering the essay now, however, in light of later revelations, Sontag seems to me to signal her private investment in the homoerotics of camp quite blatantly from the start. Very hard, for me at least, not to hear an autobiographical note in the arch (and Wildean) first sentence: "Many things in the world have not been named; and many things, even if they have been named, have never been described." The unnamed "thing" in need of description will turn out to be camp, of course— and the love that "dare not speak its name" a love of lava lamps and Doris Day films. But one feels Sontag might just as well have said "my homosexuality"—the very love, intimately embraced, that she was not to name publicly for quite a few more decades.

I think one of Sontag's reasons for disliking "Notes on Camp" later was that it was just too obvious about her own erotic orientation: the gay "coding" and the in-jokes too blatant for comfort. (Almost all of the actresses, mentioned earlier, whom she associates with camp—Garbo,

Stanwyck, Bankhead, Edwige Feuillère—were either lesbian or bisexual in inclination or noted for playing lesbian characters. She might as well be semaphoring her sapphic tastes via such a listing.) By the mid-1990s, when Sontag's relationship with Annie Leibovitz had become celebrity fodder for *Time* and *Newsweek*, the essay had already lost much of its mystery. She was no doubt annoyed by its newfound transparency: to her, I believe, it was all old news.

But at a deeper level, I believe, the older Sontag repudiated camp (and indeed her own essay on the subject) precisely on account of its symbolic registration of fierce emotions—pain, fear, abandonment, rage— and its hidden connection with real or perceived victimization. Psychologically speaking, feigning delight in the ugly and appalling is a useful response to the problem of suffering. Homosexuality—still a premier source of emotional suffering in the modern world—is often bound up with it. If it is correct to see a childhood sense of "slight" as part of camp's psychic underpinning, it is hardly surprising that the camp sensibility should flourish among gay men and women. What sort of child, apart from one mental or physically disabled, is more likely than any other to elicit parental ambivalence or dislike? Who more likely to face neglect, mistreatment, or even outright rejection? Who more likely to associate "home" with abuse and humiliation? Most straight parents today still don't want a gay or lesbian child, even when they say they wouldn't mind.

There was a kind of hurt Sontag wished not to acknowledge— at least as part of her own emotional history. Throughout "Notes on Camp" Sontag contrasts the camp attitude with something she calls "moral seriousness." (Sometimes she particularizes it even further as "Jewish moral seriousness.") Camp "incarnates a victory of 'style' over 'content,' 'aesthetics' over 'morality,' of irony over tragedy." At some point in the 1950s and 1960s the young Sontag consciously committed herself, or course, to this kind of seriousness—the exploration of "content," "morality," and "tragedy." George Eliot, the female sage, was in the end her beacon, I think—not Oscar Wilde—and "Notes on Camp" part of the process by which she assumed the public mantle of moral authority. "Seriousness" was a way of being tough and invulnerable. She resented being seen as obsessed with camp—fixed in people's mind as camp's philosopher—because her essay was in the end more about exorcism than endorsement. Like the lifelong pleasure she took in chastising other people for what she saw as their moral and intellectual defects, the contempt she felt for the essay later in life grew, I think, out of a great well of self-critical feeling. Something was unbearable and at the deepest level she blamed herself.

chaptertwo

Absolute Seriousness
Susan Sontag in American Popular Culture

DANA HELLER

Introduction: Screen Tests I

In 1964, the pop artist Andy Warhol invited the intellectual Susan Sontag to his midtown Manhattan studio, the Factory. Thirty-one years old at the time, Sontag was riding the cool wave of celebrity that began with the publication of her first novel, *The Benefactor*, and escalated with the reception of her iconoclastic critical essays—above all, "Notes on Camp"—which were hailed as groundbreaking in their attentiveness to the intersections of high and low culture. A celebrated iconoclast in his own right, Warhol already had it on good authority that Sontag didn't care much for his paintings and distrusted his sincerity. But Warhol didn't care, since by his own admission he understood that "a lot of dazzling intellects felt that way." What did matter to him, more than Sontag's aesthetic pronouncements, was that she had "a good look— shoulder-length, straight dark hair and big eyes, and she wore very tailored things."[1] So he brought her to the Factory, where she sat for what would be the first of seven four-minute silent Screen Tests.

From 1964 through 1966, Andy Warhol shot hundreds of four-minute Screen Tests, many of which are still being discovered and all of which were conducted under the simple stipulation that their subjects sit still and remain silent while being photographed. Viewing these tests, we witness repeatedly the spectacle of the subject unraveled by the demands of patent objectification. Sontag's tests (archived as ST318–ST324) are no exception, as they show her visibly disturbed by the process of submitting herself to Warhol's notoriously distracted gaze.[2] Over the course of the tests she produces a range of expressions, from dread seriousness to playfulness, and from bashfulness to intimacy. The film quality highlights her restlessness as it moves in and out of focus, from overexposure to clarity. In 320 Sontag appears bored and tired; in 321 she is lively and smiling, shifting positions in her seat, flirting with the camera as she casts her eyes up and down. She dons dark sunglasses in 321 and 322, alternately removing and replacing them, although her eyes remain dimly visible behind them. Nowhere yet evident is the fierce self-command that will eventually make her book-cover and dust-jacket images recognizable around the world.

Warhol never did cast Sontag in any of his feature films, although he would produce a film that was indirectly about her. *Camp* (1965) satirized Sontag's famous essay by reclaiming the messy gay politics that are cleansed from her well-polished conceit. However, we could say that the Screen Tests unwittingly cast Sontag in a much larger role that she would spend the rest of her career negotiating with a mixture of pleasure, irritation, and ambivalence, as she herself became transformed into an iconic piece of popular culture. Moreover, we could say that Sontag's tests serve as discursive flashpoints of mid-twentieth-century debate between the defenders of intellectual seriousness and the new champions of postmodern banality. Accordingly, we might view them as symptomatic of the shifting social relations of power and knowledge that in the 1960s would require nothing less than the refashioning of a popular American myth: the intellectual.

I begin with Sontag's Screen Tests because I see them as recognizably linked to a larger, long-standing cultural narrative that questions the power and legitimacy of the intellectual in American life even as it affirms that power and legitimacy. This narrative, or variations of it, can be found in all arenas of cultural production, but nowhere is it portioned out more generously or reliably than in the realm we know as popular culture. Here, as Andrew Ross explains, the deep ambivalence that Americans have long felt toward intellectual hauteur registers in the incorporation of popular beliefs, opinions, longings, and indignations that are reorganized in the course of the narrative, however contradictorily, to legitimate the power of intellectuals or to resist and reimagine their influence over our lives.[3]

And I believe that Sontag herself—or rather her prominent and at times sharply controversial standing as America's most famous intellectual, "the dark lady of American letters"—was an inevitable product of this contradictory process that we find in popular culture. While not intended to dismiss or diminish the value of Sontag's many trenchant, albeit ambivalent observations on the popular arts, film, literature, and photography (topics that are covered by many of the contributors to this volume) this essay takes a somewhat different approach to understanding Sontag's place within American cultural history, a place negotiated in large measure through the ways in which popular arts manage to "talk back" to intellectual authority. To this end, in the pages that follow I will consider not what Sontag said about popular culture but rather what popular culture said about her. For I believe that both sides of this conversation need to be heard if we are to understand both the role of the intellectual in American culture and the role of popular culture in American intellectual life. I also believe that neither of these roles can be understood apart from a mythology without which people never could have championed Sontag as passionately or despised her as intensely as they did—and as they continue to do.

The Intellectual: An American Mythology

In *Left Intellectuals and Popular Culture in Twentieth-Century America*, Paul R. Gorman recounts the 1988 publication of a study by the federal Department of Education that was aimed at resolving once and for all the long-contested question of whether television was destroying America's children. After analyzing decades' worth of scholarship, investigators involved in the study arrived at a conclusion, albeit one far less skeptical of television than that of the so-called experts whose labors had been mobilized to gauge its effects. Indeed, the authors of the final report found that research had been "designed to support the foreordained conclusion that television was necessarily dangerous."[4] One investigator bluntly suggested that despite scant evidence, arguments against television "seemed to satisfy some kind of need among educated people."[5] These scholars seemed set on establishing, in the language of the report, "an American mythology" that might prove television's harmful effects not with any actual facts but with the vain hope that by repeating the unfounded claim often enough it might become accepted truth.

Reading between the lines, however, the study's findings also betray unmistakable aspects of an American mythology of intellectual fakery. Although he or she comes in many guises and forms, we know the model character who motivates the myth: irrelevant, elitist, and undemocratically invested with authority that permits the exploitation of knowledge for shady personal rather than public interests, the intellectual fraud is typically an affiliated member of the professional-managerial class, an agent of bureaucratic intractability, a mind machine as unmoving as the advanced technologies that he retains unlimited and exclusive access to. But we also recognize that this character is ultimately no less a product of institutionalized discourse than the narcotized child deranged by Muppets. In other words, the intellectual is in no small part a social fiction, a fantasy that gives pleasure and satisfies needs that are no less powerful, no less interested, and no less contradictory than the latent needs of the educated elite.

But here we confront a curious omission in the archives of historical knowledge, for while much has been written about American intellectuals' engagements with popular culture, little, it seems, has been written about popular culture's engagement with the American intellectual. The omission is surprising, especially when we follow Ross further in acknowledging that any history of American popular culture is "a history of intellectuals," a fact reflected not least of all in popular culture's fascination with intellectual heroes and antiheroes.[6] This fascination remains very much alive not in spite of our culture's increasingly hostile antirationalism—a condition lamented afresh in such recent jeremiads as Susan Jacoby's *The Age of American Unreason*—but precisely because of the need to continuously rejuvenate and rejustify it. To this end, intellectual heroes and antiheroes are persistently invoked within popular culture as lightening rods for debate over (among other things) the status of popular culture itself and its alleged dumbing-down effects. From the *New York Times* editorial page to Fox TV's *Are You Smarter Than a Fifth Grader?* these debates are anxious projections of a deeply ingrained distrust of intellectual authority and, at the same time, of an equally profound desire to accord respect to those who possess advanced knowledge.

Before anyone accuses me—a popular culture scholar—of spreading the disease for which I now propose a cure, let me say that the lack of attention to intellectuals in popular culture is worth taking seriously. To ignore it is to ignore the power of mass entertainments to influence our shared notion of the life of the mind along with our common understanding of who the intellectual is or might be. Arguably, this denial owes as much to the history of American anti-intellectualism as to the history of American intellectualism, a condition well documented in works such as Richard Hofstadter's study of the hegemonic shift in early American Christianity away from traditional, learned religious styles towards enthusiastic movements that held powerful sway with rural portions of the populace that had little formal schooling.[7] Eighteenth-century churches, once centers of refined literacy and enlightened moral and political debate, would be replaced by universities, colleges, and their established seminaries in what would amount to a sweeping institutional reorganization of American intellectual life.

While a comprehensive treatment of the complex history of American intellectual life is beyond the scope of this essay, it is fair to say that the modern image of the American intellectual as synonymous with secular left politics arises generally out of the development of organized labor, itself a response to late-nineteenth- and early-twentieth-century immigration and urbanization and the acceleration of an unchecked industrial capitalism that culminated in the crash of 1929. In the politically turbulent, war-riven decades that followed, intellectuals would gradually become integrated as service "experts" into the "cultural apparatus," C. Wright Mills's term for the new artistic, information, intellectual, entertainment, and scientific managers whose labors were increasingly tied to bureaucratic operations of state and corporate administration, despite the Popular Front's belief in a progressive culture-industry politics.[8] In Michael Denning's formulation, their absorption into the institutions of state and culture would be interpreted by generations of radical writers and intellectuals—from James Farrell, to the expatriate members of the Frankfurt School, to the critics of the anti-Stalinist left—as capitulation to what C. L. R. James would later term the "bureaucratic-administrative-supervising castes," a betrayal of struggling workers around the world and, worse, a rejection of the very essence of the unaffiliated intellectual.[9] Out of these debates, a heroic counterimage of an embattled, politically disenfranchised, and socially alienated intellectual emerged. This mythology, spun on the back of the American left's romantic reliance on "the classic modernist notion of the intellect as an unattached, avant-garde, and anti-bourgeois sensibility," would prove profoundly influential.[10] Not only would it shape the identities of future intellectual movements, including both the New Left and the conservative movements, but it would also inform popular culture's own vision of the heroic intellectual as isolated blue-collar victim of Sennett and Cobb's "hidden injuries of class"[11] (think of Matt Damon's character in *Good Will Hunting*) or of a romanticized, organic link between genius and mental disorder (think of Russell Crowe's portrayal of the schizophrenic mathematician John Nash in *A Beautiful Mind*).

Of course, what the left's intellectual mythology could not account for were far-reaching changes in American social and economic organization that, between the First and Second World Wars, would expose not only the ideological fault lines of modern industrial capital but the emerging postmodern fault lines of race, gender, sexuality, and ethnicity. The national triumph of mass education and mass culture, the Southern Migration, the Harlem Renaissance, and the declining influence of the Works Progress Administration and the Congress of Industrial Organizations all contributed, in varying degrees, to a realignment of the national labor anatomy. The funneling of W. E. B. Du Bois's "talented tenth"[12] into the new post-Fordist economy, in addition to the growth of economic sectors for educated women, the increasing visibility of gay and lesbian urban subcultures, and the integration of the children of second-wave immigrants into the growing class of "cultural workmen" (in Mills's phrase) opened up opportunities for many who did not identify as "fellow travelers" of the Popular Front.[13] Rather, they were creative agents of the "Commercial Front," whose haphazard journeys towards enfranchisement suggested at least the possibility of reclaiming intellectual commitments in the name of self-representation and ownership of the cultural apparatus, the essence of Harold Cruse's argument in *The Crisis of the Negro Intellectual* in 1967.[14] But the old cultural battle lines remained drawn, hardened by the divorce that was at least ideologically finalized in the 1940s split between the Leninists and the Trotskyists. That battle and the fog that lingered into the postwar period would, according to Denning, transform the term "intellectual" itself into a vacuous "honorific,"[15] a label that Susan Sontag, at the age of fifty-nine, would uncomfortably react to during a famous 1992 interview on *The Charlie Rose Show*. Rose, upon referring to Sontag as "America's leading intellectual," sees her expression of puzzlement and discomfort and asks, "Do you reject that?" "I would never want to deny the label intellectual," Sontag responds haltingly, "but . . . it's a sociological or journalistic label. . . . I never think of myself as an intellectual . . . well, if people want to be sociological about it, they call me an intellectual."[16]

The New York intellectuals of the postwar period would carry this discomfort forward, retaining a deep nostalgia for modernist authenticity and the interior voice of originality while denouncing the corruption of the new "sociological" class of middlebrow cultural workers, writers, and artists, even as they themselves contributed to its output as consultants, journalists, authors, and university instructors. Their distrust of the new intellectual breed, their sense of having lost control of the imprimatur as their due and inheritance, was in many ways a rarefied—albeit maligned—version of the populist distrust of expertise that had already giving rise to a mainstream commercial self-help industry, a response to the desire to reappropriate power from so-called skilled professionals, whose social authority suggested an increasing loss of autonomy and control over access to basic needs and the exercise of common know-how. To the extent that this resistance to authority—both in its rarefied and populist forms—has animated popular culture's representation of the intellectual, we can say that its mythologies derive as much from the defensiveness of anti-intellectual tastes as from the defensiveness—the sense of betrayal and deflation—that is part of American intellectual history. In other words, in the popular mythology of the intellectual, history from below boisterously bumps heads with history from above. And it is my contention that to be a public intellectual in the era of pop culture's hegemonic influence—an era that we might trace to the 1960s and to Sontag's ascendancy to the mantle of iconic tastemaker—is to lay bare the lumps, so to speak.

Of course, to accept this description of Sontag—and of the intellectual in general—is to accept her not as the flesh-and-blood woman that she was but as the complex and contradictory avatar into which she was discursively molded. It is also to accept a particular view of popular culture as never ideologically unified but rather dialectical, marked by incessant border skirmishes over questions of elitism and populism, power and subordination, knowledge and exclusion, resistance and consent. And those who came of age grateful for Sontag's defense of seriousness while at the same time immersed in a popular culture that gleefully cannibalizes everything in its wake could not help but follow with interest, if not amazement, the sensational incantations of the avatar.

But why, we might wonder, when so many forms of popular culture express outright contempt for the pretensions of educated tastes, should we who honor knowledge and ideas pay attention to their organization of scatological pleasures and mawkish satisfactions—all the unfiltered racist, sexist, and homophobic ranting—only to be gratified in discovering that Pierre Bourdieu was right about the "powerless power" of symbolic capital: a lesson we might as well have taken from our own intimate, day-to-day encounters with visceral skepticism? In my own case as a university teacher of popular culture, I am routinely faced with such encounters, both by the students who are outspokenly offended by the dopiness of *American Idol* and the students who righteously defend their guilty pleasures by balking at the seriousness with which the others take it. If they ever do agree, it is typically when they can concretely apprehend, however fleetingly, the inevitable contradictions that are part and parcel of living within consumer capitalism's cultural apparatus. Often, these contradictions come into focus as embodied media "figures"—well-known people such as politicians, celebrities, and noted intellectuals who function as "discursive relay stations" (to use John Fiske's term for bodies of discourse, either fictional or nonfictional, through which contests of circulated "meanings are made visible and audibly public").[17] By examining such "figures" as "discourse events"[18] rather than self-governing agents, enlightened critical practices and the most vulgar satisfactions can appear momentarily nonexclusive and perhaps even mutually constitutive. And it is here that we are most likely to discover what is truly at stake in the "new politics of popular knowledge."[19]

Screen Tests II

Contrary to the stock description of her as humorless, Susan Sontag could appreciate a good joke, or at least she understood the comedic dimensions of the cultural ambivalence toward intellectual seriousness. Why else would she have agreed to lampoon the public intellectual—or the documentary tradition of marshaling their solemn expertise—in Woody Allen's *Zelig*? The film, released in 1983, is a mockumentary that purports to trace the history of the "human chameleon" Leonard Zelig, who becomes a popular sensation in the 1920s as a result of his amazing ability to transform his physical appearance to resemble whatever kind of person he happens to be around. When his condition is discovered, Zelig is hospitalized and meets a young female psychiatrist, Dr. Eudora Fletcher (played by Mia Farrow). Dr. Fletcher discovers that the source of Zelig's uncanny ability is his powerful desire for approval and social acceptance. By the film's conclusion, she manages to cure Zelig, although it is love—far more than psychotherapy—that finally wins the day.

In *Zelig*, Sontag plays Sontag, appearing in cameo color segments that contrast with the black and white vintage footage that Allen alters through the use of blue-screen technology. Along with Irving Howe, Bruno Bettleheim, Saul Bellow, and John Morton Blum, Sontag provides her straight-faced assessment of the "Zelig" phenomenon in terms that echo her arguments in *Against Interpretation*. "I don't know if you could call it a triumph of psychotherapy," she says to the camera. "It seems more like a triumph of aesthetic instincts because Dr. Fletcher's techniques didn't owe anything to then current schools of therapy, but she sensed what was needed and she provided it. And that was in its way a remarkable creative accomplishment."[20]

Although generally read as a satirical critique of the malleable and alienated American character, *Zelig* is actually a parody of our cultural reliance on experts—medical, historical, aesthetic, and intellectual—to unify character and discourage the kind of radical self-determination that is Zelig's talent and his sickness. The film's conventional faith in love's curing properties underscores its academic inside joke that doctors and professors are necessary and yet somehow superfluous, mere middlebrow window dressing. And while Sontag's appearance in the film should not be mistaken for self-mockery—in fact, she took herself much too seriously for that—it can be appreciated as mockery of the insipid "sociological or journalistic" label that the culture had, in 1983, already officially assigned to her and what remained of her New York ilk. The age of the partisan intellectual as radical reformer was over. The "new" intellectual was an entertainer and commentator, a fig- ure comfortably in league with a trend-driven, consumer-oriented so- ciety. In this sense, what Sontag and her intellectual cohort perform in *Zelig* amounts to a kind of intellectual minstrelsy, as their cameos both disparage and reinforce the popular visual and mannerly affects through which late-twentieth-century America saw intellectuals—as tightly framed televised talking heads delivering ex-officio commentary in front of well-stocked library shelves on PBS broadcasts.

Above all, *Zelig* lampoons the myth-making processes through which American culture manufactures the aura of seriousness. In that sense, Sontag's appearance in the film may be ironic, although we can- not count it among the moments that made her iconic in her own right. These moments or, more precisely, the contradictory crisscrossing of publications, public appearances, academic urban legends, print pho- tographs, and secondhand commentary—all the things she said and all the things said about her—seemed, like Leonard Zelig, to mutate in relation to each new context as her career took dramatic turns and as the focus of her attention shifted away from the nouvelle roman and European revival houses to American foreign policy, freedom of ex- pression, the metaphor of illness, and her own literal battles with can- cer. Although she exerted marginal discursive control over the public's image of her, this never stopped her from intervening, quite haughtily at times, on her own behalf. Always, she was acutely aware of the prob- lems posed by the fact of being an attractive, brainy woman. When she arrived in New York and began writing for the *Partisan Review*, her "good look" and early expatriate existence in France spurred rumors that she had been Jean-Paul Sartre's mistress (she had *actually* lived in his former apartment in Paris) and prompted at least one unfortunate but probably inevitable reference to her as "a cross between a Jamesian heroine . . . and Audrey Hepburn in *Funny Face*."[21] In the United States, she became a poster girl for the academy's manufacturing of celebrity, a position foisted upon her by those who claimed to care about the fate of modernism and then used against her to diminish the seriousness of her work and to make her appear capricious and trivial. For example, in his acerbic review of her novel *Death Kit*, Ted Solotaroff describes her criti- cal tone as indecisive and irritating, similar indeed to "the celebrity that [she] appears to court with her left hand and disclaim with her right."[22] Later in her career, when Sontag spoke with evangelical decisiveness, as she increasingly did with respect to political morals, she was condemned as an opportunistic gold-star member of the "self-castigating left."[23] At times, Sontag was pressed to defend herself against her own proclamations, as when in late middle age she exempted her own gathering literary strength from her assertion that writers produce their best work in youth.[24] And in the end, even the things Sontag left unsaid became fodder for the tabloid apparatus: the fact that she had romantic relations with women during her life but chose not to "come out" publicly as a role model for seekers of lesbian and gay rights has been offered as evidence of self-loathing, hypocrisy, latent homophobia—and all conceivable combinations therein—by both the gay press and mainstream journalism. In fact, one of the first books on her life, the unofficial biography *Susan Sontag: The Making of an Icon*, amounts to a sensational (and mostly discredited) exposé of her romantic liaisons, her shortcomings as a mother to her only son, and her calculated efforts—along with her lifetime publisher Roger Straus—to create a public image of moral duty and drama.[25]

Of course, the cinematic moment that probably solidified Sontag's popular fashioning as a "discursive relay station" for the realignment of gender and power norms appears in the film *Bull Durham*, a 1988 romantic comedy about minor-league baseball players and fans. Kevin Costner stars as Crash Davis, a seasoned minor-league catcher who is hired by North Carolina's Durham Bulls to train a young rookie pitcher, played by Tim Robbins, for the major leagues. Their contentious relationship is further complicated by the introduction of Annie Savoy, played by Susan Sarandon. Annie, a part-time junior college professor and baseball groupie, selects one player every season as a bed partner and apprentice in the pursuit of aesthetic wisdom and bliss. Her initial expression of interest in both men is curtailed by Crash's refusal to "try out" for the role of her lover. And, in what has become the most referenced and revered scene in baseball film history, Crash rejects Annie's advances by telling her what he believes in.

> Well, I believe in the soul, the cock, the pussy, the small of a woman's back, the hanging curve ball, high fiber, good scotch, that the novels of Susan Sontag are self-indulgent over-rated crap, I believe Lee Harvey Oswald acted alone, I believe there ought to be a constitutional amend-

ment outlawing Astroturf and the designated hitter, I believe in the
sweet spot, soft-core pornography, opening your presents Christmas
morning rather than Christmas Eve, and I believe in long, slow, deep,
soft, wet kisses that last three days.[26]

In *Bull Durham*, the inevitable romantic dénouement is strangely fore-
told here, in a moment that establishes Crash's authenticity through a
demystification of Sontag's aura. Generally, the speech pits the earthy
pragmatism of baseball's masculine hero against the intellectual frigidity
of Modern Literature 101. However, the mismatched reference to Sontag's literary celebrity turns the speech into something slightly more personal, an assertion of conventional culture's sensual triumph over the
sterility of high culture. That an intellectual who was considered radical in the 1960s for championing soulful sensuality should be shrugged
aside by the late 1980s in defense of same is probably no less surprising
than the film's closing capitulation to the power of American letters. In
the final voice-over, Annie (who has abandoned her Cindy Lauper garb
for modest prairie attire) quotes from Walt Whitman on the national
virtues and healing properties of baseball. "You can look it up," she
assures us, although the point has already been driven home that fact
checks and footnotes are irrelevant to matters of the heart.

Bull Durham's Sontag is the empress who has no clothes, the fall
girl for what Kevin Myers, a British journalist who "ran into her once"
while covering the siege in Sarajevo, dubs "wretched, credulous, self-
hating American academia" and their misplaced values.[27] However, in
the post-Vietnam era, and again following her remarks on the misnam-
ing of the 9/11 pilots as "cowards," Sontag's name appears as a cipher
for anti-Americanism and a virulent sense of outrage against a perceived loss of white male authority resulting from civil rights, multicul-
turalism, affirmative-action policies, and the generalized feminization
of the culture and its time-honored institutions. This outrage finds expression in popular culture narratives that directly and indirectly challenge the institutional doctrine of "political correctness" and its logic
of entitlements. And this remains—to this very day, in fact—a criticism of an academic world against which Sontag routinely sought to repair her popular image. Indeed, of all the demeaning associations that
Sontag tirelessly defended herself against, the one that she persistently

debunked was her image as "academic" or, again in Solotaroff's words, "a lady English professor looking for signals in Paris."[28] This is not to say that Sontag thought she had nothing to teach people. In fact, she once assured an acquaintance of her son's that she could learn more living for a year in her apartment than she could learn in six years at an American university.[29] Throughout her career, despite occasional teaching and lecturing jobs that she accepted in order to pay bills and make a living, Sontag adamantly refused affiliation with the American university and especially with a professoriate for which she expressed frank distaste, at best, and unconcealed contempt, at worst. At times, she finessed this dissociation: "I am in part a product of the university culture," she explained in an interview. "Most books that I read are scholarly books. Most books that I own are published by university presses. But I don't operate within the bounds of the university. I don't have that kind of language and I don't have that view of the writer."[30] However, in less artful moments, she could be quite brutal about the derelictions of academic anemia: "I've seen the best writers of my generation destroyed by teaching," she is reported to have often remarked, in a pointed paraphrase of Allen Ginsberg's opening line from *Howl*.[31] In fact, the Beat reference may not be entirely coincidental, since she saw the academy as anathema to creativity.

Nevertheless, in American culture, Sontag's name remained largely synonymous with academia, and this shaped her image in accord with the tensions that underwrite popular culture's depiction of even our highest-ranking academic institutions. Again, we might recall Matt Damon's character in *Good Will Hunting*, a working-class autodidact who labors as a janitor at Harvard University, making a sparse living off the littered floors of the nation's elite institution of higher learning and secretly solving backbreaking mathematical problems left on the chalkboards of darkened classrooms. However, when his genius is discovered, we learn that Will's failure to harness the powers of his sizable brain is not the result of class disenfranchisement but psychological injury, more specifically, childhood abuse. Once again, the expertise of the psychiatric profession is called upon to provide the cure, which— thanks to the efforts of one genuinely caring Cambridge doctor, himself an abuse survivor—arrives in the form of Minnie Driver, a co-ed whose own fortunes lie out west, at Stanford Medical School. In the end, Will chooses to accompany her, leaving behind his painful past, an overzealous, self-absorbed professorial mentor, and many lucrative job offers that could assure his upward mobility.

Or take *Legally Blonde*, a 2001 film comedy recently adapted into Broadway musical that tells the unlikely story of Elle Woods, a wealthy California sorority girl and fashion major whose foremost passion is shopping and whose sole ambition is to marry her college boyfriend. When he breaks up with her after gaining acceptance to Harvard Law School, on the premise that he now needs to "get serious," she decides to win him back by following him to Cambridge, a strategy requiring that she, too, be admitted to Harvard. Through sheer determination and an application video that seduces the tweedy, bow-tied members of the admissions committee more with flesh than legal aptitude, Elle gains entrée to Harvard, where her snobbish classmates instantly dismiss her as a West Coast bimbo. In one particularly satirical scene, she is introduced to her cohort—a neurotic Russian literature major, a lesbian-feminist activist with a Ph.D. in women's studies, and a physicist who claims that Stephen Hawking stole his theory of the universe from his fourth-grade paper—all model members of academia's upper echelons.[32]

The linking of academic accomplishment with lunacy, sexual deviancy, feminist militancy, and megalomania is part of a fantasy in which the ivied aura of Harvard represents all that is most enviable and yet most unhealthy and cultish in the American mythology of the learned. Indeed, *Good Will Hunting* and *Legally Blonde* are films that center on innocents who, when given the chance to "get serious" among the nation's academic elite, survive by redefining knowledge in terms that harmonize structures of pleasurable human feeling with the rigors of thinking. But in the end, neither film suggests that their protagonists' lives would have been better without Harvard or without the benefits of rigorous learning. Despite anxieties about elitism and social inequality and despite their claims that antipathy toward intellectual institutions is justified, both films demonstrate that "doctors and professors and those who hold advanced degrees really do know best."[33] Thanks to the rigors of individual therapy, Will Hunting successfully completes an oedipal rite of passage that enables him to light out for the unknown territory of love's knowledge. And in *Legally Blonde*, Elle proves that Aristotle is not incompatible with Gucci, as she acquires theoretical and practical knowledge of the law that is wholly consistent with feminine consumer arts and individual empowerment yet allows her to assist women who lack power and social privilege. The intellectual mythology is thus re-worked to integrate the heroic image of expertise with the buoyant beat of neoliberal gender equality.

Conclusion: Modernism, She Wrote

In *The Mask of Socrates*, Paul Zanker begins where this essay ends, with the recognition that every society and "every age creates the type of intellectuals that it needs."[34] In our own age, I believe that creative process plays out vigorously, although not always successfully, in our popular arts through the ongoing reorganization of contradictory values and viewpoints that speak to the American past as well as to the present, to the discourse of common sense as well as to the nobility of learned seriousness, and to a native anti-intellectualism that distrusts authority as well as to our inevitable need for and reliance on intellectual expertise. And although popular culture lays bare the contradictions, its stories cannot tell us—as audiences, critics, and fans—what finally to make of them. As Ross acknowledges:

> Some of the audience may, in fact, take to heart the discourse of disrespect, take it home and apply it in confronting or negotiating with figures of authority, while, for others, it may only cement their respect for the naturalized authority of experts. But the stories won't do any of these things if they don't provide the pleasures of recognition and identification, *of knowing one's place*: in this case, identification with the pleasure that arises from imagining oneself in control of one's environment and contesting others' usurpation of that control, even as that fantasy is devalorized.[35]

However, while some of us, like Ross, have diligently followed intellectual treatments of popular culture as sites of contestation, popular culture has been treating intellectuals as sites of contestation for its own populist purposes. These two treatments are actually linked materially as well as symbolically, and to see them operating together is to better understand not only the range and ubiquity of debate over discrepancies of knowledge and power in American society, but to understand more fully than we yet have the speed and depth of changes in the social blueprint for the kind of intellectual that society needs to make for its survival, changes that left Sontag admittedly stranded in her own lifetime.

She admitted it in 1979, when she addressed—without naming it as such—the paradigm shift that would come to be known as "the postmodern turn." Modernism, she wrote, had in the final analysis, "proved acutely compatible with the ethos of an advanced consumer society."[36] Indeed, the culture industries were either writing off aesthetic seriousness altogether or incorporating its techniques into their own corporate proliferation of vulgar satisfactions. But what Sontag did not prognosticate quite as clearly was that the intellectual, stripped of her heroic adversarial stature, had also become necessarily commoditized, a feature of the highbrow lifestyle that had been remade, packaged, and sold in accord with advanced consumer capitalism's niche-marketing tactics. And while I imagine that she would reject the notion, Sontag had become by the end of her long career a franchise, a solid brand name created by a culture that needed her to serve both as specialist and as corporate decoration. She was aware of this and could never wholly reconcile herself to the compromises that she made. "Beckett wouldn't do it," she'd reportedly say when debating with herself over whether to accept television appearances or an interview in *People* magazine.[37] But she did accept these invitations because to refuse would be a retreat into a culture that simply no longer existed. And she had encouragement. For example, it was her partner, the photographer Annie Leibovitz, who convinced her that a PR photo she'd taken of her seated at her desk might be appropriately and subtly retouched for Absolut Vodka's ad campaign. The ad made a limited appearance in 2000, showing Sontag gazing off dreamily into the distance, while on the desk immediately before her, as if it were one of her own manuscripts, sits Absolut's 1991 ad featuring only a black thumbprint on white with copy reading, "Absolut Evidence" (see fig. 3). Her novel, *In America*, is positioned visibly on the desk also, which reinforces the sense that the Absolut ad is something that she might have created.

Of course, the ad is open to many possible interpretations. Just as Absolut sought to leave its hauteur thumbprint on the art and marketing worlds with its revolutionary advertising campaigns, Sontag here lends her own imprint to the culture's successful suturing of high culture to elite consumer patterns. After her death, the Absolut ad was pointedly remarked upon by several eulogists, almost as if it provided Absolute

Figure 3 "Absolut Evidence," Absolut Vodka ad. *Source*: Under permission by V&S Vin & Sprit AB (publ). Absolut vodka. Absolut country of Sweden vodka and logo, Absolut, Absolut bottle design and Absolut calligraphy are trademarks owned by V&S Vin & Sprit AB (publ). ©2008 V&S Vin & Sprit AB (publ).

Evidence that Sontag had finally sold out to the commercial pop culture she'd come to despise, despite her youthful appreciations of certain popular forms. But in fact, these eulogies tell us far less about Sontag than they do about the kind of intellectual that our society may no longer need to create for itself. The question I want to end this essay with, then, is what kind of intellectual will we need to make in an age of savvy global consumerism, the seemingly intractable unaccountability of state and corporate interests, and mass culture's blunt immunity to the complex and compelling intellectual labors that have historically shaped the national identity? One possible answer is that we look to the technological and cultural labors of alternative wired communities working within the niche spaces of a largely commercialized digital infrastructure. A new generation of creative global intellectuals—fully networked and understanding of the unfinished histories they represent—is reshaping the cultural debate over knowledge and power, subordination and exclusion. In contexts that may not reveal their individual identities, they are nevertheless inventing the concepts and acquiring the recognitions that will provide the basis for current and future social dialogue.

How will popular culture speak of Sontag in the future? My thought is that if popular culture once stripped Sontag of her authority it will be popular culture that gives it back to her—if we only know where to look. Granted, YouTube may not be the Thalia and MySpace may not be the *Partisan Review*, but they do have the undeniable advantage of reaching beyond the social, geographical, and mythological limits of New York City. Indeed, what we can find here are spaces for the investigation of new intellectual mythologies, activities, and passions, along with creative and often surprising interventions against corporate authority and coercive ideological control. Some of these spaces are disdainful, some respectful, while some acknowledge that disdain and respect go hand in hand in the American politics of knowledge. For example, listed under "entertainment" on YouTube, Sandy Wells has produced and posted a tribute to Susan Sontag that features, in Wells's own words, "photos from [Sontag's] life taken by many notable photographers over the years and illegally harvested off the internet and edited . . . without copyright agreements or likewise for the sole purpose of appropriating the beautiful Susan Sontag to the world. So, sue me."[38] The video, which imagines Sontag as a darker and more furrow-browed Lady Di, is set to Luther Vandross's cover of the Letterman's "Going Out of My Head," and it concludes with the caption: "Susan Sontag was one of the most brilliant philosophical, yet simultaneously—albeit privately—tragic figures of our era." What exactly Wells believes to have been the apocalyptic tragedy of a life successfully lived and long to be remembered is unclear. But the pure longing for iconic seriousness—the almost mythical desire to fashion an image of intellectual immortality—belongs to everyone.

Notes

1. Andy Warhol and Pat Hackett, *POPism: The Warhol '60s* (New York: Harcourt Brace Jovanovich, 1980), 88.
2. Callie Angell, *Andy Warhol Screen Tests: The Films of Andy Warhol: Catalogue Raisonné*, vol. 1 (New York: Abrams, 2006), 188–93.
3. Andrew Ross, *No Respect: Intellectuals and Popular Culture* (New York: Routledge, 1989).
4. Paul Gorman, *Left Intellectuals and Popular Culture in Twentieth-Century America* (Chapel Hill: University of North Carolina Press, 1996), 1.
5. Gorman, *Left Intellectuals and Popular Culture*, 1.
6. Ross, *No Respect*, 5.
7. Richard Hofstadter, *Anti-Intellectualism in American Life* (New York: Knopf, 1963).
8. C. Wright Mills, *Power, Politics, and People: The Collected Essays* (New York: Oxford University Press, 1963), 406.
9. C. L. R. James, *American Civilization*, ed. Anna Grimshaw and Keith Hart (Cambridge, Mass.: Blackwell, 1993), 258.
10. Michael Denning, *The Cultural Front: The Laboring of American Culture in the Twentieth Century* (London: Verso, 1996), 109.
11. Richard Sennett and Jonathan Cobb, *The Hidden Injuries of Class* (New York: Knopf, 1972).
12. W. E. B. Du Bois, *The Souls of Black Folk: Essays and Sketches* (Chicago: A.C. McGlurg & Co., 1903), 105.
13. Mills, *Power, Politics, and People*, 418.
14. Harold Cruse, *The Crisis of the Negro Intellectual* (New York: William Morrow, 1967).
15. Denning, *The Cultural Front*, 109.
16. *The Charlie Rose Show*, "A Remembrance of Intellectual Susan Sontag," PBS, Broadcast January 7, 2005. Archived at http://www.charlierose.com/view/interview/1098, accessed March 5, 2008.
17. Jennifer Hyland Wang instructively defines and deploys Fiske's concept of "figures" in "A Struggle of Contending Stories: Race, Gender, and Political Memory in *Forrest Gump*," *Cinema Journal* 39, no. 3 (2000): 93. Fiske's discussion is found in *Media Matters: Everyday Culture and Political Change* (Minneapolis: University of Minnesota Press, 1994), 24.
18. Fiske, *Media Matters*, 6.

19. Ross, *No Respect*, 231.

20. Woody Allen, *Zelig*, feature film, Orion Pictures, 1983 (DVD: MGM, 2001).

21. David Denby, "The Moviegoer: Susan Sontag's Life in Film," *New Yorker*, September 12, 2005, http://www.newyorker.com/archive/2005/09/12/050912crat_atlarge, accessed March 4, 2008.

22. Ted Solotaroff, "Interpreting Susan Sontag," in *The Red Hot Vacuum and Other Pieces on the Writing of the Sixties* (New York: Atheneum, 1970), 261.

23. See, for example, Richard Wolin, "September 11 and the Self-Castigating Left," *South Central Review* 19, no. 2/3 (2002): 39–49.

24. *The Charlie Rose Show*, "A Remembrance."

25. Carl Rollyson and Lisa Paddock, *Susan Sontag: The Making of an Icon* (New York: Norton, 2000).

26. Ron Shelton, *Bull Durham*, feature film, Orion Pictures, 1988 (DVD: MGM, 2002).

27. Kevin Myers, "I Wish I Had Kicked Susan Sontag," Telegraph.co.uk, January 2, 2005, http://www.telegraph.co.uk/comment/3613939/I-wish-I-had-kicked-Susan-Sontag.html, accessed March 4, 2008.

28. Solotaroff, "Interpreting Susan Sontag," 262.

29. Sigrid Nunez, "Sontag Laughs," *Salmagundi*, no. 152 (2006): 14.

30. Charles Ruas, *Conversations with American Writers* (New York: Knopf, 1985), 196.

31. Nunez, "Sontag Laughs," 16.

32. Robert Luketic, *Legally Blonde*, feature film, Metro-Goldwyn-Mayer, 2001 (DVD: MGM, 2001).

33. Ross, *No Respect*, 3.

34. Paul Zanker, *The Mask of Socrates: The Image of the Intellectual in Antiquity*, trans. Alan Shapiro (Berkeley: University of California Press, 1995), 1.

35. Ross, *No Respect*, 4.

36. Denby, "The Moviegoer," 6.

37. Nunez, "Sontag Laughs," 16.

38. Sandy Wells, "Susan Sontag," youtube.com, posted March 24, 2007, http://www.youtube.com/watch?v=81cgYC5056Y, accessed March 4, 2008.

chapterthree

"Not Even a New Yorker"

Susan Sontag in America

BARBARA CHING

I love to travel, in every sense of the word, rather more intellectually than literally, but also literally. . . . I also like to come back; I'm always coming back to my country.
—*Conversations with Susan Sontag*

In spite of her fame, Susan Sontag revealed little of herself to the public. She wrote her groundbreaking work *Illness as Metaphor* (1989) without mentioning that her father had died of tuberculosis and that she herself was suffering from cancer, the two diseases discussed at length in the book. Her first essay collection, *Against Interpretation* (1966), which famously argues for an "erotics of art," says little about the author's personal tastes or experiences. Indeed, Sontag agonized over the amount of self-exposure required to sustain her career as an American writer and intellectual. "Beckett wouldn't do it" was her touchstone and whip, recalls friend Sigrid Nunez, as she reluctantly agreed to magazine interviews and television appearances.[1] But unlike Beckett, who left Ireland to live as a French writer, the well-traveled Sontag chose round trips over emigration and exile. No wonder, then, that when she did reveal herself directly, in emotional moments during interviews, in her "Trip to Hanoi" essay (1968), in the short stories collected in *I, Etcetera* (1978), in her memoir "Pilgrimage" (1987), and in the opening pages of *The Volcano Lover* (1992) and *In America: A Novel* (2000), she frequently expresses shame and embarrassment.

Her childhood "in the farthest reaches of provincial America" seemed to shame her (*CSS*, 145).[2] She longed for the urbane sophistication of the European intellectual and grew up to claim her fame as an analyst of the cosmopolitan and the contemporary. But as my epigraph indicates, Sontag's round trips—the constant "return to my country"— also defined her and her work. Taking my cue for reading an intellectual career from Sontag's method in *Under the Sign of Saturn*, where she states that "one cannot use the life to interpret the work. But one can use the work to interpret the life" (111), in this essay, I draw a portrait of Sontag the American.[3] I will focus on self-reflexive and self-revealing moments in her work when she optimistically portrays herself not as a misplaced European but rather as an American provincial who hopes that her country's birth in revolution allows an ethics and aesthetics untainted by the sophistication and sad history of the old continent. Drawing attention to the moments when Sontag avows her American roots, I argue that these are also the moments when she wholeheartedly feels and professes her commitment to *both* ethics and aesthetics. Reading both major works and obscure occasional pieces, I argue that Sontag's ethical commitment to a revolutionary rustication became more pronounced and more connected to American ideals as her career progressed—even as she was ever more scandalously accused of anti-Americanism for her expressions of dismay about 9/11 and its aftermath. Finally, I will argue that her conception of literature, another ideal that grew in importance to her, however rooted in European masters, merges into her American idealism. Although she never gave up what she called the "Idea of Europe," which she defined as "the polyphonic culture within whose traditions, some of them, I create and feel and think and grow restless, and to whose best, humbling standards I align my own" (*WSF*, 285), she significantly subtitled her 1988 speech on this subject "One More Elegy."

Pilgrimages

"Pilgrimage" (1987), an account of a visit Sontag and a friend paid to Thomas Mann while they were high-school students in southern California, exemplifies this nexus of American roots, deeply rooted shame, and a budding skepticism about the "idea of Europe." Published in the *New Yorker*, the first line announces that "everything that surrounds my meeting with him has the color of shame" (38). While critics such as Sohnya Sayres and Susan Suleiman cite this memoir to argue that Sontag's ethics and aesthetics were primarily European,[4] I underscore the ways in which Sontag's shame grows out of her disillusion with European ideals. Although the gap in their status explains some of her discomfort—she is a mere student at North Hollywood High while "Thomas Mann was not a Californian but the presiding genius of the Magic Mountain, Europe"—disappointment also plays a role. The young Sontag seems already aware that Mann's Europe no longer exists even though reading *The Magic Mountain* allows her to exult in the "discoveries and recognitions" it contains. "All of Europe fell into my head—though on the condition that I start mourning it," she notes (42). When she comes face to face with this European god rusticating in southern California, she again confronts the decay of Europe. She has to repress her disappointment with the frail man who greets them, speaks in phrases that have already suffused his essays and public pronouncements, and, worse, condescendingly treats them as if they are "representative" (rather than exceptional) Americans, fans of Hemingway and Jack London (53).

Most intriguing, though, is the way that this meeting with a European idol prompts Sontag to cast herself as a criminal guilty of despising the life that America offered her. She both opens and closes "Pilgrimage" by calling attention to the shame and hubris of aspiring to emulate a European writer.[5] Drafts of the memoir reveal that she chose the title "Pilgrimage" late in the composition process; the original title, "Doing Time," emphasizes crime and punishment.[6] She describes herself as an imposter in her family home, wearing a girlish "casing of affability" (38). Her omnivorous reading habits wreak symbolic violence on her parents since "to read was to drive a knife into their lives" (38). Her escape into literature also mirrors stealth in several forms. Recounting her bookstore visits, she confesses that she stole books when her allowance ran out: "Each of my occasional thefts cost me weeks of self-revilement and dread of future humiliation" (39). During the visit to Mann, awed by his book collection, she lets her friend do the talking while she tried "to case the library" (48).

The last paragraph of "Pilgrimage" reinforces Sontag's guilt and subsequent repentance by averring that "I never told anyone of the meeting" even as the memoir, now complete, tells everyone (54). The denouement also implies that Sontag paid her debt to society since she compares herself to a friend from this era who ended up doing time in San Quentin. At the same time, his incarceration contrasts to her own liberation. He literally does time while Sontag's metaphoric prison sentence comes to an end when she leaves California for the University of Chicago. Her childhood over, she begins to enjoy a life much like the one she imagined for herself at age fourteen, although that life unfolds not in Europe but in other parts of America (53). This journey, I would argue, is also a "pilgrimage." As Sontag moves across America, Mann moves away. And although she describes his return to Europe as a release from prison, her language also hints at a fall. He "had been doing time here" only to return to the "*somewhat leveled* magic mountain of Europe for good" (54; emphasis added). Conversely, she concludes the memoir by looking into her own brighter future, modulating into rhapsodic clarity as she announces that she has not yet identified the final stop on her journey. Her admiration for Mann, like her admiration for other artists, she says, liberated her "from childhood's asphyxiations."

Unlike Mann, who moved back, Sontag moves forward, toward a "far horizon" (54). The pilgrimage takes Sontag's favorite form, as described in my epigraph, a trip that ends at home, back in her country. Thus, once she becomes a world-famous writer herself, Sontag accepts—even chooses to suffer—heightened forms of the intrusive indignity that she felt she had thrust upon Mann. Neither Mann nor Beckett wrote memoirs, but Sontag, with "Pilgrimage," explicitly did so. In a 1997 letter to Stephen Dowden about the inclusion of "Pilgrimage" in his *Companion to Thomas Mann's Magic Mountain*, she insists that "it's a memoir—not, as you call it in your letter, an 'essay'—so do reassure me that you're not referring to it as an essay in any descriptive material about the contents of your volume."[7] In offering these revelations, Sontag plays the role of writer greeting her public, not only because she, like Mann, is a famous writer, but more importantly, because she is an American. To refuse, she explains, would be "as if I were saying to everybody, 'I am superior to all of you.' The democrat in me with a small 'd' could not bear it. After all, I'm not even a New Yorker. I

Figure 4 Sontag and Rieff show off their western-wear collection. *Source*: Photograph by Thomas Victor. Courtesy of Harriet Spurlin, the estate of Thomas Victor.

grew up in Southern Arizona and California; and I would just laugh at myself" (*CSS*, 181). While it once pained her to have Thomas Mann see her as a representatively rugged American aesthete pondering Hemingway and London, as a writer she embraces this provincial democracy—most obviously in a 1978 *People* magazine profile in which she and son David Rieff represent themselves as Americans by showing off their collection of western wear (see fig. 4).

Coming Back to My Country

Throughout her career, Sontag revisited her complex and productive affiliation with European cosmopolitanism and American provincialism. "In matters of beauty," Sontag wrote, "we are all born country bumpkins."[8] To remedy the situation, she conducted a sort of charm school in her earliest publications. Distinguishing herself from the New York intellectuals who reigned over the *Partisan Review*,[9] Sontag displayed her Europhilia even as she drew energy and an audience from the mass mediation of American culture. She got America to take note of camp, explained "happenings," and in an essay that appeared in *Mademoiselle* before it capped off her first essay collection (*Against Interpretation*), she advocated for a "new sensibility" that could appreciate equally the "beauty of a machine . . . the solution to a mathematical problem . . . a painting by Jasper Johns . . . a film by Jean-Luc Godard, and . . . the personalities and music of the Beatles" (*AI*, 304). She combined this didactic aestheticism with political activism in 1964 when she began to participate in the antiwar movement. At the same time, she subtly began to return from an intellectual journey to Europe. She obliquely narrates this development in the sequencing of her second essay collection, *Styles of Radical Will* (1969), which also demonstrates her movement from the Europeanized cultural avant-garde to American political radicalism. Although the essays originally appeared between 1966 and 1968, the book does not merely collect them; rather than republishing them in the order in which they appeared, the arrangement instead progressively amplifies Sontag's doubts about the political and ethical efficacy of modern art, or perhaps art itself, especially in its irony-drenched European modes (such as that exemplified by Thomas Mann and other European masters).[10] Without a preface or introduction to set expectations, the collection allows the reader to experience the movement from impersonal meditations on the dilemmas of modern art to a closing section containing two more personal *and* more political essays.

The book opens in a European mode with "The Aesthetics of Silence" (1967), an essay that concludes with an abstract expression of Sontag's concerns: "there still remains a question as to how far the resources of irony can be stretched. It seems unlikely that the possibilities of continually undermining one's assumptions can go on unfolding indefinitely into the future, without eventually being checked by despair or by a laugh that leaves one without any breath at all" (34). In the middle of the collection, "Theatre and Film" (1966) begins by arguing that the critical distinctions between the two art forms have been oversimplified. Yet Sontag concludes with an arresting jolt away from her complex discussion of radical positions on these specific art forms to embrace a form of simplification that she originally appeared to condemn. Adopting an oracular tone, she declares broadly, "For some time, all useful ideas in art have been extremely sophisticated. . . . We need a new idea. It will probably be a very simple one. Will we be able to recognize it?" (122).[11]

The last section of the collection recounts her own moment of recognition and places it in America. It begins with "What's Happening in America," a questionnaire in which Sontag stridently denounces Western civilization ("the white race is the cancer of human history") and declares that "this is a doomed country." This despair, however, dissolves in the next essay, the book's last. Written two years after the questionnaire, "Trip to Hanoi" describes the style of radical will that Sontag chooses. Clearly setting the stage for the resolution of a dilemma, she opens by noting that when she received an invitation to visit Hanoi, she had not yet found a way to entwine her writing with her "radical political convictions" (205). She had not expected her trip to do that for her, either, and had undertaken it with no plans to write about it. Her initial impression of the Vietnamese, who all seem to speak in repetitive revolutionary slogans without a trace of doubt or irony, only confirms her frustration. "What's painfully exposed for me, by the way the Vietnamese talk, is the gap between ethics and aesthetics," she complains (217). In an observation presaging lines she would write about her reaction to the flesh and blood Thomas Mann, she describes her jejune emotional reaction: "The first experience of being there absurdly resembled meeting a favorite movie star . . . and finding the actual person so much smaller, less vivid, less erotically charged" (209).

The trip, however, disrupts the hackneyed ironic narrative of innocence followed by experience followed by disillusion. Instead, Sontag tells about renewed idealism, offering an interesting contrast to "Pilgrimage" (written after, but taking place before, her journey to Hanoi). As she did in her visit to Mann, she feels typecast as a representative American; here, however, she admits just how American she is. "They may be nobler, more heroic, more generous than I am, but I have more on my mind than they do. . . . My consciousness . . . is a creature . . . accustomed to being fed by a stream of cultural goods, and infected with irony. . . . The gluttonous habits of my consciousness prevent me from being at home with what I most admire and—for all my raging against America—firmly unite me to what I condemn" (223). Because she does in fact benefit from America as it stands, her trip to Hanoi, like her visit to Thomas Mann, results in another confession of symbolic theft or imposture. She feels like "a fraud" (213) and begins to "question [her] right to profess a radical politics at all" (227). She can claim her right to radicalism when she realizes that her time in Hanoi, a consciousness-transforming, mind-altering, and stumbling, humiliating "trip," taught her to identify with the Vietnamese. As she traces their democratic and optimistic outlook to their history of "fiercely independent peasantry" (261), she decides that their history offers her a model for being American.[12]

The metaphor Sontag chooses to reclaim her idealism actually articulates the link to travel and tripping: "It's hard to step over one's feet," she declares (272), but the North Vietnamese leave footsteps that she can follow. After "renounc[ing . . . her] conviction of the inevitability of irony" (237), she can revise her opinion about Vietnamese simplicity, asserting that "it is not simple . . . to hope without self-mockery" (263). Such hope for a better communal future, she concludes, defines patriotism (as opposed to chauvinism), and if the Vietnamese can experience it, she could, too (266). In Vietnam, she decides, sincerity (as opposed to irony) is not a reflection of an oppressive linguistic restriction but rather "a mode of ethical aspiration" which gives her "intimations . . . of the possibility of loving my own country" (269). Compare this conclusion, in both style and content, to her commentary in "Notes on Camp," written five years previously: "One is drawn to camp when one realizes that sincerity is not enough. Sincerity can be simple philistinism, intellectual narrowness" (AI, 288). In Hanoi, Sontag reconfigures the relations between sophistication and simplicity, making them potential allies rather than opposing sensibilities. Indeed, it is possible to argue that she never again wrote anything as complex as "The Aesthetics of Silence."

To be both radical and patriotic, she recognizes, will require her to give up her "old posture of alienation," the very posture that Thomas Mann strikes in California and that she explores, admires, and undermines in the European heroes she limned in the first part of Styles of Radical Will and even later in Under the Sign of Saturn.[13] Indeed, in Under the Sign of Saturn, she conflates irony and alienation. As she introduces Walter Benjamin's belief that "irony is the most European of all accomplishments," she asserts that "irony is the positive name which the melancholic gives to his solitude, his asocial choices" (133). Alienation, then, is the negative name, and such criticism may contribute to the shame she expresses in "Pilgrimage" as she remembers her encounter with master ironist Mann. In this respect, the final title choice, "Pilgrimage," shows Sontag still drawing upon the "resources of irony," a tone that suits the evocation of her Europe-besotted past. Writing about her own experience in Hanoi gave Sontag a creative release from alienation. In 1973, she wrote a preface to the Vietnamese translation of "Trip to Hanoi" confirming the cultural revolution the trip had wrought in her. "Everything that I have written now seems to group itself as before or after "Trip to Hanoi." Although she confesses that she initially adopted a "subjective tone" as a rhetorical "tactic" to increase audience appeal and originality (since the American public already had scores of books and articles about Vietnam available), she concludes that she has "evolved" enough to say that "on this second trip to Hanoi, I feel as if I have returned home."[14]

Just as Sontag's visit to Thomas Mann ultimately undermined her fealty to the European pantheon, her "Trip to Hanoi" leads her to the horizon of her own literary tradition. In his reading of this essay, Leo Marx notes that Sontag structures her narrative according to "a well-established American design," a "hybrid joining traditional pastoralism and the nineteenth-century travel romance."[15] Indeed, as he notes, she seems almost embarrassed to find a "pastoral ideal" in North Vietnam. "If some of what I've written evokes the very cliché of the Western left-wing intellectual idealizing an agrarian revolution that I was so set on not being, I must reply that a cliché is a cliché, truth is truth, and direct experience is—well—something one repudiates at one's peril. In the end I can avow that armed with these very self-suspicions, I found, through direct experience, North Vietnam a place which, in many respects, deserves to be idealized" (SRW, 259). Earlier, she described it as an "ethical fairy tale where I am paying a visit, and in which I do believe" (215). In this very revelation, Marx argues, Sontag distinguishes herself from other American pastoralists who ironize the literary convention that Sontag here sincerely avows.[16] As an example, Marx cites Robert Frost's conclusion to "New Hampshire": "Well, if I have to choose one or the other, I choose to be a plain New Hampshire farmer / With an income in cash of, say, a thousand / (From, say, a publisher in New York City)."[17] In contrast, Sontag struggles against an easy retreat into the aesthetic with her embarrassing self-revelation, particularly of her own reluctance to give up intellectual luxuries like irony and well-stocked private book collections subsidized by New York publishing houses.

Letters from Home

Intellectual and real journeys to Thomas Mann's home and to Hanoi allowed Sontag to step over her own feet but also caused her to reflect on what it means to be at home in America. More importantly, the homecomings allowed her to enact the irony-eschewing "mode of ethical aspiration" she observed in Hanoi: she turns away from the aesthetics of silence, transforming her experience into personally revealing prose. In the last sentence of "Trip to Hanoi," Sontag reports that "what happened to me in North Vietnam did not end with my return to America, but is still going on" (274). Retrospectively, she also realized that the decision to write about herself in "Trip to Hanoi," undertaken at the time as a "conscious sacrifice" gave her "a certain freedom as a writer" that she carried into her later autobiographical fiction (CSS, 124) and, more concretely, into her word choices, what she calls "linguistic decisions" (SRW, 217). While many writers labor over the "mot juste," the decisions that Sontag places under this rubric involve choosing historically, politically, and personally laden terms and using them without irony in order to merge ethics and aesthetics. She uses, for example, "some elements of Marxist or neo-Marxist language" that she had earlier renounced (and would renounce again later) because of their past use as "a tool in the hands of dishonest people" (217).[18] The use of the word "trip," too, with its evocation of both stumbling and recreational drugs, resonates more deliberately than, say, "journey" or "voyage" or even "pilgrimage." Glossing the word in *Illness as Metaphor* (1978), she notes "it is not an accident that the most common metaphor for an extreme psychological experience viewed positively—whether produced by drugs or by becoming psychotic—is a trip" (36). The act of writing, for her, can even be such an experience. Indeed she confesses that she occasionally resorts to amphetamines to get her own writing moving;[19] thus publicly recounting her trips extends them to her audience.

Her experience of homecoming, "viewed positively," resonates in her use of the ideologically and idealistically charged word "America" in *Styles of Radical Will*. In the last two essays, she rarely refers to her country as the "United States," although she will use the term as an adjective (such as "U.S. foreign policy"). The slight twist Sontag gave to the title of "What's Happening in America" subtly indicates her commitment. When her response to this questionnaire appeared in the *Partisan Review* (1966), the title (created by the editors) was the more sinister and fatalistic "What's Happening *to* America." As she concludes her response, she praises the youth movement, proclaiming that these "young people . . . are alienated as Americans" (204) as opposed, implicitly, to the detached European style of alienation. Neither traitors nor expatriates, dissident youth participate in the American tradition of "inflaming people, from Emerson and Thoreau to Mailer and Burroughs." She hopes for "an incredible burst of creativity" from this "powerful but frustrated spiritual energy" (203).

She explored some fruits of this spiritual energy in 1975, in a largely forgotten but at the time widely distributed *Vogue* article written with Rieff, "Notes on Optimism" (see fig. 5), one of eighteen short pieces on the topic solicited by the magazine. Modeling an intergenerational faith in the future, mother and son pronounce America a "uniquely promising place" and "the freest country on the planet."[20] Although they praise European artists of despair such as Francis Bacon and Beckett, their examples of optimism rely on American radical will such as the protests that brought an end to participation in the Vietnam war. Drafts reveal that work on the essay recapitulated the movement from sophisticated to simple that "Trip to Hanoi" narrates. An early version took the form of a Socratic dialogue entitled "In the Last Days of the Republic." Socrates, philosophizing peripatetically outside of a Chase Manhattan bank, meets up with Glaucon and Aidemantus (from Cleveland) and leads them to lunch at McDonald's. Over cheeseburgers, he praises the value of optimism while they praise his irony.[21] In the straightforward final version, Sontag and Rieff use a title and form that echoes "Notes on Camp." But "Notes on Optimism" proposes a broader argument to a broader audience, unironically praising the communal action brought about by free Americans, a very different group from those who share the urban, cliquish, "disengaged, depoliticized" camp sensibility (*AI*, 277).

How to be an optimist now

Start by tuning out the me-too gloomsayers; then, read this encouraging eight-page section: eighteen top thinkers—Pulitzer Prize winners, best-selling authors, respected minds—explaining their reasons for optimism in 1975, ways you can think positively about America's future.

NOTES ON OPTIMISM

Susan Sontag and David Rieff

"Yes, Virginia, there are alternatives to despair"

David Rieff is a young writer (b. 1952) living in New York. Susan Sontag (b. 1933), a writer (examples: Death Kit, 1967; Journey to Hanoi, 1969; both, Farrar, Straus & Giroux) and filmmaker, has the good fortune to be his mother. When filmmaker Sontag directed her latest (Promised Lands, 1974), her assistant was David Rieff. Further mother-son collaboration produced the following notes on the possibilities for optimism in 1975.

100

So great is the prestige of pessimism these days that Vogue—a magazine not noted for rubbing its readers' noses in unpalatable realities—feels it appropriate to collect suggestions about what there might be, in 1975, to be optimistic about. A good deed that runs the risk of thickening the gloom. First thought: things must really be pretty bad.

● Who would not feel obliged to come on as a pessimist, if the choice were between being Cassandra or Pollyanna? Luckily, it isn't. And that's the first thing to feel good about.

● Perhaps being pessimistic is mostly our peculiarly "modern" way of staying optimistic, while hedging our bets. People have not just accepted pessimism, they have embraced it: modern pessimism is a spiritual wantonness. Instead of trying to sail between Scylla and Charybdis, people land on each in turn and feed gluttonously. Pessimism is the latest fad in the history of the senses, encouraging people to treasure their alienation and, pretty much, to go on doing what they have been doing all along. Ours is a consumer's pessimism, the status quo's best friend.

There are classics of pessimism. When Beckett writes about the end of things, his words toll 'the

final passion. The twisted screaming figures in the canvasses of Francis Bacon navigate through real agony. Despair has given us magnificent art, *our* art. But it may be too familiar now. A mood that was passionate is now flip. It reeks of self-pity. It sniggers.

● Most pedagogues of hopelessness preach a slothful ahistoricism. Actually, the world is less "dehumanized" than is usually claimed. History shows two splendid, perhaps (alas) antithetical, developments in this century toward a more humane life. One is a real rise in the quality, intensity, and integrity of community (and of altruistic feelings) in some parts of the world—such as China, North Vietnam, and Cuba. The other is the very real victories for tolerance in countries that enforce competitive relations between people—notably, our own.

The heroic struggles undertaken on behalf of tolerance are, at most, a few centuries old. And instances of the pre-modern norm are well within most people's memory. Twenty years ago in the United States, teachers under FBI investigation got a black mark for having copies not just of Marx but also of books by Ruth Benedict or Margaret Mead on their shelves; thousands of professional (Continued on page 148)

Figure 5 Sontag and Rieff, "Notes on Optimism." *Source*: *Vogue* magazine, 1975.

Travel Literature

As her career progressed, Sontag not only became more politically committed and more engaged with the potential of American ideals, she also assimilated these interests with her aesthetic concerns. She conflated literature, in particular her own acts of writing, with American optimism.[22] She explains in her 2003 Friedenspreis acceptance speech that her "childhood orgy of reading," however "clandestine," gave her "real experiences," particularly in comparison to the "cultural desert in which I lived" (*AST*, 206). Because literature does time by imagining the future, it prophesizes (195) and creates a "zone of freedom" (209). While Sontag drew her first inspiration from European models, she asserts that what literature spreads is a state of being much like America: "whether it is called democracy, or freedom, or civilization—[it] is part of a work in progress, as well as the essence of progress itself. Nowhere in the world does the Enlightenment dream of progress have such a fertile setting as it does in America" (202).

Sontag explores this fertile setting in the tellingly named short story collection *I, Etcetera* (1978). Just as she did in shaping *Styles of Radical Will*, Sontag reordered and, in some cases, retitled previously published pieces for *I, Etcetera*. Written between 1963 and 1977, the stories encompass both the pre- and post-Hanoi stages of Sontag's career. Beginning and ending with round trips, from "Project for a Trip to China" to "Unguided Tour," *I, Etcetera* returns to the shaming sense of contrast with European culture that structures the Thomas Mann pilgrimage, but it also builds on the American idealism that emerges from *Styles of Radical Will*. The first word of the title announces the autobiographical component of the collection, and the second opens it up to Sontag's environment. In *Reading Susan Sontag: A Critical Introduction to Her Work*, Rollyson argues that this book is a meditation on what it means to be an American,[23] a theme that comes out most obviously in the third story, "American Spirits." Laura Flatface, the heroine, supports herself through occasional prostitution as she travels across America inflamed by American icons ranging from Benjamin Franklin to Ethel Rosenberg. Sontag's oblique parsing of the title in "Debriefing," the second story, also sounds the note of shame when she subtly compares herself to a prostitute by echoing the collection's self-referential title in her description of a woman serving a prison sentence "for being a etcetera" (37).

Other stories offer "literature" as a redemption and escape, a new way to walk the streets and find intimacy. The first story, "Project for a Trip to China," superimposes familial relationships with international travel. Beckettian in its sparse theme and variable form yet also auto-biographical, the story evokes Sontag's childhood. The narrator, like Sontag, is the daughter of fur traders who worked in China. She, too, longs to go there and feels so alienated from her provincial American upbringing that she tells her classmates that she was born in China. Although the backward-glancing adult recognizes this origin story as her first "lie" (6), she also comes to understand it as an act of literature (a lie redeemed) and a quest for understanding her identity. "Investigate possibility that I was conceived in China though born in New York and brought up elsewhere (America)," she tells herself (5). Her first investigations take place during her "desert childhood" as she digs a hole in the backyard in hopes of arriving in China with no grown-up worries about the difficulty of walking over her own feet. She envisions herself "bursting out the other end, standing on my head or walking on my hands" (8). Her claim that she bought "the first Chinese object I acquired on my own" in Hanoi (a pair of sneakers) strains credulity (11), but it also evokes the image in "Trip to Hanoi" of walking over one's own feet (sneakers make it easier). Similarly, the trips to both Asian countries inspire Sontag to focus on building a bridge between ethics, aesthetics, and her own history, particularly her relationship to her parents and her country. "Moralism is the legacy of the past, moralism rules the domain of the future. We hesitate. Wary, ironic, disillusioned. What a difficult bridge this present has become" (20). Indeed, the story begins and ends with Sontag imagining herself crossing a bridge between Hong Kong and China (see fig. 6).

This trip, like the trip to Hanoi, holds the possibility of an ethically uplifting simplification. Invited by the Chinese government, the narrator looks forward to a "pilgrimage" during which she will encounter a "simpler," unironic source of goodness (12, 22). The trip also offers a psychological and logistic opportunity to reconnect with her family. The whole story collection is dedicated to Sontag's mother ("for you, M"). The return trip will include a stop in Honolulu, her mother's current

Figure 6 Chinese wear. *Source*: Photo by Peter Hujar. Copyright 1966, the Peter Hujar Archive, LLC. Courtesy Matthew Marks Gallery, New York, N.Y.

home, since the narrator is "exhausted by the nonexistent *literature* of unwritten letters and unmade telephone calls that passes between me and M" (28; emphasis added). Assuming that her actual trip will be a "direct experience" shaped by competing agendas and guided by a "bureaucratic Virgil" (27), the narrator places her emphasis on the future with her final statement: "perhaps I will write the book about my trip to China before I go."[24] This trip thus culminates, like Sontag's other pilgrimages, in "Literature, then. Literature before and after if need be" (29) and ends as it begins, in America.

The fourth story, "Old Complaints Revisited," further explores the nature of literature as it, too, explicitly revisits "Trip to Hanoi." The title, with its subtle indication of a return trip, also suggests that Sontag continues to struggle with her attachment to old vices like those described in "Trip to Hanoi." Here, the story's narrator, whose gender is deliberately left unclear thanks to the English language's freedom from grammatical gender (127), tries to break with a secret society (126). While critics have suggested that the group is a radical political organization, the members could just as easily be a group of apolitical intellectuals deeply invested in formalist criticism. A translator by profession, this narrator clearly seeks liberation into literature. But as the group's leader tells her, "literature . . . is for the others—the nonmembers" (105). Members focus on their "movement's unhappy history, . . . the four-volume *Commentaries* and the reading of the anthology of quotations *What Must Be Done*" (107). Nonmembers, by implication, look to the future. Joining them, for the narrator, means speaking in one's own voice and enjoying respite from work "at the service of other writers" (112) and from a "skull crammed with quotations" (104). Deliberately echoing "Trip to Hanoi," the narrator's lover in "Old Complaints Revisited" discourages her desire to break away by warning, "you can't walk over your own feet" (129).[25]

You can in literature however. The narrator of "Project for a Trip to China," who also expresses discomfort with the way "we are ruled by quotations" (26), makes a list characterizing literature as:

—The impatience of knowing
—Self-mastery
—Impatience in self-mastery
(29)

Likewise, the would-be apostate in "Old Complaints Revisited" imagines that the leader will criticize her desires as impatient and characterize her expression of them as "literary" (103). She nevertheless persists: "If I could be silent, maybe I could walk over my own feet. But if I'm silent, how can I reason? And if I can't reason, how can I ever find a way out? . . . I need words for that (129–30). Words, then, replace feet as a means of transport, and the backward-glancing title (*revisited*) and the literature that is unfolding on the pages before us demonstrate that the narrator *did* find the imaginative freedom to walk over her feet.

The way out is the return home—at least that is what "Unguided Tour," the last piece in the collection, suggests. In this story, literary and touristic clichés drown the "direct experience" so vaunted by Sontag in "Trip to Hanoi": "Worth a detour? Worth a trip! It's a remarkable collection. Still possessed its aura" (237).[26] The narrator exemplifies Sontag's "country bumpkin . . . in matters of beauty." In the story's opening line, she tells her seductive interlocutor that she "took a trip to see the beautiful things" but her experience culminates in bathos when instead of gushing over the glories she witnessed, she anticlimactically notes that "they're still there." She goes on to explain that "whenever I travel, it's always to say goodbye" (233). The beautiful things of other times and places, in other words, have little impact beyond the (always already) guided tours of longing and nostalgia for them that happen at home before, and perhaps after, the trips take place. The truly unguided tour seems to be the experience of freedom that comes from saying goodbye to all that. "Say to yourself fifty times a day: I am not a connoisseur, I am not a romantic wanderer, I am not a pilgrim" (237). This linguistic decision may remain in the fictive realm of literature, but it also makes a pledge to the future: the trips and pilgrimages will end where they begin, in her country. In the story's last segment, the narrator speculates on cures for wanderlust. She lives, after all, in an exceptionally hopeful place: "does every country have a tragic history except ours?" (240), she rhetorically wonders. Quoting John Locke's Second Treatise on Government (without attribution), "in the beginning all the world was America" (246),[27] this closing story gives final shape to the collection by rejoining the opening "Project for a Trip to China" in a quest for an American starting and resting point. Even the collection's much-discussed cover photograph, portraying the cowboy-boot clad author reclining in a large window with a hazy New York skyline at her back, illustrates this dynamic (see fig. 7). While Carl Rollyson and Lisa Paddock reproduce this image on the cover of *Susan Sontag: The Making of an Icon* as an epitome of Sontag's artfully constructed glamour, the photograph also illustrates Sontag's account of

Figure 7 Sontag turns her back on New York City. *Source*: Photograph by Thomas Victor. Courtesy of Harriet Spurlin, the estate of Thomas Victor.

her provincial American childhood—a westerner living in New York but not fully a New Yorker.[28]

The Home Stretch

Sontag's final novels, one set in Europe and the other in America, most fully explore her American identity and its relation to her Europhilia. In both, she appears as herself in the opening section. She began work on *The Volcano Lover* two years after she published "Pilgrimage."[29] Indeed, as I have argued elsewhere, *The Volcano Lover* is Sontag's own *Magic Mountain*, even as the novel's subtitle—"A Romance"—implicitly asserts her difference from the European model. Commenting on the subtitle to a *New York Times* interviewer, she asserts: "I don't want to express alienation. It isn't what I feel. I'm interested in various kinds of passionate engagement. All my work says be serious, be passionate, wake up."[30] Likewise, in a *Paris Review* interview, she explicitly connects her favorite novel to her nationality: "Nobody but an American would have written *The Volcano Lover*." Here she explains the subtitle as a reference to Hawthorne's use of the term "romance," and she goes on to aver that "my imagination is very marked by nineteenth-century American literature."[31]

The theme of theft, first played in "Pilgrimage," also sounds early in *The Volcano Lover*. Likewise, her journal entries also indicate her concern with it, particularly its relation to quotation. In *Swimming in a Sea of Death*, David Rieff quotes an entry from the 1980s in which she seems to condemn her borrowings: "'I write the way I live [and] my life is full of quotations.' Then she adds: 'Change it.'"[32] Twenty-five years later, on the opening page of *The Volcano Lover*, she describes herself haunting a flea market and defensively notes that "I am not a thief" (3). Yet the eponymous volcano lover, the hypercultivated, beauty-besotted, ironic courtier and compulsive collector William Hamilton *is* a thief, pilfering treasures from the excavations of Pompeii to add to his collections. He, and his entourage, are condemned by a feminist revolutionary in the novel's last lines, which Sontag said she had in her mind when she began writing: "They thought they were civilized. They were despicable. Damn them all" (419).[33]

In America (2000) puts a cultivated European woman center-stage as it imaginatively resolves Sontag's complex of love and shame about her country. The title echoes Sontag's earlier essay "What's Happening in America," and the epigraph, Langston Hughes's "America will be" alludes to Hughes's complaint about the injustices of American history balanced by hope for its future:

O, yes,
I say it plain,
America never was America to me,
And yet I swear this oath—
America will be!

(Similarly, the last lines of her infamous statement on the September 11 attack on America echo Hughes's use of the infinitive: "'Our country is strong,' we are told again and again. . . . Who doubts that America is strong? But that's not all America has to be" [*AST*, 107].) Here, in comparison to Europe, America *is* strong. Dedicating the book to her "friends in Sarajevo," Sontag, like the characters she creates, and no doubt like her Jewish grandparents, expresses her disillusion with Europe's seemingly endless history of tribal warfare, assuming that they all have recovered from "that . . . mighty illusion with a capital E" (10).

As she does in "Pilgrimage" and *I, Etcetera*, Sontag opens this novel by "revisiting" her early history. She clearly identifies herself with this novel's heroine, the Polish actress Maryna Zalenska, who makes the moral decision to leave her European celebrity in order to establish a commune in Anaheim (as did Helena Modjeska, the real actress who inspired Sontag). Going even farther back than her conception in China, Sontag imagines herself in Poland, invisibly observing and embellishing a dinner party among Polish artists and intellectuals. She notes that "all four of [her] grandparents were born in this country . . . around the very year [1875] to which I'd traveled in my mind in order to co-inhabit this room" (23). While the adolescent Sontag dreaded her encounter with Thomas Mann, in this imagined scene, she confidently believes that the group would welcome her around their table if she were visible (17). Like them, she possesses a moral fervor and sincerity similar to the "mode of ethical aspiration" she had identified in the North Vietnamese years earlier: "much of the fascination of these people, of their time, is that they knew, or thought they knew, what 'right' and 'wrong' were. . . . I was moved by the way they possessed these words and regarded themselves bound by them to actions. . . . Dare I say I felt at one with them?" (7–8). Inspired by their reading of Fourier and Ignacy Krasicki's utopian novel *The Adventures of Mr. Nicholas Wisdom*, their decision to establish a "perfect, rustic comity" in America exemplifies the catalytic relation between literature and the hopeful image of America, and, it, too, returns Sontag to her roots.

Even the comity's rapid dissolution reflects a hope in America. Leaving behind her southern California comrades, Maryna triumphs over the American stage and relentlessly tours the country. Just as Maryna redeems her initial American failure, Sontag symbolically rectifies and displaces her provincial shame and embarrassment. Maryna first balks at American-style publicity, and, much like Sontag, she expresses reluctance to grant interviews. But "as a modern artist," Maryna, like Sontag, seeks to reach as many people as possible (318). By the novel's end, she cheerfully stretches the truth for the sake of giving interesting interviews and shamelessly endorses a "tooth polish" (354–55), enjoying "being part of the wave of the future" (330).

Theft, too, metamorphoses into a building block of the future rather than an illicit link to the European past. Literary theft, or plagiarism, a charge that came to haunt Sontag's last works, make a prophetic appearance here in an anecdote about *Nadjezda*, a play about Poland's struggle for liberation that Maurice Barrymore wrote for Helena Modjeska. After she tired of performing it, Barrymore passed it on to Sarah Bernhardt, who evidently turned it over to her lover, Victorien Sardou. Sardou then pillaged it freely for his *Tosca*; Giacomo Puccini, in turn, based his opera of the same name on the play. Sontag herself used it as one of the subplots in *The Volcano Lover*. No wonder, then, that "Maryna was unmoved by Maurice's distress. . . . It sounded to Maryna as if [Sardou] had much improved Maurice's play" (366).[34] When Sontag was subsequently accused of plagiarizing from a host of sources for this novel, she defended herself in similar terms: "Modjeska was quite forgotten. She was a great figure. I made her into a marvelous person. The real Modjeska was a horrible racist." More importantly, she redeems the practice of quotation, even unattributed, by arguing that such borrowing and disguising is not theft but rather the nature of literature: "I've used these sources and I've completely transformed them. I have these books. I've looked at these books. There's a larger argument to be made that all of literature is a series of references and allusions."[35] *In America*, then, exemplifies the transformative freedom of literature just as life in America epitomizes the possibilities for human freedom.

Sontag died in late 2004 with no explicit burial instructions; she was convinced, her son says, that she would survive this bout of cancer as she had the others. He decided to bury her in Paris, at the Montparnasse Cemetery, near Samuel Beckett, Emil Cioran, Simone de Beauvoir, Jean Paul Sartre, and Baudelaire (*SSD*, 171). Rieff admits that "my decision to bury my mother in Montparnasse had little to do either with literature or even with her lifelong love of Paris. . . . The decision was mine alone . . . and I had to bury her somewhere" (173). New York's cemeteries are ugly, he claims, and his mother had no particular attachment to other places in America. Thanks to Rieff, in death Sontag does what Beckett would do. But her work maintains the difference. In 2002, Sontag sold her papers, correspondence, and personal library to UCLA, a decision that increased her self-exposure. According to Rieff, the sale included her private journals, which will become available for all to see: "If I had her journals in my possession after she died, and they were simply mine to dispose of as I wished, I don't think I would have published them."[36] Sontag's own words put it more happily: "I am delighted that my papers are going to UCLA, thereby renewing an old connection with Southern California. There are sentimental reasons: my mother grew up in Los Angeles during and after World War I, and I spent the later part of my childhood here." In her rhetoric here, Sontag echoes the heroine of *In America*, whose initial love for New York City gives way to her attachment to California: "She had to remind herself that this was not America but only New York, so self-important and so sweaty, so narrow and so filled up. Home . . . was not New York, where the immigrant's America begins, but where America runs into the next ocean and ends. Bogdan [her husband] needed California, the ending, the last beginning, and so did she" (327). With these late words about the fate of her library, her manuscripts, and her private affairs, Sontag, too, ensured that the life and the work remain in America.

Notes

1. Sigrid Nunez, "Sontag Laughs," *Salmagundi*, no. 152 (2006): 16.

2. Sontag explicitly labeled the conflicts between American and European culture in her 2003 "Literature Is Freedom" speech (upon receipt of the Friedenspreis des Deutschen Buchhandels [Peace Prize of the German Book Trade], October 28, 2003), concluding that America is "the Antithesis of Europe" (5). She characterizes the differences as "the perennial literary—or cultural—quarrel: between the ancients and the moderns" (6). Sontag, of course, is a modern. For a full discussion of the tradition of associating the provincial U.S. with rusticity, see Gerald W. Creed and Barbara Ching, "Recognizing Rusticity: Identity and the Power of Place," in *Knowing Your Place: Rural Identity and Cultural Hierarchy*, ed. Barbara Ching and Gerald W. Creed (New York: Routledge, 1997), 1–38.

3. I have also found Cary Nelson's approach enormously helpful. He locates "recurrent verbal patterns" in Sontag's work, noting that "when one essay is pitted against another, the logical connections give way to deeper impulses" ("Reading Criticism," *PMLA* 91, no. 5 [October 1976]: 807). Also see his "Soliciting Self-Knowledge: The Rhetoric of Susan Sontag's Criticism," *Critical Inquiry* 6, no. 4 (Summer 1980): 707–26.

4. Sohnya Sayres, "For Susan Sontag, 1933–2004," *PMLA* 120, no. 3 (May 2005): 836; and Susan Suleiman, "Culture, Aestheticism, and Ethics: Sontag and the 'Idea of Europe,'" *PMLA* 120, no. 3 (May 2005): 840. See also Elaine Showalter's *Inventing Herself: Claiming a Feminist Intellectual Heritage* (New York: Scribner's, 2001), where she suggests that Sontag's embarrassment masks her disillusion (232).

5. Her tribute to Roland Barthes in *Under the Sign of Saturn* recounts an equally humiliating encounter with the French writer who, at their last meeting, greeted her as if she were a dog: "His interest in you tended to be your interest in him. 'Ah, Susan. Toujours fidèle,' . . . he greeted me, affectionately. . . . I was, I am" (176).

6. UCLA Special Collections, Susan Sontag Papers, collection 612, box 118, folder 13.

7. UCLA Special Collections, Susan Sontag Papers, collection 612, box 77, folder 11.

8. Susan Sontag, "Beauty: How Will It Change Next," *Vogue* (May 1975): 116.

9. See Liam Kennedy's extended discussion of Sontag's coded refutation of the New York intellectuals' cultural criticism in his book *Susan Sontag: Mind as Passion* (New York: Palgrave Macmillan, 1997), esp. 16–45.

10. Elizabeth Bruss makes a similar, although more abstract observation about the form of this collection, arguing that it reveals Sontag's work-

ing through of "the language barrier": "she . . . arranged the book . . . to chart the progress of a dilemma from its first, quizzical appearance . . . to its eventual (although far from final) resolution" (*Beautiful Theories: The Spectacle of Discourse in Contemporary Criticism* [Baltimore, Md.: Johns Hopkins University Press, 1982], 226). See also Liam Kennedy's discussion of the collection as a "narrative of engagement and disburdenment" in *Mind as Passion*, 47. Cary Nelson, too, discusses the unity of the collection in "Soliciting Self-Knowledge," esp. 713–21.

11. In her book on Sontag, volume contributor Sohnya Sayres notes that this "longing for rectitude and simple truth" occurs throughout Sontag's work (*Susan Sontag: The Elegiac Modernist* [New York: Routledge, 1990], 8).

12. Paul Hollander and others who accuse Sontag of anti-Americanism ignore this turn in Sontag's argument. See his *Political Pilgrims: Travels of Western Intellectuals to the Soviet Union, China, and Cuba, 1928–1978* (New York: Oxford University Press, 1981), 265–68.

13. Among her collection of books by and about Thomas Mann are many clippings of annotated articles and reviews including one of Erich Heller's early study, *Thomas Mann: The Ironic German*, UCLA Special Collections, Susan Sontag Library, collection 892, box 329.

14. UCLA Special Collections, Susan Sontag Papers, collection 612, box 102, folder 3. While Sontag's career has involved continual self-revisions, I would argue that this new relationship has remained a constant. As I wrote in "High Regard: Words and Pictures in Tribute to Susan Sontag" (*American Quarterly* 59, no. 1 [2007]: 157–64), Sontag's essay on the Abu Ghraib snapshots "brought her to a simultaneously more horrified and hopeful vision of what photography might do in the world and how Americans, the first person plural used in her essay, might look at photographs: "Yes, it seems that one picture is worth a thousand words. And even if our leaders choose not to look at them, there will be thousands more snapshots and videos. Unstoppable," she concluded. Earlier in the essay she proclaimed that "the photographs are us" because they show American policy at work (26). But by the end, the photographs are us because we must respond to them and "our leaders" with "many thousands of words" (162). The Sontag quotations are from "Regarding the Torture of Others," *New York Times Magazine*, May 23, 2004.

15. Leo Marx, *The Pilot and the Passenger: Essays on Literature, Technology, and Culture in the United States* (New York: Oxford University Press, 1989), 300–301.

16. Marx, *Pilot and the Passenger*, 307.

17. Marx, *Pilot and the Passenger*, 311–12.

18. Linguistic decision making, as it turns out, is a work forever in progress, and Sontag's willingness to revisit her decisions also takes part in the American tradition of "inflaming people." In 1982, during a rally held at New York City's Town Hall in support of Poland's Solidarity workers' movement,

Sontag spoke out against leftists who had failed to confront the horrors of communism. In spite of the chorus of indignation and accusations of hypocrisy this denunciation sparked, Sontag did not explicitly retract any of her praise for North Vietnam.

19. Victor Bockris, "Susan Sontag: The Dark Lady of Pop Philosophy," *High Times*, March 28, 1973, 23.

20. Susan Sontag with David Rieff. "Notes on Optimism," *Vogue*, January 1975, 148.

21. UCLA Special Collections, Susan Sontag Papers, collection 612, Box 75, folder 24.

22. As Bruss notes, "Project for a Trip to China" contains "its own miniature theory of the nature of literature" (212).

23. Carl Rollyson, *Reading Susan Sontag: A Critical Introduction to Her Work* (Chicago: Ivan R. Dee, 2001), 133.

24. Carl Rollyson and Lisa Paddock note that Sontag "planned a trip to China that would culminate in a book. . . . In January 1973, Sontag took a three-week tour of the country. Except for 'Project for a Trip to China,' written before her voyage . . . she never published another word about it" (*Susan Sontag: The Making of an Icon* [New York: Norton, 2000], 158).

25. Liam Kennedy also notes this "deliberate intertextual allusion" (*Mind as Passion*, 105).

26. On this point, see Sara Meyer's excellent article on "Project for a Trip to China" and "Unguided Tour": "Susan Sontag's 'Archeology of Longings,'" *Texas Studies in Literature and Language* 49, no. 1 (Spring 2007): 45–63.

27. Sontag also cites this passage in her 1984 essay "Questions of Travel" in order to exemplify journeys "to something better" (*WSF*, 275).

28. Angela McRobbie also discusses this photograph in "The Modernist Style of Susan Sontag," *Feminist Review* 38 (1991), concluding that "this is an image which pleases the author. At home, with books, wearing black" (1).

29. The acknowledgements on the verso of the novel's title page note : "I am grateful to the Deutscher Akademischer Austauschdienst (DAAD), which brought me to Berlin in 1989, when I began *The Volcano Lover*."

30. Leslie Garis, "Susan Sontag Finds Romance," *New York Times*, August 2, 1992.

31. Sontag, interview, "Susan Sontag: The Art of Fiction CLXIII," *Paris Review* (Winter 1995): 186.

32. David Rieff, *Swimming in a Sea of Death* (New York: Simon and Shuster, 2008), 149. In a journal entry dated April 6, 1967, Sontag asserts that there are "two ways to be—a saint or a thief"—itself a reference to Jean Genet's *A Thief's Journal* and to Sartre's admiring biography of him, *Saint Genet* (unacknowledged, but who carefully footnotes a journal?). I thank Jennifer Wagner-Lawlor for calling my attention to the first journal entry, and Julia Walker for the Genet reference.

33. Sontag, "The Art of Fiction CLXIII," 200.

34. Similarly, a kleptomaniac who visited the commune and stole a set of cherished jewelry from Maryna abjectly returns it when she makes her American acting debut (*IA*, 255).

35. Doreen Caraval, "So Whose Words Are They: Susan Sontag Creates a Stir," *New York Times*, May 27, 2000.

36. Steve Paulson, "Sontag's Final Wish," interview with David Rieff, *Salon*, February 13, 2008, http://www.salon.com/books/feature/2008/02/13/david_rieff/index1.html, accessed September 15, 2008.

chapterfour

Romances of Community in Sontag's Later Fiction

JENNIFER A. WAGNER-LAWLOR

I

In a July 2000 interview, Evans Chan was coaxing Susan Sontag into describing her final two novels as examples of "historical novels," a generic label she was resisting as too limiting and conventional. "Maybe," she proposes instead, "these novels should be viewed as books about travel, about people in foreign places." She continues by noting that she traveled more after her first two novels, and came to value experiencing the world "not just in aesthetic terms, but also with moral seriousness. . . . I want for myself to take in more reality, to address real suffering, the larger world, and to break out of the confines of narcissism and solipsism."[1] In the context of the interview, Sontag seems to be alluding to her previous two novels, *The Benefactor* (1963) and *Death Kit* (1965), both of them aptly characterized (and negatively, by many critics) as narratives measuring "the confines of narcissism and solipsism."

What does Sontag gain from this correction of her interviewer— and indeed from this acknowledged adjustment in the trajectory of her own fiction writing? A great deal, it turns out. Sontag's remark here signals a clarification that becomes characteristic of her later work: a decisive turn toward the idea of a community of "militant readers." The metaphor of travel, while always useful to Sontag as to many writers attempting to record the journey of their own experiences and those of their characters, deepens from a merely formal dimension to a psychological and finally ethical one. These dimensions come together in Sontag's own later fiction, which consciously takes advantage of the travel or quest format so characteristic of the romance and, later, the genre of the novel. But Sontag's fiction moves beyond the confines of the novel's "mandate of its own normality" (*AST*, 89) as she employs one of the subgenres she left out of her piece "Outlandish: On Halldór Laxness's *Under the Glacier*", collected in *At the Same Time*, which treats on "innovative or ultraliterary or bizarre" narratives. In the 2004 essay, Sontag casts her eye upon the kinds of narratives "that deviate from this artificial norm and tell other kinds of stories" (89): among these subgenres she includes novels that "proceed largely through dialogue"; novels that are "relentlessly jocular"; novels "with characters who have supernatural options, like shape-shifting and resurrection; novels that evoke imaginary geography" (90). Her catalog of "outlandish" narratives includes "science fiction. Tale, fable, allegory. Philosophical novel. Dream novel. Visionary novel. Literature of fantasy. Wisdom lit. Spoof. Sexual turn-on" (90).

Among the novels she sees as occupying "the outlying precincts of the novel's main tradition" (90) she names one—*Candide*—that is specifically identified as the precursor of her own first novel, *The Benefactor*; as with all narratives searching for "best possible worlds," the real journey is, as *The Benefactor* makes clear, a psychological one, though the journey of her hero, Hippolyte, fails for precisely the reason Sontag identifies in the 2000 interview: the protagonist's narcissism and solipsism. But *Candide* also haunts, in a more complex way, the pages of Sontag's final two novels as well, and I will argue that this has to do with Sontag's interest in getting "beyond the confines" of her earlier narratives' peculiar claustrophobia. Utopian narratives are only superficially concerned with the "mapping" of new surroundings; after the initial strangeness of the arrival wears off, such novels usually drag thanks to the programmatic effort to limn in full detail the unfamiliar landscape, customs, clothing and architecture. What *engages* the reader of such texts is the experience of the narrator, whose unexamined beliefs and habits are wrenched out of place, challenged, her mental maps redrawn, her sensibilities reoriented, her desires redirected, temporally, psychologically, fundamentally. And while Sontag's novels employ the trappings of conventional novels, the prowling presence of Sontag "herself" *as narrator* disrupts convention and "stretch[es] our world" by extending the boundaries of the narratives she specifically identifies in subtitles as, in one case, "A Romance"—*The Volcano Lover* (1992)—and in the final case as "A Novel"—*In America* (2000). That "stretching" is "why we need fiction," says Sontag in her 2004 Nadine Gordimer Lecture (*AST*, 228): "To be a traveler—and novelists are often travelers—is to be constantly reminded of the simultaneity of what is going on in the world, your world and the very different world you have visited and from which you have returned 'home.' It is a beginning of a response to this painful awareness to say: it's a question of sympathy . . . of the limits of the imagination" (228). This is, she concludes, the novelist's "necessary ethical task."

Given this extension into the ethical, I wish to explore Sontag's final novels as specifically *utopian* narratives that are designed to lure us into a community of readers bound by a new kind of social contract: a commitment to sympathy, plurality, and what Sontag refers to as "the exercise of freedom." What Sontag comes to describe as the "mental traveling" offered by art, literature, and critique takes each reader on an outlandish journey that, unlike the quest narrative of a novel, does not—indeed *must* not—end. The imperative there is critical: reading and writing are moral acts, and to end the quest—to stop the mental traveling—risks the loss of what is "humane" about humanity: our sympathy toward others, at one level, our hope for "a better world," at another: "Literature was mental travel: travel into the past . . . and to other countries. . . . And literature was criticism of one's own reality, in the light of a better standard" (*AST*, 179). Sontag is not talking about standards of taste here, but standards of thinking, acting, living, and loving.

Because utopian narratives typically conclude with a (usually *unde*sired) return home, the text "itself" becomes a retrospective accounting of one-time disorientation framed by the narrator's palpably nostalgic yearning to return to that site. Ironically, now that he has reentered his old community, he is alien. What motivates such stories is precisely that yearning to be rejoined with the alternative, the other, the possible; the narrator vies for the reader's sympathy as she recreates the experience of the contact *between* the familiar and the strange, from the ironical point of view of the narrator's retrospective double consciousness of the real and the ideal. What motivates the *narrator* is a yearning for a partner in this new mental landscape, a fellow traveler, a commitment to her own desire: the aim of the utopian traveler—and the utopian author—is to create a community of sympathizers, affiliates in desire, fellow lovers of the other world. Indeed, utopian narratives have long been characterized as "allegories of desire," and the origins of European utopian narrative in early modern travel literature points toward the utopianist's radical search not simply for "other places" but for other ways of thinking and knowing.

More recently, according to Tobin Siebers, postmodern utopia, and the narratives describing such a notion, go a step further. Postmodernists, he argues, do not insist that they know what they want: "They are utopian because they know that they want *something else*. They want to *desire differently*. . . . For postmodernism, like all utopian thinking, is concerned with what lies beyond the present moment, perhaps beyond any present moment."[2] The futurity of this position, and the implications of that for aesthetics and the "work" of art is the central concern of Siebers's meditation upon the *heterotopian* nature of postmodern utopianism, with its attention to "desiring differently." Moreover, he argues, the postmodernist's utopia is a "romance of community" based upon the metaphor of the couple, an ongoing and powerful "grand theme . . . passed from Romanticism to modernism and postmodernism."[3] Siebers goes on to explain how this metaphor extends even to aesthetics, and this is where Siebers can cast light on Sontag. The imperative of "desiring differently" is a radical impulse at work throughout her fiction, though, as I have suggested, the failure of the two earlier novels lies not simply in the adolescent feel of their European pretensions but in the failure of Sontag's (anti)heroes. *The Benefactor* teaches us that the narcissism of her own celebrated "camp" sensibility takes one so far and no further, creating a decadent dystopia of fetishized self-consciousness; *Death Kit* stalls in a similarly solipsistic project. The success of the later two novels lies in the "break[ing] out of the confines of narcissism and solipsism" in her own fictional work—and the discovery and exploration of her own utopian sensibility. Out of the recognition of her own sense of what Siebers describes as the "romance of community," central to utopia, emerges Sontag's commitment to desire differently, as well as her increasingly sure commitment to an "erotics of art" that comes with ethical and inherently future-oriented affiliations.

Sontag scarcely qualifies as a "postmodern thinker," and her increasingly fervent commitment to art and to a certain moral aestheticism makes it impossible to see her as an advocate of postmodern relativisms. And yet the recalibration of Sontag's own affiliations translates her fiction from the early anti-bildungsroman narratives into open-ended romances of community that reject "the formal necessity of Utopian closure."[4] These late novels, both meditations on the relationships of history and politics, consciousness and will, hold open the possibility (though hardly the certainty) of change and progress—of "the future as disruption" as Jameson puts it, but a disruption whose center is itself "utopia" and whose representation art alone can most rigorously and most usefully explore.[5]

II

"Objects of art, like romances of community, are allegories of desire."
—Tobin Siebers

The shift from the narcissistic to the utopian hero is captured first in the plot of *The Volcano Lover*. Sontag's commitment to utopia in this novel is nothing like a "blueprint" for perfect government, though the novel's two protagonists are primary agents of a volatile period in European history and politics and by the narrative's close an unexpected character emerges as the novel's visionary. Rather, Sontag is interested in the governance of sympathy and will, alternative faculties that energize individual agency toward the foundation of a different kind of community. Her lurch toward utopia in this novel is centered by what Siebers describes as a postmodern "romance of community" that is founded quite simply "on the romance of the couple." Who would have thought that so rugged and nonnostalgic an intellect as Sontag would appear so committed to "love" or romanticism? And yet the hoped-for ecstasy of romance—whether in relation to art or to lovers, whether ideal or embodied—is precisely what anchors the utopic sensibility of its famous protagonists.

The novel is interested—as so much of Sontag's work is—in the nature of "the work of art": in terms of both the individual pieces that Sir William Hamilton so obsessively collects during his trips and residence in Italy and also of the "work" that art does to embody or materialize an imaginative vision or ideal form. The novel's meditations on the Cavaliere link his obsession with impossible perfection to the utopian quest that urges him and any collector on the quest to keep looking:

> So the collector is a dissembler, someone whose joys are never unalloyed with anxiety. Because there is always more. Or something better. You must have it because it is one step toward an ideal completing of your collection. But this ideal completion for which every collector hungers is a delusive goal.
>
> A complete set of something is not the completeness the collector craves. . . . A complete collection is a dead collection. It has no posterity. After having built it, you would love it less each year. Before long, you would want to sell or donate it, and embark on a new chase.
>
> The great collections are vast, not complete. Incomplete: motivated by the desire for completeness.
>
> (VL, 72)

The quest of the collector is indeed, as the novel's subtitle announces, a romance quest, one that the narrator, Sontag "herself," also embarks upon.[6] "Why enter," she asks herself in a self-reflexive passage describing herself "prowling"[7] around an outdoor flea market in Manhattan in 1992. "I tell myself what I want to hear. Yes, there's enough. I go in" (VL, 4). Thus she accepts the principle of hope that drives any utopianist toward a "degraded experience of pure possibility" (4). The Cavaliere's great passion is focused upon collecting the two things that are, inevitably, the least attainable: the volcano, Vesuvius, and the various faces and acts of love of his second wife, Emma. Of the first object, he believes that "no object could be less ownable" (28); only later does he learn that he was wrong, as it is Emma herself, that other "object" of desire, who is unattainable. Both represent great ideals to him. The volcano is the joining of "inorganic mass" and "vertical" space, earth and heaven, lava erupting from deep within the rock and spewing far into the air. The woman is the "Embodiment" (130), the juncture of flesh and art. From her the Cavaliere collects attentions and displays of beauty (as long as that lasts), skills of acting offered to him and her audiences; from Emma, in other words, he collects the traces of love ("He never tired of cataloguing the play of her moods" [131]) that originally drew him into the sympathetic circle of Emma's admirers. This was Hamilton's short-lived utopia, a "romance of community" founded in the "authority of beauty" (132).

The fragility of this bifocal romance haunts the Cavaliere, who despite his best efforts to remove his collection from war's violence, ironically loses nearly the entire cargo to nature and to human carelessness, even as he loses his wife to another. The Cavaliere clings to his hopeful idealism, which is most clearly evident in the contrast between him and his extravagant kinsman, William Beckford, contractor of the outrageous Fonthill Abbey ("the mighty forerunner of all the aesthete palaces of surfeit and synesthesia" [344]). Also a collector, Beckford's motivations could not be farther from any utopian community; his collections shore up a profound disgust with humanity that Hamilton appears not to recognize: "This was the Cavaliere's first experience of collecting as revenge" (338). Beckford can be no utopianist, as he is utterly without hope: "Nothing is more odious to me than thinking about the future." But his commitment to decadence in this central scene is matched by Hamilton's commitment to romance: "If you do not see and touch what you possess," Hamilton tells his cousin, "you do not have the experience of beauty, which is what all lovers of art—all lovers, he was about to say—desire. . . . To surround oneself with enchanting and stimulating objects, a superfluity of objects, to ensure that the senses will never be unoccupied, nor the faculty left unexercised—this the Cavaliere understood well" (339–40). Revenge, however, is not beautiful, enforcing exclusion rather than promoting inclusion: "When I have properly housed the rare and beautiful objects I possess, I will not need ever to go out, ever be obliged to see anyone again. Thus fortressed, I can cheerfully contemplate the destruction of the world, for I will have saved all that is of value in it" (337). His sensibility isn't just decadent; it's a dead end.

What is ironic, however, about the Fonthill Abbey scene is how clearly it recalls the Cavaliere's own detachment from and lack of sympathy toward the world, emblematized by his obsession with the volcano: "He was high up, looking down. A human dot. Far from all obligation of sympathy, of identification: the game of distance" (111). Hamilton's tragedy is that he fails so entirely as an artist of his life and dies understanding that life as a truly "degraded experience of pure possibility." Nevertheless, in him there is the desire for a community of like-minded aesthetes to admire his precious collections. As Siebers points out in his work on postmodern heterotopia, "the desire to assemble is . . . as much a metaphor for community as for aesthetic creation."[8] So we see in Beckford, decadently, and in Hamilton, distantly, alike: "I collect, therefore I am" (112). But Hamilton's vision of inclusion is too solipsistic to be transformative. As a courtier he is continually watched, and he revels in this fact: "The House of Lords is a stage, the court is a stage, a dinner party is a stage—even a box in a theatre is a stage" (330). But while he knows himself to be a kind of performer, he is singularly ineffective in his political performances, vastly overshadowed by the spectacular accomplishments of "the Hero," Admiral Nelson, and by Emma, a spectacle in her own right but also a much more skilled manipulator of human beings.

While the Cavaliere exemplifies a kind of utopic sensibility represented by his aesthetic devotions, he falls short through a certain lack of will that many around him recognize. The novel introduces him as an elegant courtier, detached, "managing brilliantly" (20), but he is gradually revealed to be only half the man he should have been, sterile in more ways than one. Though he actually reads *Candide*, we learn, he is singularly unsuccessful in actually transforming his life toward any ideal of community. He craves the possession of art because it brings mind and matter together, materializes his desire for beauty. He craves Emma for the same reasons, although her beauty is only skin deep to him, and she finally becomes an embarrassment and a liability. But what he craves most and most fails to achieve is *sympathy*, in the romantic sense, as a kind of imaginative network that connects everything that would at least reach toward something sublime and perfect, like the volcano he so admires.

What's lacking in the Cavaliere, surely centered somewhere in the "vortex of melancholy" (20) that his early enthusiasms disguise, is made up for in his larger-than-life counterpart, "the Hero," Lord Horatio Nelson. A different sort of romantic figure himself, Nelson is granted the bittersweet experience of paradise—"our paradise" (356)—of the love of Emma Hamilton, enjoyed mutually and both emotionally and, according to detailed passages, deeply physically, even as the Hero suffers his battle wounds. The closest to paradise Hamilton reaches is the space carved out for him by art. In a passage reminiscent of Hippolyte's search for an ideal space in *The Benefactor*, the Cavaliere (invoking Voltaire just as Hippolyte does) muses about his own "elsewhere":

> No, to read was precisely to enter another world, which was not the reader's own, and come back refreshed, ready to bear with equanimity the injustices and frustrations of this one. Reading was balm, amusement—not incitement. And reading was mostly what the Cavaliere did in these first weeks while he was still feeling ill, including rereading an essay on happiness by Voltaire. It was the best way to endure the elsewhere of exile: to be in the elsewhere of a book. And as he became stronger, he could gradually be where he was.
>
> (231)

And perhaps the Cavaliere is not so different, however unintentionally, from his strange cousin after all, even not so different from Hippolyte, "enjoying the waning tribulations of subjectivity and the repose of a privacy that is genuine" (*The Benefactor*, 231); in either case, he is a failure, in love and politics.

Surprisingly, the novel's last and strongest words come from one of the least visible characters: the executed Neapolitan revolutionary, Eleonora Pimentel, whose dramatic monologue closes the novel. In a characteristically self-reflexive, Sontagian move, Eleonora is explicitly (if anachronistically, metafictionally) associated with the author of the novel. What does this final identification signify, and what kind of sympathy does Sontag feel with a heretofore incidental character? Like her author, this fictional Eleonora has, as Cary Nelson says, "found a successful voice"; Eleonora's rhetoric shares the same "cool, self-regarding detachment" that Nelson sees in Sontag's criticism.[9] But beyond that, this character avows (to use one of Sontag's regularly "valorized terms" [Nelson, "Soliciting," 722]) an *active* partisanship not simply with aesthetic ideals (like the Cavaliere) but also with actively political, indeed utopian ones.[10]

As much an artist as Emma Hamilton, Eleonora makes a "performance" (*VL*, 412) of her death as she did of her life, choosing an appropriate costume, props, and even the timing and blocking. She, alone of all the characters in the novel, according to her posthumous statement, "was not nostalgic about the past. I believed in the future" (418).

She also, alone of the primary characters in the novel, "did not drown in the love of a single person" (418). She dies for love—but for love on a wider stage: "I will not allow that I was moved by justice rather than love, for justice is also a form of love" (419). She dies for a better humanity. A true believer in *this* ideal, she alone dies together in the community of "her friends," fellow prisoners from the Neapolitan insurgency: "my joy at seeing my friends again—I was to be hanged in good company, with seven of my fellow patriots—suddenly gave me the impression that I was not afraid to die" (413). She alone lived for someone other than herself, a partisan with an earnest, even "ecstatic" commitment to "set[ting] an example" (419). She alone in the novel possesses both sympathy and will, and they together fuel her desire to "be pure flame" (417), erupting and burning through social and political injustices. Eleonora is a utopianist and a political diva who stages her final appearance before a national and international audience, and her public execution inflames the hearts and minds of the political body in ways that Emma Hamilton's ultimately campy attitudinizing (designed, Eleonora suspects, simply to please her men) could not hold a candle to. Eleonora alone is aroused by the romance of a community that might defuse the violence of her times. Even if that romance comes to a violent end for her personally, she achieves something no one else in the novel does, filling the demands both of the personal and the communal through a rhetoric, whether poetic or political, that modulates—to borrow a phrase from Cary Nelson's description of Sontag's own critical voice—between "intimacy and abstraction" ("Soliciting," 720).

III

In her award-winning novel *In America* (2000), Sontag's pursuit of a utopian romance of community achieves fuller exploration. Maryna Zalenska, this novel's protagonist, most closely resembles not the Cavaliere, though she possesses his civilized sophistication, nor Emma, though she shares Emma's theatrical genius. Rather, she is an extension of the fearless Eleonora, for she, too, is a diva, and what Sontag calls a "striving woman."[11] Maryna is extremely work-ful; she is equally idealistic, equally desirous of love, but persuaded in a way that Hamilton was not of the ways in which "work," and especially the "work of art," *can* not only create but transform society. Picking up the tropes of theatricality from the earlier novel, where they are mostly associated with Emma's theatrics and their erotic efficacy, in this novel acting is professional work and is presented as uniquely liberatory in the ability of an actor to move in and out of identity at will—and to capture the aesthetic and, maybe, the social imagination of her audience.

In *In America*, Sontag signals interest in utopian aspirations even before the narrative begins. Its epigraph, from Langston Hughes, reads simply, "America will be," announcing that the essence of America— or, at least, the essence of the *myth* of America—is its state of constant transformation into something else, its active futurity, its constant modernity. David Morris reminds us that America "in some sense *is* postmodernism,"[12] and the crux of Sontag's novel becomes squaring that assertion with the association of America with a historical utopia. While reviewers of *In America* have argued about the novel's problematic status generically because of its "typically" postmodern metafictional devices, one aspect of the issue has been overlooked: the novel, postmodern or not, falls squarely into the formal genre of utopian narrative. In an opening chapter, labeled "Zero" to signal a sort of proleptic prehistory to the narrative, the narrator, Sontag "herself," speaks out of the present, with obvious references to the author's own work and allusions to her own biography. The narrator describes herself as "so exotic a stranger" (17) to the persons whose lives she will be tracing in this novel; in other words, she is the typical outsider of utopian narrative, like William Morris's "Mr. Guest," who intrudes in order to observe and record. Like Morris/Guest, Sontag is a time traveler,[13] though in this novel "traveling back to the past" (19) rather than to the future in order to glimpse the "seeds of prediction" (23) that would determine what America's future, Sontag's present, and beyond would look like.

Still, Sontag's work, like her heroine's, is for the future. Indeed, what interests Sontag about the work of her latest protagonist is its relation to art—and especially this particular kind of work's transformative power.[14] The heroine of this novel is an actual historical figure, a famous Polish actress named, originally, Helena Modrzejeswska, who emigrated in 1876 with her family and a small entourage of friends to the American frontier in Anaheim, California, which is now, of course, only a few miles from that quintessentially American utopia, Disneyland. Having had a "dry run" on a remote Polish mountain, where the cohort would summer in order to "inscribe their own vision of an ideal community" (63), this heroine (renamed Maryna Zalenska in the novel), her husband, and several other Polish couples set up an explicitly Fourier-based phalanstery, seeking the "unencumbered freedom" (65) they could not find anywhere in Poland. This taste of freedom is what brings them ultimately to California, a "LABORER'S PARADISE" (121). She has to explain her emigration to puzzled friends and stricken fans: "'Since when have you believed in paradise?'" her friend Henryk asks. "'Always. Since I was a child. And the older I get, the more I believe in it, because paradise is something necessary'" (38). And thus she and her friends dedicate themselves to new social roles, no longer as discontented intellectuals but as farmers remaking the land in the image of their bookish utopian blueprint.

But Maryna's utopian ambitions took form in the theater, as she realized the ways in which "work," and especially the "work of art," can liberate an actor, who moves in and out of identity at will. According to the narrator, "the theatre seemed to her nothing less than the truth. A higher truth. Acting in a play, one of the great plays, you became better than you really were. . . . You could *feel yourself* being improved by what was given to you, on the stage, to express" (32; my emphasis). Maryna's drive is to make this condition of self-improvement and subjective freedom permanent, residing equally in the imagination and in the world, and not a temporary thrill lasting for just a few hours of performance on a Polish stage. Her goal is thus fully engaged in the theater's promise of futurity, new identities, new spaces of performance. Her theatricalized sense of space and action will offer something the "Helena" from the Old World decides she can only discover on "this rude stage" (136), America itself, where freedom is tied closely to the belief that any American can, will-fully, "make herself" and become, as we say, a "made" man or woman, one who has "made it."

The association of acting with futurity is essential to the novel's reconstruction of utopian aspirations and potentialities: "Yes," says Maryna early on, "that's what preparing a role is, it's like looking into the future" (48). The Anaheim adventure is clearly another great drama, a rewriting of personal and national history: a freeing from the past and an opening up to the future—a transformation of a social and personal history that are conveniently joined in the figure of this great actress, long since dubbed Poland's "national treasure." Her insistence on bringing her immediate family and a cadre of devotees along was justified in more ways than the merely personal: after all, she says, only slightly facetiously, "one can't do plays without other people" (78).

But it is her delight in the idea that she can leave history behind, her own personal and national histories, in coming to America that so appeals to her. Maryna believes that her compatriots, "natural pessimists" (223), falsely chain History and Fate together and that individual Poles, including herself, are left with too limited a stage upon which to act. Maryna and her husband, Bogdan, talk about the way in which the Polish people come to believe that failure is a romantically noble thing, justifying a tragic history of national conquest from without and national underachievement from within. Over and over again Maryna refuses to acknowledge that "the past is a fate" (223) that cannot be escaped, and she resists her compatriots' general expectation of, and compensatory admiration for, lack of success as a historical and psychological bondage stalling cultural progress and limiting human agency. While still in Poland, Maryna sees the theater as the only possible mode of resistance: "Acting," she observes, "was a program for overcoming the slave in myself" (135), but the temporary freedom "on the boards" was hardly enough for so ambitious and expansive a personality: "It's a new life, the life I want" (178) she says time and time again, "rewriting the past" (268). And for this reason Maryna insists, to the dismay of nearly every acquaintance and fan, on emigration, rejecting the "sentiment of *Europamüde*, tired of Europe," as Sontag puts it in a 1984 essay, "Questions of Travel."[15] For in America, Bogdan remarks, "it is hard to think that failure has its nobility" (225). Maryna's own belief in the art and the work of self-transformation on the stage leads to her pursuit of the dream of "mak[ing] it [her vision of an alternative life] real" (117) on the much larger stage of her own life and history, capturing the aesthetic and, hope-fully, the social imagination of her audience in her own quest for the "freedom" that America offers.

What's strange about this book, though, and numerous reviewers accurately note this, is that the work they set out to do—the work of farming, the work of community—is not taken all that seriously. As the novelty of manual labor and living off the land wears off and tensions increase within the group, the expansiveness of the rhetoric in letters sent back home starts to ring false. Indeed, this highly self-conscious group realizes rather quickly that the fantasy of returning to pastoral bliss is just that, a fantasy, and they begin to admit to a certain unintended falseness to their efforts. Maryna acknowledges the accusation of one of her entourage, her eventual lover, Richard, who frames it in the theatrical terms that pervade this novel: "Tell me that you don't feel you are acting in a play. Tell me that there isn't one Maryna who is kneading dough, . . . and the other, standing beautifully tall as only you do, who gazes at herself with amazement and incredulity" (206).

Indeed, this ironical self-regard soon prompts her to return to the theater, which she continues to believe is a more authentic arena for the enactment of both personal and social progressiveness and personal freedom than scraping out a living on the California hills. The community members admit their ineptitude and give up on the enterprise rather quickly.[16] Maryna and company have gotten a little browner, a bit leaner, and their hands have developed some calluses. But this kind of labor on the land, however equally distributed, however bracing and healthy, does not advance the horizon of utopia very far. The commune disbands with little regret on anyone's part, and the land in Anaheim, "our Arden" (323), is eventually sold off.

The California experience has particularly little direct effect on Maryna, the one who dragged everyone there in the first place, except insofar as it reinvigorates her will to self-invention. What America has offered her already is the sense of a constant present, a continuous sense of possibility, a constant intuition of the future. As Maryna's husband notes in his diary, "The Past is not really important here. Here the present does not affirm the past but supersedes and cancels it" (223). Maryna turns away, without nostalgia, from the romantic scheme of the "utopian household," which she has come to view as "so cramped, so ungenerous a stage" (153) rather than as the "perfect setting for a transformation," as she had once described California.[17]

Instead, she turns toward the wider public stage of America itself, where her project of American self-invention begins in earnest. Removing from mothballs her diva's mask, Maryna will be satisfied with nothing less than the conquering of another nation. Only after abandoning the pragmatic commune work and again taking up the work of transforming herself does she understand the full implications of her musings: "Surely you see," she says in a letter, "that I'm thriving on being stripped of almost all that made me distinctive to others and to myself" (173). For a woman who revels in "impersonating and transforming" (319), this stripping away is the beginning of a liberation from the "slavery," as she put it earlier, of the past, and the beginning of her project of truly *re*making herself in earnest. This cannot take place according to a "blueprint" model for another utopian commonwealth but instead according to transformative *act*ion on a much wider, new, and constantly changing stage, "this rude stage" (136), America, which she proceeds to tour from coast to coast, from north to south. And at this work of transformation she works far more energetically, passionately, and extravagantly than she did at commune building. She pushes herself to mental and physical limits with a zeal that alarms even her husband who, though accustomed to her extravagancies, is amazed by her inexhaustible demand for success, her fierce refusal to be limited by the past, and her drive to cultivate her new persona and new audiences. In a session with an acting student named Krystyna, Maryna tells the other woman to

> make the role your own, don't feel shadowed by how I portray her. . . . When the great Rachel brought her Scottish lady [Lady Macbeth] . . . to London and was told that their great Mrs. Siddons had already exhausted every possible idea for playing the sleepwalking scene, Rachel replied, Surely not *every* idea. I intend to lick my hand. Your wildest fancy, Krystyna. (320)

Novelty—or, perhaps better, *modernity*—is more important to Maryna now than any memory of greatness. Make it new. By the end of the novel, "Maryna liked being part of the wave of the future" (330), and when she is acclaimed, finally, no longer as a great Polish actress but as a great "American" one, she triumphs in her new nobility, not the nobility of failure that fed Polish defeatism but a nobility of the modern, of the successful.

IV

> But paradise is always being lost.
> —Sontag, "Questions of Travel"

Tracing the frank failure of the Anaheim farm to Maryna's "self-made" American identity, we might think Sontag denies positive utopian possibilities. In an early interview with Edwin Newman, Sontag mentions "having a kind of disillusionment about the possibilities of community, or even what people are capable of" (*CSS*, 16–17). Maryna echoes this skepticism when she asks, "Where is the community of friends I believed in?" (304). The novel certainly rejects a naïve view of utopia; indeed, maybe there were hints the commune was doomed from the start, notably in the hovering narrator's suspicion that her cultured protagonists were already too ironical (no "coven of tardy romantics" [*IA*, 10]).[18]

And there is a more serious charge, against Maryna herself. Her husband, Bogdan, whose diary provides a running counternarrative to Maryna's increasingly false note of romanticism, remarks that the natural optimism characteristic of Americans and rooted in their denial of the past has a paradoxical effect on their character, which clearly Maryna now shares: "The weakness of any attachment to the past is perhaps the most striking thing about the Americans. It makes them seem superficial, shallow, but it gives them great strength and self confidence. They do not feel dwarfed by *anything*" (223). Maryna's complex heroism brings with it an embodiment of certain quintessentially American virtues: drive, adaptability, faith in the will and in the future. But she also reflects aspects of America that Sontag, in much of the rest of her work, admires least. As the author remarks in an interview with Michael Cathcart, "I am depicting in this book someone who adapts to the United States, to a culture that is both very money-minded and very moralistic." Maryna's own drive for utopia in this novel is similarly and essentially self-centered—*New York Times* reviewer Michiko Kakutani calls her a "simple narcissist."[19]

The heroine's vision of the world has little to do with community and more to do with a vision of modernity—which for her is itself utopia, a "being in the future" that takes her from what she was, what she *is*, and allows her to ask herself what she *could* be. In her groundbreaking essay "On Style" (1965), Sontag described the history of art generally as "the history of different attitudes toward the will," a study of "the new ideas of self-mastery and of mastery of the world, as embodying new relations between the self and world";[20] any single work of art is "the signature of the artist's will."[21] This is an apt description of Maryna's extravagant "way of being" in this new world, with her insistence on paring down experience to nothing but the enacting of modernity, the continuous creation of those "new relations" with the world. But those "new relations" come at a cost—to old affiliations and to her sense of alliance with old friends, with her own past, and with, as we are too frequently reminded by the hurt and critical commentaries of her husband, her lovers. Is this what Sontag meant by "adapting to America," this unique individualism, tied so closely to will, to work, and to success—and so lacking in loyalty and sympathy to the dreams of others? And what then becomes of Sontag's intentions toward recuperating the viability and seriousness, for our own time, of utopia?

In a damning review of *In America*, Carol Iannone describes the novel as the epitome of Sontag's career in its display of intellectual affectation and irresponsible posturing and counterposturing. No surprise, then, that the reviewer compares the character of Maryna to certain aspects of Sontag herself, both figures "now largely retired from [their] utopian endeavors but still seeking metamorphosis in art."[22] But Iannone misses the import of *In America*'s deeply ironical conclusion. If there is a "utopic sensibility" to be found in Sontag's novel, as I have suggested there is, to expose it requires that we shift our frame slightly, by looking away from the theatrical history of Maryna herself and to the textual frame within which that drama is played out. The novel's form, for all its connections to the theatrical, has a generic agenda of its own, and Sontag's fictional work actively engages that generic agenda. In 2001, Sontag identifies the "education of feeling" as the primary aim of novels generally,[23] and certainly this is the case with every one of her own. But Sontag's approval of the novel's sensibility of "feeling" is reanimated with something more modern: the interest in embodiment and display that theatricality offers. In other words, in these novels Sontag begins to reconnect the novel's education of feeling with her interest in theater's political possibilities, insisting upon its crucial role in deconstructing the many possibilities—both abject and oppositional—of human agency.

The exposure of this sensibility lies in *In America*'s peculiar last chapter. If Sontag had believed unreflectively in the twin powers of theater to transform and transcend, she would not have written this lengthy monologue, which touches on Maryna's performance in *The Merchant of Venice* and is spoken by the most successful American actor of the nineteenth century, the great Edwin Booth. In her essay on Roland Barthes, Sontag describes the theatrical as "the domain of liberty, the place where identities are only roles and one can *change* roles, a zone where meaning itself may be refused"; the "triumph" of this position, "the aesthete's position," is its "refusal of the tragic"—as such a position also refuses "the tragic of its finality" (*WSF*, 82). Surely Maryna is in such a position, but in becoming the "wave of the future" has she not lost more than she admits to by abandoning her past? Does her achievement of self-sufficiency and self-determination really bring her the wholeness of an authentic utopian happiness?[24] These questions, uncomfortably posed in the final chapter, create an ironized network of tropes and narratives that complicate what appears at first glance to be too innocent a belief either in theater, in the "self-made" success of America, or, certainly, in the myth of America as a utopia.

Booth's role in this final act of the novel is to reintroduce the tragic into the fictional drama, and in doing so to resist Maryna's all-too-American facility of action. The monologue—complete with italicized stage directions that significantly blur the boundaries of novel and drama—is apparently motivated by an interpretive error on Maryna's part. Booth disavows Maryna's facile "I feel your pain" gesture of touching Shylock's shoulder because she injects this sign of empathy just when Shylock's paradoxical status as human and not-human is most appallingly on display and when his demand on the sensibilities of his audience is most insistent and difficult. At the same moment, the corporate nature of the theatrical audience is paradoxically most and least social; that is, Shylock here forces every member of every audience to turn back upon him- or herself and measure Shylock's responses against his or her own sympathies, prejudices, and ethical understandings. Shakespeare's genius was to make this a deeply uncomfortable moment for any honest person. Booth thus charges this gesture with inauthenticity, since it allows Maryna's character to get away with a facile expression of sympathy. *Fear* of Shylock's pain would have been a more realistic response, he asserts, for "being in pain is very combustible" (370) and to touch Shylock at this moment could never soothe his emotions but only ignite them ("*Nel petto un Vesuvio d'avere mi par*," once again).

Edwin Booth should know about facile underestimations of theater's political and emotional dynamics. We meet him drunk, self-indulgent, and morbid, aware of his brilliance and success but haunted by historical reality: his brother is the Booth who murdered President

Lincoln, in the theater. No one knows better than this Booth how "even a box in a theatre is a stage" (*VL*, 330); while he famously stars on stage for the imagined histories of *Hamlet* and *Richard III*, he is condemned to see himself playing a bit part in a singular historical tragedy of his own time. This actor's life stands as an ironic critique of aesthetic detachment: Is it a mere accident, a coincidence of historical contingency, that one of the most politically dramatic moments of American history is enacted in a theater by the brother of America's most celebrated actor? Perhaps, but in America the myth of a constant present and the irrelevance of the past obscures the effects of willfully ignoring the influence of historical contingency. Such willed ignorance, now in the early twenty-first century as then in the late nineteenth, threatens the ethical and political progressiveness of an idealized American national character as often as it promotes it.

Booth's pathetic sense of hollowness, despite (or because of) his exemplary skills as an actor and his celebrity, challenges Maryna's ascendancy, asking her, and us, to consider whether this diva's mask, however flush with success, admiration, and money, is not perilously brittle. Maryna's interpretive error may seem trivial, but in fact it's a critical error and a typically American one: the conflation of "willing strenuously and taking for granted" (*IA*, 344), the easy, self-aggrandizing solution. Minor characters like Booth, here, and like Bogdan throughout the rest of the novel, help to correct Maryna's strenuous willfulness. "'Our community is like a marriage,'" Bogdan's journal quotes Maryna as saying; "and suddenly I'm on my guard. I don't mean *our* marriage, she says, laughing. I mean a marriage that's matured by compromises and disappointments and abiding goodwill" (219). Thus, here at the end of the novel, Booth invites us, along with Maryna, to find the compromise between the purity of the ideal and the complexity of the real: "Every marriage, every community is a failed utopia," remarks the narrator; "Utopia is not a kind of place but a kind of time, those all too brief moments when one would not wish to be anywhere else" (175). If Bogdan and Maryna have found compromises within their romance of community, so, too, have Booth, her "'husband in art,'" and Maryna, who is "'as naked [to Booth] as if you were my bride'" (387).[25] Thus partnered here at the end, Booth can gently propose to Maryna that we can improve the moment. Maybe, I'm not sure, you *can* touch me. I'm not entirely averse to a new piece of business here. I am not so pledged to tradition. And I have an absolute loathing of empty repetition. But I hate improvisation. An actor can't just *make it up*. Shall we promise each other, here and now, always to tell first when we're going to do something new? We have a long tour ahead of us.

(387)

The reconciliation here is between thinking and feeling, intellect and sympathy, self and other: these meet in the commitment to sincerity that Edwin Booth requests, played out onstage as experiments of gesture during future rehearsals and performances before their American audience.[26] Through her recreation of these romantic forbears, Sontag proposes to us—the audience beyond Maryna's and Edwin's—a utopic sensibility that Maryna herself notably lacks. Booth's crucial lesson is that the cultivation of *sympathy* should be the highest ideal for an artist, for only sympathy's sincere intention can turn an audience away from the specter of historical tragedy and toward a cautious intimation of hope.[27] "*Utopia [is] at the horizon of a voyage (travel),*" says utopian theorist Louis Marin;[28] it may be that Maryna discovers her utopian freedom only now, in these critical moments, when the "work" of art is laid bare during the nomadic journey through America's theatrical spaces.

With such an open-ended (indeed un-novelistic) conclusion—Booth and Maryna will continue to travel, perform, and *trans*form audiences through the intersubjective work of performance—the utopic sensibility offered by the novel's *author*, notably present "in the wings" as the self-consciously contemporary narrator, comes to the foreground. The novel offers a model for an ongoing performative that promises a contingent humanism rooted in a fragile communion of performers, both with each other and with their anticipated audiences. Such moments align themselves with just those "utopian performative moments" described by Jill Dolan, in which "we can experience emotionally and affectively, as well as intellectually and aesthetically, politically and spiritually, the possibilities of a world purposefully, revealingly, out of joint. In the rupture of the possible into the real, we can feel our way elsewhere."[29] Richard Dyer puts it another way in his discussion of entertainment generally:

"the utopianism [of entertainment] is contained in the feelings it embodies. It presents . . . what utopia would feel like rather than how it would be organized. It thus works at the level of sensibility."[30]

Gestures of affiliation or sympathy performed willfully, either through art or through political action, stage the best hope for a positively transformative society, as such moments reconnect one individual with another and recall their responsibilities *to* each other. Sympathy urges a common cause, a communality and a communion, an affiliation with progressive possibilities for the self and her community. Sontag's own highly criticized appearance in Sarajevo as director and the success of a controversial production of *Waiting for Godot* in 1993 exemplifies the most rigorous biographical instance of the alliance of Sontag's own political sensibility and political commitment through "an ethical idea" of the theater,[31] and it is the exposure of just such "an ethical idea" that *In America* seeks again.

V

"Nowhere in the world does the Enlightenment dream of progress have such a fertile setting as it does in America."
—Susan Sontag, "Literature Is Freedom"

Susan Sontag seemed surprised "thirty years later," at the anniversary of the 1966 publication of *Against Interpretation*, that she should have been so central to what now seems to her "indeed a utopian moment";[32] she was even more surprised, though gratified, that not only was she taken so seriously—as "seriousness itself was in the early stages of losing credibility in the culture at large" ("Afterword," 312)—but the idea of utopia was as well. Thirty years later, she looks back bemusedly at seriousness so "quaint, 'unrealistic'" (312). And yet as she closes this essay she offers, "lurching from nostalgia to utopia," a hopeful gesture: "My hope is that its republication [*Against Interpretation*] now [in 1996], and the acquisition of new readers, could contribute to the quixotic task of shoring up the values out of which these essays and reviews were written" (312). We might be surprised that a thinker so dedicated to critique should commit herself, yet again, to such high seriousness, even given her ironical acknowledgment of her beginnings as "a pugnacious aesthete and a barely closeted moralist" (309). We should be touched, though, at her faith in her earliest ardors, even from the knowing perspective that "a certain irony," born of maturity and cultural shift, imposes.

Sontag's history of exploring the ironies of ideology and the limitations of modernity casts a long shadow on *In America*'s fragile conclusion;[33] it's wise to remain mindful of Cary Nelson's warning years ago that many of this critic's pronouncements "include overt advocacy, but it is rarely uncomplicated or uncompromised" ("Soliciting," 709). Indeed Sontag was called upon throughout her life to "explain" such compromises, and many didn't "buy" the explanations. But as she understood it, the necessity of utopia's impossible demands is allied with the necessity of art and with an insistence on the value of ideals even (or especially) in a time that "is experienced as the end—more exactly, just past the end—of every ideal" (*WSF*, 271). What has remained consistent throughout Sontag's career is a continued call for faith in art's fundamental power to change human sensibility. This is the message of Sontag's latest writings, which, like her final novel, exhort us toward a *reconciliation*—her term—of the nostalgic and the utopic in our modern world. This sense of reconciliation, between old and new, real and ideal, pervades her 2003 Friedenpreis presentation keynote in Berlin:

> "Old" and "new" are the perennial poles of all feeling and sense of orientation in the world. We cannot do without the old, because in what is old is invested all our past, our wisdom, our memories, our sadness, our sense of realism. We cannot do without faith in the new, because in what is new is invested all our energy, our capacity for optimism, our blind biological yearning, our ability to forget—the healing ability that makes reconciliation possible.
> (*AST*, 203)

This stance is anticipated in *In America*, in which the marriage of Maryna and Bogdan and, later, the "artistic marriage" of Maryna and Edwin are not destroyed by the abandonment of naïve idealism but are strengthened by willing compromise to the demanding and endless dynamic of reality and desire. This dynamic, Sontag teaches us, can only finally be negotiated by the cultivation of sympathy: "If literature has engaged me as a project," remarks Sontag, "first as a reader and then as a writer, it is an extension of my sympathies to other selves, other domains, other dreams, other words [*sic*; for "worlds"?], other territories."[34] This recent remark echoes her much earlier statement, in the NPR interview with Elizabeth Farnsworth previously cited, where she notes that novels "aren't just pleasure, I think they are an education of feeling. They extend your feeling. They make you . . . they should make you more compassionate, more . . . have more empathy with other human beings. They struggle against this dryness, this dryness that a lot of people feel."

While *In America*'s final chapter disavows the idea that America is "simply" the utopia of individualism, it nevertheless avows its author's belief in a utopic sensibility based on an ideal of a sympathetic community, including the author's own speculative audience. In contrast to Sontag's earlier novels, *In America* foregrounds a utopic sensibility that resists the fetishization of the individual and avows the centrality of a social space joined by the twin poles of action and imaginative feeling. "Who would we be if we could not sympathize with those who are not us or ours? Who would we be if we could not forget ourselves, at least some of the time? Who would we be if we could not learn? Forgive? Become something other than we are?" (*AST*, 205). Over the arc of her career, Sontag's novels point to the imperative of the utopia that art offers: not a place, but an ongoing act-ivity or "work" of reading, seeing, critique, and action that is simultaneously aesthetic, political, and ethical in its judgments. The projection of this ideal community, a communing or dialogue among "other selves" with "other dreams," traveling toward horizons elsewhere, is her best vision for realizing a humane and progressive future.

Notes

1. Evans Chan, "Against Postmodernism, Etcetera—a Conversation with Susan Sontag," http://www.iath.virginia.edu/pmc/text-only/issue.901/12.1chan.txt, accessed January 8, 2009.

2. Tobin Siebers, "Introduction," in *Heterotopia: Postmodern Utopia and the Body Politic*, ed. Siebers (Ann Arbor: University of Michigan Press, 1995), 3.

3. Siebers, "Introduction," 9.

4. Fredric Jameson, *Archaeologies of the Future: The Desire Called Utopia and Other Science Fictions* (New York: Verso, 2005), 211.

5. In saying this, I am supposing that Sontag, while employing postmodernist literary devices and engaging certain strains of postmodernist thought, would be happy to be counted out of the community of postmodernists who would claim that postmodernism's "general crisis of representation" (Jameson, *Archaeologies*, 212) also means that we are now in an era of postutopianism. Sontag, as I will discuss, would be the last to propose blueprints for society, but art's role in critiquing and understanding the relationship of subject to history is, for her, a self-evident truth. I suspect she would accept, instead, Jameson's offer that "there is no reason to fear that postmodern Utopias will not be as energizing in their new historical context as the older ones were in previous centuries" (212). The most complete explication, and most satisfying engagement with postmodernism's challenge to utopia's relevance (or even possibility) is Jameson's monumental *Archaeologies of the Future*, as well as Siebers's earlier text.

6. See Brigitte Peucker, "Looking and Touching: Spectacle and Collection in Sontag's *Volcano Lover*," *Yale Journal of Criticism* 11, no. 1 (Spring 1998): 159–65, on this and other aspects of this novel. Also see the interesting discussion of this novel in Julie C. Hayes, "Fictions of Enlightenment: Sontag, Süskind, Norfolk, Kurzweil," *Bucknell Review: A Scholarly Journal of Letters, Arts and Sciences* 41 (1998): 26–29, where she discusses this novel's "fusion of passion and classification, aestheticism and appetite" (26).

7. In her essay "A Double Destiny: On Anna Banti's *Artemisia*," Sontag writes that "an author who may be described as a lover of sorts is, inevitably, one who insists on being there—brooding, interrupting, prowling about in her book. Relentlessly dialogical (it is in the nature of the language of love to be dialogical), the novel offers an impassioned mix of first- and third-person voices" (*AST*, 41). She states that the author's "presence in the novel is at the heart—is the heart—of the novel" (42). This describes quite precisely the so-called postmodern intrusiveness of Sontag "herself" as narrator of both this novel and *In America*.

8. Siebers, "Introduction," 10.

9. Cary Nelson, "Soliciting Self-Knowledge: The Rhetoric of Susan Sontag's Criticism," *Critical Inquiry* 6, no. 4 (Summer 1980): 720, 721.

10. This self-identification with a strong female character is only one of the things that infuriates Bruce Bawer in his crabby review of "that Sontag woman," and *The Volcano Lover* in *New Criterion* 10, no. 9 (1992 May): 10–17. Carol Iannone concurs, finding the author's intrusions irritating, "the still unfinished work of the essayist usurping that of the novelist" ("At Play with Susan Sontag," *Commentary* 111 [February 2001]: 57). Sontag's biographers Rollyson and Paddock describe Sontag's self-mythologizing in her reminiscences and also, by extension, in her fiction not as "hypocritical" but as "an endearing effort to maintain her vision of herself and of the writer's career which is not infected with cynicism" (*Susan Sontag: The Making of An Icon* [New York:

Norton, 2000], 60). Nancy K. Miller's memorial essay, "Theories and Method-ologies: Regarding Susan Sontag," *PMLA* 120, no. 3 (May 2005): 828–33, also looks at this self-presentation as a "woman intellectual," but in the context of Sontag's (ambiguous) relation to feminism and to a rejection of political passiv-ity that became even more prominent in her last years. Maryna herself touches on this relation in *In America*; see *IA*, 134–35.

11. Elizabeth Farnsworth, "Conversation: Susan Sontag," interview, *NewsHour with Jim Lehrer*, February 2, 2001, http://www.pbs.org/newshour/conversation/jan-june01/sontag_02-02.html.

12. David Morris, "Postmodern Pain," in *Heterotopia: Postmodern Uto-pia and the Body Politic*, ed. Tobin Siebers (Ann Arbor: University of Michigan Press, 1995), 151.

13. "Mr. Guest" is William Morris's narrator-self in *News from Nowhere* (1890). Sontag's "A Double Destiny: On Anna Banti's *Artemisia*," which de-scribed Banti's way of "prowling" around her own text (see n. 7) is also inter-ested in the character—whether fictional or authorial—who functions as "a time-traveler, a visitor" (43).

14. On this relationship of utopia, imagination, and work see Louis Marin, "Frontiers of Utopia: Past and Present," *Critical Inquiry* 19 (1993): esp. 413–15: "Utopia is the infinite work of the imagination's power of figuration. Uto-pia is the infinite *potential* of historical figures: it is this infinite, this 'work,' this *potential* that the Greek negation *ou* allows to be understand as a prefix to the name *topos*. Utopia is the plural figure of the infinite work of the limit or fron-tier or difference in history. *Totality and infinity: Utopia at the horizon of a voy-age (travel)*" (413).

15. *WSF*, 277. Also directly relevant to the contrast of this *Europamüde* with the promise of America is Sontag's more recent speech, "Literature and Freedom," presented upon her acceptance of the Friedenpreis in October, 2003, where she remarks upon the history of the contrast: "The authors of recent popular tracts promoting the idea of an inevitable clash of interests and values between Europe and America did not invent these antitheses. Foreign-ers brooded over them—and they provide the palette, the recurrent melody, in much of American literature throughout the 19th century, from James Feni-more Cooper and Ralph Waldo Emerson to Walt Whitman, Henry James, Wil-liam Dean Howells, and Mark Twain. American innocence and European so-phistication; American pragmatism and European intellectualizing; American energy and European world-weariness; American naïveté and European cyni-cism; American goodheartedness and European malice; American moralism and the European arts of compromise—you know the tunes" (*AST*, 194).

16. Kenneth Roemer notes the frequent gap between ideal and real in the records of actual utopianists and their need to acknowledge contingency and lim-itations—unlike a utopianist author dwelling only in the imaginary: "A utopist, the author of a literary utopia, is free to imagine any setting that will adequately

express his concepts of goodness or, in a dystopia, badness. The founders of utopian communities, on the other hand, are severely constrained by nagging realities. 'The pigs ate up all the potatoes on the flat today; also the squash. Oh, Hell!'
reads a diary entry by a founder of a utopian community in California" ("Defining America as Utopia," in *America as Utopia*, ed. Kenneth Roemer. [New
York: Burt Franklin, 1981], 4). He adds, however, that the author's freedom
is "exposure"—something Sontag will always be aware of: "Utopists cannot
hide; they set the ground rules for their utopias. Therefore, they consciously or
unconsciously reveal their deepest desires and fears as they describe the worlds
they have created with their imaginations" (*IA*, 5). In choosing as her setting an
historical utopian experiment that rather quickly failed, Sontag signals her interest not in utopia per se but in what I am calling the utopic sensibility of an
individual.

17. Judith Sklar, "What Is the Use of Utopia?" in *Heterotopia: Postmodern Utopia and the Body Politic*, ed. Tobin Siebers (Ann Arbor: University of
Michigan Press, 1995), surveys some of the major American utopian experiments, including the type of Fourierist efforts that Maryna's community in
nineteenth-century California represents. Generally speaking, she notes, these
American phalanxes "tended to fail due to inefficient management. They went
broke, and they suffered an unusual number of fires. The real trouble, it seems
to me, was that the sort of people who would do well in a Fourierist phalanx
would do well in American life anyhow and would therefore be unlikely to
join. As models for the eventual transformation of a society, of hardship and
painful work into ease and pleasurable production, Fourier's enterprises went
nowhere. . . . Hence the sad ending of both utopian enterprises: one to liber-
ate eros, the other to render labor fulfilling in a planned harmonious environment" (50).

18. Sontag refers at this point in the text to an eighteenth-century version
of More's *Utopia* by Polish writer Ignacy Krasicki: his "Nipu" is "an ideal, con-
summately isolated community . . . that stern blueprint for a stripped-down life
of perfect, rustic comity" (*IA*, 9–10).

19. Michael Cathcart, "Interview with Susan Sontag," Radio National
(February 6, 2000), www.abc.net.au/rn/atoday/stories/s133826.htm. The rest
of Kakutani's review remains similarly negative, describing the novel generally
as "flat," expressing ideas that "the gifted Sontag" has expressed "more per-
suasively and with far more nuance and subtlety many times before" (Michiko
Kakutani, "'In America': Love a Distraction That Gets in the Way of Art," review, *New York Times*, February 29, 2000, www.nytimes.com/library/books/
-022900sontag-book-review.html.). This charge is also lobbed by *New Republic* reviewer James Wood, who also objects to the "stageyness" not only of
Maryna's world but of the postmodern narrativity of the novel's form ("The
Palpable Past-Intimate," *New Republic*, March 27, 2000, www.powells.com/
review/2001_07_26.html).

20. "On Style," in *A Susan Sontag Reader* (1963; New York: Vintage Books, 1982), 151.

21. Sontag, *Reader*, 152.

22. Iannone, "At Play," 7.

23. Farnsworth, "Conversation: Susan Sontag."

24. Michael Silverblatt, "For You O Democracy," *Los Angeles Times Book Review*, February 27, 2000, 1–2, a review of the novel, describes this final monologue, along with the opening chapter "Zero," as an "anti-sentimental" foil to Maryna's "lacquered self-deception."

25. Jill Dolan's description of certain dramatic moments seems an apt one to describe this rapprochement between Maryna and Booth: "Perhaps in these moments of communal, almost loving rest, when the flesh stops and the soul pauses, we come together, at attention and relieved, to feel utopia" ("Performance, Utopia, and the 'Utopian Performative,'" *Theatre Journal* 53 [2001]: 477). Dolan's faith in "the politically progressive possibilities of romanticism in performance" (479) strikes me as a less careful version (she admits to the risk) of Sontag's own hopes for art.

26. Such moments represent the kind of "gestic moments of clarity" that Dolan sees as theater's transformative moments ("Performance, Utopia," 475). Dolan stresses the connection of utopic performance to a "practice of reception": "In some ways, utopian performatives are the received moment of *gestus*, when those crystallized, moving pictures of social relations become not only intellectually clear but felt and lived by spectators as well as actors" (Dolan, introduction to the special issue "Utopian Performatives," *Modern Drama* 47 [2004]: 172). The "utopia" for her lies in the moments of solidarity or empathy, however brief, and does not require that such moments "translate" into action: "by its very nature, [the utopian performative] can't translate into a program for social action, because it's most effective as a *feeling*" (169).

27. Michael Wood eloquently sounds a note of caution in his review: "*In America* displays the same unrequited love, but converts it into utopia, the place we can't go beyond and don't wish to leave. The vision is alluring, and Sontag is suggesting we need both to understand its appeal and to shake it off. It is not a style of radical will but rather the reverse: a longing for a historical time when wishing was an option, and for the fantasy time when wishing was enough" ("Susan Sontag and the American Will," *Raritan* 21, no. 1 [Summer 2001]: 147).

28. Louis Marin, "Frontiers of Utopia: Past and Present," *Critical Inquiry* 19 (1993): 413.

29. Dolan, introduction, 167.

30. Richard Dyer, *Only Entertainment* (New York: Routledge, 1992), 18.

31. Peter Brooks describes Sontag as "ethically noble but utopian" in her argument in *Illness as Metaphor* ("Death of/as Metaphor," *Partisan Review* 46

[1979]: 443). Also see Erica Munk on Sontag's "ethical idea" of the theater ("Only the Possible: An Interview with Susan Sontag," *Theater* 24 [1993]: 31).

32. "Afterword: Thirty Years After . . . " (1996), in *Against Interpretation and Other Essays* (New York: Macmillan, 2001), 311.

33. See Christine Brooke-Rose's observations in her essay entitled "Eximplosions," *Genre* 14 (1981): 9. Sohnya Sayres opens "For Susan Sontag, 1933–2004," *PMLA* 120, no. 3 (May 2005): 834–38, her *PMLA* memorial to Sontag, with a discussion of this scene (see esp. 834–35).

34. Liam Kennedy notes that "Sontag's opposition to moral assumptions and unifying demands of humanism is remarkably consistent": "she criticizes a 'sentimental humanism' in Edward Steichen's famous 'Family of Man' exhibition, for wrongly assuming 'a human condition or human nature shared by everybody'" ("Precocious Archaeology: Susan Sontag and the Criticism of Culture," *Journal of American Studies* 24 [1990]: 25).

chapterfive

Sontag, Modernity, and Cinema
Women and an Aesthetics of Silence, 1960–1980

E. ANN KAPLAN

The noun "Sontag" covers many different intellectual periods and physical embodiments: in light of all the knowledge quickly gathered about Sontag since her death, we now know just how many different art forms she dealt with, how many performances and productions she was involved in, how much she traveled, how much she knew—all this aside from the major works we are all already familiar with. Why is it that only on a scholar's death do others find time to fully attend to her?

My chapter focuses on the years 1960 through 1980 because it was in this early intellectual period in her career that Sontag wrote about and made her films. If she ceased writing about film, it was because she had moved on to other art forms—photography, painting, theater—and not because she lost interest in cinema. Indeed, Sontag loved cinema and saw more films from around the world than many of us in cinema studies.[1] She was endlessly curious about the new and was drawn to 1960s European cinema as an innovative form like little else in the period. Her brilliant essays discussing directors she admired—Godard, Bresson, Antonioni, Resnais, Bergman—were written before cinema studies developed as an academic field, and especially before "high theory" dominated film studies.[2] These essays may be less well known than the devastating critique of Leni Riefenstahl in "Fascinating Fascism" (1974), which was one of the few Sontag essays to be included in anthologies geared for teaching film in the academy and which contributed a good deal to discussion of film and politics.

I

Sontag burst onto the U.S. intellectual scene on the cusp of the major theoretical changes of the 1970s and (increasingly) the 1980s. This is what makes her 1960s criticism refreshing to read now. However, Sontag's creativity might be missed unless her work is situated in its specific historical moment and in relation to her own conception of what she was doing. In her 1966 prefatory "Note" to the paperback edition of essays written between 1962 and 1965, Sontag describes the pieces not as "criticism proper" but rather as "meta-criticism"—"case studies of (her) evolving sensibility," written with "passionate partiality" (*AI*, ix–x). This is where Sontag dares to depart from New Criticism as such. Indeed, browsing through the 1964 issue of *Partisan Review* in which "Notes on Camp" first appeared, I was struck by just *how* different that intellectual moment was from our own, and how impressive Sontag's intervention was.[3] For if her criticism accords in a general way with the methods of New Criticism that were then dominant, the objects Sontag is drawn to—cinema, the new novel, popular culture (including the "camp" she invented)—were not being noticed by the U.S. intellectuals (William Phillips, Philip Rahv, Richard Poirier, editing *Partisan Review*) whom Sontag managed to connect with after arriving in New York from California and Chicago.[4] It is in the 1960s essays collected in *Against Interpretation* (1966) and a bit later in *Styles of Radical Will* (1969) that one finds the interests that energize her creative work. Sontag's critique of the New Criticism she is associated with is evident in her very concept of being "against interpretation," since "interpretation" would seem to be at the heart of New Criticism.[5] "By reducing the work of art to its content and then interpreting *that*" Sontag notes, "one tames the work of art. Interpreting makes art manageable, conformable" (*AI*, 8).

Sontag, that is, was ahead of her culture in being attracted to what I see as the "late" modernism of post–World War II Europe, which had barely yet had an impact in the United States. This era spawned a generation of artists reflecting a new sensibility touched by trauma—the Holocaust, Hiroshima—and that set the stage for 1960s revolutionary movements, including feminism. (The deaths of Antonioni and Bergman in 2007, that of Robbe-Grillet in February 2008 [Rivette marked his eightieth birthday at the same time] underscore the passing of a generation that greatly influenced Sontag.) It should not be surprising that the late modernist techniques that interested Sontag seem first to emerge in postwar France, given the strong French modernism of the 1920s and 1930s and the relative stability of many French intellectuals during WWII. And given her frequent visits to Europe in the 1960s, her close relations with European artists and critics, and her sensitivity to traumas of World War II, it's not surprising that late-modernist themes preoccupy Sontag and find their way into her films as also into those of directors, such as Duras, Godard, Bergman, Bresson, and Antonioni, who particularly interested Sontag.

A sign of the cultural times—the academic and critical temperature of 1969 in America—is revealed in the critical reaction to Sontag's first film, *Duet for Cannibals*, evident in an interview of Sontag and Agnès Varda with Jack Kroll, then senior editor at *Newsweek*. It speaks well for Richard Roud, chair of the New York Film Festival Selection Committee at the time, that Sontag's and Varda's films were chosen for the 1969 screening of new films. But the interview with Sontag and Varda (whose *Lion's Love* was the film selected) shows how daring and controversial both their films were in 1969.[6] Among the first female directors to be shown in the festival, Sontag and Varda seem conscious of their roles as innovators and renegades. Kroll, clearly well versed in Sontag's writings, seems genuinely bewildered by and uneasy with the themes in both women's films, seeing them as "very unusual" if not incomprehensible—works he says that could not have been made earlier. He says Varda's film has upset people and finds the characters in the films "grotesque" (a concept both directors reject). Kroll is genuinely at a loss as to how to categorize each film. His attitude is barely tolerated by either woman, with Sontag seeming the most scornful of Kroll's stance.

There is an implicit feminist sense to the way Sontag and Varda resist Kroll's efforts to interview them—a sort of siding of the two against him that was typical of feminists at the time. This stance anticipates Sontag's little recognized public identification with the women's movement in her early-1970s writing, which includes a long 1972 essay published in Paris in French, "Réflexions sur la Libération des Femmes (Réponses aux Questions)," that appeared in *Les Temps Modernes*.[7] Sontag's difference from her male *Partisan Review* peers is obvious here (although they were willing to publish an essay, "The Third World of Women," in 1973), and her writings confirm prowomen sentiments found especially in her second film, *Brother Carl*.[8]

Sontag was known for her critical essays and status as a public intellectual, although she felt she was most herself as an artist rather than a critic. Writing before cultural studies emerged, and as popular culture was only just beginning to be taken as a serious object of study for intellectuals, Sontag nevertheless wrote brilliantly on Hollywood science fiction, and on pornography *avant la lettre*. But as a high modernist, she was not, in general, drawn to popular culture.[9] But she was also not a strict New Critic either. Her polemic against interpretation is perhaps most obvious not in the essay by that name alone but in her discussion of Ingmar Bergman's *Persona*, made in Sweden shortly before Sontag directed her films there. I will later point out certain common themes in *Persona* and *Brother Carl*, but for now Sontag's objections to how critics treated Bergman's film—objections that suggest her sympathy for a kind of phenomenology while not undermining her strong interest in Freud—are what interest me.[10] Sontag berates critics of *Persona* for interpreting the relations between the mute protagonist, Elizabeth, and her husband, or imagining Elizabeth's feelings about her nurse Alma when in fact what we see on the screen does not justify the meanings critics claim.

Sontag uses a similar phenomenological approach in her discussion of Godard's *Vivre Sa Vie*: Sontag states that "*Vivre Sa Vie* is an exhibit, a demonstration. It shows *that* something happened, not *why* it happened. It exposes the inexorability of an event" (*AI*, 199). She notes that "despite appearance Godard's films are drastically untopical. An art concerned with social, topical issues can never simply show that something is. It must indicate *how*. It must show *why*. But the whole point of *Vivre Sa Vie* is that it does not explain anything. It rejects causality" (*AI*, 199). To sum up the point, Sontag says Godard "does not analyze. He proves." Proof, she says, differs from analysis: "Proof establishes that something happened. Analysis shows why it happened" (*AI*, 198). Sontag in fact makes Godard into a formalist while still claiming that his films are "emotionally exalting, even when they are being most deadpan and cerebral" (*AI*, 201). If her own films share a similar interest in refusing to provide meaning—an interest in enigma similar to that in some of Antonioni's films—they are also still emotionally alive.

The style of Sontag's films would seem to prohibit the interpretation she feared; arguably, for Sontag, the lack of information about who characters are, what their past together is, and what events have taken place before the story starts forces the viewer to give up trying to figure things out and to focus on each scene, each shot; to watch the camera; and to register the powerful emotions in play in each scene. "What matters in *Marienbad*," Sontag says in her essay "Against Interpretation," "is the pure, untranslatable, sensuous immediacy of some of its images, and its rigorous if narrow solutions to certain problems of cinematic form" (*AI*, 9). While this may be accurate about *Marienbad*, Sontag's films are equally about emotionality as about cinematic form. Indeed, Sontag objects to the fact that Resnais's films "lack tonicity and vigor, directness of address. They are cautious, somehow, overburdened and synthetic" (*AI*, 241). She concludes that Resnais's films "do not go to the end of the idea or of the emotion which inspires them which all great art must do" (*AI*, 241). I would argue that Sontag's brilliance lies in taking this lesson to heart and managing (especially in *Brother Carl*) a perfect combination of emotions and form. It is meaning that is unclear: Sontag deliberately frustrates our desire for it, inviting us to think otherwise, to function in a different kind of relationship to her screen than we are accustomed to, especially, but not only, in conventional Hollywood.

II

Shortly after writing so much about film, in 1969 Sontag tried her hand at directing, making *Duet for Cannibals* in Sweden for the Sandrew Film and Teater Production Company, followed by *Brother Carl* a year or so later, also made in Sweden for the same company.[11] Little known and rarely shown, these films offer insight into Sontag's intellectual and aesthetic concerns in the late 1960s and 1970s and amplify interests in the film essays. The films also, I'll argue, demonstrate Sontag's insights into gender imbalances of the period that worked against women's happiness—and this before the women's liberation movement developed its full-fledged critique of patriarchy.

One can find cinematic techniques and what I referred to above as late-modernist themes in Sontag's films that one also finds in Godard, Bergman, Bresson, and Antonioni, such as a certain abstraction, an interest in mystery/spirituality, a disillusionment with leftist politics (which by no means entails abdication of politics),[12] a refusal of causality, a despairing view of human communication, and a focus on human inability to find and keep love. Sontag's knowledge of 1930s modernist innovators (such as, in France, Antonin Artaud, Marcel Duchamp, Samuel Beckett, Jean Genet, André Gide) is evident in her essays, but in the wake of the horrors of World War II, her themes (like theirs) become more despairing, elegiac even, to use Sohnya Sayres's term.[13] Sontag certainly knew and avidly consumed movies by European directors also touched by the war during her time in Paris, Rome, and Sweden, before their films were readily available in the United States.[14] She knew some of the directors (especially the female directors, such as Agnes Varda and also Marguerite Duras), but this hardly means her art is derivative.[15] Sontag's films are unique both in terms of overall theme and cinematic techniques. They are made with a care and attention to detail rare in first films.

That Sontag's three feature films (1969, 1971, 1983) and her complex 1974 documentary are not widely available or much discussed in academic film studies is perhaps partly a result of their varied places of production as well as their enigmatic nature. The first two feature films, as noted, were made in Sweden, and the third, in Italy. All had low critical visibility in the United States (although her second film, *Brother Carl*, gained notice in Paris). Films by an American director but, in one case, spoken in Swedish and featuring Swedish actors and, in the second, using French and Swedish actors and, in the third, spoken in Italian and made for Italian TV, would likely not attract exhibitors. And documentaries are always hard to market.

Both Sontag's films thematize silence as a response to male violence, though they fall short of dealing directly with the more general haunting of Western cultures by violence, oppression, and death, such as one finds in a late-modernist director like Duras. Sontag's metaphysical interests are closer to Ingmar Bergman, who is an obvious reference point for Sontag's films; in addition to her profound 1967 essay full of admiration for *Persona* and *The Silence*, her feature films were made after Sontag had been lecturing and presumably seeing Bergman's films in Stockholm. *The Silence (Tystnaden)* (1964) and *Persona* (1967) appeared just as Sontag was preparing her first film, *Duet for Cannibals* (1969) and perhaps provoked themes concerning silence and emotion that Sontag already had in mind.

Few critics explicitly relate the strategic use of silence to questions of affect, but such linkage illuminates Sontag's attention to embodiment and affect. I am interested here not only in how Sontag's films evoke feminine or feminist issues (although in both cases this perspective is relevant) but especially in their deployment of an aesthetics of silence as illuminated by reference to Gilles Deleuze's concept of affect. In *Proust and Signs* (1964), Deleuze argues that affect or emotion triggers profound thought. "Thought," he says, "is nothing without something that forces and does violence to it"; sensations are the signs that, he says, force him "to bring out of the darkness what (he) had felt and convert it into a spiritual equivalent."[16] Following Deleuze, Brian Massumi distinguishes affect and emotion, using experimental psychological studies. He sees affect as autonomic, an intensity registered on the skin while emotion, he argues, is "subjective content, the socio-linguistic fixing of the quality of an experience, which is from that point onward defined as personal."[17] Both affect and emotion require language (neither Deleuze nor Massumi pretend otherwise), but affect connotes feeling as trace, resonance, uncertainty, while emotion indicates fixing on a specific feeling. Sontag's films have sequences relying on affect and others on emotion in Massumi's sense. It is the tie-in with the aesthetics of silence that interests me here. Visual culture offers a unique possibility for moving beyond words and also close to the body, while inevitably within a sign system functioning as a kind of language.

If I had to categorize Sontag's films as belonging to a world of either emotion or affect, her first film would typify a work built on emotion, the second on affect. However, both films inevitably use both techniques; it's a matter of which prevails. The world of *Duet for Cannibals* might well be called "artificial and artistic," to use Gabriele Schwab's phrase from a discussion of experimental art.[18] This is a highly self-conscious work, deliberately playing with narrative voice and performance, perhaps with a nod to the Godard of *Breathless*, *La Chinoise*, and *Vivre Sa Vie. Duet* is about intellectual arrogance and psychological manipulation—a kind of psychic cannibalism denounced in Greek tragedy and resonant of plays by Racine (as a French reviewer of the film noted).[19] A young left-leaning couple, who admire Dr. Bauer (the opening shot shows the wife, Ingrid, nailing a poster of Bauer to a wall), an apparently leftist political leader (he has a splendid cigarette lighter given to him by Brecht), are caught up in, and terrorized by, a kind of game that the middle-aged Bauer and his beautiful, apparently schizophrenic wife, Francesca, play with them. There's not really any plot as such, but the film is structured rather like a chess game, with one or another of each couple making moves to which the others respond. For the most part, the Bauers are by far the better because more experienced players, and they almost win the game.

Tomas, the young husband pursuing a Ph.D., agrees to work for Bauer tabulating and organizing manuscripts relating to his past secret political engagements. The tension between Tomas and Ingrid increases when Bauer insists Tomas live in his house. We know nothing of the couples' lives before they come together in this way, and we will know nothing of what happens once the young couple finally leave the Bauers' house. One watches with anxiety and interest the ways in which the Bauers manage to seduce Tomas first, and then Ingrid, anticipating the famous so-called Stockholm syndrome (after a 1973 robbery in Stockholm);[20] each younger person crosses the interpersonal boundary to shade into the older one, until what they desire is what the other desires, no matter at what personal cost, succumbing to what is now called a "borderline" pathology. The Bauers recall the monstrous couples in Shakespeare or Racine. Sontag knew and wrote a great deal about modern drama, and she staged plays and other works. Indeed, there is something theatrical about the way scenes in the Bauers' house are staged, something Brechtian in the distancing from the characters. As we will see, there is more of Shakespeare and Racine in the implicit evil at work in *Brother Carl* and in the intense emotionality of rejected love and betrayal. Is it coincidence that in her introduction to the script of *Brother Carl* Sontag calls the film "a winter's tale" (Sontag, *Brother Carl: A Filmscript*, x–xi)?

The viewer experiences mixed emotions watching this dizzying alternation of Tomas's desires and fantasies (in one scene we think he is in bed with Ingrid but soon it seems Francesca is there), sometimes

SONTAG, MODERNITY, AND CINEMA

exasperated that he does not leave, and furious with the manipulations of the Bauers. But Sontag keeps us at a distance, rather in the manner of Godard or the Brecht her protagonist mentions when pointing out the cigarette lighter to Tomas (Sontag evidently wanted to signal this playwright, whom she admired and wrote about in several essays, including "Spiritual Style in the Films of Robert Bresson" [AI, 177–82]).

Ingrid, as a wife losing her man, is the only character one can possibly identify with. Francesca is beautiful and seductive, and her Italian is lovely (in a Godardian scene, Francesca recites Dante by heart), but she is too mad for us to relate to.[21] Bauer is alternately pathetic and revolting; in one dinner scene, he eats greedily and then proceeds to vomit his meal. Tomas and Francesca sit at the table while the sounds of Bauer's retching fill the sound track.

The main back-and-forth tussle is between Ingrid and Tomas over Tomas's dedication to Bauer and increasing infatuation with the seductive Francesca. Ingrid risks losing her husband, whom she loves, and at first fights from the outside to keep him from going back to the Bauers. Finally, realizing this will not work, she enters the game being played by Bauer and Francesca while Tomas walks out in a rage. If Francesca at first seemed to be a pawn in her husband's game, once Ingrid joins the couple, Francesca appears to have a game of her own. This creates a somewhat comic reversal, such that Ingrid ends up being the older couple's slave, just as her husband was before. Sontag has a lot of fun with the play between Ingrid and Francesca. Francesca seduces Ingrid, and they exchange clothes, put on wigs, and end up looking alike. Androgynous, if not queer overtones predominate in an era long before the term "queer" was invented and when even lesbianism was not openly displayed. The relationships develop into a comic ménage à trois (reminding one of the film Bob and Ted and Carol and Alice). There is throughout a nod to the Godard of Breathless (which itself parodies American film noir) not only in the stark black-and-white photography but more literally in the scene where Bauer sends Tomas in a black sedan to deliver secret documents to another car in a garage somewhere. The screeching tires and shiny black cars common in film noir and in Breathless suggest Sontag's having fun with the genre. The silly hat that Bauer insists Tomas wear—and we later see Bauer wearing—adds the comic touch frequent in this film (note scenes where Bauer puts on a thin beard, later seen on Tomas, or plays with hats while looking in a mirror). Sontag is suggesting that these people are actors, performing roles and putting on costumes, and that identities are fluid, floating. She invites viewer to wonder if all human interaction is a performance, an act, lacking any depth.

The leader's lies and manipulations remind one of Elizabeth's vampire-like treatment of her nurse, Alma, in Bergman's *Persona*. In both cases, the younger person is vulnerable to the seductions and abuse of the older one and unable to sustain a stable subjectivity. Bauer reminds one of a dangerous psychoanalyst (there are many such images in Hollywood film) in his manipulation of Tomas. One might note that Elizabeth in *Persona* also psychoanalyses Alma in her notebooks. Perhaps Bauer reflects Sontag's suspicion of psychoanalysis as therapy while believing, like her cultural peers Norman Brown and Herbert Marcuse, in psychoanalysis "as a project for the transformation of human culture, and as a new and higher level in human consciousness as a whole" (*AI*, 258).[22] Bauer represents a disillusionment with leftist politics in the late 1960s that Sontag shared as increasing information about Stalin's abuse of power in the Soviet Union reached the West. Bauer's charisma comments on that of many totalitarian leftist leaders.

The Bauers finally end the game. Guns and bandages have been symbols throughout the film, suggesting violence, injury, and death. Bauer has long pretended that Francesca has threatened to kill him, and he gave Tomas a gun to protect himself. Francesca played a game with Tomas that involved bandaging his head, and later on Bauer also appears with a bandaged head. Early in the film, Francesca suddenly and violently breaks a window, the glass shattering over the floor. Now Bauer pretends he has killed her in self-defense. Ingrid and Tomas run from the house, and the film ends with a shot of Bauer and Francesca staring out of the window of their house at the departing couple, perhaps planning their next game and their next vulnerable couple.

Shot in black and white to symbolize (as with *Brother Carl*) the stark metaphysical polarities that preoccupy Sontag at this time, *Duet* is beautifully photographed and efficiently edited, and its symbols (cutting, breaking, guns, bandaging, imprisoning) are carefully used to suggest underlying emotional violence without being in the least heavy-handed. Shot on location in Stockholm (Sontag didn't want to use sets), the images are as stark as those of a documentary (there are scenes of Ingrid and Tomas walking in the city or traveling shots over Stockholm before the camera discovers Tomas and Ingrid on a roof outside their attic); some scenes are lush and elaborate (especially those inside the Bauers' house, as in the scene where Tomas reads and Francesca recites or when Tomas peeks through an elaborate wooden grille to where Bauer and his political visitors are secretly meeting). The image of shattered glass is at once terrifying and beautiful, as is the image of Tomas cutting himself in the opening sequence. The several scenes of eating reflect on the cannibalism of the title, with Bauer's vomiting perhaps suggesting how disgusting psychic devouring is. Throughout, an apparently contradictory tension prevails between the underlying threat and violence and a playful, comic reflection on human nature. The impossibility of normal, loving human communication or of pleasurable sex is perhaps one overriding theme. This, along with lack of motivation, causal explanation, narrative or character "development," and disillusionment with leftist politics, signals the late modernism of Sontag's film.

III

By the time Sontag came to publish the script of *Brother Carl*, she had had time to reflect on her experiences making her first film and the benefit, perhaps, of the many French reviews of *Carl*, most of which also referred back to *Duet*. Her comments on her choice regarding language show her interest in language and its emotional effects: In the first film, she has Swedish actors speaking in Swedish but translates the script into English subtitles. In the second, she wanted her Swedish and French actors to speak English partly because she felt that their slightly strained pronunciation would indicate the tense emotions among the characters. Sontag wanted the play of accents, the hesitations and displaced rhythms to show how the stiffness of the plot turns on the dilemmas of speaking, being silent, finding it hard to speak at all.

Sontag's introduction to her script also indicates how *Brother Carl* came to be made. Göran Lindgren, president of Sandrew Film and Teater Company, after screening *Duet* invited her to return to Sweden the following year (1970) to make a second film. Against Lindgren's wishes for a color film, Sontag insisted on black and white to support her "winter's tale." She found *Carl* harder to write than *Duet*, although she had the new film in her head and was grateful to Florence Malraux for acting as her interlocutor as she wrote the script. Sontag was happy that Gunner Lindblom, whom Sontag admired in Bergman's *The Silence*, agreed to play the part of Lena, since she had written it with Lindblom in mind. Laurent Terzieff, whom Sontag had also imagined for the part, readily agreed to play Carl partly because he saw links to the relationship between Diaghilev and Nijinsky. Sontag notes that the characters of Martin and Carl had long lived in her head as "emblems of the dramaturgy of silence (or voluntary mutism)" that had been a recurrent theme in her novels, where several mute figures appear (Sontag, *Brother Carl: A Filmscript*).

Sontag suggests commonalities between these two feature films, including the theme of mutism, but to me they are vastly different projects. It's true that each film involves two couples. In *Carl*, these are Martin, a worn-out theatrical director, and his estranged wife, Lena, and their friends, Peter and Karen, who have a mute child, Anna. In addition, there is Carl, who was Martin's protégé but is now schizophrenic and also voluntarily mute. He lives in a cabin near Martin's house on an island. Most of the film's action takes place in this remote place where Martin has retired for the time being.

While mutism is a common theme, the voluntary mutism of Francesca in *Duet* is part of a game, while that of Carl (and Anna, too) is a response, as perhaps in Bergman's Elizabeth, to deep trauma. In Carl's case this trauma is psychic abuse by a monstrous personality, while Anna may be responding to deep conflict between her parents. The films do share the late-modernist themes noted earlier and a basic structure of the two couples with complex, intertwining relationships. Each film (as Sontag also notes) has a monstrous male figure at the center, a powerful personality who abuses other characters for unknown reasons. Narcissistic, self-absorbed, monomaniacal, Martin and Bauer each control the other characters; each is cold, unloving, ambitious. However, Martin, Sontag notes, is a Bauer past his prime; he has already done maximum damage and in a state of exhaustion, revulsion, and weary cynicism has almost lost his appetite for playing games.

Women are the main victims in both films, although in *Carl* Sontag shows that men can also victimize other men, as is the case with Martin vis-à-vis Carl. Sontag's sensitivity to the thwarting of female desire is even more powerful in this film than in *Duet*, where Ingrid suffers but manages to retaliate with some success. In *Carl*, Lena's fervent wish to rekindle the sexual fire in her husband (as he kindles a literal fire in an early scene) is doomed to failure. Martin's coldness and selfishness make sure that she will never regain his love, that "the wounds of love" (to quote a French reviewer) will not be healed.[23] But I anticipate. The main point for now is that this film confirms that Sontag is a feminist *avant la lettre* in her depiction of Lena.

Carl shares some themes with the Bergman's *Persona* and *The Silence* (the voluntary mutism, twinning, enigma), but the tone and style of Sontag's film are vastly different. Where Bergman keeps his distance from his characters, examining them almost as scientific specimens, in *Carl*, at least, Sontag comes close to her characters. Hers is a cinema of the intellect and emotion brilliantly combined. If the French title, *Les Gémeaux*, suggests the twinning that happens in *Persona* between Elizabeth and Alma, here the implied twinning is between Carl and Anna, even if there is some linking of Karen and Lena through their relationships to both Martin and Carl (both women are attracted to both men in their different ways and engage in sex with them). Martin's emotional violence toward both women is communicated powerfully through editing, music, and silence. Sontag is far from a detached observer.

Sontag's interest in silence (what she calls "voluntary mutism") was of long standing and was deeply personal. In a sense, Sontag shows that those who speak, like Bauer, are inauthentic; they abuse language. Silence is a way to communicate that avoids the deception of words. It's no accident that the directors Sontag talked about so brilliantly in the early 1960s were often those whose films moved slowly and involved less narrative (or dialogue) as such than visual imagery. In her essay "The Aesthetics of Silence," Sontag supports what she calls the "serious" use of silence in Valéry and Rilke, "as a zone of meditation, preparation for spiritual ripening, an ordeal that ends in gaining the right to speak" (*SRW*, 6). While Antonioni came to mind at times as I watched *Carl*, especially in the device of the enigma (just as Anna disappears suddenly in *L'Avventura* and her absence is never resolved, so in *Carl* the enigma of the crime and its reasons remain unresolved), Antonioni's practice of silence veers more toward what Sontag sees in her "Aesthetics of Silence" essay as the modern artist's reluctance to communicate, reflecting an ambivalence about making contact with the audience (*SRW*, 6). Her own project aims to communicate but not necessarily through dialogue and more via image, sound, editing, and lighting.

Sontag's use of language, sound, and silence in *Carl* is self-conscious; she added the sound after shooting so as deliberately to introduce an abrasive, partly artificial track that would acquire a presence in the film that the on-location sound she used in *Duet* could not produce. She wanted an abstract musical element not just for sense but to offer a certain resistance to the dialogue. The film opens with a focus on the mute child Anna, and the sounds she listens to obsessively dominate the soundtrack: the loud ticking of a clock, the phone's dial tone, her hand knocking on the glass of a window. Later, the insistent, painful, high-pitched violin of Torbjön Lundqvist's music, specially composed for the film, sounds almost like screeching and tears at the viewers' consciousness, enabling us to feel viscerally the characters' pain. Anticipating the recent theories about emotion and narrative that I noted earlier, Sontag says, "Against language itself, which is a kind of colonization of the feelings, the film evokes the deeper but more dangerous contact between people that is created by the challenge of a mute presence—an inability or an unwillingness to speak" (*SRW*, xiii).[24]

Silent Carl's forlorn beauty is expressed in several remarkable scenes. The first shot of him, through Karen's eyes, finds him standing on a rock over the water, handling with immense grace a huge net for catching fish. The light catches the net as Carl swings it with almost painfully beautiful grace, his body bending and moving as he manages the object. This shot follows Karen's breathless rush from the intensity of Lena's attempt to kindle Martin's love against his resistance. The camera finds a correlative for her anxiety and dis-ease by moving with her as she rushes through the woods to the edge of the lake. Together, these sequences, accompanied by the natural sounds of the sea and the wind in the trees, as well as music, express first anxiety and a need to get away and then a kind of desire for the silent beauty Carl elicits. The challenge of Carl's mute presence reflects the more dangerous contact that Sontag mentions in her script of the film, but also, in accordance with Sontag's comments on Godard's *Vivre Sa Vie*, in *Carl* she proves rather than analyzes. Before the action of the film, a terrible event took place, and Sontag "proves it." But she does not analyze it. We never know exactly what happened or why. For this reason the film's universe is that of trauma, and as in trauma, so with Carl in the film. An event has happened, but we do not know the cause. We cannot analyze it; it is not available in any way that would allow it to be represented, shown, or explained.[25]

Martin's crime has resulted in Carl's sinking from a theatrical star and a dancer trained by Martin, to a mute, schizophrenic, extremely fragile, and vulnerable young man.

Purportedly an abused child, Carl constantly returns to live in a hut near Martin's house. We learn of this abuse in a long, strange scene, shot in the darkness of the woods as the group finishes a picnic, where Martin retells, at Carl's insistence, a story of Carl's wizened, rejecting parents.[26] Martin seems to want to repair Carl's horrible childhood as well as his own monstrous act: in one scene, we see Martin trying to engage Carl in dance moves; in another, Martin bathes the dependent Carl in an outside tub, drying and then dressing him. The enigma about the crime seems even more insistent the harder Martin tries to repair the wound. It seems that Martin is waiting for a letter from Carl—perhaps hoping to be forgiven—and Carl does finally write such a letter. In a powerful sequence, Carl hands Lena a letter to give to Martin. It is early afternoon on a bright sunny day. The scene shows Lena walking in the woods, the light dappling the leaves; the only sound is the rustle of these leaves. Carl appears and hands Lena a letter, which she reads in silence. Viewers are not allowed to see what she reads. Lena tears up the letter and scatters the fragments to the winds.

This letter figures powerfully in the film's ending. Like the famous letters in Poe and Shakespeare (and in commentaries by Lacan and Derrida), the letter is the sign that links Lena, Martin, and Carl in deadly conflict.[27] After trying to make Martin jealous by unsuccessfully seducing Carl (as Karen tried before her), Lena confronts Martin directly about their relationship. When Martin declares that he does not and will not love her, Lena wonders what reason there is for her to live. Martin will not give her any. When Lena mentions her destruction of Carl's letter, Martin is finally roused, furious that Lena not only tore the letter up but will not reveal its contents. Soon after this exchange, Lena commits suicide. Carl finds her and lovingly tries to revive her, to no avail. Lena's death, however, appears to produce the miracle at the end of the film.

In her introduction to *Carl*, Sontag mentions this miracle, and the influence on her interest in miracles of Dryer's film *Gertrud*, the films of Jean-Marie Straub, and Japanese Bunraku theater. She also comments that miracles are the only subject of profound interest left for art. Karen returns to Peter, and Carl comes to live with them and Anna. Perhaps through his identification with Anna's mutism, Carl is able to engage Anna's attention as no one has yet been able to do. In a wonderful concluding scene by the sea, watched from afar by Karen, Peter, and Martin, Anna finally smiles and speaks to Carl, apparently ending her mutism. This is the "black-to-white" movement of the film that Sontag alludes to; the black-and-white film was needed to represent the specific black (horrendous crime) to white (healing) that the miracle of Anna's return to speech represents.[28] Lena's thwarted desire and the complex intertwining emotions among the couples in the film somehow produced this opening to life for the child. The child's mutism perhaps stood as a sign of adult failure to communicate, to speak to one another, to describe the feelings locked up inside them. As one reviewer put it, Sontag's characters seem people ready for psychoanalysis—or for something to allow them access to speech.[29] But I think Sontag's point lies elsewhere, namely, in the late modernist despair about humanity in the wake of two World Wars and the catastrophes of the Holocaust and Hiroshima. It would seem that silence is the only possible response to such horrors— or at least, it is one response that makes a certain amount of sense.

IV

Sontag's late-modernist themes, linked to the post–World War II, era also include a focus on women's thwarted desire—and the newfound ability in late modernism for such desire to be a self-conscious aspect of women's art—a critique of male domination and female acquiescence to it. Sontag often brings a female perspective to bear on her late-modernist themes, and this makes her 1970s work original. If Karen and Lena are set against Alma and Elizabeth in Bergman's film, it is at once apparent that Sontag conveys powerfully what one French reviewer called "les blessures de l'amour." She does this through mobilizing cinematic techniques that thematize affect while Bergman is after something more abstract and theoretical. If Sontag's is a cinema of intelligence, as critics often call it, that's not to deny its strong emotional pull, its evocation of trauma and pain, suffering and guilt in different ways from Bergman. In Deleuze's terms, affect is the force that produces thought in Sontag's films. While I have stressed Sontag's intellectual affinity with European late-modernist intellectuals, one could also trace some American and British alliances that might account for the emotionality of *Brother Carl*. Sontag's tormented couples share something with those in Edward Albee's *Who's Afraid of Virginia Woolf* (1962), and Carl's schizophrenia has more to do with 1960s British Reichian views of mental illness than with Freud.[30]

For intellectual women born before World War II, feminist attitudes were complex and more subjective than for younger women gaining their feminism through the movements of the 1960s and 1970s. This is sometimes forgotten by feminist critics (such as Wiseman) who do not think in terms of generation and do not take into account the negative cultural norms about intellectual women prevailing when Sontag was growing up. Feminist attitudes for these women came through subjective experiences, but in the postwar years, gender relations were only just beginning to be rethought. If inevitably at first male-identified (there were no women's studies departments for intellectual women going to college in the 1950s), women living through the war inhabited an implicit feminism. The war shaped politics for women of Sontag's generation in terms of gender but also disillusionment about humanity. Moreover, as a public intellectual who moved easily between Europe and the United States, Sontag exemplified a cosmopolitanism only possible in the wake of the war, which I discuss elsewhere. Her project from 1960 to 1980 was an intense dissection of what she calls the "new" novel and the "new" films, and penetrating the form of genius she discovers in the artist.

Much changed for Sontag in later years. Her many years living with photographer Annie Leibovitz stimulated her to think newly about women, photography, and a beauty forced on females, as evidenced in her introduction to Leibovitz's book imaging diverse women. Sontag's illness had a profound effect and changed the direction of her concerns somewhat.[31] One of her last acts was to mount a production of Samuel Beckett's *Waiting for Godot* in war-ravaged Sarajevo. In her interview with Bill Moyers and also in a recorded lecture at New York University at the turn of the century, Sontag talks about her need to contribute and, after writing so much about war, to finally find out about war by personal experience. Going to Sarajevo at the time was dangerous, and she could easily have been killed. But her need to act took precedence. Beckett's protagonists, impotently waiting for something to happen, for some relief, effectively addressed the situation in Sarajevo. That the play she put on was about silence and the inadequacy of language brought her back, full circle, to earlier interests and themes.

Notes

1. In private conversation, David Rieff, Sontag's son, noted his mother's curiosity about everything and her energy for the new. He also stressed how different her world view was from the stripped down one of authors like Beckett whom she nevertheless admired. A friend and colleague of Sontag's, Steve Barclay, confirmed Sontag's incredible curiosity about international cinema and noted her frequenting of film archives in both Los Angeles and New York. As early as 1960, Sontag was writing film criticism for the student-directed *Columbia Daily Spectator*, under the pseudonym "Calvin Koff"—articles that reveal her already amazing knowledge about early and contemporary cinema and its history. See Sontag, "Some Notes on Antonioni and Others," reprinted with a preface by Colin Burnett in *Post Script* 26, no. 2 (Winter–Spring 2007): 137–41. Sontag includes material from this article in *Against Interpretation* as "A Note on Novels and Films" (1966).

2. In a longer version of this essay, I discuss in some depth the burgeoning development of film studies in 1960 in Britain (where I was teaching film at the time) under the auspices of Paddy Whannel and others at the British Film Institute. Sontag was thinking about cinema and its history at around the same time in the United States, but not necessarily with any knowledge of what was ongoing in England. In France (where Sontag traveled regularly) the group around the *Cahiers du Cinema* magazine was also engaging in 1960 with film history, especially with Hollywood. *Cahiers* provided the formative experience for later directors of New Wave cinema such as Truffaut, Godard, Rivette, and others. Charles O'Brien also discusses the relationship of Sontag's 1960s film criticism and concept of aesthetics to film studies in "Sontag's Erotics of Film Style: Between Meaning and Presence," *Post Script* 26, no. 2 (Winter–Spring 2007): 41–52.

3. This was also my own formative intellectual moment, since in 1964 I was a graduate student at Rutgers University with a research assistantship at *Partisan Review*. My trajectory, however, was different from Sontag's (whom I saw at a distance at one of the big conferences William Phillips and the editors organized). I was already involved with Students for a Democratic Society, having met Tom Hayden, who was organizing a community action project in Newark, while I and my then-husband Ralph Kaplan, who had cowritten the Port Huron Statement with Hayden and others at the University of Michigan, were organizing a similar project in downtown New Brunswick. Sontag was

revolutionizing aesthetics while we struggled with activism. This is by no means to deny the incredible importance of what Sontag was doing nor her later activist interventions. Rather, I seek just to situate what she was drawn to against what else was going on at the time.

4. The 1964 issue of *Partisan Review* shows U.S. culture on the brink of change. That is, some tired aesthetic arguments (see for example John Simon's polemic against Sontag's "Notes on Camp") coexist not only with Sontag's fresh views but also with those of Steven Marcus and Gore Vidal. The terms of the debate largely about popular or marginal cultures now seem quite dated in the new universe of cultural studies, if not exactly moved beyond. Sontag's criticism, however, still energizes, interests, and alerts.

5. This concept also intimidates a critic like me, who might be tempted to read into her films meanings that Sontag would argue have not been *demonstrated* on the screen.

6. Jack Kroll, interview with Susan Sontag and Agnés Varda, *Camera Three*, host Jim McAndrew, prod./dir. Merrill Brockway, writer Stephan Chodorov, CBS-TV, October 12, 1969, videocassette, Creative Arts Television Archive, Kent, Conn., 1977.

7. This essay ranges widely into the history of gender difference, touching upon biological, economic, social, and political aspects of women's oppression over the ages. Sontag stresses that the extraordinary women who invalidated prevailing concepts of women as passive, domestic, and unequal to men were considered exceptions rather than seen as challenging norms. The essay shows Sontag's identification with the ideology underlying the women's movement but does not really add anything to what feminists across many academic disciplines were already saying in 1972. Ideas in the *Temps Modernes* essay were repeated in a 1973 essay, "The Third World of Women," in *Partisan Review* and in articles in newspapers. In an interview in the mid-1990s, Sontag reflects on her being labeled as an "exceptional" woman: she warns that such labeling does a disservice to women in general in making visible women outside of the norm, as if one would not expect most women to participate in public culture. I disagree with much of Susan Wiseman's argument about Sontag as an elite and isolated intellectual in light of her interest in the women's movement; see "'Femininity' and the Intellectual in Sontag and Cixous," in *The Body and the Text: Hélène Cixous, Reading and Teaching*, ed. Helen Wilcox et al. (New York: Harvester/Wheatsheaf, 1990), 98–113. While we would not today use the term "Third World of Women," Sontag did not have the benefit in 1973 of postcolonial and ethnic studies.

8. Sontag has not generally been credited for her prowoman stance, perhaps because the text of her French article was not known and certainly her films (where I argue this stance shows) were not readily available. This may account for statements like Angela McRobbie's, suggesting that "the intellectual space which [Sontag] has defined as her own is one in which gender does not

figure." McRobbie agrees with my position here that in "high or late European modernism . . . there was no available space to speak as a woman" ("Susan Sontag: Modernist Style," in *Postmodernism and Popoular Culture* [New York: Routledge, 1994], 79). McRobbie's is a far more sympathetic and contextualized position than that of Susan Wiseman's 1990 criticism of Sontag in comparison to Hélène Cixous referred to in note 7.

9. For a discussion of Sontag and the issue of popular culture, see McRobbie, "Susan Sontag: Modernist Style."

10. Sontag was married to Philip Rieff when he was writing his now classic *Freud: The Mind of a Moralist* (New York: Viking Press, 1959). As I speculate later, Sontag's influence may be seen in the discussions of Freud's attitudes to women. Indeed, the entry on "Susan Sontag" in *Current Biography* 30, no. 6 (June 1969): 41–43, notes her collaboration with Rieff on the book. In their useful *Susan Sontag: An Annotated Bibliography, 1948–1992* (New York: Garland, 2000), Leland Poague and Kathy A. Parsons comment regarding Philip Rieff's book that Sontag "agreed to Rieff's claim of sole authorship in their divorce settlement," and further cite many ways in which Sontag's intellectual interests proliferate in the volume (513, 518).

11. I will limit my discussion to these two feature films since I could not find a subtitled version of *Unguided Tour* and my themes developed in tandem with Sontag's critical writings on film do not pertain so obviously to *Promised Lands*, which I will discuss in other Sontag research.

12. Sontag was always politically aware if not always activist. Clearly she knew her Marx and was vocal in opposition to the Vietnam War. In the interview cited in note 6, Kroll mentions the "smell" of disaster and the theme of apocalypse in the 1969 selection of films for the New York Film Festival. Varda and Sontag see their films as "political," each in its own special way. Sontag's unfortunate polemic against all totalitarian regimes during the Vietnam War created a burst of anti-Sontag rhetoric from the left.

13. In a slim volume written before Sontag's death and the resulting renewed attention to and appreciation of Sontag's amazing oeuvre, Sohnya Sayres calls Sontag, in a subtitle, "The Elegiac Modernist." This smart book touches on numerous aspects of Sontag's writings, films, and fiction without going into great detail, and its project dovetails with mine in seeing Sontag's aesthetics as those of late modernism. See Sayres, *Susan Sontag: The Elegiac Modernist* (New York: Routledge, 1990).

14. In New York, however, as of 1956 one could see foreign films, thanks to the film distribution company Janus Films, especially at the Fifty-fifth Street Playhouse, which Sontag no doubt frequented. Sontag might also have seen European New Wave films at the famous Brattle Cinema in Harvard Square, owned by Bryant Haliday and Cyrus Harvey, who also owned the Fifty-fifth Street Playhouse. As innovators teaching film in the academy in 1970, we relied on Janus's 16mm collection to bring European cinema to our students.

15. In related research, I am exploring links between Sontag and Duras in regard to a cinema of silence and other late-modernist aspects the two artists share as women in the period from 1960 to 1980. See my "Women, Trauma, and Late Modernity: Sontag and Duras, 1960–1980," paper presented at the Society for Cinema and Media Conference, Philadelphia, March 8, 2008.

16. Gilles Deleuze, *Proust and Signs*, trans. Richard Howard (New York: George Braziller, 1972), 95, 96.

17. Brian Massumi, "The Autonomy of Affect," *Cultural Critique* 31 (1995): 88.

18. Gabriele Schwab, *The Mirror and the Killer-Queen: Otherness in Literary Language* (Bloomington: Indiana University Press, 1996), notes what she calls "highly experimental and commonly considered difficult to read" texts (xi), which refuse easy access, tending to "withhold their 'meaning' and refrain from telling coherent narratives" (xi). This strategy of withholding "seems to render them all the more powerful and enables them to draw readers into their artificial and artistic textual worlds" (xi).

19. See review by Henri Chapier, review of *Les Gémeaux*, *Combat* (Paris), January 24, 1973, 1.

20. I was curious about Sontag's making a film that anticipates the "Stockholm syndrome." In the 1973 robbery, the robbers held employees hostage from August 23 to August 28. The victims became emotionally attached to their victimizers and defended them after their release. Nils Bejerot, a criminologist and psychiatrist, named the syndrome in a news broadcast about this case.

21. For example, in one scene, she gets in Bauer's car, refuses to come out, and, as Tomas watches horrified, she lets Bauer in, starts to make love to him, and then grabs a can of shaving cream with which she proceeds to completely cover the windscreen.

22. In her essay "Psychoanalysis and Norman O. Brown's *Life Against Death*," Sontag appears to agree with Brown that in the unconscious "mankind is unalterably . . . in revolt against sexual differentiation and genital organization" (*AI*, 259). Sontag appears to agree that the important thing is to live in the body and to accept the androgynous mode of being; human neuroses arise from man's (*sic*) incapacity to live in the body.

23. See Claude Mauriac, "Les blessures de l'amour," review of *Brother Carl*, *Express* (Paris), January 29, 1973. There were many French reviews of Sontag's second film, partly because it starred French actors, Geneviève Page and Laurent Terzieff. In each case, some space was also given to her first film.

24. I have in mind here work by Brian Massumi, partly inspired by Gilles Deleuze, on the difference between what Massumi calls "quality" (narration in which emotions are fixed by being linked to cognition) and "the expressive event" (an intensity that is experienced on the body without or before cognition fixes the feeling); see "The Autonomy of Affect." Sontag also notes in her 1968 essay on Godard that "while images invite the spectator to identify with what

is seen, the presence of words makes the spectator into a critic" (*SRW*, 185). In her essay on Bresson, Sontag contrasts "art that involves, that creates empathy" with art (like Brecht's and Bresson's) that "detaches, that provokes reflection." Yet she claims that "great reflective art is not frigid. It can exalt the spectator, it can present images that appall, it can make him weep" (*AI*, 177).

25. For a more detailed analysis of trauma and a lengthy bibliography see my *Trauma Culture: The Politics of Terror and Loss in Media and Literature* (New Brunswick, N.J.: Rutgers University Press, 2005).

26. Parenthetically, I wondered if this was some sort of parable or allegory of Sontag's own unhappy childhood, about which we hear next to nothing in her work. The fullest account I have yet found is in Sayres's book on Sontag, in the chapter "Biographical Notes." We learn that Sontag's parents, export traders, left her in the care of grandparents and then much later an Irish nanny. Certainly Carl's bitterness about his parents would seem to reflect Sontag's feelings about her parents.

27. It is hard not to think of the many letters that go astray in Shakespeare and Racine, to say nothing of Poe's "Purloined Letter" and Lacan's and Derrida's commentaries on it.

28. In a touching and rare moment of personal comment, Sontag notes that while making the film, she had been trying to perform a miracle that was the deepest personal source for the film. Shortly after finishing the film, she learned that her miracle had failed. Nevertheless, she says, she still believed in miracles. Critics speculate that Sontag had in mind a close friend's suicide that happened at this time.

29. See review, "Les Gémeaux," by Jean-Luc Douin in *Télérama*, February 3, 1973.

30. I do not have space to develop these possible alliances. I want to thank Helen Cooper and Adrienne Munich for suggesting I follow these up after I gave a talk related to this chapter.

31. David Rieff writes lucidly and with obvious pain about his mother's clinging to life despite her recalcitrant cancer in his *Swimming in a Sea of Death: A Son's Memoir* (New York: Simon and Schuster, 2008). Sontag did not want to go quietly into the dark but fought a courageous battle to the end. Her love of the new, of discovery, and her curiosity had been an energizing life force that she could not bear to relinquish. Many of us share her desire to keep on learning and discovering the new. Her comment in an afterword (written in 2006, when Sontag was well over seventy years old) to a new edition of *Against Interpretation* is telling in regard to aging: "To look back on writings of thirty or more years ago is not a wholesome exercise. My energy as a writer impels me to look forward, to feel still that I am beginning, really beginning, now, which makes it hard to curb my impatience with that beginning writer I once was in a literal sense" ("Afterword: Thirty Years After . . ." [1996], in *Against Interpretation and Other Essays* [New York: Macmillan, 2001], 307).

chaptersix

Sontag on Theater

JULIA A. WALKER

Of the tributes that followed Susan Sontag's death in December 2004, few made reference to her work in and on the theater. Most emphasized her criticism, reading her landmark 1964 essay "Notes on Camp" as a bellwether of cultural studies. Others focused on her translation of European theories into an American idiom. Some reflected upon her contributions to contemporary American literature, offering qualified praise for her later novels such as the National Book Award–winning *In America* (1999). A few addressed her provocations as a public intellectual, recalling her incendiary (if sometimes ill-phrased or ill-timed) rebukes of racism, communism, and post-9/11 jingoism. And nearly all commented upon her celebrity, noting the iconic photographs that frequently appeared in popular magazines throughout her lifetime as well as those taken by Annie Leibovitz as memento mori of her departed lover. But almost none gave serious consideration to Sontag's work in the theater.[1]

Even during her lifetime, Sontag's critics had little to say about her theatrical interests. Neither Sohnya Sayres nor Liam Kennedy addresses at any length Sontag's work in and on the theater in each of their book-length studies.[2] While Carl Rollyson does acknowledge her criticism of and directorial work in the theater in his *Reading Susan Sontag: A Critical Introduction to Her Work*, he does not discuss her playwriting in any of the book's main chapters, having dismissed *Alice in Bed* (1993) in his "Chronological Overview" with the assertion that "the essayist predominates over the dramatist."[3]

In this chapter, I'd like to entertain the possibility that Sontag, the dramatist, predominates over Sontag, the essayist, the novelist, and even the activist. Or rather, I propose to demonstrate that the theater, for Sontag, was not simply one art form among many (and a minor one, at that) but provided a powerful metaphor that informed the very foundations of her thought. That metaphor—of actors acting on a world-historical stage—appears in nearly all of her work, not only in her overt activism but also in her more "literary" meditations, including the later novels, which thematize performance. Once so obvious as to not bear mentioning, this particular formulation of the metaphor derives from the philosophical movement of existentialism, a signature intellectual preoccupation of the 1950s, when Sontag came of age. Once obvious, perhaps, the existentialist context of Sontag's early work is nonetheless worth noting, especially in our own moment, when existentialism has been "eclipsed" (in the historian François Dosse's words) by poststructuralism and, now, new materialisms.[4] We might recall that the *Partisan Review*, where Sontag began her career, helped introduce existentialism to American readers. And, as newly released excerpts from Sontag's journals confirm, Jean-Paul Sartre and Simone de Beauvoir were among her most important intellectual models.[5]

In its staunchly humanist orientation, its affirmation of individual agency, and its emphasis upon the responsibility that comes with freedom, existentialism provides many of the key ideas that resonate throughout Sontag's work. But where these ideas are treated primarily as themes in Sontag's early writing (including her theater reviews), they increasingly inform the formal attributes of her later work, as when she realizes the metaphor of actors acting in the world to scold the West for its political passivity toward the genocidal siege in Bosnia in her 1993 production of Samuel Beckett's *Waiting for Godot* in Sarajevo. In this chapter, I show how Sontag's interest in the theater, while overlooked by her eulogists and critics, appears consistently throughout her career, especially in her unwavering belief that, at its best, art has a cathartic power to inspire its audience to take moral and political action. As we'll see, that belief increasingly led Sontag to explore drama and performance as formal means by which to resolve the social, aesthetic, and phenomenological problems that she could not solve satisfactorily in other genres.

Spectator/Critic/Commentator

Evidence of Sontag's profound and long-lived interest in the theater is easy to find: simply look in the table of contents in any of her essay collections. *Against Interpretation* (1966) contains an appreciation of Sartre's analysis of playwright Jean Genet, a critique of Eugene Ionesco's plays, a meditation on the current state of the theater (in the form of several reprinted reviews),[6] a testy engagement with Lionel Abel's critical assessment of modern drama, and a pioneering analysis of the performance-art precursor known as "happenings." *Styles of Radical Will* (1969), dedicated to Open Theatre founder Joseph Chaikin, includes a sustained deliberation on the formal differences between theater and film. *Under the Sign of Saturn* (1972) reprints her analysis of Antonin Artaud, the artistic visionary who called for a "theatre of cruelty"; it first appeared as an article in the *New Yorker* and was later expanded into the long introductory essay that prefaces the volume of Artaud's writings that Sontag later edited. Finally, *Where the Stress Falls* (2001) contains a typically sharp denunciation of recent avant-garde theater for enthralling its audience with Richard Wagner's emotional, visual, and stereophonic effects without troubling it to engage the magnitude of his ideas.

Even her seemingly non-theater-related essays bear an imprint of the theater's influence. "Notes on Camp," after all, is dedicated to playwright Oscar Wilde, who, in his life and work, practiced a sensibility that is in love with theatrical artifice and exaggeration. Similarly, her portrait of Walter Benjamin, the title essay in *Under the Sign of Saturn*, interprets his life and career not through his influential and frequently cited essays "The Work of Art in the Age of Mechanical Reproduction" or "Theses on the Philosophy of History" but through the melancholy mood of his dissertation on the *Trauerspiel*, or German mourning play.

Her allusions to non-theater-related works often reveal that she read them through the lens of the contemporary theater. Her essay "Marat/

Sade/Artaud" (in *AI*), for example, echoes Barthes's *Sade/Fourier/Loyola*, suggesting that, whether or not Barthes was influenced by Peter Weiss's play *Marat/Sade* (which is not unlikely), Sontag understood him to have engaged the ideas that Weiss had dramatized, and perhaps that director Peter Brook had materialized in his legendary 1964 production. Her essay implicitly expands Barthes's intellectual genealogy to include Artaud, whom she considered to be one of the two most important influences on twentieth-century theater (the other being Bertolt Brecht).

In the introduction to her 1976 edited collection of Artaud's writings, Sontag establishes the fact of his importance through her sustained analysis of his life's work.[7] Unlike Jacques Derrida, who takes *The Theatre and Its Double* as a synecdoche for Artaud's entire corpus,[8] Sontag provides an overview of that corpus that attends to the evolution of Artaud's thought. As her chronological arrangement of his poems, essays, letters, plays, and manifestoes suggests, Artaud redefines the problematic of expression every time he shifts the medium in which he writes; early in his career, for example, Artaud sought to express himself in poetry, only to find that written language deadened his thought. In (silent) film and theater, however, Artaud theorized that communication could transgress the limitations of written language by taking bodily form. Of course, this proved a disappointment, too, as he discovered when he tried to realize his screenplays and dramas in production. From these failed experiments, Artaud returned to verbal language, hoping to divine the magic locked within its limits of signification through the incantatory use of words. Finding himself on the other side of conventionally defined reason, Artaud resigned himself to schizophrenia, finding relief in the act of writing, even if—and perhaps especially because—it was only to himself. The irony, as Sontag wryly notes, is that this was his most productive phase.

Sontag's chronological overview provides a deeper context for a work such as *The Theatre and Its Double*, bringing it into fresh relief. For within this generic variety is a topical continuity that gives an overall coherence to Artaud's work—a continuity Sontag finds in Gnosticism, the spiritual practice based upon the belief that the world is composed of a duality between the inner psyche and the outer material realm, spirit and flesh, good and evil.[9] Although the goal is to overcome these dualisms, Gnostics typically imagine life as a struggle, with the persecuted spirit seeking to free itself from the flesh and the material realm. Sontag maps Artaud's varied career onto four stages of Gnosticism—the affirmation of the body, the revulsion from the body, the wish to transcend the body, and the quest to redeem the body[10]—reading the corpus of his work as "the first complete documentation of someone *living through* the trajectory of Gnostic thought."[11] Yet, as she shows, any or all of Gnosticism's four stages may appear in any one work. *The Theatre and Its Double*, for example, expresses both an affirmation of the body in its emphasis upon bodily modes of signification and a desire to transcend the body in its visceral assault upon the audience's senses.

Although she wrote introductions for other writers, such critical overviews are typically brief, written as favors for former lovers or those whose work she ambivalently admired.[12] Her introduction to Artaud, by contrast, reveals her strong affinity for his work, sharing as she did his understanding of meaning as a sensuous, embodied experience, as well as his problematic relationship to written forms. Indeed, if I were to read her life through her work (as she does Walter Benjamin's life through his), it is her long introductory essay on Artaud that I would choose as the clarifying lens. For underlying the variety of genres within Sontag's own corpus is also a continuity of themes and concerns. Like Artaud, Sontag believed that good art always touches a nerve, sending shock waves throughout the audience member's body, transforming it into a materialization of a new and potentially revolutionary consciousness. Although she may not have been a full-fledged Gnostic, there is something approaching a mind-body duality in her work that she seems intent upon overcoming. She was a literary intellectual engagée, after all, invested in the power of ideas to transform our relationship to the world, even as she repeatedly refused the notion that ideas could be extracted from the material forms in which they appeared, insisting that their power lay as much in the visceral appeal they made to our senses as in their supposedly rational "content."

Although this quasi-Gnostic dialectic of "form" and "content," "mind" and "body" appears throughout her work, it seems to take on an urgency in the middle years of her career, when she received her first diagnosis of cancer. It was that experience and the confusing public assumptions about what cancer *meant* that spurred her to write *Illness as Metaphor* (1978). In that cultural monograph, she famously challenges the idea that cancer—a disease of the physical body—is "caused" by psychological neuroses. Both in that book and in her follow-up *AIDS and Its Metaphors* (1988), Sontag dismisses this spurious causal link between mind and body, refusing the shame that comes with a cancer—and later AIDS—diagnosis, as if the disease is a form of psychological (if no longer divine) retribution that has been meted out as punishment to the patient's body. Tracing the history of cultural attitudes toward disease in these works, Sontag pursues a poststructuralist line of inquiry, demonstrating how language shapes our understanding of what bodies mean. In her later work for the theater, however, she begins to develop a more dialectical understanding of the relationship between language and bodiliness, exploring the body as not just a passive object but an experiential source of meaning.

Directing Consciousness

Sontag's first directorial foray in the theater came in 1979, when she directed Luigi Pirandello's *As You Desire Me*. In good Pirandellian fashion, the play concerns the contested identity of "Cia," a woman who may or may not have been abducted during WWI and later returned to her family. In the face of her unknown and unknowable past, Cia chooses a future in which she can define herself through her own actions. Leaving her family for the company of Salter, a writer, Cia symbolically chooses to authorize her own life instead of assuming the ready-made role given to women in conventional domestic arrangements. According to Rollyson, the play, interpreted by Sontag as "a modern feminist parable with operatic overtones," allowed her to confirm her own decision to abandon such roles "in a quest for self-fulfillment."[13]

Sontag's choice of Pirandello, again, suggests the profound influence that existentialism had on her thought. After all, the Sartrean motif of the mirror of intersubjectivity, where others provide one's image of oneself, was most probably inspired by Pirandello's *Six Characters in Search of an Author*. In *As You Desire Me*, these existential themes are once again in evidence, as Cia proclaims "Being! Being is nothing! Being is becoming!"[14] Indeed, Sontag may have felt that the act of enacting and directing a play was an aesthetically satisfying way of experiencing the idea of defining oneself through one's actions.

Her second experience in directing came in 1985, when Robert Brustein invited her to the American Repertory Theatre at Harvard University. There, she directed *Jacques and His Master*, Milan Kundera's dramatic adaptation of Diderot's novel *Jacques le Fataliste*. Here, again, the existential themes are well apparent, as the play uses a journey to thematize the act of self-definition as a movement into an uncertain future. Unfortunately, if we are to take Gerald Rabkin's word, the production was not a success—a failure he attributes as much to Kundera's "anemic" adaptation as to the "uniform blandness" of Sontag's direction.[15] Although the "literary critic" in him was excited about Sontag's participation in the project, the "theatre critic" ultimately remained unsatisfied. "I have no doubt," he explains, "given her critical acumen, that she had a firm conceptual model in her mind as she mounted the play. But this model remains elusive because it is not projected physically."[16] Sontag, in other words, had not yet found a way to translate her ideas into the formal material of the theater arts.

By 1993, when she directed a multiethnic, gender-blind production of *Waiting for Godot* in Sarajevo, Sontag appears to have acquired these skills, even if her critics, again, were dissatisfied. Casting three pairs of Vladimirs and Estragons—one male-male, one male-female, and one female-female—Sontag sought to expand the representational possibilities of the play. They were, Sontag explained, "three variations of the theme of the couple."[17] As for ethnic makeup, Sontag did not intentionally set out to cast representatives from each of the three major ethnic groups; instead, she relied upon the simple fact of Sarajevo's multicultural heritage. As she explained, "the population of Sarajevo is so mixed, and there are so many intermarriages, that it would be hard to assemble any kind of group in which all three 'ethnic' groups are *not* represented."[18] In this way, she set out to represent Sarajevo to itself—not the "Sarajevo" of the Western news media (the "civilized" European-style city caught between the barbarism of Serbian aggression and the threat of Muslim fundamentalism) but the "Sarajevo" that was a "secular, antitribal ideal" that, understood as such, was a target for destruction.[19]

Surprisingly, few critics chastised her for taking such liberties with Beckett's script.[20] (After all, she had vehemently objected to Joanne Akalaitis's 1984 production of *Endgame*, which set the play in a burned-out New York City subway.) When they did, they tended to cast their criticism in terms of intellectual integrity rather than a standard of fidelity to Beckett's text. Lois Oppenheim, for example, found that Sontag's translation of the play's "nowhere/anywhere" setting into "Sarajevo" "significantly reduced the [play's] universal intentions."[21] By particularizing her production to war-torn Sarajevo, Sontag altered the Benjaminian landscape of Beckett's play. These ruins were no longer the allegorical detritus of a sacred worldview to which Vladimir and Estragon remain comically committed. In Sontag's production, which took place in a theater whose walls bore the pockmarks of repeated mortar attacks, *Godot*'s ruins had become the literal ruins of a world in thrall to an all-too-human will to power.

To be sure, mortar attacks, power outages, and actors fainting from malnutrition particularized Sontag's production, reducing rehearsal times to such an extent that Sontag decided to present only act 1. Although she rationalized that it lays out the action of the entire play, she also realized that "there is a difference between Act I and the replay of Act I which is Act II. Not only has one more day gone by. Everything is worse. Lucky no longer can speak, Pozzo is now pathetic and blind, Vladimir has given over to despair. Perhaps I felt that the despair of Act I was enough for the Sarajevo audience, and that I wanted to spare them a second time when Godot does not arrive." But "Maybe," she continued hopefully, "I wanted to propose, subliminally, that Act II might be different."[22]

Whatever meanings were lost in the abridged length and particularization of the play's setting, Sontag's production of *Waiting for Godot* appears to have completed her apprenticeship in translating intellectual concepts into visual terms (pace Rabkin's critique). What's more, it appears to have emboldened her to continue her hand at playwriting. The three plays she wrote—*A Parsifal* (1991), *Alice in Bed* (1993) and *Lady from the Sea* (1997)—appeared in fairly rapid succession, interrupted only by her production of *Waiting for Godot* in Sarajevo (1994) and her performance-conscious novel *The Volcano Lover* (1994), to be followed closely by *In America* (1999), her fictional biography of actress Helena Modjeska. All of this suggests that the theater—with its ability to stage the dialectical relationship between bodies and words—was a principal concern of Sontag's, especially at the end of her career, even when she wasn't directly writing for it. When she did, she returned to problems she had not satisfactorily solved in her essays and cultural monographs, often using the theatrical form as a way to find an answer.

A Parsifal

In *A Parsifal*, her first play, for example, Sontag takes up the problem of what we might call "active identification," a problem she broaches first in *On Photography* only to return to it more emphatically in *Regarding the Pain of Others*.[23] This problem concerns the ability of a work of art to engage and activate its viewers' sympathies. The assumption here is that any such engagement necessarily bears within it a responsibility to move the viewer to action, where "action" involves, at the very least, a phenomenological reorientation toward the subject at hand. *On Photography* registers Sontag's ambivalence toward the photographic medium, revealing her doubt about its ability to invite this kind of active identification. The photograph's implicit claim to reproduce reality, coupled with its status as an object that can be held in one's hand, invites the viewer to assume a passive—rather than active—attitude of looking at and relating to the world it depicts. In *A Parsifal*, Sontag again concerns herself with the problem of active identification, but, instead of indicting photography for inducing a passive response in its audience, she indicts passivity itself—both as figured by her central character, Parsifal, and as experienced by her own audience, whether it identifies with him or refuses to do so.

Published in 1991, *A Parsifal* can be read as an attempt to skewer the empty politics of sympathy that sustained television talk shows and later came to be associated with candidate Bill Clinton's oft-repeated claim to "feel your pain." It was also written at the outset of the Bosnian conflict, when Sontag issued her *"j'accuse,"* calling on Western governments to stop the violence and on intellectuals to serve as witnesses to their governments' failures. Few of either, as we know, heeded her call. But where *Regarding the Pain of Others* attempts to explore why the images of that conflict were not enough to prompt intervention, and where her production of *Waiting for Godot* attempts to stage that absence *as* an absence to show the effects of that unheeded call, *A Parsifal* is an angry indictment of those who stayed home. It is also an attempt to explore how identification functions—both when it works and when it doesn't—which is why she turned to the dramatic form. It is the drama, after all, that Aristotle theorized in relation to identification, the mechanism by which audiences are moved toward catharsis (usually translated as a purgation of socially destructive emotion).

Taking up the problem of how to invite an audience to actively *dis*identify with indifference, violence, and stupidity (and the political forces that rely upon them), Sontag retells the medieval quest narrative of the innocent knight, which was probably suggested to her by Hans-Jurgen Syberberg's 1981 film of the Richard Wagner opera. To be sure, Wagner's musical drama serves as the play's primary intertext. But where Wagner follows the basic narrative of *Parzifal*, Wolfram von Eschenbach's late-twelfth-century epic poem, Sontag radically condenses his five-act opera into a six-page scene in which Parsifal, updated as a contemporary soldier, is held to account for his various acts of violence. Where Wagner's Parsifal undertakes a journey—which, within the terms of the Christian allegory, represents a spiritual quest for the redemption of all of humanity—Sontag's Parsifal is an antihero who—reinterpreted for the postsacred world of existential humanism—is incapable of being moved to sympathy. Where Wagner abides by Aristotle's conception of the drama as an "imitation of an action," staging Parsifal's physical and spiritual journey as movement, Sontag invokes Benjamin to stage Parsifal's spiritual and political inaction as stasis, the pure spatialization of time.

The play begins with Parsifal breaking the "fourth wall" of conventional realism to introduce himself to us, his audience. His immediate interlocutor is the Ostrich (Sontag's invention), who functions as a chorus figure, watching and commenting upon the action as it unfolds. As such, the Ostrich facilitates our sympathetic engagement with the play, inviting us to pivot in and out of identification, such as when he deliberately shifts the pronoun in his statement "I watch" to the command, "You watch," as Parsifal declares he is "passing through."

Adding a frankly absurdist element to the play, the Ostrich would also seem to represent both the proverbial head-burying refusal to engage with reality and the need for eternal vigilance. As the Ostrich explicitly tells us, female ostriches are said to hatch their eggs by gazing at them; if they look away, the egg is thought to be addled. Thus, according to folk tradition, ostriches who bury their heads in the sand are leaving their brood unprotected. Only concerted attention can guarantee the future well-being of the flock.

"Further," the Ostrich continues, "we are told that if an egg is bad the ostrich will break it. . . . This is why in Eastern Orthodox churches ostrich eggs are often suspended from the ceiling. As the ostrich will break an addled egg, so will God deal with evil people."[24] Not just attentive care, in other words, but justice is needed to protect the world represented by the egg. Both responsibilities—the Ostrich insists—must be understood as actions. Although watching might seem to be passive, requiring little effort on the part of the observer, Sontag suggests that it should involve just as much energy as the destruction of evil. Sontag's metaphor is meant to cross the footlights much like Parsifal's direct address. You, the audience, she seems to say, are being called to action: Watch with engaged attention, and act with justice.

When Amfortas, the King of Pain, crosses the stage on a motorized gurney, Parsifal remains unmoved. Although, in Wagner's version, Parsifal fails to express sympathy the first time he encounters Amfortas, he does eventually ask after his condition upon completing his quest and learning that compassionate action is his divine mission in life. In Sontag's version, innocence becomes not the necessary state that gives way to transcendent knowledge, but a cynically deployed legalistic plea by which to avoid culpability for his actions. Interrogated by a squadron of knights, Parsifal submits to a press conference, holding aloft a glowing red microphone.

For those who recognize the parodic gesture, the glowing red microphone is meant to recall the Holy Grail that King Amfortas raises in Wagner's opera. A stunning moment in the opera, when music, scene, and narrative unite to signify Parsifal's transcendence from innocence to the incipient awareness of divine knowledge, the apotheosis of the Holy Grail is, in Wagner's theory of the *Gesamtkustwerk*, meant to be experienced viscerally as well as cognitively by the audience. Sontag's treatment of this scene is antipathetic, especially in its substitution of the microphone—a postmodern symbol of self-glorification—for the Holy Grail. Here, there is no transformation. Nothing changes. At most, Parsifal—our representative of humanity—admits to having lived a life of banal evil, but he shifts responsibility for his actions, claiming that "they" "organized everything." One can imagine him directing that "they" at the audience, inviting us to inhabit that interpellation with considerable discomfort. But that is Sontag's point: we are meant to recognize our own complicity in the structure of violence that authorizes Parsifal's actions.[25]

The play ends with Parsifal, slowly mounting a scaffold, remarking in Beckettian fashion, "This is a play, this is a death, this is slowness. If we slow down enough we will never die. (*Reaches top of scaffold.*) If we move, we move into the future. We will die. (*Remains motionless. Lights up.*) We will not die."[26] Unlike the guileless fool who knows no better, Sontag's Parsifal understands well what he must do to end the suffering of others. Yet, at the play's conclusion, he chooses not to move into the future, not to act with compassion, even as he refuses to take responsibility for those choices. Humanity remains unredeemed.

By asking her audience to both identify and disidentify with Parsifal, Sontag puts us in an impossible—but aesthetically satisfying—double bind. Whichever sympathetic alignment we make, we are discomfited by the moral and ethical implications of our choice. Insofar as we identify with him, we must feel frustration at his inability to take responsibility for his actions and move with compassion into the future. Insofar as we refuse to identify with him, we are identified as the "they" that authorizes and is culpable for his violence. Thus, formally as well as thematically, *A Parsifal* interrogates the problem of active identification. By casting the problem in dramatic form, Sontag asks her audience to directly inhabit that problem and—by leaving them in a state of discomfiture—enact its resolution.

Alice in Bed

Sontag's interest in the moral imperative of sympathetic engagement continued to motivate her dramatic writing. In her next play, *Alice in Bed* (1993), she turned her attention to a problem that she had begun to identify earlier in her work on illness and was addressing concurrently in her novel *The Volcano Lover*: the problem of sympathy and how to understand it as not just a private subjective experience but one that has social and political implications. Where *Illness as Metaphor* and *AIDS and Its Metaphors* examine how sympathy for those suffering from illness can be diminished by moralizing cultural attitudes, *Alice in Bed* approaches the problem from the perspective of the patient. Here, Sontag seeks to understand sympathy as a phenomenological experience of the body that defines one's relationship to oneself and to others in the world.

The title character of *Alice in Bed* is Alice James, sister of the philosopher William and the novelist Henry James. Making explicit reference to Virginia Woolf's observation that if Shakespeare had had a sister, she would not have been able to realize that same talent, Sontag's play concerns the frustrations that Alice James experiences in a patriarchal culture that keeps her from publicly expressing, let alone acting on, the stuff of her imagination. Just as her ideas are confined to her head, so is she confined to her bed, unable to enter into the realm of possibility.

This metaphor of confinement is elaborated throughout by an alternation of scenes that take place in her head and in her bed. The first two scenes explore the existential terms of Alice's confinement, as she and her nurse argue over whether she *can*not or *will* not get out of bed. Where scene 1 takes place on a darkened stage, casting the debate in psychological terms, scene 2 makes us laugh as that debate is recontextualized in concrete terms: once the lights are up, we see that Alice is physically unable to get out of bed since she is smothered under ten thin mattresses on which the nurse is sitting. The nurse—dressed in striped ticking, visually aligning her with the mattresses that threaten to suffocate Alice—represents the medical establishment and its control over women's bodies. Unlike Charlotte Perkins Gilman's *The Yellow Wallpaper*, in which the horror of that control is represented in the narrator's loving deference to her doctor-husband, Sontag's play represents it as a bitter joke; even if the nurse and the medical establishment physically confine her, Alice is complicit in her own incarceration, using it as an excuse to avoid active engagement with the outside world. Sontag's heroine is sympathetic but not a victim; she bears some responsibility, even if only for the choice of inaction.

The link with *A Parsifal* is clear. Where Parsifal won't act, Alice both won't and can't. Insofar as she is a woman defined by a patriarchal order that subjects her to its rules of gender decorum, she can't; insofar as she internalizes its strictures, she won't. For example, we see her refusal to act on her own desires at the end of scene 2, when she asks for the mattresses to help her repress her murderous desires, and in scene 3, when she asks her father—the apparent object of those murderous desires—for permission to kill herself. He refuses to cooperate, insisting that she take responsibility for her decision, asking only that—if she does decide to commit suicide—she do it gently so as to spare her family unnecessary distress. Confronted with his stoicism (figured as an unfeeling wooden leg—a historical detail that Sontag exploits), Alice is metaphorically disarmed. For, though patriarchal authority doesn't have a leg to stand on, Alice can do little more than swoon in its thrall. Like the title character of Lewis Carroll's *Alice's Adventures in Wonderland*, Sontag's same-named heroine seeks a hole to fall into; like *Parsifal*'s quixotic enchantress, Kundry, she seeks to avoid responsibility in sleep.

These are the two primary intertexts in this play. Carroll's story provides the hallucinogenic visual vocabulary for Alice's imaginings. Wagner's opera provides the musical accompaniment to her real-world encounters in its repeated motif of "pain." Here, as in *A Parsifal*, Sontag jettisons the Christian allegory in Wagner's source materials in order to focus on the existential implications of her character's plight. Alice (like the playwright) is a talented, intelligent, ambitious woman who is caught in a painful double-bind. Pace de Beauvoir, she is not born a woman but becomes one—imperfectly—by trying to respond to the conflicting intersubjective cues that are directed at her. Sontag represents these conflicting cues by skewing the perspectives and scales of her scenes. For example, while much of the play's action takes place in Alice's bedroom, scenes 2, 4, and 7 each depict it from a different angle, with scene 6 magnifying everything in it so as to make Alice seem very small. These shifting perspectives not only convey Alice's disorientation expressionistically but create the effect that the audience is caught in this intersubjective web of the double bind as well, both sending and receiving the conflicting cues.

Sontag's interest in the existentialist notion of intersubjectivity is further registered in scene 4, where Alice's brother "Harry" attends her at her bedside. Of course, we recognize him as the author Henry James, whose paraphrastic style was meant to capture the psychological complexities of his characters' thoughts and feelings. In like manner, Harry narrates Alice's life, fixing its shape and significance, much as Sartre's grandfather did when he deemed young Jean-Paul a "writer:"

> HARRY "Her tragic health was in a manner the only solution for her of the problem of life—as it suppressed the lament of equality, reciprocity, etc."
> ALICE What a terrible thing to say. Why should equality, reciprocity be more of a problem for me than for you. Tell me. Are you saying this of me.

HARRY Not yet. It's what I will say of you two years after you have
   died, at the age of forty-three—
ALICE Don't tell me.
HARRY Of course not.
(*He leans forward to caress her cheek.*)
ALICE No no I don't mind. I find I am more curious than I thought.
   Well let's have it all. Do I, I mean will I, tenses are strangely potent
   aren't they, commit suicide.
HARRY You don't take your life.
ALICE After all that talk. I should be ashamed of myself.
HARRY (*smiling tenderly*) Yes.
ALICE So I didn't commit suicide. And I'll have, I gather from your dis-
   creet silence, a real illness. Much preferable to this tiresome neuras-
   thenia. I never quite saw myself as Elizabeth Barrett, being unable
   to envisage for myself either the literary gift or the ardent rescuer.
   (*Pauses*) Cancer.
HARRY Alas.
(*AB*, 30–31)

So, there she has it: her destiny in a nutshell. Despite her protesta-
tions, Harry gets the last word. He gets to name "the problem of [her]
life" and give it the gestalt of significance. Alice is shamed by the knowledge that her threats of suicide were mere self-dramatizations, as if they
were merely the empty words of an actor (elsewhere she identifies the
vice of self-dramatization with Sarah Bernhardt). And yet, even if only
empty words, they have shaped her relationships with everyone around
her. Harry, brought to tears by the thought of her unhappiness, urges
her to will herself into wanting to live. Alice comforts him, wryly noting
that that is her role: "Well I am a woman and that is a woman's job, to
comfort and reassure men, even from the bed, sickbed deathbed birth-
bed, to which the man has come, on tiptoe, to visit and comfort, is it
not" (*AB*, 39–40). Thus, caught in an intersubjective web, Alice plays
the roles defined for her by patriarchal society, resisting them as best she
can by remaining bedridden and thus choosing not to act, by inflecting
her lines with sarcasm and thus giving a bad performance, or by creating an alternative mise-en-scène in her head.

Scenes 5 and 6 offer such alternative sites of action: a tea party and
an imaginary trip to Rome. Sontag described the tea party in scene 5 as

a Lewis Carroll–style fantasia, inspired by the happy coincidence of a shared name (*AB*, 115). But her Alice's tea party is as much an homage to Caryl Churchill's play *Top Girls* (1982), with its feminist banquet attended by historical and fictional women, as to Carroll's *Alice's Adventures in Wonderland*.[27] In Sontag's version, each woman for whom the table is set represents a psychological facet of her protagonist: Margaret Fuller (an intimidating intellect), Emily Dickinson (a closeted talent, preoccupied with death), *Parsifal*'s Kundry (pain and guilt, seeking respite in sleep), and *Giselle*'s Myrtha (anger, in the figure of a woman scorned). Although her encounters with these women provide Alice with some self-awareness and—more important—self-acceptance, the uninvited specter of her mother haunts this space of provisional freedom, calling her back to the traditional feminine roles she seeks to escape. Margaret, however, leaves her with a glimmer of hope—the thought of Rome—where one of her brother's female characters both experiences freedom and contracts encephalitis (significantly, for this stifled intellectual, the swelling of the brain). Scene 6 is a monologue in which Alice imagines that space of freedom. But any such heady thoughts find themselves tethered back down to the Benjaminian ruins deposited around that open city, as Alice finds herself unable to transcend space and time without encountering evidence of "the life I do not lead, the suffering I do not know" (*AI*, 84).

Scene 7 situates us back in Alice's bedroom, where a sleeping Alice is roused by an intruder. Indeed, as a representative of the real world, he steals into her space as stealthily as he seeks to take her possessions. Alice surprises him, though—both by startling him and by acceding so quiescently to his demands. In fact, she implores him to steal her mirror in a comic gesture of existential self-denial. Reversing the power dynamic in the relationship between possessor and dispossessed, Sontag burlesques the burglary to show how little Alice has to lose.

In the final scene, Alice's room is bare, the curtains stripped from the windows, as the sun sets into the horizon. It would appear that Alice's struggle is finally over, her body, having succumbed to breast cancer, brought into alignment with her psychological state of nonexistence. But the sadness the audience must feel from knowing that Alice is dead is leavened by a sense of relief offered in the form of a bright light that increasingly fills the room until blackout. It is a provisional transcendence, suggesting that, while Alice has been released from a body that has been the site of culturally inscribed limitations, we, the audience, who have imaginatively inhabited that body by means of our sympathetic identification with her, are returned to our own bodies at play's end. The white light, in its emptiness, invites us to write new inscriptions—both upon the historical trace that is Alice's body and upon the corporealities that are our own. Insofar as those meanings are self-authorized, they promise us a greater freedom than Alice was able to realize.

Sontag claimed that, while she wrote the play in January 1990, she first dreamed it ten years earlier, while directing Pirandello's *As You Desire Me* in Rome. Indeed, both plays deal with the theme of self-authorization, even if Sontag negates that theme by presenting a character indisposed from authorizing her own life. Pirandello's heroine, Cia, leaves her husband and the conventional gender roles he assigns her for her lover, a writer, who represents the freedom of authorizing one's own life. Perhaps this narrative formula also put Sontag in mind of Henrik Ibsen's 1888 play, *The Lady from the Sea*. This would provide her with the basis for her next and last play, the article-less *Lady from the Sea*—an ironic adaptation meant to correct what Sontag took to be Ibsen's "profoundly flawed" ending.[28] Revisiting issues first addressed in Sontag's feminist essays "The Double Standard of Aging" (1972) and "The Third World of Women" (1973), *Lady from the Sea* offers a critique of the "freedoms" available to women subject to patriarchal—and perhaps heteronormative—prerogatives, while exploring the problem of unfulfilled female desire.

Lady from the Sea

As Sontag notes in the short article in *Theatre* magazine that introduces her adaptation, Ibsen's *The Lady from the Sea*, in which his heroine Ellida chooses not to leave her husband and run away with the mysterious lover from her past, is based upon "two quite contradictory ideas"—the folkloric theme of the mermaid, on the one hand, and the portrait of a bourgeois marriage that is the hallmark of domestic realism, on the other:

Two kinds of material, which point to two quite different resolutions. A realistic study of a marriage may well end with a reconciliation of the estranged spouses. But such an ending is defiantly at odds with the folk-loric materials which Ibsen thought the heart of his play. In the many tales of sea-women who try, for love of a well-intentioned man, to live a land-life . . . the woman is invariably obliged to return to the sea. . . . The sea-woman in Ibsen's play will remain on land, reject the tempta-tion of a demon lover, and accept happiness with her human mate.[29]

Clearly, Sontag finds the metaphorical mermaid's return to her land-locked husband unbelievable or—if believable within the terms of do-mestic realism—tragic. She thus denounces the "happy" ending of Ib-sen's play for not being "true to the story that he is telling."[30]

In her adaptation, Sontag retells Ibsen's story but adds a thick layer of irony, inviting her audience to question its "truth." In scene 2, for ex-ample, Sontag employs a Brechtian alienation effect to question Ibsen's picture of the freedom and equality that are available to women in a bourgeois marriage. In a direct address to the audience, Ellida narrates the mermaid legend, only to be interrupted by her husband's reassertion of patriarchal authority. (Although Ibsen refers to him by his paternal name, "Wangel," Sontag identifies him by his first name, Hartwig, em-phasizing the existential—if not cultural—equality between him and his wife.)

> ELLIDA (*to audience*): Seals are actually people who of their own free will have plunged into the ocean and drowned. Once each year, on Twelfth Night, they get a chance to come ashore and take off their sealskins. Then they look just like everyone else.
>
> HARTWIG: I don't believe this story.[31]

Ellida goes on to recount how, on one such Twelfth Night, a young boy stole the sealskin belonging to a mermaid who was frolicking on the beach. Knowing she would follow him to retrieve it, he leads her to his home—and to his bed—where he "make[s] her an ordinary woman" and "make[s] himself a man."[32] Together they have children and appear to lead a happy life. All the while, the man keeps his wife's sealskin locked up in a chest. "Now something sad happens," Hartwig interjects.

> HARTWIG: The man from Mikladur was happy with his seal wife. Hap-piness has to end.

ELLIDA: One day he went fishing with other men from the village, and while he was sitting out at sea, pulling in fish, his hand brushed his belt where the key usually hung. He was dumbfounded to realize that he must have forgotten the key at home. Choking with grief he cried out, "This evening I'll be without a wife!" He rowed home as fast as he could, he ran to his house, and sure enough, his wife was gone.

The children were sitting quietly. So that they would not hurt themselves while they were alone in the house, his wife had put out the fire and locked up all the knives and sharp objects.

HARTWIG: How considerate of her!

ELLIDA: She had indeed found the key and opened the chest, and when she saw the sealskin, she had to take it, after which she had run down to the beach, pulled on her sealskin, and plunged into the sea. This is where the old saying comes from: "He couldn't control himself any more than a seal that finds its skin."

HARTWIG: Couldn't control herself? She didn't really love him, that's all.

ELLIDA: When she leaped into the sea, her seal mate found her, and they swam away together. All these years he had been waiting for her to come back to him.

HARTWIG: You see! She'd never loved her husband!

ELLIDA: When the children she had with the man from Mikladur went down to the beach, a seal could be seen just off the shore watching them, and everyone thought that it was their mother.

HARTWIG: She never loved the children either!

ELLIDA (*addressing Hartwig directly for the first time*): How can you contradict a legend?

HARTWIG: Cold. Like the sea.[33]

Where Ellida tells a story of female self-fulfillment outside the bounds of bourgeois marriage, Hartwig imposes his own interpretation, reading it as the story of a particular marriage that fails due to the woman's duplicity (figured here as a literal "double-ness"). Sontag thus asks her audience to understand the story that Ibsen tells (and that she retells) as Hartwig's story, its patriarchal ideology naturalized by the emotional cues he prompts us to feel.

But in reading Ellida's decision to stay with Hartwig as a capitulation to patriarchal authority, Sontag fails to consider Ibsen's play within the context of his larger corpus. To be sure, she places Ellida alongside

Hedda Gabbler, Nora Helmer, and Rebecca West as examples of his "neurotic" heroines, but she fails to see how the drama, taken in its entirety, plays out one of the possible permutations for resolving the story of an unhappy marriage: wife leaves husband (*A Doll's House*), wife stays in unhappy marriage, producing unhealthy children (*Ghosts*), husband kills wife/wife kills husband (*Rosmersholm*), wife kills self (*Hedda Gabler*), wife returns to husband who reforms but fails to realize her ideals (*The Master Builder*), wife returns to husband, both of whom reform (*The Lady from the Sea*).[34]

Granted, Wangel's "reform" is only briefly sketched in Ibsen's play, but it definitively triggers the resolution. After he threatens to have the stranger arrested for a crime committed long ago, Wangel quickly realizes that his marriage is endangered less by the stranger himself than by the mysterious pull of the sea and the freedom that he and it represent. Ellida tells Wangel that while he has the "means and the power" to keep her legally tied to him, "all my thoughts, all the longings and desires of my soul" cannot be bound. "In quiet sorrow," Wangel realizes she is right and so releases her from the "bargain" they had made in which he would take her back to Skjoldviken, the coastal town where she was born, in exchange for her commitment to stay with him. "Now you can choose your own path," he tells her, "in perfect—perfect freedom."[35] Surprised, Ellida asks him why he's changed his mind, to which he replies, "because I love you so dearly."[36] Valuing her happiness over his own, Wangel continues, "Now your own true life may resume its real bent again, for now you can choose of your own free will, and on your own responsibility, Ellida."[37] She is dumbfounded. "Of my own free will, and on my own responsibility! Responsibility, too?" Ellida stammers epiphanically. "That changes everything."[38]

For Ibsen's Ellida, what changes is both her husband's realization that his love must include a recognition of her own autonomy and her realization that their marriage is founded upon that sense of love. This love, rather than the possessive love offered by the stranger, is what ultimately sets her free. Ibsen isn't departing from the folkloric narrative so much as reinterpreting it in abstract terms: his Ellida returns not to a lover who represents the sea and a provisional sense of freedom but to a love that is freedom itself.

Without explicitly narrating the mermaid legend, Ibsen uses it both as an implicit structuring principle and as a rhetorical device by which to heighten his audience's surprise at Ellida's decision. This isn't a flaw, however; it is classic Ibsen. For if they're surprised by Ellida's decision, Ibsen's audience will have to attend closely to her reasons for making it. Those reasons are clearly stated in the dialogue, where Ellida distinguishes between a freedom from and a freedom of. The stranger has offered her a kind of freedom—a freedom from the conventional constraints of marriage—but Wangel offers her another type of freedom—a freedom of action premised upon the principle of individual autonomy that both expects and requires her to take full responsibility for her actions. It is this second type of freedom (a remarkably Sartrean notion of freedom) that Ellida chooses and Sontag (also remarkably) neglects.

But even if his audience is taken by such surprise at her decision that it fails to understand the distinction Ellida makes between the "freedoms" offered her, Ibsen provides a narrative means by which to comprehend her transformation. It lies in the parallel narrative of Bolette's engagement to Arnholm. The eldest daughter from Wangel's first marriage, Bolette likens herself to a carp in a pond, trapped in a backwater town, never to explore the wide world around her. Arnholm, her former tutor (representing worldly knowledge), has returned for a visit, mistakenly assuming that she has feelings for him. Although the mistake is quickly brought to light, Arnholm proposes to her, having come to develop feelings for her in imagining hers for him. He knows she longs to see the world and so promises to show it to her if she will be his wife. Although she is momentarily disappointed at the prospect of marrying a man so much older than she, Bolette consents, accepting the bargain he has proposed. Intelligent, compassionate, and gentle, Arnholm isn't a villain. Nonetheless, what he offers is nothing less than emotional blackmail. His is much the same "bargain" that Wangel offers Ellida but later retracts when he realizes that it satisfies his own needs more than hers. Ibsen includes this parallel narrative in order to show a fundamental difference between the conventional arrangement of Arnholm and Bolette's marriage and the transformed union of Ellida and Wangel. Sontag also includes the parallel, but only as a reiteration of the female captivity narrative she wants to tell.

Like Ibsen, Sontag ends her play with Ellida choosing Hartwig over the mysterious stranger from her past. That stranger, however, is not represented by another actor; as if to underscore the elusive freedom that he represents, Sontag presents him as a literal absence that the actor portraying Ellida must make present. Alternating between conventional realist acting ["(*To the Foreigner*) What do you want here? What are you speaking to me like this? Who are you looking for?"] and Brechtian narration ["(*To the audience*) He says I am looking for you"], the actor portraying Ellida enacts her choice as an internal conflict between the lure of a freedom that is uncertain and the comfort of an unfreedom that is familiar.[39] Realizing that unfreedom, itself, is a choice, Ellida exclaims, "So now that I am free to choose I can even choose you." "Yes!" Hartwig affirms. "But will I still be free, Hartwig, if I choose you?" she asks, to which he responds, "There are no certainties in freedom. That's why it's so beautiful. That's why everyone dreams of being free."[40] Although, as in Ibsen's play, Ellida is free to make her decision, in Sontag's play she calls upon that freedom to choose unfreedom in order to avoid responsibility for all but this one action. After all, Hartwig has already defined freedom as a "flash of light" that is over before you can even say the word. In the final scene, Ellida, dressed in a high-necked dress, sits on the veranda, embroidering, imagining violent and self-liberating actions that she (like Alice) will never undertake. Unnerved by the responsibility she bears for the one decision she has made, she asks Hartwig if she made a mistake, to which Sontag's figure of patriarchal authority answers, "Just the opposite. No," he continues, invoking Ibsen's metaphorical language, "you learned to *acclimatize* yourself."[41]

Thus ironizing Ibsen's "happy" ending, Sontag asks her audience to regard it as its own type of fairy tale and resist the comedic satisfaction of its affirmation of marriage. But Sontag does not simply unsettle Ibsen's ending; she invites her audience to imagine an alternative ending through its dialectical negation. Its antithesis exists in the folkloric materials Sontag makes explicit early in her play. For the mermaid—unlike Ellida—escapes from a life defined for her by her male counterpart; she is free (as the ocean suggests). With its trope of a "second skin," the mermaid legend offers a way of imagining a transcendence of the patriarchal inscriptions that define the female body. But, unlike *Alice*'s white light, which clears a space for the writing of new meanings onto the body, in *Lady* the transcendence seems peculiarly material. After all, the mermaid returns to her original sealskin and to a mate who, as a seal, is thus "homomorphic." To her human mate, this half-seal/half-woman is necessarily "heteromorphic," with all of the agonistic features that such a relationship implies. Written at a time when Sontag was beginning to publicly acknowledge her bisexuality, *Lady* thus may be read as refusing not only the patriarchal gender roles of a conventional bourgeois marriage but also the heteronormative disciplines exercised upon queer bodies. Perhaps, like the sea, the experience of lesbian desire called Sontag to rehabilitate a body that not only had been culturally denied her but that she, at times, had denied herself.

Conclusion

The theater, as I have tried to demonstrate, was fundamental to Sontag's thought. As referent in many of her critical essays, as metaphor for her political activism, and as medium of her later creative work, the theater informed her thinking and shaped her habit of mind. Although Sontag experimented with various genres throughout her career, exploring the expressive possibilities of each, her work is knit together by a special fascination with the dialectical relationship between form and content, where form is often imagined through the metaphor of the body, and content, of the "mind." Although the form-content dialectic is a function of all art, nowhere is its correlation to the metaphor of mind and body made more palpable than in the theater, where words are embodied, ideas made flesh.

Like Artaud, whose work she so admired, Sontag may have been drawn to the theater because it allowed her to stage this dialectic in both formal and thematic terms. Perhaps, like Artaud's corpus more generally, Sontag's contributions to the theater may be clarified with reference to Gnosticism. For if Sontag's four stages of Gnosticism are mapped onto her theatrical contributions, what comes clear are the affirmation of the body in her directorial work (where the body's ability to create meaning is affirmed), the revulsion from the body in *A Parsifal* (where she repels her audience's identification from the embodiment of political passivity), the wish to transcend the body in *Alice in Bed* (where her audience is asked to imagine a state of freedom beyond the patriarchal disciplines imposed on women's bodies), and the quest to redeem the body in *Lady from the Sea* (where the mermaid seeks to return to her original sealskin).

Of course, the mermaid's return is refused in Ibsen's original and ironically negated in Sontag's adaptation. Written toward the end of her life when Sontag was beginning to experience a recurrence of cancer, *Lady from the Sea* also suggests a revulsion from the body, insofar as the mermaid rejects her human body. But if we consider the photographs that Sontag would seem to have authorized Annie Leibovitz to take of her toward the end of her life, we might come to another conclusion. Those photographs—of a postorgasmic body luxuriating in bed, of an enervated body quickened by an IV, of a lifeless body soon to be interred in earth's diurnal course—those photographs suggest another type of quest for the body's redemption. Ever the existential humanist, Sontag appears to have followed Sartre's dictum that "existence precedes essence." Her body was her life; having reached a state of Being in death, she was the sum of what she had done. And what she had done—as an essayist, novelist, director, filmmaker, playwright, and activist—was act—with conviction both in and on her world.

Notes

1. See, for example, Bonnie Marranca and Gautam Dasgupta, "Art and Consciousness," *Performing Arts Journal* 80 (2005): 1–9. While they remark that, among American intellectuals, Sontag was "unusual in attending seriously to the theatre and the other non-literary arts" (1), they don't develop this observation into a consideration of how that serious attention informed her writing or thinking more generally; it serves primarily to introduce a reprint of their 1977 interview with her. See, too, Paul Berman, "On Susan Sontag," *Dissent* (Spring 2005): 109–12. Although he cites Sontag's production of Samuel Beckett's *Waiting for Godot* in Sarajevo as an example of her activism and intellectual bravery, he treats the play simply as an occasion for her political activism rather than an integral site of it (109).

2. Sohnya Sayres, *Susan Sontag: The Elegiac Modernist* (New York: Routledge, 1990); Liam Kennedy, *Susan Sontag: Mind as Passion* (Manchester: Manchester University Press, 1995). To be fair, Sayres's study predates Sontag's playwriting career, and Kennedy's appeared in print only two years after the publication of *Alice in Bed*, which explains why they do not analyze her plays. Still, in discussing Sontag's interest in Artaud, for example, both critics treat him as if he were some kind of abstract theorist of modernism, making scant reference to his work in the theater.

3. Carl Rollyson, *Reading Susan Sontag: A Critical Introduction to Her Work* (Chicago: Ivan R. Dee, 2001), 40.

4. François Dosse, *A History of Structuralism*, trans. Deborah Glassman, 2 vols. (Minneapolis: University of Minnesota Press, 1997). As Dosse points out, the zeitgeist that goes by the name of "poststructuralism" didn't disprove the fundamental premises of existentialism so much as replace them with an anti-foundationalist model of subjectivity. He sees this "eclipse" as a shift in intellectual fashion.

5. Sontag, "On Self: From the Notebooks and Diaries of Susan Sontag, 1958–67," *New York Times Magazine*, September 10, 2006, 52–58.

6. Rollyson asserts that "Sontag's only real regret was writing theatre criticism for *Partisan Review*. She was not that kind of critic—one who goes to plays and passes judgment—and she felt she was being forced into the mold of Mary McCarthy, who had established her reputation writing theatre criticism in the same publication" (*Reading Susan Sontag*, 184). In the reprint of her 1977 interview with Marranca and Dasgupta, Sontag indeed dismisses that type of criticism, referring to it as the work of "monitoring productions and giving out grades—the kind of consumer reporting that decides whether something is good or not good, well performed or not well performed" ("Art and Consciousness," 3). However much she wished to distinguish herself from professional theater critics, Sontag was nonetheless an avid theatergoer, and her essays on the theater were important to her, as evidenced by their inclusion in these published collections.

7. Susan Sontag, introduction to *Antonin Artaud: Selected Writings*, trans. Helen Weaver (New York: Farrar, Strauss and Giroux, 1976).

8. Jacques Derrida, "The Theatre of Cruelty and the Closure of Representation," in *Writing and Difference*, trans. Alan Bass (Chicago: University of Chicago Press, 1978).

9. Sontag, introduction to *Antonin Artaud*, xlv.

10. Sontag, introduction to *Antonin Artaud*, xlviii.

11. Sontag, introduction to *Antonin Artaud*, li.

12. See, for example, Susan Sontag, preface to *Plays: Maria Irene Fornes* (New York: PAJ, 1986). See also Alexis Soloski, "A Parsifal," *Village Voice* 51, no. 9 (March 1–7, 2006): C59, who notes that her play *A Parsifal* was apparently written in lieu of a requested introduction to the published catalogue of Robert Wilson's set designs. Only her introduction to *A Barthes Reader* would seem to be an exception, but it is an exception that proves the rule insofar as Barthes, like Artaud, was profoundly important to Sontag's thought. Susan Sontag, introduction to *A Barthes Reader* (New York: Hill and Wang, 1982).

13. Rollyson, *Reading Susan Sontag*, 26–27.

14. Luigi Pirandello, *As You Desire Me*, trans. Samuel Putnam (New York: Dutton, 1931), 145.

15. Gerald Rabkin. "Milan and His Master." *Performing Arts Journal* 9, no. 1 (1985): 21–22.

16. Rabkin, "Milan and His Master," 20.

17. Susan Sontag, "*Waiting for Godot* in Sarajevo." *Performing Arts Journal* 47 (May 1994): 92. Rollyson observes that many of the themes she treats in the plays she chose to direct were also addressed in her own novels and films. He reads her production of Pirandello's play, for example, alongside her film *Brother Carl*, both of which introduce characters with uncertain pasts (*Reading Susan Sontag*, 26). Similarly, he compares her production of Kundera's play to her film *Duet for Cannibals* as well as her television essay on dancer Pina Bausch, noting that all three introduce variations on the "couple relation" (35). Rollyson is right to emphasize these continuities for—throughout her career— Sontag continually returned to core themes and ideas. But with each return, Sontag explored the formal possibilities of expression that were offered by a new genre.

18. Sontag "*Waiting for Godot* in Sarajevo," 92–93; emphasis mine.

19. Sontag, "*Waiting for Godot* in Sarajevo," 93.

20. See her response to these unnamed critics in Sontag, "*Waiting for Godot* in Sarajevo." Evidently, some attacked her for being frivolous—putting on a play (of all things!) in a war zone. Others accused her of being narcissistic—drawing attention to herself, Madame Directeur, rather than the people of Sarajevo whom she was purportedly "helping." Dismissing her critics, Sontag insisted, "What my production of Godot signifie[d] to [the residents of Sarajevo], apart from the fact that an eccentric American writer and part-time director volunteered to work in the theatre as an expression of solidarity with the city (a fact inflated by the local press and radio as evidence that the rest of the world 'does care'—when I knew, to my indignation and shame, that I represented nobody but myself), is that this is a great European play and that they are members of European culture. . . . Culture, serious culture from anywhere, is an expression of human dignity" (90).

21. Lois Oppenheim, "Playing with Beckett's Plays: On Sontag in Sarajevo and Other Directorial Infidelities," *Journal of Beckett Studies* 4, no. 2 (1995): 39.

22. Sontag, "*Waiting for Godot* in Sarajevo," 97.

23. Susan Sontag, *A Parsifal, Antaeus* 67, no. 3 (1991): 180–85.

24. Sontag, *A Parsifal*, 181–2.

25. See *RP*, 101–3, where she makes this insight explicit.

26. Sontag, *A Parsifal*, 185.

27. As Michael Feingold notes in his review of Ivo von Hove's production, Sontag's play is even more closely evocative of Joan Schenkar's play about Alice James, *Signs of Life*, which also includes a Churchill-esque feminist tea party. See "Pity the Poor Theater, Sick and Bedridden—Except When It Gets Up to Dance," *Village Voice*, November 21, 2000, 79.

28. Sontag, "Rewriting *The Lady from the Sea*," *Theater* 29, no. 1 (1999): 89.

29. Sontag, "Rewriting," 90.

30. Sontag, "Rewriting," 91.

31. Sontag, *Lady from the Sea, Theater* 29, no. 1 (1999): 94.

32. Sontag, *Lady*, 95.

33. Sontag, *Lady*, 95–96.

34. Apparently, Sontag hadn't read *Ghosts*. Claiming *The Lady from the Sea* "reeks of the playwright's ambivalence toward his subject," Sontag invites her reader to speculate on the "pressures" Ibsen surely must have felt, "after the still (to this day) shocking resolution of *A Doll's House*, to provide a story of a discontented wife who does not leave her husband" ("Rewriting," 90). In *Ghosts*, Ibsen did provide that story, along with the lesson that society should not tolerate a morality that values the marriage contract over the health and happiness of the man and woman bound by it. If anything, the cultural "pressures" upon Ibsen that Sontag imagines as having resulted from *A Doll's House* may explain why he took such pains to deemphasize the mother-child bond as a factor in Ellida's decision to stay in this play.

35. Henrik Ibsen, *The Lady from the Sea*, in *A Doll's House, The Wild Duck, The Lady from the Sea*, trans. R. Farquharson Sharp and Eleanor Marx-Aveling; rev. Torgrim and Linda Hannas (1910; London: J. M. Dent, 1985), 239.

36. Ibsen, *The Lady from the Sea*, 239.

37. Ibsen, *The Lady from the Sea*, 239.

38. Ibsen, *The Lady from the Sea*, 240.

39. Sontag, *Lady*, 107.

40. Sontag, *Lady*, 111.

41. Sontag, *Lady*, 112; italics mine.

chapterseven

The "Counterculture" in Quotation Marks
Sontag and Marcuse on the Work of Revolution

CRAIG J. PEARISO

In the last two decades, a number of authors have looked to Susan Sontag's "Notes on Camp," seeking either to reassert and build on its critique of the camp sensibility's apolitical tendencies or to condemn Sontag's reading for its apparent failure to understand the nuances of queer subcultures.[1] The remarks that follow may rankle those on both sides. In this essay, I return to "Notes on Camp," attempting to resituate this work in the context of the broader analysis of 1960s American culture presented in Sontag's *Against Interpretation* (1966). Ultimately, my goal will be not just to reinterpret "Notes on Camp" in light of these other works but to reinterpret *all* of the essays found in that volume historically by reading them against the contemporary thought of philosopher Herbert Marcuse. In the essay "Against Interpretation," Sontag wrote of an "erotics of art" (*AI*, 14), a form of direct engagement with aesthetic works that would distance the viewer from a society dominated by an overwhelming tendency to separate form from content and to understand "Being-as-Playing-a-Role." Yet throughout the essays collected in the volume of the same name, Sontag struggled time and again with notions of authenticity and theatricality in relation to what she deemed the "new art." The more she tried to separate the "Camp sensibility" from the "new sensibility," the more inextricable the two came to seem. More importantly, neither one appeared capable of achieving any true critical distance from the new technological and social realities of post-war culture. For this reason, Marcuse's account of "one-dimensional society" and its conquest of "higher culture," published in the same year as "Notes on Camp," provides a fascinating complement to many of Sontag's writings of this period, especially given her acknowledged debt to Marcuse's social-historical analyses of the mid-1950s.[2]

As the historian Gerald Howard has written, the "coolly ironic mood so characteristic of so much of Sixties art seems to contradict the heated idealism, political activism and self-exploration so equally characteristic of the Sixties."[3] By revisiting Sontag's analysis of these "sensibilities," and in relating those sensibilities to the works of Marcuse, it will become apparent that whether or not one agrees with the judgments issued in her "Notes," camp just might be the hinge between cool art and the heated work of revolution that interests Howard. In ways that even Sontag herself may not have realized at the time, camp may have been the dominant political and aesthetic sensibility of that era.

I

It's striking to recall that for Herbert Marcuse, writing at approximately the same time that Sontag wrote "Notes on Camp," political and aesthetic opposition seems to be almost entirely ineffectual. In his 1964 *One-Dimensional Man*, he writes that contemporary society is "irrational as a whole." It is a "society without opposition," one in which citizens submit to the "peaceful production of the means of destruction, to the perfection of waste, to being educated for a defense which deforms the defenders and that which they defend."[4] To be sure, Marcuse never denied that difference endured in this society, but the oppositionality necessary for dialectical thought, and thus for any meaningful, radical transformation had, he argued, effectively vanished. "The manifold processes of introjection seem to be ossified in almost mechanical reactions," he wrote.

> The result is, not adjustment but *mimesis*: an immediate identification of the individual with *his* [sic] society and, through it, with the society

as a whole. . . . In this process, the "inner" dimension of the mind in which opposition to the status quo can take root is whittled down. . . . The impact of progress turns Reason into submission to the facts of life, and to the dynamic capability of producing more and bigger facts of the same sort of life.[5]

Contemporary society had eradicated virtually all resistance. Difference, promoted only to enhance the illusion of inclusiveness, had ceased to be meaningful. One of the ways in which this could be seen most clearly, he argued, was in the liquidation of oppositionality from the realm of "higher culture."

In one-dimensional society, the aspects of the work of art that once enabled it to stand against the dominant social reality have been expunged. "This liquidation . . . takes place not through the denial and rejection of the 'cultural values,'" Marcuse explains, "but through their wholesale incorporation into the established order, through their reproduction and display on a massive scale."[6] Rather than delivering the potential liberation that Walter Benjamin saw in its mechanical reproducibility, mass culture, according to Marcuse, has done just the opposite. It succeeded in the total conquest of individual consciousness. It did so, he explained, by purporting to deliver the happiness that art once only suggested. Unlike earlier artworks, whose *promesse de bonheur* was invariably, necessarily deferred, the products of mass culture presented themselves as the true fulfillment of individual desires. One-dimensional culture appeared to have eliminated the social strictures that had produced the work of "higher culture" as a necessary form of sublimation. "Higher culture" was meaningful, Marcuse argued, "because its authentic works expressed a conscious, methodical alienation from the entire sphere of business and industry, and from its calculable and profitable order."[7] One-dimensional society rendered this mode of culture obsolete by blending "harmoniously, and often unnoticeably, art, politics, religion, and philosophy with commercials."[8] It brought these different cultural manifestations, along with the individual consciousnesses responsible for their creation, into alignment with their common historical denominator: the commodity form. Sublimation no longer seemed necessary, therefore, for the desires of the individual appeared to have been accommodated within the social structures they once contradicted. They were reconciled with the society that once worked to exterminate them. The utopian moment of art was thus superseded by suggestions of a utopia achieved within mass culture.

Two years later, in his essay on "Repressive Tolerance," Marcuse's tone conveyed an unmistakable despair. The "abstract tolerance" of American liberal democracy—abstract "inasmuch as it refrains from taking sides"—offered nothing, he argued, but a mockery of true tolerance.[9] Though contemporary social and cultural institutions allowed all sides of a given debate to be heard, "the people," those called upon to evaluate contrasting positions, had been left incapable of making crucial distinctions between differing points of view. The tolerance that purportedly made them "free" individuals had in fact subjugated them. They were able only to "parrot, as their own, the opinions of their masters."[10] What appeared to be tolerance was little more than a mirage; individuals are stripped of any sense of the potential social import of their actions. "Real opposition" is replaced by "the satisfactions of private and personal rebellion."[11] One could do or say virtually anything without posing a significant threat to the status quo. In the name of self-fulfillment, individuals had allowed themselves to be nullified, subsumed within a social order that only worked against their best interests.[12]

These were the conditions Marcuse believed to be responsible for the "repressive desublimation" of human sexuality. In "Repressive Tolerance," he argued that desublimation, as it existed in contemporary culture, was truly injurious to the individual. It "weaken[ed] the necessity and the power of the intellect, the catalytic force of that unhappy consciousness which does not revel in the archetypal personal release of frustration . . . but which recognizes the horror of the whole in the most private frustration and actualizes itself in this recognition."[13] Society's ultimately enslaving "liberation" of art and sexuality had rendered the individual incapable of recognizing his or her own unhappiness. Any sense of emancipation one might have felt within the technological society was nothing more than that society's "conquest of freedom." And much like the artist, whose statements of alienation had become easily assimilable, those who attempted to flout the rules of this social order succeeded only in strengthening its grasp: "Zen, existentialism, and beat ways of life, etc. . . . are no longer contradictory to the status quo. . . . They are rather the ceremonial part of a practical behaviorism, its harmless negation, and are quickly digested by the status quo as part of its healthy diet."[14] Rebellion had been reduced to a set of signifiers so that it might become the ultimate in conformity. Even sexual perversion, which in *Eros and Civilization* was said to be thoroughly irreconcilable with a society that attempted to subjugate all sexuality to the logic of labor, had been successfully co-opted. The forms of eroticism in which Marcuse and Sontag had placed their hopes no longer seemed to offer the same opportunity for transcendence. One could "let go," as it were, and yet leave the "real engines of repression" entirely intact. Asking the reader to consider the difference between "love-making in a meadow and in an automobile, on a lovers' walk outside the town walls and on a Manhattan street," Marcuse explained:

> In the former cases, the environment partakes of and invites libidinal cathexis and tends to be eroticized. In contrast, a mechanized environment seems to block such self-transcendence of libido. Impelled in the striving to extend the field of erotic gratification, libido becomes less "polymorphous," less capable of eroticism beyond localized sexuality, and the *latter* is intensified.[15]

The body's increased sexualization precluded its true re-eroticization. Perversion, desublimated only to be safely compartmentalized as a leisure activity, no longer upheld the possibility of the erotic as an end in itself. Nevertheless, to paraphrase Sontag, the nausea of the replica seemed to have been transcended.

While Marcuse had not abandoned all hope for a radical, total revolution, the source from which that revolution might spring proved increasingly difficult to identify. Art, sexuality, alternative ways of life: nearly all forms of opposition had become easily, inherently absorbed into the dominant culture. Compelled, therefore, in spite of his own arguments, to designate a source of potential social transformation, Marcuse alluded to the "substratum" of the technological society, "the exploited and persecuted of other races and other colors":

> They exist outside the democratic process; their life is the most immediate and the most real need for ending intolerable conditions and institutions. Thus their opposition is revolutionary even if their consciousness is not. Their opposition hits the system from without and is therefore not deflected by the system; it is an elementary force which violates the rules of the game and, in doing so, reveals it as a rigged game. . . . The

fact that they start refusing to play the game may be the fact which marks the beginning of the end of a period.[16]

The experience of racial oppression, in other words, would provide the exteriority necessary for true critique. Writing in the early 1960s, Marcuse praised the members of the Civil Rights Movement for their courage. The power of their willingness to "face dogs, stones, and bombs, jail, concentration camps, even death" lay "behind every political demonstration for the victims of law and order."[17] By 1966, however, his perspective had changed slightly. In "Repressive Tolerance" he wrote that

> the exercise of political rights (such as voting, letter-writing to the press, to Senators, etc., protest demonstrations with *a priori* renunciation of counterviolence) in a society of total administration serves to strengthen this administration by testifying to the existence of democratic liberties which, in reality, have changed their content and lost their effectiveness. In such a case, freedom . . . becomes an instrument for absolving servitude.[18]

Apparently, the willingness to face dogs, stones, bombs, etc. was no longer sufficient. The turn in Marcuse's thought clearly reflects the public transition from the nonviolent Civil Rights Movement of the 1950s and early 1960s to the openly confrontational politics of Black Power. All the same, the potential catalyst of historical transformation would still be found in the oppositional strategies of "other races and other colors." For Marcuse, in the face of a virtually totalizing system of repressive tolerance, the opposition of racial minorities maintained an element of purity and authenticity otherwise lost.

II

For Sontag, too, in the mid-1960s, artistic practice was at a turning point. Artists were developing new forms that seemed to delight in stonewalling critical analysis. In some sense, she argued, this should come as no surprise. For more than a century, the relationship between the critic and the work of art had been approaching an impasse, thanks primarily to the critic's blatant disregard for the work of art's objectivity. "In most modern instances," Sontag believed, the critic simply rendered art "manageable, conformable" (*AI*, 8). By seeking to interpret aesthetic works, the critic implicitly assumes that form and content are somehow distinct, thereby doing a certain violence to the work itself: "Interpretation, based on the highly dubious theory that a work of art is composed of items of content, violates art" (*AI*, 7). In response to this critical aggression, Sontag argues, modern artists began making works that actively thwarted any and all attempts at interpretation by appealing directly to the senses. These artists looked to "elude the interpreters . . . by making works of art whose surface is so unified and clean, whose momentum is so rapid, whose address is so direct that the work can be . . . just what it is" (*AI*, 11). Among her listed examples of this new, more insistently "present" work: the "theatre of cruelty" of Antonin Artaud; the happenings of Alan Kaprow; the novels of Alain Robbe-Grillet; and the films of directors like Michelangelo Antonioni, Jean-Luc Godard, and Robert Bresson. The value of these works, she claims, is that they defy translation. They force one to acknowledge the work's "pure, untranslatable, sensuous immediacy . . . and its . . . solutions to certain problems of . . . form" (*AI*, 9).

In "One Culture and the New Sensibility," published just a year after "Against Interpretation" and "Notes on Camp," Sontag explains the tension between these artists and their critics in terms of a clash between contrasting sensibilities. "What we are witnessing," she wrote, "is not so much a conflict of cultures as the creation of a new (potentially unitary) kind of sensibility"; one era in the history of "human sensory awareness" is being supplanted by the next (*AI*, 296). New artists, she argues, had begun transforming a flood of new experiences into a new kind of work. The result is not the end of art but rather a shift in its function from being a "magical-religious operation . . . passed over into a technique for depicting and commenting on secular reality," into being as "a new kind of instrument, an instrument for modifying consciousness and organizing new modes of sensibility" (*AI*, 296). For the viewer, this means the experience of the new art would seem almost painful, as the effort to organize "new modes of sensibility" necessarily redefines the notion of pleasure. "In one sense," she explains,

> the new art and the new sensibility take a rather dim view of pleasure. . . . The seriousness of modern art precludes pleasure in the familiar sense—the pleasure of a melody that one can hum after leaving the

concert hall, of characters in a novel or play whom one can recognize, identify with, and dissect in terms of realistic psychological motives, of a beautiful landscape or a dramatic moment represented on a canvas. If hedonism means sustaining the old ways in which we have found pleasure in art (the old sensory and psychic modalities), then the new art is anti-hedonistic. Having one's sensorium challenged or stretched hurts. The new serious music hurts one's ears, the new painting does not graciously reward one's sight, the new films and the few interesting new prose works do not go down easily.

(*AI*, 302–3)

Given the inherent difficulty of the new art, it is surprising that Sontag finds the "new sensibility" from which it arises inherently populist. This paradox does not spring from any explicit political program—she found the "new art," after all, to be "notably apolitical and undidactic, or rather, infradidactic"—but because those who share this sensibility seem to demand "less content in art" (*AI*, 300, 303). The eradication of "characters in a novel or play whom one can recognize, identify with, and dissect in terms of realistic psychological motives" had been carried out not in order to bring an end to pleasure per se, but to force the audience to attend solely to the pleasures of the form itself. And it is from this reorientation that the unpleasant challenging and stretching of the sensorium would inevitably result.

Or would it? At the end of the essay, Sontag writes that one "important consequence" of the new art and the new sensibility is that "the distinction between 'high' and 'low' culture seems less and less meaningful. For such a distinction . . . simply does not make sense for a creative community of artists and scientists engaged in programming sensations, uninterested in art as a species of moral journalism" (*AI*, 302). For those conforming to the "new sensibility," and taking pleasure in form rather than content, a song by the Supremes or Dionne Warwick—both Sontag's examples—could prove just as exciting or rewarding as the writings of Samuel Beckett or the films of Godard. As she put it, the "fact that many of the most serious American painters . . . are also fans of 'the new sound' in popular music . . . reflects a new, more open way of looking at the world and at things in the world, our world" (*AI*, 303). Now, one can almost certainly hum the melody of "Baby Love"

after leaving the concert hall, or after turning off the radio for that matter, but for Sontag, this seems to be beside the point. Her argument suggests not that the Supremes were representative of the "new art" but
that the "new artists," with sensibilities reshaped through their intense
engagement with the modern world, had reached a point of sensory
sophistication that allowed them to appreciate the formal qualities of
"Message to Michael" as much as those of *Malone Dies*.

Yet not all young artists who appeared to appreciate popular culture were engaged in this project of formal directness. As Sontag points
out, the works of artists like Andy Warhol seemed to be characterized
by a peculiar type of *in*directness. In contrast to the brute materiality of
the "theatre of cruelty," Pop Art had frustrated any attempt at translation and domestication by using "a content so blatant, so 'what it is,'"
that efforts to move beyond the surface of the object were ultimately
denied. But upon introducing this idea of indirectness as an alternate
path to immediacy, one that required the viewer to make reference to a
work's content before being forced to contemplate its form, Sontag runs
head-on into a historical dilemma. Simply put, the "new art" and the
"new sensibility," whether or not they involved "the renunciation of all
standards," were in the end reconcilable with the demands of postwar
consumer capitalism (*AI*, 304).

Sontag's stumbling over this problem is particularly interesting given
the theoretical precedents for her position. The urgency with which she
pressed for a critical "erotics of art," she explained, was rooted in the
reformulation of psychoanalysis presented by Marcuse and Norman O.
Brown in the 1950s. Like them, she believed that the political biases implicit in Freud's theories of sexuality were deeply problematic; Sontag
explains that they are two of the first thinkers to indicate the "revolutionary implications of sexuality in contemporary society" (*AI*, 257). In
Eros and Civilization, published in 1955, Marcuse argues that Freud's
belief that human culture is necessarily repressive amounts to little more
than a defense of the status quo. The repression Freud saw as integral
to any orderly and efficient society was, according to Marcuse, "surplus repression," the subordination of individual desires and impulses
to the demands of industrial capitalism. The corrective to this surplus
repression was to be found, he argued, in the remembrance of the developmental stage of "polymorphous perversity," a moment prior to the

restriction of eroticism to the genitals. If the entire organism could be re-eroticized, Marcuse argued, the body would be freed from its status as an instrument of alienated labor.

Similarly, in his 1959 text *Life Against Death*, Brown calls for the rejoining of mind and body. Unlike "revisionist" American Freudians, he believed that psychoanalysis holds the key to healing both society and the individual. This cure would be achieved not through the reeducation of the mind but through the recognition of the mind's dependence on the body; if the primacy of the body could be acknowledged, and an androgynous mode of existence accepted, the neuroses resulting from sexual differentiation and "genital organization" could be overcome. As Sontag summarized this argument, "The core of human neurosis is man's [*sic*] incapacity to live in the body—to live (that is, to be sexual) and to die" (*AI*, 259). Following Marcuse and Brown, Sontag's "erotics of art" thus constitutes a move toward this re-eroticized individual. For Sontag, the attempts of "new artists" to reeducate the senses are not just aesthetic obligations but social imperatives. Through the direct experience of these works as a material refusal to submit to the demands of "critical" thought, she believed individuals could be transformed. Nevertheless, the "Surrealist sensibility" at play in these works also gave rise to the works of artists like Warhol, which were far more difficult to reconcile with her notions of formal directness. Like the surrealists, all of Sontag's "new artists" sought to "destroy conventional meanings" and to create new ones through the use of "radical juxtaposition."[19] But where Kaprow and Artaud actively challenged viewers' senses and sensibilities, Pop Art, according to Sontag, ultimately looked only to entertain them. Warhol and others like him were merely the legatees of those surrealists who made it fashionable for the French intelligentsia to frequent flea markets. The particular form of "disinterested wit and sophistication" in which they specialized may have stymied critical interpretation, but it failed to acknowledge the more urgent task facing the artist: the personally and socially "therapeutic" work of "re-educating the senses" (*AI*, 271). Pop Art, therefore, was plagued by its dependence upon the more insidious form of the "Surrealist sensibility" known as camp.

The "Camp sensibility," Sontag argues, is not a way of changing the world through aesthetic experience but rather of "seeing the world as an aesthetic phenomenon" (*AI*, 277). In some sense the opposite of the "new sensibility," which enabled one to take pleasure in the formal qualities of certain products of popular culture, the camp sensibility viewed those products as an image of failure. It attended to the forms of individual works but only to point out the extent to which those forms were incommensurable with their purported content. In "Notes on Camp," Sontag wrote that the camp sensibility was "the love of the exaggerated, the 'off', of things being-what-they-are-not . . . Camp sees everything in quotation marks. . . . To perceive Camp in objects and persons is to understand Being-as-Playing-a-Role" (*AI*, 279–80). Unfortunately for Sontag, the camp sensibility proved exceedingly difficult to pin down for this very reason. Following a few introductory remarks on the necessity of understanding Camp as a sensibility, she literally reverses her position. "Not only is there a Camp vision, a Camp way of looking at things . . . Camp is as well a quality discoverable in objects and the behavior of persons. . . . It's not *all* in the eye of the beholder" (*AI*, 277). It seems that in order to access the camp sensibility, she felt it necessary to work backwards from "campy" objects—things like Tiffany lamps, the *National Enquirer*, Flash Gordon comics, and the famous Brown Derby restaurant in Los Angeles. From these examples, drawn from "the canon of Camp," she believed it would be possible to extrapolate those characteristics that appealed to—and conditioned— "the Camp eye" (*AI*, 277). Through a brief survey of these objects, she surmised that Camp could not be overly serious, overly important, or overly good: "Many examples of Camp," she explained, "are things which, from a 'serious' point of view, are either bad art or kitsch" (*AI*, 278). The camp object was one that proclaimed, whether naively or consciously, its own silliness, extravagance, or artificiality. Simply put, it was an object in which form and content failed to coalesce.

But it was camp's practitioners—as opposed to its objects—that Sontag found more worrisome. As she understood it, camp amounted to the reformulation of dandyism in the world of mass culture. Camp's intimate ties to mass culture had effectively expunged the dandy's "quintessence of character and . . . subtle understanding of the entire moral mechanism of this world" (*AI*, 290). In place of this character and understanding was mere "aestheticism." Camp's affected pleasure in the imperfections of the everyday was thus reducible to the latest moment in the "history of snob taste" (*AI*, 290). It was not a sophisticated appreciation of the formal qualities of pop culture but a patronizing send-up of that culture, focusing on its inability to deliver what it promised. What is more, camp had only taken hold at a moment when "no authentic aristocrats in the old sense exist . . . to sponsor special tastes." And in the absence of a true upper class, "an improvised self-elected class, mainly homosexuals," had come to serve as the "aristocrats of taste" (*AI*, 290). Camp's appreciation of the mundane, its celebration of the art of the masses, could never have been mistaken for a truly populist—or even avant-garde—project. Rather, it was precisely the opposite.[20] Unlike "true" artists, those who appreciated camp were virtually incapable of developing any new or deeper understanding of the world. Rather than providing a challenge to critical thought, they had simply inverted its standards.

Once again, however, for Sontag, the most profound challenge to critical thought would proceed not through the intellect but through the senses. It was for this reason, among others, that when faced with camp she experienced a "deep sympathy modified by revulsion" (*AI*, 276). On one hand, the camp sensibility actively thwarted any attempt at easy interpretation: hence her choice to approach the phenomenon through a series of "notes" rather than attempting to fix its meaning in an essay. At the same time, the ironic immediacy of campy objects seemed to hold no real social or political promise. Camp thus problematized the sensuous immediacy that was so important to Sontag's "erotics of art." As she observed, "Camp . . . makes no distinction between the unique object and the mass-produced object. Camp . . . transcends the nausea of the replica" (*AI*, 289). For Sontag, that is, camp's emphasis on surface and the presentation of self as performance was less about foregrounding the tensions that might be contained within those surfaces and performances and more about finding a clever way of accepting or even celebrating them. One might say that the camp sensibility seemed to take the wrong kind of pleasure in its images. Sontag's accusation of "aestheticism," therefore, opposed camp not to the real but to the modernist notion of the aesthetic as a lever of social change.

For Sontag, one of the most repugnant aspects of camp was its virtual inescapability. Indeed, this was so troubling that she feared her own attempt to define the camp sensibility would ultimately result in "a very inferior piece of Camp" (*AI*, 277). In spite of her attempt to avoid this fate by approaching camp obliquely, her efforts to distinguish camp from non-camp nonetheless ended in frustration. This is because, as Fabio Cleto has written, in her search for the "contemporary *Zeitgeist*," Sontag "was depicting . . . postwar culture as a camp landscape of . . . indifference of original from derivative, of high from low culture, of subject from object."[21]

The revulsion Sontag felt in response to the camp sensibility was rooted in a wish to present the "new art" as an example of a potentially revolutionary sensuous immediacy, but, as Cleto points out, it was the obsolescence of this type of immediacy to which camp alluded. Camp thus exposes the social aspirations of formalist criticism as a farce. The sociohistorical conditions that gave birth to camp left nothing untouched. Everything, to paraphrase Sontag, had been placed "in quotation marks"—not by camp but by the material and cultural conditions of its production. It was for this reason that such foundational oppositions as original and copy, aristocrats and masses, and subject and object could no longer provide the grounds from which critique might proceed. That the "Camp sensibility" should emerge at the same moment as the "new sensibility," therefore, should have come as no surprise.

IV

This critical dilemma mirrored the political dilemma that many, intellectuals and activists alike, faced in the mid- to late 1960s. According to Jacob Brackman, Sontag's "disjunct essay" in *Partisan Review* "was read by tens of thousands, but its reverberations affected the culture consumed by hundreds of millions."[22] What was once preserved within the "classy preconscious" of American culture had, following the publication of Sontag's essay, surfaced as a part of the popular consciousness. As a result, critical judgment had been "clog[ged]" and aesthetic standards "scuttle[d]."[23] Although Sontag "had been describing a method of appreciation, her rules were embraced as principles of manufacture."[24] Brackman himself tried to respond to this deadlock by developing in a 1971 monograph his own theory of the "put-on"; following Sontag, he began his account by seeking to resuscitate a system of clear distinctions between concepts like original and copy, high and low, and producer and consumer. While it's tempting to dismiss Brackman's project for its apparent failure to recognize the historical dilemma encountered by both Sontag and Marcuse, it is nevertheless productive to accept his invitation to reconsider the relationship among Sontag's camp sensibility, aesthetic practice, and the forms of grassroots political opposition.

It is important to recognize that strategies such as camp (or Brackman's notion of the "put-on") must not be presented as correctives to foolishly "authentic" statements of political commitment. This would be to rearticulate the standard opposition between purity and co-optedness that both modes of performance exposed as historically meaningless. Rather, such practices as "camp" demand that we be more attentive to the nuances and subtleties of speech and action in this era of American history, that we recognize that in many cases the two modes of "consciousness" were inextricable. Marcuse and Sontag had hoped for an authentic form of eroticism or aesthetic practice capable of distancing the individual from the commodity form and the logic of capital, but later critics such as Brackman pointed to a new dilemma: that such strategies themselves acknowledge the impossibility of achieving that distance, whether through art, an unfettered Eros, racial or sexual difference, or any other purported mode of transcendence.

As several of the essays in this volume show, Sontag herself could not sustain and eventually repudiated the kind of political distancing that "camp" celebrated. But in teasing out the relationship of Sontag to contemporary critics like Marcuse, we can begin to better appreciate the tremendously complex relationship between "the sixties" and our own historical moment—and between Sontag's early aestheticism and her later turn from an erotics of art to something like an ethics of art.

Notes

1. See, for example, Andrew Ross's now classic essay "Uses of Camp," in *No Respect: Intellectuals and Popular Culture* (New York: Routledge, 1989), 135–170; or the essays collected in Moe Meyer, ed., *The Politics and Poetics of Camp* (New York: Routledge, 1997); and David Bergman, ed., *Camp Grounds: Style and Homosexuality* (Amherst: University of Massachusetts Press, 1994).

2. Sontag makes Marcuse's influence on her work most explicit in the essay "Psychoanalysis and Norman O. Brown's *Life Against Death*," reprinted in *AI*.

3. Gerald Howard, ed., introduction to *The Sixties: The Art, Politics, and Media of Our Most Explosive Decade* (New York: Marlow, 1995), 16.

4. Herbert Marcuse, *One-Dimensional Man: Studies in the Ideology of Advanced Industrial Society* (Boston: Beacon, 1964), ix.

5. Marcuse, *One-Dimensional Man*, 10–11; emphasis in original.

6. Marcuse, *One-Dimensional Man*, 57.

7. Marcuse, *One-Dimensional Man*, 57.

8. Marcuse, *One-Dimensional Man*, 58.

9. Herbert Marcuse, "Repressive Tolerance," in Herbert Marcuse, Barrington Moore Jr., and Robert Paul Wolff, *A Critique of Pure Tolerance* (Boston: Basic Books, 1969), 85.

10. Marcuse, "Repressive Tolerance," 90.

11. Marcuse, "Repressive Tolerance," 115.

12. Marcuse, "Repressive Tolerance," 115.

13. Marcuse, "Repressive Tolerance," 115.

14. Marcuse, *One-Dimensional Man*, 14.

15. Marcuse, *One-Dimensional Man*, 73.

16. Marcuse, *One-Dimensional Man*, 256–57.

17. Marcuse, *One-Dimensional Man*, 257.

18. Marcuse, "Repressive Tolerance," 84.

19. According to Sontag, surrealism, as a sensibility, looked to shock audiences by presenting them with the "creative accidents of arrangement and insight," a practice she described as the "collage principle." See Sontag, "Happenings: An Art of Radical Juxtaposition," in *AI*, 269–70.

20. In "Uses of Camp," Andrew Ross makes a similar point. According to Ross, camp was not marked by the "democratic esprit" of Pop Art but by an adherence to the logic of cultural capital. As Sontag wrote in 1964, the "ultimate camp statement" says of its object, "it's good because it's awful." One must also, Ross points out, read this "ultimate statement" "from the point of view of those whom it indirectly patronized, especially those lower middle-class groups whom, historically, have had to bear the stigma of 'failed' taste." Camp, in Ross's account, extracted its cultural capital from both "forgotten forms of labor" and the sincerity of those who consumed the products of that labor. Just as the "discovered" object of Pop Art could never rid itself of its essential obsolescence, he argues, the resurrected object of camp can "hardly shake off its barbaric associations with the social victimization of its original taste-audience." Thus, where Pop Art claimed to be the result of a passive engagement with and enjoyment of mass culture, the pleasure of camp could only be "the result of the (hard) *work* of a producer of taste, and 'taste' is only possible through exclusion *and* depreciation." See Ross, "Uses of Camp," 153.

21. Fabio Cleto, introduction to *Camp: Queer Aesthetics and the Performing Subject*, ed. Fabio Cleto (Ann Arbor: University of Michigan Press, 1999), 46.

22. Jacob Brackman, *The Put-On: Modern Fooling and Modern Mistrust* (Chicago: Henry Regnery, 1971), 9.

23. Brackman, *The Put-On*, 26.

24. Brackman, *The Put-On*, 9. If, as Brackman points out, the pronouncements of the stereotypical "Militant Negro," the "hippie," the gay liberationist,
and others were in many cases put-ons, campy plays on stereotypical personal
and political identities, then how are we to make sense of the "politics of authenticity" so commonly associated with late-1960s America? Should one dis-
count these put-ons, assume that the perpetrators simply "missed the point"?
Or should one read these political gestures in relation to the figures of noncon-
formity they embellished, as performances highlighting the extent to which "the
revolution" had been reconciled with the culture it sought to overthrow?

chaptereight

A Way of Feeling Is a Way of Seeing
Sontag and the Visual Arts

LESLIE LUEBBERS

Sontag and Hodgkin

In 1991, Susan Sontag and Howard Hodgkin's work, *The Way We Live Now*,[1] a limited-edition artist's book, was published after four years of collaboration. A trade edition,[2] which was a modification, not a facsimile, came out the same year, and the proceeds for both were donated to AIDS organizations in the United States and Britain. It is likely that Sontag and Hodgkin met in New York. Sontag was a persistent presence in New York's gallery scene, where Hodgkin's work was shown at Kornblee Gallery in 1973 and at Knoedler Gallery, which became his U.S. representative, in 1981, 1982, 1984, and 1986. He was more appreciated in America during the earlier years than he was in Britain, and, as he had spent several childhood years near New York, he felt quite at home in the city, where, beginning in 1977, he came to work with the master lithographer Judith Solodkin at Solo Press.

By 1984, Howard Hodgkin was a star. That year, he represented Britain in the Venice Biennale, an international assembly of about 500 artists. Robert Hughes wrote in the July 2 issue of *Time*:

Not since Robert Rauschenberg's appearance at the Biennale 20 years ago has a show by a single artist so hogged the attention of visitors or looked so effortlessly superior to everything else on view by living artists. . . . Hodgkin paints small, and his work combines the intimate and the declamatory. Every image seems to be based either on a room with figures or a peep into a garden from a window, and is regulated by layered memories of conversation, sexual tension and private jokes. But this is conveyed by an extraordinary blooming, spotting, bumbling and streaking of color, an irradiation of the mildly anecdotal by the aggressively visual.[3]

Presented in the galleries of the British Pavilion, the works were generously spaced on walls painted a Nile green that lent the interior a time-and-space-altering lambency, within which the radiant painted objects seemed to possess supernatural brilliance and clarity. The following year, Hodgkin won the Turner Prize, Britain's most prestigious award for visual artists, and an expanded version of the Biennale show toured internationally, including at the Phillips Collection in Washington and the Yale Center for British Art in New Haven, collecting enthusiastic reviews. By 1987, Hodgkin and Sontag were collaborating on *The Way We Live Now.*

Howard Hodgkin

It takes no mental gymnastics to imagine an affinity between Sontag and Hodgkin, who were the same age and of similar renown in different but related professions and who shared intellectual passions as well as rigid defenses against intrusions into their private lives, above all into their post-marriage-and-children conversions to homosexuality.

Hodgkin is the product of a long-established clan of Quaker origin with high accomplishments in medical science, social and educational reform, law and public service, art and scholarship, and entrepreneurship. But there is no doubt that the extended Hodgkin family possessed the broad intellectual sensitivities as well as the means to foster Howard Hodgkin's artistic inclination, though his mother valiantly, if futilely, discouraged it.

Hodgkin was born in August 1932 in London, where his father was a manager of Imperial Chemical Industries and an avid amateur horticulturist. Early in World War II, the family decided to send Howard, his mother, and his sister to the United States, where they lived in a grand manse on Long Island for three years, visiting New York often. Hodgkin frequently relates spending hours (at age nine or ten) in the Museum of Modern Art, admiring the work of French artists Vuillard, Bonnard, Leger, and Matisse, who were not yet collected in Britain. Back in England in 1943 and not happy about it, he specialized in running away from one elite school after the other, including Eton, which, however, was redeemed to some extent by Wilfred Blount (brother of the art historian/spy), who introduced him to Indian miniature paintings, an immediate fascination that later resulted in a carefully accumulated and fine collection. Eventually, after several rounds of psychological counseling that Howard seems to have managed to his advantage, including a prescribed summer with the former New York hosts, he was allowed to enroll in a school for artistic youth, then Camberwell School of Art and Bath Academy of Art. In 1954, now in his early twenties, he began teaching art in secondary schools as a means of supporting his painting and, within a few years, his wife, Julia, also an artist, and two sons, Louis and Sam. In 1964, he traveled with the assistant keeper of Indian Miniatures of the Victoria and Albert on the first of many trips to India, which became an enduring source of inspiration.

During the 1970s, Hodgkin experienced radical upheavals. Surviving a life-threatening occurrence of latent amoebic hepatitis that he had contracted during the initial Indian journey, he managed to produce his first major retrospective exhibition, organized in 1975 by the Arts Council of Great Britain to travel throughout the British Isles. The same year, he was appointed CBE (Commander of the British Empire), more for his efforts on behalf of modern art as an influential trustee of the Tate Gallery (1970–1976) than for his painting, and, after an "encounter," so described by Bruce Chatwin in a catalogue essay, he dissolved his marriage.[4]

Many critics and art historians see in Hodgkin's art a definitive rift between the work of his heterosexual life and his homosexual life. Hodgkin rejects this premise, arguing that transitions in his work are continuous and based on his evolving understanding of how to make pictures that are "representational of emotional situations" experienced in the past. Throughout his career, his work has been compared, not surprisingly, to the *intimism* of Vuillard and Bonnard, who at times specialized in compressed compositions on themes of domestic life, as well as to Matisse's formal manipulations of saturated color to evoke spatial and figure-ground relationships. But beginning in the mid-1970s, writers start describing the sensuality that had always been essential to Hodgkin's work in boldly sexual language. In an interview for the catalogue of the Venice Biennale exhibition, Hodgkin admits a change from earlier observed situations to ones in which he is passionately involved.[5] In the same interview, however, he insists on continuity in his work:

> Somebody once said to me that I always claimed that my pictures were about feelings, whereas he thought they were always resolved in terms of the pictures, in terms of pictorial language and in terms of the physical object. And he's quite right, because they are pictures and they have to be resolved in those terms. But the impetus for that resolution comes from feeling, which is what they are all about. And if I have succeeded, I've turned the original feeling, emotion, or whatever you like to call it, into an autonomous object, which I look at exactly the same way you do . . . as strange or interesting or whatever to me as it does to any other spectator.[6]

The Way We Live Now

Sontag's text for *The Way We Live Now* was first published in the *New Yorker* in 1986.[7] It gathers and assembles into a generational portrait the denial and dread that accompanied the phenomenon of an unpredictable and incurable disease. Written in the form of telephonic streams of consciousness, one or another of the twenty-six characters (Aileen to Zak) relates one another's conversations about the latest developments in the illness of an unnamed bisexual friend:

> At first he was just losing weight, he felt only a little ill, Max said to Ellen, and he didn't call for an appointment with his doctor, according to Greg, because he was managing to keep on working at more or less

the same rhythm, but he did stop smoking, Tanya pointed out, which
suggests he was frightened, but also that he wanted, even more than
he knew, to be healthy, or healthier, or maybe just to gain back a few
pounds, said Orson, for he told her, Tanya went on, that he expected
to be climbing the walls (isn't that what people say?) and found, to his
surprise, that he didn't miss a cigarette at all and reveled in the sensation of his lungs being ache-free for the first time in years.[8]

Guided by her "exhortations" in her book *Illness as Metaphor* (followed by *AIDS and Its Metaphors* in 1988), Sontag's narrative device
allows the victim's friends to describe the course of the disease in conversation without employing the military metaphors of illness that, Sontag
insisted, mystify and moralize illness and isolate and distract the patient
from understanding the disease and demanding appropriate therapy. In
The Way We Live Now, the protagonists, all busy young New Yorkers,
strive to convince themselves that their friend is unchanged, except perhaps in barely noticeable ways—not all bad, that "the disease" is just a
disease, that acknowledging its characteristics, treatments, and causes
is rational and right. But despite congratulating the patient and themselves on becoming able to use the name easily, "AIDS" never appears
in the text, and discussion of prognosis is avoided or blurted hopelessly
and then retracted.

Remarkably, Sontag manages to individualize the alphabet friends
through their emerging histories with the patient and their reactions to
his malady. In the midst of their chatter of news, observations, or occasional bitchiness, most of them express remorse for past recklessness
and fear of its consequences for themselves, sexual partners, and friends.
"Well, everybody is worried about everybody now, said Betsy, that seems
to be the way we live, the way we live now."[9] Finally, though the friend
is "still" alive, the by-now unsurprising but unwelcome truth is uttered,
"We're learning how to die, said Hilda, I'm not ready to learn, said
Aileen."[10] The patient exemplifies their fears:

And in all his talk about the future, when he allowed himself to be
hopeful, according to Quentin, he never mentioned the prospect that
even if he didn't die that . . . it was over, the way he had lived until now,
but according to Ira, he did think about it, the end of bravado, the end
of folly, the end of trusting life, the end of taking life for granted, and of

treating life as something that, samurai-like, he thought himself ready to throw away lightly, impudently.[11]

Howard Hodgkin is said to have worked for more than three years on producing the complex, hand-tinted color etchings for the luxurious limited-edition book. The titles of the four pieces are linked fragments of Sontag's text. Each one, except for the facing-page endpapers, folds out in two, three, or four horizontal panels. Even though Hodgkin undoubtedly shared the terror of AIDS with Sontag and her subjects, the literary source of these images, unusual as the starting point for Hodgkin's work, may account for the amount of time and labor they required, even for a famously slow artist.

The most representational piece, *In Touch, Checking In*, is a huge, flop-eared rendition of a black dial telephone decorated with a rakish red aura, red finger openings and a black spiral tail. Its appealing domesticity is rendered ominous by an insistent, fluorescent green dial. Like all of the works in *The Way We Live Now*, it is a lift-ground etching, a technique that produces characteristic grainy, porous areas of pigment. Each color is printed separately from copper plates and then hand-painted with one or two more hues. In relation to Hodgkin's paintings, the lift-ground etching process achieves a quality that is entirely different from but equally as tactile as his lush sweeps of paint.

As You'd Been Wont—Wantonly, Wantonly Eros Past is an ochre field of repose, recognizable with some effort as the back of a reclining head, upper torso and arm, hemmed in by a busy, rippling pattern of orange, gray, and black, with a gray veil encroaching on Eros from the right margin.

The Hospital Room Was Choked with Flowers, Everybody Likes Flowers, Surplus Flowers . . . The Room Was Filling up with Flowers is a stifling luxuriance of brushy red splotches and green lozenges and swoops minimally held on the page by rust and black rectangles recalling the distinctive painted frames around Hodgkin's works that set the pieces apart from their surroundings. Floating within *The Hospital Room*, however, the shapes suggest architecture overwhelmed by effulgent, nearly suffocating nature spilling over and into the world.

But He Did Stop Smoking, He Didn't Miss Cigarettes at All, a quotation from the opening paragraph of the story, is composed of a series of slightly diagonal, overlapping stripes and patterned fields of clear red and green with a hopeful rectangle of marine blue in the lower right corner, as if the world had tipped slightly with the diagnosis of AIDS.

The endpapers, *Fear Gives Everything Its Hue, Its High*, consist of a ground of wide, roughly shaped check marks or reverse C-shapes printed in vermillion red and then hand colored with irregular brush strikes of cobalt blue. They resemble blood chemistry gone awry. "I can't stand them coming in here taking my blood every morning; what are they doing with all that blood, he is reported to have said."[12] At the same time, the barely differentiated continuous pattern resembles Sontag's tapestry of words, a weaving of run-on thoughts that creates a seamless composition of anxiety.

Sontag on Hodgkin

Sontag wrote "About Hodgkin" as one of three texts in the catalogue that accompanied the 1995 retrospective exhibition, Howard Hodgkin Paintings, which was shown in Fort Worth, New York, Düsseldorf, and London. By this time, she and Hodgkin were very well acquainted, judging by the book project and an Annie Leibowitz photograph of them from 1993 on the deck of a Nile cruise ship that serves as the frontispiece for *Writers on Howard Hodgkin*, a later book containing the essay (which was also included in *Where the Stress Falls*). Writing about Hodgkin's work also brought Sontag into the unusual territory of abstract (or semi-abstract) painting, a territory that seemed tailored for the "erotics of art" she had asserted three decades earlier in "Against Interpretation" (*AI*, 14). But while the project of recovering our sensual responsiveness to art as a thing in itself was as vital in 1995 as it had been in 1964, the obstacles had multiplied. In "Against Interpretation," Sontag assailed modern interpretation that

> excavates, and as it excavates, destroys; it digs "behind" the text, to find a sub-text which is the true one. The most celebrated and influential modern doctrines, those of Marx and Freud, actually amount to elaborate systems of hermeneutics, aggressive and impious theories of interpretation. . . . In a culture whose already classical dilemma is the

hypertrophy of the intellect at the expense of energy and sensual capability, interpretation is the revenge of the intellect upon art.
(*AI*, 6–7)

In a similar vein, Sontag introduces "About Hodgkin" with an analysis of the embattled state of modernism in which artists have retreated into the blank white cube (*WSF*, 151). Motivated not simply by the modernist notion of ineffability or of the inability of one art form "to be paraphrased or transposed into another medium," artists and others who continue to value art for its own sake remain mute to avoid being vilified as elitists (*WSF*, 152).

Rehearsing a list of widely and, by this time, routinely disparaged modernist notions, Sontag introduced Hodgkin's practice in the frameworks of "the unsayable," "thingness" and "style," attributes Hodgkin (still) insists upon. He is stubbornly mute about his paintings, although he speaks easily in interviews about artists whose work he admires. He insists that his pictures are "objects," not images, and no one disputes that his style is unique, uniquely identifiable, and filled with a limited inventory of marks and techniques and an intense palette. In an oblique reference to Hodgkin, Sontag observes that "for those whose principal interest is neither to come clean about adventures in selfhood nor to speak on behalf of fervent communities but rather to perpetuate the old, semi-opaque continuities of admiring, emulating and surpassing, prudence may suggest saying less rather than more" (*WSF*, 152).

In "Against Interpretation," Sontag denied the notion that art should not or could not be discussed and posed the question, "what would criticism look like that would serve the work of art, not usurp its place?" Her answer is "what is needed, first, is more attention to form in art" (*AI*, 12). In writing "On Hodgkin," Sontag attempts this approach:

A first observation about Howard Hodgkin's work: the extent to which everything by Hodgkin looks so unmistakably by him.

That the pictures are done on wood seems to heighten their rectangularity—and their "thingness." Usually modest in size by current standards, they seem boxy, blunt, even heavy sometimes because of the proportions of frame to interior of the picture, with something like the form, if not the scale, of a window, displaying a ballet of plump shapes which either are enclosed within thickly emphatic brush strokes that frame (or shield) or are painted out to the edge of the raised frame. The pictures are packed with cunning design and thick, luscious color. (Hodgkin's green is as excruciating as de Kooning's pink and Tiepolo's blue.) Having renounced painting's other primary resource, drawing, Hodgkin has fielded the most inventive, sensuously affecting color repertory of any contemporary painter—as if, in affecting the ancient quarrel between *disegno* and *colore*, he had wanted to give *colore* its most sumptuous exclusive victory.

(*WSF*, 153–54)

Sontag's descriptions of Hodgkin's work are not unusually illuminating or successful when compared to other essays in *Writers on Howard Hodgkin* or elsewhere, and neither is her fascination with his work unique.'

· Operating on a border very much of his own devising between figuration and abstraction, Hodgkin has made a sturdy case for regarding his choreography of spots, strips, discs, arcs, swaths, lozenges, arrows and wavy bands as always representational.

"I am a representational painter, but not a painter of appearances" is how he puts it. "I paint representational pictures of emotional situations." Note that Hodgkin says "emotional situations," not "emotions" (*WSF*, 156). These "representations of emotional situations" defined Sontag's, and many other critics', attraction to Hodgkin, and it is likely that Sontag's doggedness as a champion of the sensory experience of art was her allure for him. But the difficulty of writing about the "unsayable" is not easily resolved. In the conclusion of her essay "On Style," Sontag summarizes, "In the greatest art, one is always aware of things that cannot be said . . . , of the contradiction between expression and the presence of the inexpressible" (*AI*, 36).

Sontag's contribution to the critical conversation about Hodgkin's work is to argue against autobiography as the "content," a point of view he emphatically shared. However, his habit of supplying enigmatic, diaristic titles for his work provided for many critics an opening to discuss personal meanings that Sontag and Hodgkin separately refuted. In an epistolary exchange with John Elderfield originally published in the same volume as "About Hodgkin," the artist replied to a host of questions and propositions about his subjects: "The subject matter of my pictures is of primary importance—I couldn't make a picture that was not 'about' anything. . . . But what does that mean?"[13] What it means is that the subject, expressed sometimes obliquely in the title, is a point of departure, a hint, a summary of the accumulation of marks that, over time, become the materialization of a memorable (emotional) circumstance.

Sontag relies on the titles to discuss Hodgkin's pictures, yet she uses these suggestions of autobiographical content to argue against autobiography as meaning: "What is on display is not the emotional state of the artist" (*WSF*, 156). She notes that frequently the subjects are events that occurred during Hodgkin's excursions to exotic places. "Two passions which we associate with this painter, traveling and collecting, are both expressions of ardent, deferential feeling for what is *not* oneself. . . . Both pursuits, traveling and collecting, are steeped in elegiac feelings" (*WSF*, 157).

Sontag offers no elaboration on collecting, but of the travel, she writes, "*After the Shop Had Closed, The Last Time I Saw Paris, When Did We Go to Morocco, Goodbye to the Bay of Naples* . . . many titles focus on time ('after'), on the awareness of finalities" (*WSF*, 157). Memory alone, unsubstantiated by notes, sketches, photographs, or any other on-the-spot descriptive aid, informs Hodgkin's paintings. Several writers who have gained access to his huge sky-lit studio claim that it is pristinely white; many paintings in progress are hidden behind large stretched canvases of the kind most artists use as their substrate. Hodgkin uses them to conceal all the panels except the one under his immediate scrutiny; some may remain out of sight for months. As Sontag writes: "What is worth painting remains in, and is transformed by, memory. And what survives the test of long-term deliberation and countless acts of re-vision. Pictures result from the accretion of many decisions (or layers, or brush strokes); some are worked on for years, to find the exact thickness of feeling" (*WSF*, 158). Emotion and visualization are inseparable. "A way of feeling is a way of seeing" (*WSF*, 158).

A Way of Feeling Is a Way of Seeing

Sontag's phrase addresses the painter's process, not the viewer's response. The analogy in music would be, "a way of feeling is a way of playing" or in dance "a way of feeling is a way of moving." In her call for an erotics of art, Sontag proclaimed, "The aim of all commentary on art now should be to make works of art—and by analogy, our own experience—more, rather than less, real to us. The function of criticism should be to show *how it is what it is*, even *that it is what it is*, rather than to show what it means" (*AI*, 14).

In "About Hodgkin," Sontag demonstrates this approach and succeeds in showing how the artist arrives at his paintings as the embodiment of feeling. Sontag acknowledges that an artistic creation can usefully be considered as a "statement being made in the form of a work of art" (*AI*, 21). Works of art refer to the world in which they are produced:

> But, their distinctive feature is that they give rise not to conceptual knowledge (which is the distinctive feature of discursive or scientific knowledge—e.g., philosophy, sociology, psychology, history) but to something like an excitation, a phenomenon of commitment, judgment in a state of thralldom or captivation. Which is to say that the knowledge we gain through art is an experience of the form or style of knowing something, rather than a knowledge of something (like a fact or moral judgment) in itself.
> (*AI*, 21–22)

This statement bears resemblance to the argument of Susanne K. Langer, in her work on the philosophy of art, *Feeling and Form*. Making a comparison between the logical form of language and the logical form of music, and by extension other "non-discursive" forms, Langer writes:

> Because the prime purpose of language is discourse, the conceptual framework that has developed under its influence is known as "discursive reason." Usually, when one speaks of "reason" at all, one tacitly assumes its discursive pattern. But in a broader sense any appreciation of form, any awareness of patterns in experience, is "reason"; and discourse with all its possible refinements . . . is only one possible pattern. For practical communication, scientific knowledge, and philosophical thought it is the only instrument we have. But on just that account there are whole domains of experience that philosophers deem "ineffable."[14]

The answer, then, to the question of what art does to make our experience more real is that it can give access to realms of knowledge
or understanding that discursive reason cannot unlock. Based on Ernst
Cassirer's *Philosophy of Symbolic Forms*, Langer makes a case that all
understanding, whether related to discursive or nondiscursive forms, is
based on intuition or insight.[15]

The central argument of Langer's philosophy of art concerns symbols. "Art is the creation of forms symbolic of human feeling."[16] Language is a symbolic system of words, each of which has a direct correlation, agreed upon by convention, with human experience—objects,
actions, qualities, and so forth. In her terms, "A complex symbolic function such as a sentence is an *articulate form*. Its characteristic symbolic
form is what I call *logical expression*. It expresses relations."[17] *Feeling
and Form* is the extension of Langer's aesthetics of music, *Philosophy in
a New Key*; thus, she introduces the later work by summarizing the difference between language and music as articulate symbolic forms:

> Why, then, is it not a *language* of feeling, as it has often been called?
> Because its elements are not words—independent associative symbols
> with a reference fixed by convention. Only as an articulate form is it
> found to fit anything; and since there is no meaning assigned to any
> of its parts. . . . We are always free to fill its subtle articulate forms
> with any meaning that fits them; that is, it may convey an idea of any-
> thing conceivable in its logical image. So, although we do receive it as
> a significant form, and comprehend the processes of life and sentience
> through its audible dynamic pattern, it is not a language, because it has
> no vocabulary.[18]

In her essay "On Style," Sontag writes, "Style is the principle of a
decision in a work of art, the signature of the artist's will" (*AI*, 32), and
she emphasizes that these decisions, though they may follow certain recognized "rules," are ultimately arbitrary. "The sense of inevitability that
a great work of art projects is not made up of the inevitability or necessity of its parts, but of the whole" (*AI*, 33). Describing Hodgkin's process, Sontag refers to his palette and methods of paint application, the
wood support and incorporated frames, the inventory of shapes, and
the long process of layering these into a successful whole. As Langer
writes, "An artistic symbol . . . involves all the relationships of its ele-

ments to one another. . . . That is why qualities enter directly into the form itself, not as its contents, but as its constitutive elements."[19] In his interview for the catalogue of the Venice Biennale exhibition, Hodgkin described his measure of a successful painting: "I've turned the original feeling, emotion, whatever you like to call it, into an autonomous object, which I look at exactly the way you do . . . as strange or interesting."[20]

Sontag and Langer address the phenomenon described by Hodgkin: that a work of art as an autonomous object is estranged or set at a distance from the world; for both writers the quality of otherness, difference, semblance, or transparency is essential to the idea of artistic creation and to its function. The artistic will, or style, guiding the artist's decisions, writes Sontag, "both abolishes the world and encounters it in an extraordinarily intense and specialized way" (*AI*, 30). Langer credits Schiller with first understanding that "*Schein*," or semblance, "liberates perception—and with it, the power of conception from all practical purposes, and lets the mind dwell in the sheer appearance of things."[21] An artist, much the way Hodgkin describes his creative process, produces an object that exists in the world physically, yet stands apart from it as an articulate symbol that can communicate any idea appropriate to its symbolic form. Thus all successful works, even representational ones, are abstract in this sense of estrangement from the world. "As though in evidence of the symbolic nature of art," writes Langer, "its peculiar 'strangeness' has sometimes been called 'transparency.'"[22] Sontag asserts, "*Transparence* is the highest, most liberating value in art—and criticism—today" (*AI*, 13).

Art and Beauty

Sontag and Hodgkin show *that* a painting is a form of feeling and *how* a painting is a form of feeling; this is the work—the real and only work—of an artist. But when the painting emerges from the studio to be placed on a gallery wall, it seems fair to ask *what it does* and *how it does what it does*. How do works of art make our own experience more real? What is transparence, and how does the critic's task engage it?

Sontag's article "About Hodgkin" makes a case against the artist's work as autobiography and asserts that the spectator engages a painting as an autonomous object; thus questions about the artist's history, intent, or message are entirely irrelevant. The transparence of an artistic object is the quality that allows it to be independent of its maker or the circumstances of its making and to be perceived uniquely by each viewer. As Langer writes:

> The art lover who views, hears, or reads a work from "the audience standpoint" enters into a direct relation not with the artist, but with the work. . . .
>
> There is an actual emotion induced by its contemplation . . . [that] is not expressed in the work, but belongs to the percipient; it is the psychological effect of his artistic activity, essentially the same whether the object that holds his attention be a fragile bit of poetry, a work of terrible impact and many torturing dissonances like Joyce's *Ulysses*, or the serene Parthenon frieze; the "aesthetic emotion" is really a pervasive feeling of *exhilaration*, directly inspired by the perception of good art. It is the "pleasure" that art is supposed to give.
>
> Every good work of art is beautiful. . . .
>
> The entire qualification one must have for understanding art is responsiveness.[23]

Sontag, too, came to use "beauty" as a cultural touchpoint. "Beauty" is not a word encountered frequently in her work, but one of her last articles is "An Argument About Beauty," published originally in the 2002 issue of *Daedalus* titled "On Beauty," which includes several essays by scholars and cultural critics, including Arthur Danto and Dave Hickey, each of whom in recent years has contributed to the revival of beauty as a topic in art criticism.[24] In her essay, Sontag takes aim at relativism and the gradual erosion of beauty as a standard in art, of taste as an instrument of discernment, of judgment as a standard of objectivity, and of binary discourses that allow the opposition of good and bad, the beautiful and the ugly. "Beauty," she writes in her schematic rehearsal of its fate in the twentieth century, "continues to take a battering in what are called, absurdly, our culture wars" (*AST*, 8).

Sontag's reluctance to use the term "beauty" in her writing seems entirely justified by its inherent ambiguity in the discourse of modernity. In his essay in the *Daedalus* volume, "The Abuse of Beauty," Danto uses the lens of a century of art and philosophy to provide a far more detailed account of beauty's history. In a contemporary situation when anything can be art and not everything is beautiful, he argues that the relationship between art and beauty, if not meaningless, is either hostile or circumstantial.[25] In Sontag's somewhat different interpretation of the same phenomenon, she says, "The subtraction of beauty as a standard for art hardly signals a decline in the authority of beauty. Rather it attests to the decline in the belief that there is something called art" (*AST*, 5–6). But Sontag maintained belief; throughout her career she insisted on art, insisted on beauty, and insisted on their personal and social importance. In "On Style," she asserted:

> The moral pleasure in art, as well as the moral service that art performs, consists in the intelligent gratification of consciousness. . . . Art performs this moral task because the qualities that are intrinsic to the aesthetic experience (disinterestedness, contemplativeness, attentiveness, the awakening of feelings) and to the aesthetic object (grace, intelligence, expressiveness, energy, sensuousness) are fundamental constituents of a moral response to life.
> (*AI*, 24–25)

Thirty-five years later, in "An Argument About Beauty," she proposed that "the wisdom that becomes available over a deep, lifelong engagement with the aesthetic cannot . . . be duplicated by any other kind of seriousness. Indeed, the various definitions of beauty come at least as close to a plausible characterization of virtue, and of a fuller humanity, as the attempts to define goodness as such" (*AST*, 12). This is, as she says, serious. In her presentation in 2004 of the first Nadine Gordimer Lecture, "At the Same Time: The Novelist and Moral Reasoning," which provides the title of Sontag's posthumously published essays and lectures, she offers an ironic distillation of Kant's categories of time and space in *A Critique of Pure Reason*: "Time exists in order that everything doesn't happen at once . . . and space exists so that it all doesn't happen to you" (*AST*, 214). In the development of her argument, the point of this quote is that the novel (and by extension, though she doesn't offer this, other art forms), focuses attention on certain aspects of the tumultuous simultaneities of our world. Later in the lecture, Sontag asserts, "To be a moral human is to pay, to be obliged to pay, certain kinds of attention" (*AST*, 226).

Art selects and art provides an essential kind of knowledge that can only be acquired through attentiveness to the form of feeling that is art. However, a response to "forms of feeling," or any discursive or nondiscursive symbols, requires the viewer's receptivity. Sontag acknowledges

> the peculiar dependence of a work of art, however expressive, upon the cooperation of the person having the experience, for one may see what is "said" but remain unmoved, either through dullness or distraction. Art is seduction, not rape. A work of art proposes a type of experience designed to manifest the quality of imperiousness. But art cannot seduce without the complicity of the experiencing subject.
> (*AI*, 22)

This, then, is the obligation of the art critic to the artwork and its audience: not to interpret the work, thereby making of it an illustration of a meaning, but to conduct the viewer through thickets of time and space, through the fogs of unfamiliarity, through the veils of prejudice to a direct, personal engagement with the artwork that results in the exaltation of intuitive understanding—and a lifetime pursuit of similar seductions.

A way of feeling is a way of seeing.

A way of feeling is a way of knowing.

An erotics of art links the ways.

Notes

1. The limited edition book is Susan Sontag, *The Way We Live Now*, illus. Howard Hodgkin, lim. ed. (London: Karsten Schubert, 1991). It can be found in collections of prints and illustrated books in several museums, including the Museum of Modern Art in New York.

2. Susan Sontag, *The Way We Live Now*, illus. Howard Hodgkin (London: Jonathan Cape, 1991). All citations in this chapter are to this version of the publication.

3. Robert Hughes, "Gliding Over a Dying Reef—the Venice Biennale," *Time*, July 2, 1984, 76–77.

4. Bruce Chatwin, "Howard Hodgkin: Indian Leaves," in *Writers on Howard Hodgkin*, ed. Enrique Juncosa (Dublin: Irish Museum of Modern Art, 2006), 66.

5. David Sylvester, "Interview with Howard Hodgkin," in *Howard Hodgkin: Forty Paintings, 1973–1984*, ed. John McEwen and David Sylvester (London: Whitechapel Art Gallery, 1984), 99.

6. Sylvester, "Interview with Howard Hodgkin," 98–99.

7. Susan Sontag, "The Way We Live Now," *New Yorker*, November 24, 1986, 42.

8. Sontag, *The Way We Live Now*, 7.

9. Sontag, *The Way We Live Now*, 12.

10. Sontag, *The Way We Live Now*, 29.

11. Sontag, *The Way We Live Now*, 23–24.

12. Sontag, *The Way We Live Now*, 29–30.

13. John Elderfield and Howard Hodgkin, "An Exchange," in *Howard Hodgkin Paintings*, by Michael Auping, John Elderfield, and Susan Sontag (New York: Harry N. Abrams, 1995), 68–69.

14. Susanne K. Langer, *Feeling and Form* (New York: Charles Scribner's Sons, 1953), 29.

15. Langer, *Feeling and Form*, 378–79.

16. Langer, *Feeling and Form*, 40.

17. Langer, *Feeling and Form*, 31.

18. Langer, *Feeling and Form*, 31.

19. Langer, *Feeling and Form*, 51.

20. Sylvester, "Interview with Howard Hodgkin," 99.

21. Langer, *Feeling and Form*, 49.

22. Langer, *Feeling and Form*, 52.

23. Langer, *Feeling and Form*, 395–96.

24. *Daedalus* 131, no. 4 (Fall 2002).

25. Arthur Coleman Danto, "The Abuse of Beauty," *Daedalus* 131, no. 4 (Fall 2002): 35–37.

chapternine

Metaphors Kill
"Against Interpretation" and the Illness Books

JAY PROSSER

"Against Interpretation" (1964) is arguably Sontag's signal essay: polemical, serious, full of grand claims, and written with great style.[1] Sontag's rejection of interpretation and metaphors hinges on a problem with meaning and how in effect we make sense of living and dying, the creating, finding, and understanding of significance in our lives and deaths. She offers a straightforward meaning, so transparent as to be almost not an interpretation but rather a bald statement, of interpretation:

> By interpretation, I mean here a conscious act of mind which illustrates a certain code, certain "rules" of interpretation.
>
> Directed to art, interpretation means plucking a set of elements (the X, the Y, the Z, and so forth) from the whole work. The task of interpretation is virtually one of translation. The interpreter says, Look, don't you see that X is really—or, really means—A? That Y is really B? That Z is really C?
>
> (*AI*, 5)

Rather than this arbitrary and distracting act of interpretation, Sontag urges that before the work of art we take up a stance of unconscious absorption. Emerging in fact again and again in her writing is this demand that we pay attention, with sensuality and energy, to the thing in itself. Our reception of the work of art should be less an experience of the sublime than our absorption into the physical body of the work before or beyond words, our incorporation or embodiment of art. Interpretation comes to be figured as not only the supplement to but the spoiling, polluting of this embodiment. Over the course of Sontag's career, a startling connection among interpretation, metaphors, and illness is made. Reading "Against Interpretation" followed by *Illness as Metaphor* and *AIDS and Its Metaphors*, we see how a posturing polemic in an essay by someone at the start of her writing career is carried in the two illness books to a sincere and compassionate plea for confronting the failures of the body, the limits of life, and the reality of death—even if, in Sontag's own illnesses and in the interpretation of her death, attention to the body's suffering reality proves unsustainable and metaphors return as inevitable.

Sontag's refusal of interpretation rejects a process of translation that displaces the material, the thing, or what Sontag calls the world. In "Against Interpretation," interpretation is traced to a theory of art as mimesis, which first splits off art from the world and then splits form from content. When, as in mimesis, art is assumed to represent the world rather than be the world, art suffers next to the world, and art becomes "in need of defense" (*AI*, 4). This defense of art contains and effects separation between form and content, as form becomes in need of translation into content. Form not transparent as content—like art not transparent as or a statement of the world—needs exegesis. Like art in relation to the world, form is disparaged next to content. And it is the "defense" that gives birth to the odd vision in which something we have learned to call "form" is separated off from something we have learned to call "content," and to the well-intentioned move that makes content "essential" and form "accessory" (*AI*, 4). Overemphasis of the idea of content as object and form as a means to that goal leads to "the perennial, never-consummated project of *interpretation*" (*AI*, 5).

The bogey figure in this theory of mimesis is Plato. Plato and Aristotle are both held culpable in "Against Interpretation" for the rise in interpretation of art, but Aristotle at least is said to defend art rather than call for its banning. As well as in "Against Interpretation," Plato is an overshadowing presence in *On Photography*, in which the first essay is called "In Plato's Cave" and where the modern world of photography is seen to have updated our experience in the cave, extending our "confinement in the cave, our world" (*OP*, 3). But *On Photography* suggests that photographs are not images, copies in need of interpretation, because photographs are the world. In Sontag's view of photography the image is an object, a mysterious piece of world reality—although Sontag writing on photography is nevertheless engaged in a process of interpretation, of translating this material, mystical form into language. In "Against Interpretation," a decade earlier, Plato is condemned as part *of* the classical view of the world when the magic and power of myth and art were broken by "realism" (*AI*, 4). That realism appears here in inverted commas denotes Sontag's disparagement for the theory and aesthetic of realism—her distaste for and disbelief in the idea that art could represent the world, rather than being so close to it as to be magical. Real*ism* effects a displacement or translation from the real world. The theory of mimesis that Sontag resisted—the first theory of representation and interpretation—is an act of taming the magic and power of the work's material, of rationalizing the viewer's unconscious absorption. Although Sontag's writings on photography are an interpretation, in her first book on photography more than anywhere in her prose we can feel her absorption into the object, the magical and mystical power of photography. Sontag in *On Photography* is already prizing the material, an aesthetic that drew her repeatedly to write on photographs and later still to write in defense of ill bodies.

In spite of blaming Plato for originating a notion of art as less than world, at one point in "Against Interpretation" Sontag sounds like a copy of Plato—except that instead of condemning art as less than the world, she condemns interpreters for writing about art in a way that makes the world such. "To interpret is to impoverish, to deplete the world—in order to set up a shadow world of 'meanings.' It is to turn *the* world into *this* world. ('This world'! As if there were any other.)" (*AI*, 7). Here the people imprisoned in Plato's cave are not those viewing art mimetically but interpreters who create and watch the shadow world of meanings. Interpreters, like the figures in Plato's cave, separate the world through layers or figures of meanings to create an alternate world. In her polemic, Sontag even calls for a kind of banning of interpreters or, at least, of interpretation from the world: "The world, our world, is depleted, impoverished enough. Away with all duplicates of it, until we again experience more immediately what we have" (*AI*, 7). Her expulsion echoes Plato's (or Socrates') expelling artists from the republic, and for the same reasons—both Sontag and Plato seem to condemn the copy and prize the original, except that Sontag is a kind of reverse Platonist, for where Plato prizes pure form and not the material, she values the material before any splits from form.

In "Against Interpretation," Sontag's rejection of "a certain code, certain rules" of making meaning and interpretation is also a refusal of rules and codes per se, and particularly those of the essay's time. If interpretation is "perennial, never-consummated," this makes interpretation a profession, and the act of interpretation becomes professionalized. "Against Interpretation" is written at a moment of the professionalization of art and interpretive criticism at once authoritative and arcane. One has only to think of what was happening in art—critical and academic interpretation in terms of the contemporary turn to the signifier, and how this turn resulted in explanations of signification, to see how anticonventional is Sontag's position against interpretation. Certainly there is anti-intellectualism in her stance against interpretation. Interpretation is described as "the revenge of the intellect upon the world" (*AI*, 7), the world Sontag would defend from interpreters and that she sees as already impoverished and depleted. She senses that the abstraction of art at the time was a shift away from the representational and also a rejection of the art critics' attempt at explanation—the art critics among whom Sontag never fully fit: "the actual developments in many arts seem to be leading us away from the idea that a work of art is primarily its content" (*AI*, 5). Sontag is in alliance with the art against the interpreters. We are reminded that Sontag, never fully in the academy, was at the time making a transition out of the academy, leaving her job teaching religion at Columbia University in 1964 to take up a position as writer in residence at Rutgers. In opposing the professionalization of interpretation, Sontag was both ahead of her time—making a turn away from signification in what we have now learned to call the turn to the ethical or the real—and out of her time, if anything a bit reactionary, even as she charged interpretation with being both reactionary and ahead of its time, or modern. Interpretation, she writes, has become "the modern way of understanding something" (*AI*, 7), and she aligns interpretation with urbanization, industrialization, and, inevitably, pollution:

Today is such a time, when the project of interpretation is largely re-actionary, stifling. Like the fumes of the automobile and of heavy in-dustry which befoul the urban atmosphere, the effusion of interpreta-tions of art today poisons our sensibilities. In a culture whose already classical dilemma is the hypertrophy of the intellect at the expense of energy and sensual capability, interpretation is the revenge of the intel-lect upon art.
(*AI*, 7)

It is at this point in "Against Interpretation," when interpretation as part of modernization and industrialization is said to produce "hy-pertrophy of the intellect," that we come to a symptomatic moment in Sontag's stance against interpretation, which links the activity with metaphors and illness. "Hypertrophy" is not only a metaphor—an in-terpretation of the effects of interpretation—in its meaning of excessive growth or development, enlargement of a part or organ of an animal or plant, according to the *Oxford English Dictionary*. Since the *Oxford English Dictionary's* first definition makes clear that "hypertrophy" is a physiological term, Sontag uses not only a metaphor but an illness metaphor for this excessive intellect and excessive interpretation. The choice of terms is symptomatic of the inevitability of metaphors, for how can you think without metaphors, without translating and saying X is really, or really means, A? What, anyway, does it mean for some-one who became our key cultural interpreter to write "against interpre-tation"? Especially when the writing is alive, as Sontag's is, it is going to be strongly allegorical, as Sontag's was—even if the problem writ-ten against is allegory. In Sontag's illness metaphor against interpreta-tion, the professionalization of interpretation produces a growth of the intellect, at the expense of energy and sensual capability—an excessive growth that kills off energy like the cancer Sontag didn't yet have.

This is not the only metaphor in "Against Interpretation," and in-deed at moments of most feeling and absorption Sontag turns to meta-phor, especially to illness metaphors or to the military metaphors she would later condemn as illness metaphors. She again describes the effect of interpretation as growth or bacteria or disease, writing that "thick en-crustations of interpretation have taken hold" (*AI*, 8) around many au-thors. Beckett's oeuvre "has attracted interpreters like leeches" (*AI*, 8), and in a military metaphor Kafka is described as having been "subjected to a mass ravishment . . . by armies of interpreters" (*AI*, 8). In these metaphors authors are figured and interpreted as organic entities, bodies, countries, or nations to be defended, doctored, and tended from defilement and invasion before the excessive growth of interpretation.

In the opening to *AIDS and Its Metaphors* (1989), where we get an explanation of the illness book written ten years before, *Illness as Metaphor* (1978), the phrase "against interpretation" resurfaces, and Sontag makes the connection between interpretation and metaphors. The posture of beginning an independent writing career in "Against Interpretation" comes to have real content and meaning as it is rewritten and adapted, first in *Illness as Metaphor* by a forty-year-old with cancer, though without mentioning her own experience, and then, in *AIDS and Its Metaphors*, with the writer having come through the cancer to find a new disease stigmatizing a whole new social grouping of others. In 1989, reflecting back on the first illness book and returning to that early essay, Sontag begins *AIDS and Its Metaphors*, "Rereading *Illness as Metaphor* now, I thought" (*AM*, 92):

> The purpose of my book was to calm the imagination, not to incite it. Not to confer meaning, which is the traditional purpose of literary endeavor, but to deprive something of meaning: to apply that quixotic, highly polemical strategy, "against interpretation," to the real world this time. To the body. My purpose was, above all, practical. . . . The metaphors and myths, I was convinced, kill.
> (*AM*, 102)

There is a recognition here that she was not writing about the real world in "Against Interpretation," in spite of her insistent defense therein of a singular world from interpretative and representational copies. It would seem that her writing is a copy, not real, but about aesthetics. Now she is no longer protecting authors from armies of critics as leeches but engaged in a work of defending or tending the body, which here is the real world. Metaphors and interpretation are not simply polluting and distracting translation. Now the hypertrophy is real. Metaphors are deadly; metaphors kill.

Understanding here what she means by metaphor also helps build that connection to interpretation. Again she turns to Greek interpreters or philosophers of forms, now the more redeemable Aristotle. It is not until

AIDS and Its Metaphors that we learn that her understanding of metaphor comes from Aristotle's *Poetics* and learn also how crucial metaphor is to understanding, and indeed to the interpretative expression of understanding.[2] "Saying a thing is or is like something-it-is-not is a mental operation as old as philosophy and poetry, and the spawning ground of most kinds of understanding, including scientific understanding, and expressiveness" (*AM*, 93). It is not until *AIDS and Its Metaphors* that she tells us how ancient and inevitable is metaphor, though she herself had begun *Illness as Metaphor* with an outlandish and notable metaphor of travel, of the sick inhabiting "the night-side of life," a different country with different citizenship—so that readers unconsciously absorbed in the work, not having their interpretive wits about them, may have thought she meant the metaphor. But here she says she deliberately prefaced the polemic "with a brief, hectic flourish of metaphor, in mock exorcism of the destructiveness of metaphorical thinking" (*AM*, 93). For indeed, she says in retrospect and qualification of *Illness as Metaphor* and "Against Interpretation," as she echoes the phrase, "Of course one cannot think without metaphors. But that does not mean there aren't some metaphors we might well abstain from or try to retire. As, of course, all thinking is interpretation. But that does not mean it isn't sometimes correct to be 'against' interpretation" (*AM*, 93).

"Some metaphors" and "sometimes" being against interpretation are important qualifications. Sontag would seem to be not against metaphor and interpretation per se but rather against particular metaphors and interpretations on particular occasions. Both illness books show and condemn the processes and effects of metaphorization or interpretation on illnesses and the ill. Particularly for diseases where "causality is murky and treatment not effectual," "subjects of deepest dread [become] identified with disease" (*IM*, 58). Then disease becomes a metaphor to be imposed on subjects of dread. The metaphors interpret the material body as something else. The material Sontag defends against interpretation is the body, the world now the body. Then the illness metaphors stigmatize the people who have the disease, further harming them. In short, to metaphorize is to moralize, and her rightness here can be felt in the influence of the illness books on almost all subsequent thinking on representations of cancer and AIDS in particular.[3]

As well as the process of metaphorization, the illness books also condemn kinds of metaphors. The metaphorical uses of cancer include resistance to urbanization, again evoking industrialization and pollution, and Sontag sounds like an urbanite defending her city space. Descriptions of cancer often draw on economics—figures of growth, of excess—symptomatic of our capitalist culture. But the metaphors for cancer derive, finally, not from economics but from the language of politics and especially warfare. Jews have been analogized to syphilis but also to cancer, and there is something "implicitly genocidal" in the cancer metaphor (*IM*, 84). Israel is described by a certain Arab press as "a cancer in the Arab world" (*IM*, 84). The war on cancer relies on military metaphors. Military metaphors have also come to dominate description of the medical situation with AIDS, in part because of the technologization and modernization of medicine and warfare together, the body placed under scrutiny and the battle to be fought over the body. AIDS is figured less as excessive and out of control growth than as invasion. "This is the language of political paranoia, with its characteristic distrust of a pluralistic world" (*AM*, 106). Sontag is prescient about the ways in which figures of a "war on," from cancer, to drugs, to poverty, to AIDS, to terror, will be used to displace and translate complex situations into metaphors of simple battles with clear sides. "Indeed, the transformation of war-making into an occasion for mass ideological mobilization has made the notion of war useful as a metaphor for all sorts of ameliorative campaigns whose goals are cast as the defeat of an 'enemy'" (*AM*, 99). And in a wonderful moment, she acknowledges that she is not exempt from that process of making metaphors, of ideological mobilization. "I once wrote, in the heat of despair over America's war on Vietnam, that 'the white race is the cancer of human history'" (*IM*, 84). We turn to metaphors of illness, she writes, "to be morally severe" about evil without religion or philosophy, in a world without magic (*IM*, 84).

The changing field for metaphors suggests the historicity of metaphors, the way in which they are rooted to a particular moment. And as the footnotes to both texts make clear, the idea that we can make ourselves better or worse through how we feel emotionally, the target of *Illness as Metaphor*, was very real in the 1970s when Sontag had cancer and was writing against such metaphors. In *AIDS and Its Metaphors*, she writes of the climate, "People are losing their jobs when it is learned that they are HIV-positive" (*AM*, 120). She cites Reagan's interpretation of his illness—that he didn't have cancer removed, he had something removed from within him that had cancer—and the figure for AIDS of the "gay plague." In both cases she's writing against the use of figures and language to displace and translate reality and to hypertrophy—or we could even say to hyper-trope—illness.

Yet as she herself works in "Against Interpretation" through illness metaphors, she works in the illness books via interpreting literature. Apart from Reagan, there are few references from "real life" or the world; her references come from books, as they are part of Sontag's world. In *AIDS and Its Metaphors*, some medical texts are cited, more than in *Illness as Metaphor*, but in both the predominant source material is literature. In spite of writing against the "literary endeavor" in "Against Interpretation," the illness books are a literary endeavor—an endeavor that, in the end, she prized more than her essays, like the critic she had so much in common and was in interpretive relationship with, Roland Barthes. He also would have preferred to have been a novelist, he admitted toward the end of his life. From Dickens's *Nicholas Nickelby*, Stowe's *Uncle Tom's Cabin*, and Segal's *Love Story* to Camus, Kafka, and Keats's letters and diaries, Sontag reads illness narratives in literature. Like Freud, whom she condemns in "Against Interpretation," along with Marx, as a principal propagator of interpretation, for in their hermeneutics "all observable phenomena are bracketed . . . as *manifest content*" (*AI*, 7), Sontag is producing theory from and on literature. And hers is not a huge variety of literature. Apart from *Love Story*—and as it's hard to imagine Sontag reading Segal, we may assume that she was responding to the popularization of the novel through the 1970 film—Stowe, and some late James, her reading is overwhelmingly European: along with Kafka, Mann is cited a lot, Boccaccio, and of course the Greeks. There is nothing, for instance, African American, and nothing apart from *Love Story* that is contemporary. In such literature, canonical or high modernist, almost invariably in need of interpretation, illness would, of course, appear as a metaphor, not the material reality itself. Sontag when writing about literature, by the way, only gives us interpretation—she doesn't retell the plots, provide us with the material of the texts. She is speaking to a reader who like her knows the texts well. In parallel to her reliance on literature, in writing about the linguistic transformations, displacements, and translations of illnesses into metaphors, she turns to language. To make the link between cancer and TB through consumption, crucial to tracing the historical processes of the metaphorization of illness, she turns to the *Oxford English Dictionary* and etymology. Even as she's resisting displacement of world, in this case material body, into word, she's writing about bodies in the realm of language.

And yet like her confrère Roland Barthes—who also wrote a book on photography, soon after hers, that is close to *On Photography* in its seeing in photography the thing itself—in the photography book and in the illness narratives, Sontag is drawn to the referential, the material, to what Barthes called in his first book "zero degree," by which he meant the absence of meaning, just the thing in and of itself.[4] Sontag attempts to undo meaning ("to deprive something of meaning") in "Against Interpretation" and again in the illness books, and, like Barthes, who sought to reach some ultimate material, to work interpretation backward. Barthes also struggled with codes and conventions, and in *S/Z* produced a structuralist parody of interpretation, an interpretation in reverse where no meaning is to be derived from his reading of Balzac's "Sarrasine" but only his sensual and energetic absorption in the form of text itself, his interpretation containing a complete repetition of Balzac's short story. Both writers—both wanting to be novelists and both such brilliant critics—desire, through forms of literature and photography, among others, presence. Sontag has a remarkable interpretation in *AIDS and Its Metaphors* of sex as "an act whose ideal is an experience of pure presentness" (*AM*, 160)—both a moment and fullness, no copies or shadows.

There's a purity to Sontag's wanting to pare down the growth of metaphors, to cut out the hypertrophy of figuration. "Illness is *not* a metaphor—and the healthiest way of being ill—is one most purified of, most resistant to, metaphoric thinking" (*IM*, 3), she writes at the opening of *Illness as Metaphor*. She is indignant at how patients, especially cancer patients, are lied to about their illnesses and even the causes of death. She condemns the interpretation of death as something else, its translation into, in fact, another category of illness as a result of the expansion or hypertrophy of illness as a category—life becoming ever extendable, disease ever curable in the modern world, "the modern denial of death" (*IM*, 8). Wherever she writes she abhors psychologizing, banalization, inurement, sentimentalization, the cheery optimistic worldview that life should be without suffering. That we should be happy and that the human condition is ever ameliorable are assumptions that bear the "unmistakable stamp of our consumer culture" (*IM*, 51). Freud (again) and Jung are blamed for popularizing the psychologizing that metaphorizes and euphemizes—and exacerbates the terror of—disease and death. "Psychological understanding undermines the 'reality' of a disease. That reality has to be explained. (It really means; or is a symbol of; or must be interpreted so)" (*IM*, 55). If disease is given a psychological cause, then "death itself can be considered, ultimately, a psychological phenomenon" (*IM*, 56). For Sontag, as indeed for Plato's Socrates or indeed Freud himself, a realist in a philosophical if not an aesthetic sense, "depressing emotions and past traumas . . . [are] the human condition" (*IM*, 51). Death and disease are as much a part of life as health. The dominant psychological cause attributed to cancer at her time of writing was the repression of feelings, particularly undischarged rage, according to Reich, "anesthetized feelings" (*IM*, 62). Sontag was angry, but she did discharge it and seemed to believe in deep feeling and expressing it above all. As in *On Photography*, we are absorbed in the presence of the voice in these texts, in Sontag's belief in living and speaking sincerely, and in her attention to what's real.

Reading "Against Interpretation" followed by the two illness books in order, it is clear how Sontag transformed that early polemic and moved beyond posture to change the world or at least the way people experience (interpret) the world, which may be the same thing. There's an increasing urgency in the illness books, a need to find a way to write and effect compassion, which is a term that many reviews of *Illness as Metaphor* noted as one of the admirable qualities of the book. Indeed, at the start of *AIDS and Its Metaphors*, writing about the purpose of her first book, Sontag says she wrote *Illness as Metaphor* to reduce the suffering of patients so that they could regard cancer as just a disease, without meaning. "*Illness as Metaphor* is not just a polemic, it is an exhortation. I was saying: Get the doctors to tell you the truth; be an informed, active patient; find yourself good treatment" (*AM*, 102–3). Along with paying attention to what's in front of you, suffering is always Sontag's deep subject, and often they are combined so that in reading Sontag we are paying attention to suffering.

And yet Sontag is judgmental and conservative about what treatments, particularly for cancer and AIDS, she will broach. In spite of questioning the medical scrutinizing of the body and the construction of illnesses, she maintains faith in Western science, rejecting any holism. Of those patients who seek alternative medicines, she writes that they refuse the Western medicine that could help them, "instead to seek to heal themselves, often under the auspices of some 'alternative medicine' guru. But subjecting an emaciated body to the purification of a macrobiotic diet is about as helpful in treating AIDS as having oneself bled, the 'holistic' medical treatment of choice in the era of Donne" (*AM*, 124–25). Sontag offers no evidence for what she deems the failures of the macrobiotic diet, nor even an interpretation of what she thinks the macrobiotic diet is—which consists of foods in their purest, most life-giving or biotic, state, with the goal of reducing in the body the toxins of pollution and industrialization that Sontag also opposed. Sontag is willing to countenance that distress can affect the immune system but not that emotions cause disease. She even questions—smoker until into her cancer—the connection between cancers and environmental causes such as pollutants and cigarettes. She is, above all, scathing about the relation between body as material and mind as interpretation of the world, the idea of balance and harmony in world and in mind and body, although in non-Western medicines, which tend not to construct singular illnesses, these form the central tenets of health.

Particularly in the first illness book Sontag relies on schematic contrasts. This is so in her description of the relation between TB and cancer, where she needs to show continuity between the two illnesses so that cancer comes to play the role of dominant disease metaphor over TB, and with the twentieth century the cluster of metaphors and attitudes formerly attached to TB split up and are parceled out to two diseases: romantic sufferings to insanity, "agonies that can't be romanticized to cancer" (*IM*, 36). With her historical genealogies of the discourse of disease, she comes to seem like a version of Foucault, without his footnotes and research into medical materials, accessible, interpretable. And especially when she shows the construction of disease through language and through a range of symptoms, she sounds like the French theorist who died, most probably of the different infections grouped together and known as AIDS, too early in the epidemic to analyze his own illness or to read *AIDS and Its Metaphors*. Unlike Foucault, though, in a way above all accessible to the real world, Sontag is in danger of platitudes. Is the dark continent of Africa really a metaphor contemporary to the emergence of AIDS in the 1980s? And can she not see how in describing a figure for AIDS as "a scourge of the *tristes tropiques*" (*AM*, 140), she misappropriates—translates and displaces—the very advanced but threatened non-Western civilizations Lévi-Strauss meant by this term?

And where is Sontag placed in terms of her own national and cultural belonging? Does she see no paradox between inhabiting so comfortably and proximately the material of European literature and still putting Europeans in the third person and blaming them for bringing their diseases to the world?

The fundamental question about "Against Interpretation" and the illness books is whether Sontag's argument against interpretation and illness metaphors works. Can we be ill outside of language and metaphors, the functions of narration and interpretation—which might also be ameliorative and help us make sense of suffering? Indeed, can we live and die without metaphors and interpretation? Sontag won a Lambda (lesbian and gay) book award recognizing work on AIDS for *AIDS and Its Metaphors* in 1989; Paul Monette won the same award the year before, for *Borrowed Time*. Monette's account of the loss of his lover to AIDS, a memoir written with the aesthetics of novel, relies on and is in good part effective because of its use of metaphors not only to describe to us but also to help Monette understand, with the memoir based on his journals, the illness and the death of Roger. With Roger's AIDS, an unknown disease and, yes, unspeakable, the couple feel "on the moon"[5]—on the night-side of life with which Sontag begins *Illness as Metaphor*. And above all, the couple, especially Roger, are figured as Greek warriors going into battle, a metaphor that enables Monette both to recover the lost homoerotics of classical civilization and to come to terms, through revisiting and seeing an analogy in Plato's Socrates, with Roger's stoic death. The year that Sontag won the Lambda prize, Larry Kramer's *Reports from the Holocaust: The Story of an AIDS Activist* also won, also for work on AIDS.[6] Kramer's metaphor of the Holocaust suggests the vast scale of loss from the epidemic, particularly in his gay community, which proved right, and also that there was something implicitly genocidal in world governments' stalling on putting money into research for a cure and being willing to release drugs at the earliest stage. Kramer is founder of the AIDS Coalition to Unleash Power and the Gay Men's Health Crisis, and there is no evidence to suggest that *AIDS and Its Metaphors* was used in the AIDS- or gay-activist movements, in spite of this being the closest to a gay-rights book Sontag would produce, in her criticism of the way in which AIDS had been rendered the gay plague. Indeed, in his review of *AIDS and Its Metaphors*, British gay activist Simon Watney wondered why Sontag didn't credit established gay writers on AIDS.[7]

Unlike Monette's and Kramer's books, Sontag's books about illness are not memoirs, and indeed *Illness as Metaphor* works as not-memoir. In *AIDS and Its Metaphors*, in one of the most autobiographical moments of any of her essays, she writes about why she has not written memoir, the "I" appearing to tell us why in *Illness as Metaphor*, in spite of the fact that its writer also had cancer, "I" is not there. "I didn't think it would be useful—and I wanted to be useful—to tell yet one more story in the first person of how someone learned that she or he had cancer, wept, struggled, was comforted, suffered, took courage . . . though mine was also that story. A narrative, it seemed to me, would be less useful than an idea" (*AM*, 101). With such ideals and the discipline of being "useful," Sontag's "I" appears here as a cancer patient retrospectively, only when she doesn't have cancer, and only to further spurn the uses of that "I." And yet we learn here how her experience urged her on to write the earlier book. She wrote *Illness as Metaphor* quickly, "spurred by evangelical zeal as well as anxiety about how much time I had left to do any living or writing in. . . . In the decade since, I was cured of my own cancer, confounding my doctors' pessimism" (*AM*, 101–3).

But there is now a memoir that reveals the details of Sontag's death, in 2004, from cancer, a narrative that suggests Sontag's expressed resistance to metaphorization may have left her unable to confront her own illness and death. David Rieff's book *Swimming in a Sea of Death: A Son's Memoir* tells the story of his mother's death and his experience of it.[8] Since Rieff cites from his mother's journals highly personal details (about her emotional state, her feelings about her body, her sexuality) that she had not told even him, it is possible to question the ethics of Rieff's decision to write and publish another illness narrative. That he should be so intimately biographical about Sontag, especially when he acknowledges that "her two essays on illness are almost *anti-autobiographical*," sets him up as a contrary writer on Sontag and a disloyal son (*SSD*, 28). *Swimming in a Sea of Death* unveils shocking and private emotional moments in the death of a public intellectual in a way that seems to justify Sontag's resistance to such sentimentalizing and narrativizing of illness.

Rieff's memoir is "useful" as an attempt to work out his own grief, guilt, and confusion. In his account, Sontag herself emerges as a contrary figure, facing in her death the contradictions between the life and the writing that she may have juggled all along. *Swimming in a Sea of*

Death brings home Sontag's presence, in the life as much as in her books. As the son writes of his mother, "She loved living. If I had to choose one word to describe her way of being in the world it would be 'avidity.' There was nothing she did not want to see or do or try to know" (*SSD*, 15). But when it came to death, her presence and love of life meant that "reality was elsewhere" (*SSD*, 48). Sontag is shown to refuse to accept her own dying and, worse, to panic at the fact of death. What is most unbearable for the reader who turns from Sontag's work to her son's memoir is the gap between the ideals of her work and the facts of her death: "She who could talk about anything could rarely really speak of death directly, though I believe she thought about it constantly. . . . But instead, almost until the moment she died, we talked of her survival, of her struggle with cancer, never about her dying" (*SSD*, 16–17). Without the unfounded reassurances from the doctors, Rieff tells us, his mother would have gone mad.

Against the two illness books, the son reads her private papers, which he is soon to publish: "Her journals, which she began to keep again quite soon after her surgery, tell a different story. They are punctuated with the repeated notation 'Cancer = death'" (*SSD*, 28). Rieff quotes her diaries on her own chemotherapy: "'twice a week I return/haul myself to the hospital and present my opaque body to Doctor Green or Doctor Black . . . so they can tell me how I am. One pushes and pulls and pokes, admiring his handiwork, my vast scar. The other pumps me full of poison, to kill my disease but not me.' . . . 'I feel like the Vietnam War,' she wrote. 'My body is invasive, colonizing. They're using chemical weapons on me. I have to cheer'" (*SSD*, 35). Through the diary Rieff connects the life back to the essays:

> In retrospect, my mother was painfully acquiring the cultural traits that were simultaneously the privilege and the burden of what she would later describe in her essay "Illness as Metaphor" as her new citizenship in the world of the ill. As the months passed, and as she seemed to be weathering both the toxicity of her treatment and the tremendous psychological adjustment to what she thought of as her new "maimed" self—or, more bluntly put, the damage done to her sexuality from which I do not believe she ever fully recovered—she began not only to hope in earnest that she might survive, but also to fundamentally re-

cast in her own mind what had happened to her. Early on in her illness, she wrote that, much as she might reject it intellectually, emotionally she accepted the old claim of the psychologist Wilhelm Reich . . . that cancer was mainly the product of sexual repression. 'I feel my body has let me down,' she wrote. 'And my mind, too. For, somewhere, I believe the Reichian verdict. I'm responsible for my cancer. I lived as a coward, repressing my desire, my rage.' "
(SSD, 36)

The son's insight into his mother's (repressed, damaged) sexuality makes for uncomfortable reading. But so does the sense that the writer who was our greatest critic of the metaphors of illness internalized the metaphors of cancer as death sentence, as war, and as repressed emotion. Drawing for us and for himself lessons from his mother's death, Rieff expresses the guilt not just of a survivor. He berates himself most for not correcting his mother's "magical thinking," the belief, against the evidence, that intellect could outwit death: "It was a folie à deux, I suppose: the thing she wouldn't do was the thing I couldn't do" (SSD, 73). He is still "swimming in a sea of death" — though his conclusion suggests his loss, in the midst of life, as a healthier and certainly more realistic mindset than her denial: "I wish that I had lived, while she was alive and well, with the image of her death at the forefront of her consciousness" (SSD, 177).

Because the illness narrative comes from the son and not the mother, it works out his suffering rather than hers. For this reason, it is not fair to say that the manner of Sontag's death and illness invalidates the insistence on confronting the truth in the illness books. Even the journals, fragmented and not worked through for a public, won't contain her illness narrative. But we might wonder, had Sontag written her own illness narrative in full and for publication, in one of the illness books or perhaps as a third, memoir text, what she might have seen about the inextricability of metaphors and death, and perhaps the usefulness of illness narratives. Could she have found herself less antimetaphor and at the same time more able to accept her own death?

Metaphors may kill but they also make some things sayable and bearable. Metaphors are, for most of us, as inevitable as illness and death.

Notes

1. Susan Sontag, "Against Interpretation," in *AI*, 3–14.

2. The importance of metaphor for understanding and creating reality and the significance of Aristotle as originating figure for the primacy of metaphor in Western thought had been written about, just before *Illness as Metaphor*, by Paul Ricouer, in *The Rule of Metaphor: Multi-disciplinary Studies of the Creation of Meaning in Language* (1977; London: Routledge, 1978).

3. See, for example and only as a start, Jackie Stacey, *Teratologies: A Cultural Study of Cancer* (London: Routledge, 1997); and Steven F. Kruger, *AIDS Narratives: Gender, Sexuality, Fiction, and Science* (London: Garland, 1996).

4. Roland Barthes, *Camera Lucida: Reflections on Photography*, trans. Richard Howard (New York: Hill and Wang, 1981); Barthes, *Writing Degree Zero*, trans. Richard Howard (New York: Hill and Wang, 1968); Barthes, *S/Z*, trans. Richard Howard (New York: Hill and Wang, 1970).

5. Paul Monette, *Borrowed Time: An AIDS Memoir* (San Diego: Harcourt Brace Jovanovich, 1988).

6. Larry Kramer, *Reports from the Holocaust: The Story of an AIDS Activist* (New York: St. Martin Press, 1989).

7. Simon Watney, "Sense and Less Than Sense About AIDS," *Guardian Weekly*, March 26, 1989, 28.

8. I am grateful to Nancy K. Miller for her conversations about this book and for her questions about its significance for my essay.

chapter ten

The Posthumous Life of Susan Sontag

NANCY K. MILLER

Still, there is something predatory in the act of taking a picture. To photograph people is to violate them, by seeing them as they never see themselves, by having knowledge of them they can never have; it turns people into objects that can be symbolically possessed.

—Susan Sontag, "In Plato's Cave"

I used to tease my mother by saying to her that though she had largely kept her own biography out of her work, her essays of appreciation—on Roland Barthes, on Walter Benjamin, on Elias Canetti, to name three of the best of them—were more self-revealing than she perhaps imagined. At the very least, they were idealizations. At the time, she laughed, lightly assenting.

—David Rieff, foreword to *At the Same Time*

In the mainly black and white pages of *A Photographer's Life, 1990–2005*, Annie Leibovitz reveals her companion of fifteen years in an uncommon degree of intimate, physical detail. The photographs of Sontag—asleep, naked in the bathtub, playing at the beach with Leibovitz's little daughter, terminally ill in hospital, and finally, dead—present a view of Sontag radically different from the glamorous, carefully posed, hard-edge figure that the writer over several decades offered a public hungry for celebrity culture and enamored of her stylized beauty. Some of the Leibovitz photos are touching, a few are endearing, but most are hard to look at. How does the photographer justify exposing Sontag's physical suffering, as well as the images of her private, bodily life?

Leibovitz addresses her decision to make the private public in the book's introduction: "After Susan died, on December 28, 2004, I began searching for photographs of her to put in a little book that was intended to be given to the people who came to her memorial service. The project was important to me, because it made me feel close to her and helped me to say good-bye."[1] I don't know whether Leibovitz read Barthes's *Camera Lucida*, but for those familiar with his classic study of photography, the echoes are distinct and uncanny (certainly, Sontag would have recognized them). In the second, more overtly autobiographical part of his essay, Barthes describes the experience of sorting photographs after his mother's death. What he "wanted," he said, was what Paul Valéry said that he wanted after *his* mother's death: to "'write a little compilation about her, just for myself (perhaps I shall write it one day, so that printed, her memory will last at least the time of my notoriety.'"[2] He was "looking for the truth of the face" he had loved, Barthes explains, and he found it (67).

Like Barthes, thinking about loss and how to memorialize it for himself, Leibovitz, too, looks at pictures of the woman she loved. Barthes famously decided not to publish the image of the face he loved, preferring words to image, and leaving the image to the reader's imagination. (The "truth" of that face, he reasoned, would be recognizable only to him.) In selecting images for the memorial service, Leibovitz does the exactly the opposite. And yet I want to underscore the similarity of the impulse because of the language in which the motivation for the editorial process is cast: the use of the adjective "little" and the linking of the "little book" to the author's own fame or notoriety: explicitly in the case of Barthes, implicitly for Leibovitz. For each, whatever the outcome, the identification of photographs with a view toward a book engages the process of remembrance, puts the healing process into movement. *A Photographer's Life* and *Camera Lucida* share this project of grieving through gazing at images, even if, in these elegiac enactments, Leibovitz, unlike Barthes, is also the creator of the images themselves.

Shortly before his own death, Barthes publishes his "little book," *Camera Lucida*; very much alive, Leibovitz creates an exhibit at the Brooklyn Museum. The exhibition catalogue, a very big book, details the selection process.

Going through my pictures to put this book together was like being on an archaeological dig. The work I did on assignments for magazines and for advertisements was edited and organized, but I didn't know how much other material I had. I don't take a lot of purely personal pictures. Susan Sontag, who was with me during the years the book encompasses used to complain that I didn't take enough pictures. . . . I had put a few personal pictures in the first retrospective collection of my work which covered the years 1970–1990, and I thought I would do that again for this book. Then, when I realized that I had so much more personal material than I had imagined, and that the period this book covers is almost exactly the years I was with Susan, I considered doing a book made up completely of personal work. I thought about that for a while and concluded that the personal work on its own wasn't a true view of the last fifteen years. I don't have two lives. This is one life, and the personal pictures and the assignment work are all part of it. (np)

Leibovitz defends her decision not to separate the two domains. The adjective "personal" occurs no fewer than eight times in first two pages of the introduction, and Leibovitz is succinct in her autobiographical defense: "I don't have two lives." As a writer, I respect that principle and have no wish to argue against including the personal within the sphere of the professional, however defined. (The personal, I should be clear, means not just the Sontag photos, but also the many pictures of the photographer's parents, children, and family.) Indeed, as *Camera Lucida* palpably demonstrates, the personal works effectively in counterpoint to the professional when the contrast between the two realms produces some kind of new knowledge or vision.

In *Camera Lucida*, a book whose subtitle in English is severe, *Reflections on Photography* (the French is less so: "Notes on Photography"), Barthes places the love for his mother and his grief at her loss within his own biography as a writer and student of photography. He learns about what photographs mean to him—and how they come to convey meaning—through this shattering loss, which he incorporates into his theoretical speculation. In a way, I'm suggesting, through the juxtaposition of her pictures and her framing introduction, that Leibovitz makes an analogous move as she incorporates personal details from Sontag's life into her celebrity photographer's visual diary. We are dealing, then, with two obviously distinct but nonetheless related acts of memorialization: the exposure of private grief and the construction of a public narrative that frames and gives meaning to the gesture. Is it possible to imagine that Leibovitz's Sontag adds to our earlier view of the subject, either of Sontag as a celebrity (the kind of "assignment work" that in fact was part of their relationship) or of the notion of celebrity itself?

As in any memorial project—verbal or visual—neither Barthes's mother nor Susan Sontag had a choice about having her relationship to the mourner made public. Barthes idealized his mother, and Leibovitz appears to have idealized (or at least idolized) Sontag. Nonetheless, in both cases, for the critic and for the photographer, no matter how loving the grieving subject—and in both cases we are dealing with an admiring love—the object of the photographs is necessarily imported into the story as part of the work of mourning.

Here my comparison begins to break down. Barthes decides not to show the face of the one whose loss means the end of his life as he knew it. *Not* showing is Barthes's attachment to maintaining his idealization: his mother was perfect in *his* eyes. What she was to him is not shareable. He keeps his, that, essential mother to himself. By deciding to show all, Leibovitz instead appears to need to de-idealize her love object in the eyes of the world, the better, I'm going to suggest, to claim her. She does this in two ways. First, she publishes "personal" images that reveal Sontag in unexpectedly unglamorous and awkwardly embodied poses and positions. Most readers of Sontag's books will have primarily a sense of the author's face (and hair) and not her body (with the one exception of the famous 1975 Peter Hujar portrait of Sontag stretched out like a canvas), except as an imposing (and always posing), often monumental presence. Through Leibovitz's personal photographs of her companion, we are suddenly confronted with a body surprising in its corporeal detail, and a biographical vulnerability of the flesh rarely alluded to by Sontag herself.

Almost simultaneously, in the media coverage that preceded the exhibit, Leibovitz promoted, along with the photographs, the narrative of their story as a couple, a story Sontag had never acknowledged publicly, even though it was an open secret—for those in the know. On the cover, for instance, of the weekend magazine of the *Guardian* (Oct. 7, 2006), romantic dialogue glosses the image: "I kissed her goodbye and I said I love you, and she said I love you." The caption continues: "Annie Leibovitz's farewell to Susan Sontag."[3] Wrapped entirely in a blanket on board a mysterious sunset journey, Sontag retains her familiar iconic power; a recognizable hauteur remains, despite a slightly troubled gaze, along with the dark mane of hair and its signature white stripe. But inside the magazine, the farewell takes another tone. Through a mix of poses and settings, all personal and familial, we get Leibovitz's Sontag: a maternal Sontag, holding Leibovitz's first daughter; Sontag between the sheets in a Venice hotel room; Sontag walking the beach with her literary agent; traveling in Jordan; receiving chemotherapy; and, finally, Sontag, a sleeping nude. With these images, Leibovitz locks Sontag into her incipient biopic—or at least her version of the couple—a narrative Sontag is no longer in a position to accept or reject, at least not directly.

In the similar *Newsweek* illustrated coverage of the show, there are no nudes (this is America, after all), but in both magazine pieces we see the strange, widely circulated memento mori photographs of Sontag's wounded, but exquisitely dressed, stretched out corpse. The image, taken almost immediately after her death, is composed from four segments, which contributes to the startling effect of the photograph.

There are many more images in the show and the book—including the ones of Sontag dead—that expose the body in decline, several where Sontag is swollen, almost beyond recognition, being transported on a hospital gurney, etc. Leibovitz explains to the journalist why she included these images of terminal illness, acknowledging that these were subject to contentious debate. In the *Guardian*, Leibovitz says that she consulted "a small circle of Sontag's friends" about the ethics of publishing the photographs that carry the mark of death: "Leibovitz wanted to show," the journalist explains, "what illness looks like and what courage looks like, too" (Brockes, "My Time," 30). By proxy, Leibovitz seems to argue that, thanks to her exposure, viewers also were invited to bid farewell to Sontag's public image and learn something about regarding the pain of others. In some ways, this seems fitting, if sadly ironic, for an author who took illness and images of suffering as her subject. Is it? As Leibovitz says in *Newsweek*, acknowledging (in reference to the hospital shots) that these are "very tough pictures": "I think Susan would really be proud of those pictures—but she's dead. Now if she were alive, she would not want them published. It's really a difference. It's really strange."[4]

The images of Sontag ill and dying shock the viewer, and one can see a certain logic (Leibovitz's) in publishing them, given Sontag's own desire not to flinch before images of suffering. In *Swimming in a Sea of Death: A Son's Memoir*, David Rieff takes the opposite view. Speculating about how much kinder it would have been if fate had allowed his mother to die suddenly, with no "time to be frightened," Rieff bitterly regrets the publication of Leibovitz's photographs: "She would not have had the time to mourn herself and to become physically unrecognizable at the end even to herself, let alone humiliated posthumously by being 'memorialized' that way in those carnival images of celebrity death taken by Annie Leibovitz" (*SSD*, 150). That was not to be. Sontag had exactly too much and too little time.

I find it hard to imagine Sontag wanting the revelation of the biographical information, both about her love life and her terrible death, conveyed by the Leibovitz show and book and widely circulated through the media. Reading Sontag back to *Illness as Metaphor* for her views on the uses of personal narrative, one is reminded that what she wanted to achieve in her books about illness was something beyond the individual case, not wanting to "tell yet one more story in the first person of how someone learned that he or she had cancer, wept, struggled, was comforted, suffered, took courage . . . though mine was also that story" (*IM*, 101). What mattered to Sontag was the act of description and analysis *beyond* the act of revelation: "I want to describe, *not what it is really like* to emigrate to the kingdom of the ill and live there, but the punitive or sentimental fantasies concocted about that situation" (*IM*, 3; emphasis added). In Leibovitz's photographs of a physically debilitated Sontag, a Sontag inhabiting the kingdom of the ill, Leibovitz seems determined to show exactly what Sontag declined to describe: "what it is really like" to be ill. Perhaps what the photographer illuminates instead is what it is like to *bear witness* to the illness of others, what it is like to look at the pain of others. In this sense, Leibovitz has offered a form of witness that runs parallel to Rieff's own act of witness as a writer to the unfolding of his mother's decline and demise. The problem comes from the ethics of bearing witness in public, on behalf of the other, silent partner. Whose or what interests are served by the exposure?[5]

Of course, unlike Roland Barthes's mother, Susan Sontag was committed neither to silence nor to an obscure personal figure. Not long before her death, moreover, Sontag authorized the publication of her own diaries, a segment of which appeared in the *New York Times* less than two years after her death. Dated May 1961, the first lines read: "The book is a wall. I put myself behind it, out of sight and out of seeing." The framing (and unsigned) newspaper commentary points to the tension between public persona and private life, the life behind the wall, as it were, that the diary may or may not reveal: "Her public persona was durable and unmistakably hers. But in the journals, the effort of it appears again and again."[6] It's the cost of that effort that I believe Sontag alludes to in her analysis of Barthes's last work, in her sense that he found in writing about photography "the great exemption, perhaps release, from the exactions of formalist taste" ("Writing Itself: On Roland Barthes," *WSF*, 86). We can't know yet whether the diaries, which will be "shaped" by the hands of David Rieff and others, as Rieff says in the foreword to *At the Same Time* (*AST*, xii), will tell us more of the effort of living that went on behind the wall of books, the "effort" of maintaining that ultra-cultivated public persona. At the end of her *Guardian* interview, Leibovitz puts forward her view of the diaries: "'It's funny because—although in the end she wanted her diaries published—Susan always said she felt that art really had to rise above the personal.' Leibovitz disagrees" (Brockes, "My Time," 35). About the relation of the personal to art, there is no agreement, but a distinction may be made between choosing to make your intimate matters public (the diaries) and having publication (in the name of art) taken out of your hands (the photographs).

In her conclusion to *Regarding the Pain of Others*, Sontag offers a palinode to some of her harsh pronouncements about the limits of photography in the ethical realm. But she maintains a certain skepticism about images by "certain photographers of conscience" that show "heart-rending subject matter" (*RP*, 120). Even contained in a book—rather than displayed on the walls of a museum and vulnerable to the distractions of museum going—the effect of disturbing photographs, she maintains, wears off. Characteristically, Sontag prefers the book to the exhibit: "the weight and seriousness of such photographs survive better in a book, where one can look privately, linger over the pictures, without talking" (*RP*, 121). To show or not to show? To look or look away? Sontag never resolved the contradiction. We must learn to pay attention to suffering, but how, if in the end we spectators really "don't get it" (*RP*, 125). A journalist embedded in Iraq with photographer Ashley Gilbertson neatly summarizes the dilemma: "The life of the reporter: always some-one else's pain" (*RP*, 40). This is what Sontag finally understood: "At some moment," she concludes in *Regarding the Pain of Others*, "the book will be closed. The strong emotion will become a transient one" (121). When all is said and done, the spectator stands outside the pain.

Strangely, neither Leibovitz nor Rieff mentions the other photo-graphs in the show and circulated in the media. Arguably more shock-ing, or at least surprising, than the suffering body—the inexorable deg-radation brought on by the ravages of cancer, or even the unflinching documentation of human pain in depressing hospital settings—are the full-scale nudes, the sleeping odalisque between the sheets, the kitsch domesticity: Sontag in the tub. These "personal" images, to use Leibo-vitz's word, are far less easy to defend as belonging to an ethical project and point toward the fatal flaw of the celebrity photographer: the in-ability precisely to distinguish between what is and isn't in the interest of the photograph's objectified subject.

Beyond inclusion of the nudes and the pictures of silly private mo-ments (Sontag celebrating New Year's Eve in Paris dressed in a bear cos-tume), however, perhaps the strongest (and most embarrassing) example of Leibovitz's will to publicize her intimacy with Sontag was the choice to place on the cover of her book the portrait Sontag took of the pho-tographer in their hotel room at the Gritti Palace in Venice. The book's cover is the contact sheet of a series of images from their trip, the final pick marked off in red crayon. I'm *hers*, Leibovitz seems to be longing to say, looking into the eye of the camera in Sontag's hand, just as she was *mine*.

Although the exhibition, and secondarily the book, received a great deal of media attention at the time—how could they not?—in the end, the question they pose is not so much their capacity to shock and the eth-ics of their publication as their posthumous existence in the history of the representation of the Sontag persona. Will the images of an ill, em-bodied, and coupled Sontag revealed in Leibovitz's story alter the mode of self-portrayal Sontag chose for herself early on?[7] In particular, what place will the ultimate portrait—of the dead author—occupy in the rep-ertoire of images that constitute the public narrative of Sontag's life?

The last line of "Photography: A Little Summa," a four-page essay consisting of fourteen numbered theses, originally published in 2003 and collected in *At the Same Time*, points us away from any certainty

Figure 8 In order to capture "this beautiful young face . . . for eternity," the *New York Times Book Review* cropped out all evidence of the photographer's work and the model's posing. *Source*: *New York Times Book Review*, March 11, 2007. Photo by Bob Peterson; permission from Getty Images.

about posterity: "14. There is no final photograph," Sontag concludes (*AST*, 127). Nonetheless, seen from the threshold of a history as yet to unfold, for Sontag the signature photo, I'm going to suggest, the true memento mori, will remain the author photo, a head shot from the author's beginnings.

In "TBR: Inside the List" (March 11, 2007) the *New York Times Book Review* ran a biographical note on Sontag, whose posthumous essay collection *At the Same Time* was reviewed in the same issue. The column revisits Sontag's career, including the reception of the early novels. A 1966 portrait of Sontag appears in the margins (see fig. 8), the beautiful young face preserved for eternity.

Notes

1. Annie Leibovitz, *A Photographer's Life, 1990–2005* (New York: Random House, 2006), np.

2. Roland Barthes, *Camera Lucida*, trans. Richard Howard (New York: Hill and Wang, 1981), 63.

3. Emma Brockes, "My Time With Susan," interview with Annie Leibovitz, *The Guardian*, October 7, 2006.

4. Cathleen McGuigan, "An Exclusive Look at Annie Leibovitz's Compelling—and Surprisingly Personal—New Book," *Newsweek*, October 2, 2006, 56.

5. Rieff gave Leibovitz permission to take the photographs of Sontag after her death in the funeral home, reasoning that "well, people who have an artistic bent, who cope with a death through their art—she's a person who does this all the time." The problem came with their publication. Interviewed in England, Rieff professed surprise that Leibovitz crossed that line: "it just never occurred to me she would publish them. She knows perfectly well my mother would not have wanted her to publish them, but she felt she had to do it" (Cathy Galvin, "Archive: The Intimate Secrets of Susan Sontag," *Times* [London], May 25, 2008). Rieff said much the same thing in an interview on NPR's *Fresh Air*, January 10, 2008 (http://www.npr.org/templates/story/story.php?storyId=17989334).

6. Sontag, "On Self: From the Notebooks and Diaries of Susan Sontag, 1958–67," *New York Times Magazine*, September 10, 2006, 52.

7. Although some of the late author photos, notably the glamour shot for the cover of *In America*, were taken by Leibovitz, the last one, for the posthumous collection, *At the Same Time*, which shows part of Sontag's lined and solemn face, marked by illness, was not. Possibly this was Rieff's choice to mark an end to the Leibovitz image era.

chaptereleven

In Summa
The Latter Essays — an Appreciation

SOHNYA SAYRES

In the first waves of appreciation that followed Sontag's death, just a few years ago at this writing, her stature as a woman of letters and a public intellectual of the first order were unquestioned—a gratifying, assuredly deserved, tinged-with-awe round of applause. One could not help but consider, however, that the beautiful, deeply committed portraits she had written of other "partisans" of art and ideas—a "partisan of letters" she had called Barthes in her lustrous memorial of him—had not become the model toward which one could only aspire, and many of these appreciations faltered. Her accomplishments, her standards, and her aesthetic embrace of her subjects overwhelm the usual prosaic style of acknowledgments. A pattern could be detected, not yet a consensus, of remembering her early essays as stunning, speaking about her own fiction with more reserve, being rather glum about her politics, sniping about her celebrity, and—something more subtle, and a little more telling of the times—an unwillingness to find in her life's work a project. Not to do so makes her seriousness seem inflated, discomforting. Chances are that a career as long and dedicated as Sontag's has a project; just *when* in that person's career it becomes self-evident may be elusive, though not to her, I believe. Now that all new paths have been foreclosed and the delight we take in recalling her vivifying—am I being too fusty in hesitating to use the word "sexy"?—presence is muted by the toll of her disease, the inner trajectory of her ideas lies open to be claimed.

David Rieff, Sontag's son, writing in the foreword to her posthumously collected essays, *At the Same Time*, is able to summarize easily what her project was. It was never obscure; she prepared carefully for it in her master's degrees and an almost accomplished Ph.D.—in comparative religions, modern philosophy, and literature. David Rieff writes: "It is sometimes said of my mother's work that she was torn between aestheticism and moralism, beauty and ethics. Any intelligent reader of hers will see the force of this, but I think a shrewder account would emphasize their inseparability" (*AST*, xv).

Beauty and ethics: they were ever-present in her nature of inquiring, ever foremost in her interests. However, in the objects of her inquiry, she often had to fend off one from the other, for their dynamics were too often at odds. The possibility of these being inseparable in the world would not have been a productive stance for her. Ethics requires us to act, ultimately, as does the quest for truth, which demands establishing a faith with ourselves for proceeding with ever-evolving standards. The good and the true can live in metaphysical harmony—these trustworthy old virtues—but not so surely can beauty. The beautiful is a peculiar kind of apprehension; she never tired of parsing it. It elevates us, lulls us, reassures us, in itself. Whatever else, there is the beautiful in feeling states, in ideas; we can learn to extend our appreciation of it; it may goad us to create it, own it, be near it, preserve it—we may attach it to all other values, the beauties of love relationships, the beauty of kindness, the way that health evokes beauty, the way our children seem. A deeply spiritual person may appear to us to be beautiful, while, perhaps, the reverse is not so sure, that a deeply aestheticized person is, naturally, good.

These floating attachments especially confuse the issue of separability and inseparability. Beauty, the great centripetal force, may drag the others to itself. Given a chance to choose, we will choose the beautiful where we might avoid the ethical and ignore the shaky grounds of a truth claim. In these last instances, which are frequent enough, Sontag becomes particularly engaged.

What moved her, for instance, to take up the pen once more on this subject in her last years? An off-putting comment by Pope John Paul II in 2002. In her view, his remarks were an inordinately delayed response to the scandal of sexually "predatory" priests who had been protected for years. He equivocated in just the wrong dimension, telling his cardinals that "'a great work of art may be blemished, but its beauty remains; and this is a truth which any intellectually honest critic will recognize'" (*AST*, 3):

> Is it too odd that the pope likens the Catholic Church to a great— that is, beautiful—work of art? Perhaps not, since the inane comparison allows him to turn abhorrent misdeeds into something like the scratches in the print of a silent film or craquelure covering the surface of an Old Master painting, blemishes that we reflexively screen out or see past.

Beauty, used thus, Sontag begins, has been "a perennial resource in the issuing of peremptory evaluations" (*AST*, 3).

What follows in this essay ("An Argument About Beauty") is pure Sontag. Each sentence of her swift cultural history displays her gifts as a careful writer, long familiar with the subject and able to bring it to clarity in terse phrases with fine touches, for instance, the ironies she finds in the rise and fall of positions. Against the modernist efforts to dethrone beauty to the "merely," aesthetes such as Oscar Wilde would declare: "Nobody of any real culture . . . ever talks nowadays about the beauty of a sunset. Sunsets are quite old fashioned" (Wilde, *The Decay of Lying*). Sunsets, continues Sontag, "reeled under the blow, then recovered" (*AST*, 5). She takes aim with superlatively chosen examples, such as the German officer, WWII, at the Russian front, musing on the Christmas stars, without telling us what we need to think about his grasping at straws. The infinite, without its concern for us, "deepens our sense of the sheer spread and fullness of reality, inanimate as well as pulsing, that surrounds us all. . . . beauty regains its solidarity, its inevitability, as a judgment needed to make sense of a large portion of one's energies, affinities, and admirations" (*AST*, 13).

Do be aware; don't try to "usurp" beauty for evasions and cover-ups. Sontag is at the ready. She'll make that gesture appear "ludicrous," without belittling the conceptual frame. This elegant anatomizing of a cultural artifact while appreciating its power sometimes confuses readers who do want positions. Is she attacking beauty? Backing away from her initial outrage, interrogating herself and previous stands on aesthetics to the point of complicity or self-contradictions? False questions. This kind of essay is her method, evidenced from the very first collection, *Against Interpretation*.

What is also in evidence in these last volumes is what is sometimes called the mature style. The surfaces of these essays shine with polish; the essence of her thoughts is arrived at quickly, having been given much time to ripen. Background influences are quieted. She does not need to set up a climate of antagonists, just specific ones will do. Nietzsche, so often invoked before, has slipped away. There are few Nietzschean gestures of radical inversions, or Adorno-like disclosures by way of hidden contradictions, or the French postwar intellectual gestures of hyperbole in the service of wrenching free from a disgraced past. Theirs were "aggressive" gestures. Her thoughts do not undercut themselves quite in the manner of the epigram, as they earlier had a tendency to do. Oscar Wilde is in attendance when she is specifically concerned with beauty, but when he is absurd, she lets him be just that.

In the mature style of these last essays, the object of her earlier quests has long been found. She was not apt now to worry herself over sensibilities that only moderately attracted her, and thus are likely in some part to repulse. Her early essay on camp reverberates with the side of her that will take pleasure in the gay community's identification with camp. She will find its source, make herself play, too. However, much of that essay was constructed, for all these worthy intentions, with some strain and with some not so hidden rebukes at "camp taste's" trivializing. The tension gives the essay its famous brilliant qualities. In these later essays, puzzlement no longer serves as a motive to write. Nor can she be baited, as she turns inward to herself, into an argument. She is in the "summa" stages of her thinking, as in the title of "Photography: A Little Summa."

Facts, sheer facts, at this stage of life grow larger, more fulsome, speaking mostly for themselves. That a writer may have written from an enforced exile, for example, can simply be stated as such, for she has contemplated this condition often before; as president of PEN, she made it her charge to know it well.

II

The rest of my remarks here take up Sontag's thoughts on these most venerable of critical issues—starting with the beautiful, then the good and the true—arguing that these are Sontag's touchstones, consistent in her work and never more in evidence than in these her last pieces. To understand their interaction has been her life's project.

Can there be more about beauty to be contemplated? After fifty years of doing so with a mind of a moralist? As with a photograph—she has written, "there is no final photograph"—there cannot be the final word on beauty. Who would have predicted that in this war in Iraq, American soldiers would carry their own digital cameras to plug into the World Wide Web as often as they could? Some of these will be judged aesthetically, inevitably, as Sontag considers. Beauty as Sontag refers to it needs to be understood in the classicizing tradition, for that was her sensibility. For her, form initiates, form demonstrates, form makes us care when an artifact becomes unreadable in any other way—as an object found in the sand, a captionless photograph. She drew her portraits of other writers and artists with heroic stances, dramatizing their engagement with their work in agonistic terms. Her essays are now labeled "essays of admiration," and such a method befits a universalizing, formalist set of questions.

In drawing this portrait of Sontag, I, too, confront the temptation to make her work coalesce. Nonetheless, some ideas about her work are just plain misconceived. She was not a pop culturalist, as we might use the term today. Her early work did discuss pornography, disaster films, and camp, but not from aficionado enthusiasms. She was interested in their dubious essences. Mostly she wrote on art-house films, happenings, dance, painters, photography, in distinctly intellectualized ways, even if these reviews were published in *Vanity Fair*. She did not watch TV. And if she confessed that she enjoyed rock and roll, well, she was not deaf. Between the Doors and Dostoevsky, she has written, it will be Dostoevsky. But does she have to choose?

She came into her milieu very young, in her twenties, when she sensed that the climate and controversies made by the New York intellectuals of ten or twenty years or more her senior would never be the world that she inhabited. She became attracted to postwar Paris, leaving behind an Oxford Ph.D. program, falling into its culture, the arms of lovers, and ideas.

These would be her North Star in the constellation of influences for many years. Those influences would extend to Scandinavia, Central and Eastern Europe—a "European fellow traveler," she has called herself. In all these efforts, she modeled herself on the pattern of the independent writer, with a public intellectual's responsibilities to grasp the world. When she took to the stage in times of political controversies, she spoke with a stern, corrective eye and voice. When she visited ostracized countries, as North Vietnam and China were at that time, she hesitated to write but from a self-questioning diarist's stance. In the case of China, because her father had died there when she was four years old, the form in which she chose to think was in preparatory *koans*.

She explains in the essay entitled "The Conscience of Words": "As a writer, a maker of literature, I am both a narrator and a ruminator. Ideas move me. But novels are made not of ideas but of forms. Forms of language. Forms of expressiveness. I don't have a story in my head until I have the form" (*AST*, 148).

"The defense of literature," she continues, "has become one of the writer's main subjects" (*AST*, 148). Her tone is regal, naming literature and the vocation of writing and reading a vehicle of honor and freedom. True, these statements were made in the context of accepting literary prizes, so that the restrictions of the event come into play. One might grow a little wary of her high-toned sincerity, for instance, had her own erudition, practice, and experience not been exemplary in the pursuit of understanding literature. She returns a defense of literature's authority at a time when we have become used to hearing claims against its authority. Her judgments can be sweeping, her targets too easy to name, her fears exaggerated:

> What is more true is that the hypertext—or should I say the ideology of the hypertext?—is ultrademocratic and so entirely in harmony with the demagogic appeals to cultural democracy that accompany (and distract one's attention from) the ever-tightening grip of plutocratic capitalism.
>
> This proposal that the novel of the future will have *no* story or, instead, a story of the reader's (rather, *readers'*) devising is so plainly unappealing and, should it come to pass, would inevitably bring about not the much-heralded death of the author but the extinction of the reader—*all* future readers of what is labeled as "literature." It's easy to

see that it could only have been an invention of *academic* literary criticism, which has been overwhelmed by a plethora of notions expressing the keenest hostility to the very project of literature itself.
(*AST*, 221)

Perhaps sensing that these *all*s and *no*s cannot be placed entirely on the shoulders of professors of postmodern literature, she blames television's influence. Be that as it may, her championing of the singular voice of the author is staunch. The novelist takes us through space and time not of one's own devising; it is an "act of achieved form . . . whereas broken or insufficient form, in effect, does not know, wishes *not* to know, what belongs to it" (*AST*, 224.)

Thus, the indefatigable energy of beauty. It seeks to complete itself, to act, as an "achieved form." Hypertexts, and suggestions like them, do have a pedagogic appeal, besides a false democratic one, in that we can learn how form seeks to achieve itself and take pleasure, by following the initiatives already put into motion. But, of course, we cannot be led to the heights, where beauty entices others to press onward and upward.

Sontag insists on difficult, serious work; her strong condemnations of even more vague constructions, such as American culture, would place her square in the company of neoformalist critics, but that another strain pulls in the opposite direction. To torture my metaphor a little, and to make a possibly supercilious point: allow that the good and the true do not have their eyes fixed entirely upon beauty as they climb Mount Parnassus. They cast about, in this utterly deceptive, frequently unjust, frequently brutalizing world, and must speak. In her Nadine Gordimer Lecture, "At the Same Time: The Novelist and Moral Reasoning," Sontag speaks in praise of Gordimer's commitments and to her view that "a fiction writer whose adherence is to literature is, necessarily, someone who thinks about moral problems: about what is just and unjust, what is better or worse, what is repulsive and admirable, what is lamentable and what inspires joy and approbation. This doesn't entail moralizing in any direct or crude sense. Serious fiction writers think about moral problems practically. . . . The stories they tell enlarge and complicate—and, therefore, improve—our sympathies. They educate our capacity for moral judgment" (*AST*, 213).

With a slightly playful nod towards Kant's concern about critical judgments in time and space, and with unapologetic references to standards, Sontag builds a defense for storytelling as ethics because storytellers, the good ones, must take responsibility to conclude their "felt intensity" and bring what "enlightenment" they can to the story's "resolution—which is the opposite of the model of obtuseness, of nonunderstanding, of passive dismay, and the consequent numbing of feeling, offered by our media-disseminated glut of unending stories" (*AST*, 225).

In these last pieces, not, of course, understood as such, Sontag reiterates the position she took as a younger woman. The arts educate capacities, without which moral judgments are mere norms, rules, governance of the senses and feelings, states remarkably unpersuasive and frequently too forbidding. When these moral judgments are laid upon the arts, they damage those new, fresh-springing sympathies that are about to be educated. Conversely, the arts, too, can "inure," not just when sensationalizing for the sake of sensationalizing, not just in debased, formulaic practices, but also in the sheer ubiquity of the casual, the abrupt, the slight. To gain Sontag's praise, especially now when she can think more clearly about what her own life's work has been and to whom she is indebted, artists need commitment to the demands inherent in their style of address and equally inherent in the life-world that haunts them.

This project can yield to lightness; it can seek the more profound of the comedic revelations. As Sontag describes the work of her one-time companion, the dancer Lucinda Child:

> Child's conception of dance is Apollonian: dance should be lively, playful, joyous. Beauty equals power, delicacy, decorum, unaffected intensity. What is ugly is timidity, anxiety, demagoguery, heaviness. (Other exemplars of the Apollonian style: Seurat, Mallarmé, Morandi, Ozu, Wallace Stevens.)
> (*WSF*, 169)

In her discovery of Machado de Assis, she catches the whimsy (which modulates a vein of "true misanthropy") in the garrulousness of his character-narrator, Brás Cubas. She then launches into her manner of inquiry about just what this phenomenon is:

> To natter on obsessively, repetitively, used to be invariably a source of comedy. (Think of Shakespeare's plebeian grumblers, like the porter in

Macbeth; think of Mr. Pickwick, among other inventions of Dickens). That comic use of garrulousness does not disappear. Joyce used garrulousness in a Rabelaisian spirit, as a vehicle of comic hyperbole, and Gertrude Stein, champion of verbose writing, turned the tics of egotism and sententiousness into a good-natured comic voice of great originality. But most of the verbose first-person narrators in the ambitious literature of this century have been radically misanthropic. . . .

Beckett's narrators are usually trying, not altogether successfully, to imagine themselves as dead. Brás Cubas has no such problem. But then Machado de Assis was trying to be, and is, funny. There is nothing morbid about the consciousness of his posthumous narrator; on the contrary, the perspective of maximum consciousness—which is what, wittily, a posthumous narrator can claim—is in itself a comic perspective.

(*WSF*, 37)

The arts and letters do us good because with them we discover the knowledge, the demonstration, that via the artist's effects, moral capacity grows. Because?

The nature of moral judgments depends on our capacity for paying attention—a capacity that, inevitably, has its limits but whose limits can be stretched.

But perhaps the beginning of wisdom, and humility, is to acknowledge, and bow one's head, before the thought, the devastating thought, of the simultaneity of everything, and the incapacity of our moral understanding—which is also the understanding of the novelist—to take this in.

(*AST*, 226)

Sometimes, what Sontag means by morality is just the capacity of courage when it is called upon to display itself. On the occasion of making the Oscar Romero keynote address, she reminds us that, generally, "a moral principle is something that puts one at *variance* with accepted practice" (*AST*, 182) and that variance has consequences: societies fight back. There are so many heroes, she considers, millions, just as there are millions of victims, who have fallen to their own insistence that societies actually live up to professed ideals. People, generally, much prefer to think that they "are doing the best that they can" when awareness would dispel that presumption.

For the moral life to sustain its resonance, and individual positions to reflect the good, ultimately truth must be found. Intentions and consequences both depend upon it. Resistance to social norms for its own sake becomes a form of self-righteousness, and flaunting conventions for no other sake than that gesture becomes another form of self-delusion. Sontag grows so easily definitive, proscriptive in these essays, that one remembers an old, exasperated, assertion of hers that some truths are indeed simple. Simply, moral judgment is about "assigning importance to one action over another" and "the justice of the cause does not depend on, and is not enhanced by, the virtue of those who make the assertion. It depends first and last on the truth of a description of a state of affairs that is, truly, unjust and unnecessary" (AST, 184).

How have we proceeded in this last half century or so, with the burden of finding truth, through art and critique? The sciences and other knowledge-producing disciplines barely touched her published thoughts; judgment depends on insight from deeply cultured perspectives. The truth the she writes about comes from masterpieces, grounded in intimately observed experiences and astute political awareness.[1] Above all, the truth of the masterpiece has to be on par or paired with history, so that the writing of history begins to show its own weakness of explanation, its prefigured conveyances of coincidences. "The truth of the novelist," Sontag concludes, "unlike the truth of the historian—allows for the arbitrary, the mysterious, the unmotivated. . . . The truth of fiction depicts that for which one can never be consoled and displaces it with a healing openness to everything finite and cosmic" (AST, 88).

These are old assertions about the truth in works of arts, Sontag acknowledges, although she might have also acknowledged that these assertions came long before the novel was given moral stature. In this qualification, what comes to mind are many of the troubles in the aesthetic paradise of "healing openness," in the education of the sentiments, and in the enlarged capacities for judgment that Sontag attributes to noble, complex works. Contemporary life has brought about its own revolution in aptitudes. It has made seeing, the screen and the photograph, a primary vehicle; it has made listening to gab, oratory, commentary, journalism of all sorts, and programmed or self-programmed music an hourly pastime. At present, it has placed new faith in personae that "interact" by category, quip, and overexposure to the fleeting, without the awkwardness of actual meeting. It has raised hopes of vastly extended personal empowerment and a body/identity more valuable dead than alive. Intellectual pleasure has more to do with surfing for surprises in the media onslaught.

These later conditions give Sontag's defense of the culture of literature a faintly pedantic, endearingly passé quality that Sontag hears but to which she will not yield. She has chosen her path. Her public pretends, at least, to be part of that culture. We can all be grateful.

She has long reasoned herself into this defense, or, to put in another way, for all the reasons she can stake her claims for literature with such convictions—not the least of which is her ease with philosophy—several large conclusions stand out. I am thinking especially of the case of photography. She gave inordinate critical attention to photography, above films and theater, for instance, although she had been a filmmaker and dramatist and director. Photography offers an instructive contradistinction to literature. This daemon of modern times moves in single images, beautiful, but not so truth telling, and perhaps not so morally strengthening. And then again, unlike the pleasures of the text, about which one can rhapsodize as long as the aesthetic dimension pulls the reader on, the photograph emboldens the eye alone, its sheer ubiquity amounting to another kind of mindset that had to be carefully quizzed.

At the risk of repeating myself, allow me to remark at this juncture that Sontag's pioneering work in thinking about culture proved to be a continuous inspiration to cultural studies, media studies, and offshoots such as visual culture, without overarching systems of new thought, in a manner erudite without obtuseness. However, again some qualifications on this matter are in order. When she did think about contemporary culture qua culture, it was largely with a shudder. She found most of it and its effects depressingly nihilistic. She ropes photography securely into those foundational objections.

But not individual photographs per se, about which she admits a great passion. Photographs invite both contemplation and inattention. Photography, after all, has about it the book, the gallery, the special case for inquiry that a stilled image can elicit. Yet, through appearance, thin appearance, photography seems almost the equivalent of the shadows on the walls of Plato's cave, for we can almost reach to touch its source, "out there," in the real world. It holds the promise of being the most democratic of art forms, with the power to document and an almost equal power to lay upon us too many instances of sentiments, alarm, and beautified reality until our responses are numbed and the effort toward fuller apprehension deflected. As she summarizes in an extended essay published in 1977, *On Photography*: "The powers of photographs have in effect de-Platonized our understanding of reality, making it less plausible to reflect upon our experience according to the distinction between images and things . . . [it has become] a potent means of turning tables on reality, turning *it* into a shadow" (*OP*, 179–80).

This worrisome certainty never left her. In her last essay on photography, "Photography: A Little Summa," she draws together the totalizing impact of this technology that has become the "modern way of seeing," which is to see in "fragments." "To see reality in the light of certain underlying ideas has the undeniable advantage of giving shape and form to our experience." But this way is denied, as "misleading, demagogic"; supposedly, it represses "our energy" (*AST*, 124–25): "To be modern is to live, entranced, by the savage autonomy of the detail" (*AST*, 126).

III

To give Sontag's own underlying ideas more credence, listen to their inherent trajectory, which developed in her earlier work from her forties. Already she was championing the sense that what was gained with the new sensibility was also a loss: the rejection of the "metanarratives" was replenished by a world held in our heads as "an anthology of images" (*OP*, 3). *On Photography* was received by many in the photography community with yelps of complaint. "Against photography!" they cried. Indeed, the tone is austere. In few other places has her triangle of critical concerns been so axiomatic or so urgent. With this new "ethics of seeing" come new strains to the apprehension of truth and to the preparation for action. A little review here of that older book helps to refine her purpose in *Regarding the Pain of Others*. For instance, the condition of literature is not far from her mind:

A now notorious first fall into alienation, habituating people to abstract the world into printed words, is supposed to have engendered

that surplus of Faustian energy and psychic damage needed to build modern, inorganic societies. But print seems a less treacherous form of leaching out the world, of turning it into a mental object, than photographic images, which now provide most of the knowledge people have about the look of the past and the reach of the present. What is written about a person or an event is frankly an interpretation, as are handmade visual statements, like paintings and drawings. Photographed images do not seem to be statements about the world so much as pieces of it, miniatures of reality that anyone can make or acquire.
(*OP*, 4)

In the lights cast by the good, the true, and the beautiful, photography becomes "predatory," "voracious," though always "beautiful," even when photographers affect disdain for beauty, even when they emphasize humanism. For Sontag, this humanism is only a "variety" with which they replaced "the formalist justifications of their quest for beauty . . . [and which in turn] masks the confusion about truth and beauty underlying the photographic enterprise" (*OP*, 112).

Because the eye of the camera courses within our very veins, into all forms of surveillance, into all forms of commemoration, it begins to litter life with a newly demanding detritus of very partial understandings, indispensable now in almost every way, and in almost every way commanding. In discussing the art photograph, Sontag mentions that museums have played a role in their reception that cannot be "overestimated"; yet here, too, the extraordinarily rapid transformations and influences have blended criteria into the ubiquitous and indomitable category of the "interesting."

But it is now clear that there is no inherent conflict between the mechanical or naïve use of the camera and formal beauty of a very high order, no kind of photograph in which such beauty could not turn out to be present: an unassuming functional snapshot may be visually interesting, as eloquent, as beautiful as the most acclaimed fine-art photographs.
(*OP*, 103)

Unfortunately, for all this inclusive enthusiasm, what "makes something interesting is that it can be seen to be like, or analogous to, something else" (*OP*, 175.) Images invite circular thinking, endlessly: "The photographic recycling makes clichés out of unique objects, distinctive and vivid artifacts out of clichés. Images of real things are interlayered with images of images" (*OP*, 175).

Whereas reality is discrete, imbedded, and irreproducible, images can be flipped like playing cards; journals with many photographs are by definition "flip books"; any juxtaposition becomes relevant, exploitable. Photographs make the entire world "available as an object of appraisal" (*OP*, 110). Thus the kind of knowledge gained through still photographs will always be "knowledge at bargain prices—a semblance of knowledge, a semblance of wisdom; as the act of taking pictures is the semblance of appropriation, a semblance of rape" (*OP*, 24).

Can the good be saved for this fundamental enterprise of modernity, whose appetite for acquisition, for consuming and discarding, is dependent upon the stimulant of images? In one of Sontag's best demonstrations of her critical astuteness, she ponders why the Chinese protested Antonioni's film *Chung Kuo*. How could they be offended by the very shuffling of intimacy, perspective, and personalizing that we take for granted in a filmmaker's art? Because they are subject as a nation to the ethos of the "good," which now is "one kind of dictatorship, whose master idea is 'the good,' in which the most unsparing limits are placed on all forms of expression, including images." Don't be surprised if the future offers

> another kind of dictatorship, whose master idea is "the interesting," in which images of all sorts, stereotyped and eccentric, proliferate. . . . The only question is whether the function of the image-world created by the cameras could be other than it is. . . . The present function is clear enough, if one considers . . . what dependencies they create, what antagonisms they pacify—that is, what institutions they buttress, whose needs they really serve.
> (*OP*, 178–79)

Had Sontag's intimacy with photographs not been in rich attendance, *On Photography* would wilt into denunciation. Instead, her high demands on the form confirm her love for it, so that her criticisms are remembered as lyrical admonishments—a critique in the best meaning of the term. Nonetheless, probity judges images harshly—this now "interminable dossier" of present life.

It would be twenty years before Sontag published *Regarding the Pain of Others*. In the meantime, China radically redefined its ethos of the "good" in the direction of a boom in material life unprecedented in scale in human history. It, too, needs the continuous feed of the image-world, though not yet with the "no-holds-barred" variety of the West. Though the rules of public decorum and censorship modulate from culture to culture, state to state, vehicle to vehicle, instance to instance, Sontag confesses that her earlier call for an "ecology of images" has no chance now. Actually, it was a vague idea, suggesting a sustained fertility of mind and balance of influences, as if images could cooperate and prey upon one another like living creatures. But back in the 1970s, many saw in the new concept of "ecology" hope for all sorts of human-willed yet overly complex endeavors. If economists could start talking about economies as "ecosystems" why not images? The "why not" has been answered. There will not likely be an oversight commission directing truth in images as there has been a weak board directing truth in advertising. As in gestures such as "truth in media," the agenda could be rollicking in political witch-hunts. The digital/IT weltanschauung has melted away the chances for right thinking on any governance issues. (It is now scrambling to restore some of the faith in the veracity of the image by adventuring into computer software to detect pixel cloning, irrational lighting, and flash direction in the eyes of the subjects to help determine pure fakes—but of what consequence to most present uses of photos?)

So why return to the case of photography? One use of this form's influence cannot be dispensed with in what it may tell us, what it suggests or entices, what it may harden in us, and that is what we "see" when regarding the pain of others. The image world and the unquestionably moral importance of the reality it shadows nearly overlap. The tight correspondence reinvites the world; the imaginary can fly away from the lure of daydreaming on things so beautifully evoked and toward rescue. Those in need of our help quite possibly can break through the distancing effect of aesthetic apprehension perhaps better than they can the physical distance from the event of their suffering.

IV

In *Regarding the Pain of Others*, Sontag is looking for how truth can be told beautifully in the interests of awakening conscience, then sustained long enough before the deluge of ready-made cynicism. Her choices will have to be rarified to be aligned with the fullness of her worldly, politicized analyses. She has much to remind us of.

Sontag tells us about the first photograph of an atrocity that was staged as a photograph and meant to shame—unlike battle field assemblages of the period (all periods?), which were tainted by sentiments of patriotic sacrifice.

> Beato's image of the devastated Sikandarbagh Palace involved a more thorough arrangement of its subject, and was one of the first photographic depictions of the horrific in war. The attack had taken place in November 1857, after which the victorious British troops and loyal Indian units searched the palace room by room, bayoneting the eighteen hundred surviving Sepoy defenders who were now their prisoners and throwing their bodies into the courtyard; vultures and dogs did the rest. For the photograph he took in March or April 1858, Beato constructed the ruin as an unburial ground, stationing some natives by two pillars in the rear and distributing human bones about the courtyard. (*RP*, 54)

The most ancient sin of the victorious—the unburial of the enemy dead—was laid at the feet of the British; Beato had found the means to circumvent the apologist response, perhaps the prurient and the excitable as well.

Sontag remembers that Thatcher imposed heavier media control—allowing only two photojournalists and no direct TV transmissions—around the Falkland War (April–May 1982) than had been in effect since the Crimean: "It proved harder for the American authorities to duplicate the Thatcher controls on the reporting of their own foreign adventures" (*RP*, 65). But, of course, American authorities tried very hard. Her book discusses the revelations of Desert Storm (1991), the "misinformation and media corral" successes of the U.S. military, whose plots must have taken months of planning. These were "images of the techno war: the sky above the dying, filled with light-traces of missiles and shells—

images that illustrated America's absolute military superiority over its enemy . . . [while obscuring] the fate of thousands of Iraqi conscripts who, having fled Kuwait City at the end of the war, on February 27, were carpet bombed with explosives, napalm, radioactive DU (depleted uranium) rounds, and cluster bombs as they headed north, in convoys and on foot, on the road to Basra, Iraq" (*RP*, 66). She might have been a little out of the loop at this writing—only ten years after those events and still relatively early in the second Iraq War—not to draw more implications about the swelling of voices speaking against America's war crimes. These protesting voices cite this infamous "turkey shoot" as well as Abu Ghraib. About the pornography of the images from Abu Ghraib (in the essay "Regarding the Torture of Others"), she says: "For the meaning of these pictures is not just that these acts were performed but that their perpetrators apparently had no sense that there was anything wrong in what the pictures show" (*AST*, 135). "What is illustrated by these photographs is as much the culture of shamelessness as the reigning admiration for unapologetic brutality" (*AST*, 137).

In this work on photography, Sontag is more willing to engage the medium's documentary strengths because documents keep powerful people from making up "the world" as they want it to be perceived, even if they own its resources and wield most of its influence. Sontag must reengage photojournalism from this standpoint, but the older cautions are still in place. She reminds us of Ernst Jünger's relatively early (1930s) "irrepressible identification of the camera and the gun" (*RP*, 66). So she finds faint amusement at the qualms about real violence shown on TV news, for instance:

This novel insistence on good taste in a culture saturated with commercial incentives to lower standards of taste may be . . . understood as obscuring a host of concerns and anxieties about public order and public morale that cannot be named, as well as pointing to the inability otherwise to formulate or defend traditional conventions of how to mourn. What can be shown, what should be shown—few issues arouse more public clamor.
(*RP*, 68–69)

On Daniel Pearl's early 2002 death in Karachi, preserved on video by his executioners, she writes: "Notably, both sides treated the three and half minutes of horror only as a snuff film. Nobody could have learned from the debate that the video had other footage, a montage of stock accusations" (*RP*, 69).

And with her characteristic succinctness and directness, she forges key observations, one after another. On Europe: "horror seems to have vacated Europe, vacated it for long enough to make the present pacified state of affairs seem inevitable." That impression gave "the war in Bosnia and the Serb campaign of killing in Kosovo their special, anachronistic interest" (*RP*, 71–72).

She saw in the emblematic photographs of the destruction of the World Trade Center the use of the "sublime or awesome or tragic register of the beautiful" (*RP*, 75), in contrast to other people's remarks about their "surreal" impressions of the event, which she took to be a "hectic euphemism behind which the disgraced notion of beauty cowered" (*RP*, 76).

So much attention has been paid to the photograph as both a work of art and a document in the intervening years that proscriptions—not hers—have produced "remarkable exaggerations about what photographers ought or ought not to do—suffering shouldn't be beautiful, captions shouldn't moralize," and the spectacle should not be invoked. Yet, she writes, "the spectacular is very much part of the religious narratives by which suffering, throughout most of Western history, has been understood" (*RP*, 80). She notes with some sad astonishment that even this religious, sacred use is disappearing because of ignorance.

As if to correct whatever false impression there may remain about her relationship to image and reality, she points out that she was "not being that bad" as when André Glucksmann (and by extension Jean Baudrillard and Guy Debord) made the tendentious, metaphor-driven claim of war as media in his visit to Sarajevo. The city was then under siege; Sontag was there courageously helping to stage plays.[2] How particularly objectionable such facile "postmodernisms"—that war is a media event—can be when the bombs are falling and soldiers are bayoneting and citizens fear their neighbors, the open square, the roof falling in, starvation. They were starved also for images of what was happening to them and aware, with awful certainty, that the pain of others would be infused, for some considerable time, into the aftermath. Her thoughts had never taken flight into provocative swirls of language where the ground becomes distant, vague, and suspect.

The medium was never "the message" to Sontag, any more than illness was a metaphor. That which is immanent within photography's formal properties has to be part of understanding; the dynamics among object, purpose, and reception remain paramount. For example, photography needs to wend its way through the phenomenologically difficult emotion of "shock," which she begins to demonstrate. With such demonstrations, she asks that photography stay grounded, in the lifeworld, and be brave about doing so. For *Regarding the Pain of Others* proved to be Sontag's last antiwar statement, a continuation of the arguments of Virginia Woolf in *Three Guineas* with which she frames her opening discussion. She had no intention of allowing art, the artful dodger, to slip away into the surreal, not on the matter of war.

V

I will leave these necessarily overly schematized thoughts on Sontag's last essays with one final demonstration of what her project has been. I suppose it is inevitable that on the closing of such a vigorous life one finds the impression of the person in almost all of her far-reaching efforts. As she conceded about Roland Barthes in commemoration after his death in 1980, "He is the subject of all the subjects that he praises. (That he must, characteristically, praise may be connected with his project of defining, creating standards for himself.) In this sense, much of what Barthes wrote now appears autobiographical" (*WSF*, 84).

In her essay "Unextinguished: The Case for Victor Serge," she makes clear that his life and works could only have come from a revolutionary era that is, as Sontag says it is, "so discredited in a prosperous world." His life would not be exemplary, in another critic's hands. She makes it so, with a wonderful intimacy with his times. In a series of dialogic questions about the obscurity his work has fallen into, Sontag reflects upon these outpourings from an astonishing survivor of a punishing world, who "deplores but he does not regret. He has not given up on the idea of radical social change because of the totalitarian outcome of the Russian Revolution"—for which he fought and suffered (*AST*, 63). And then she asks, "Is [he obscure] because, embattled and defeated as he was, his literary work refused to take on the expected cargo of melancholy? His indomitability is not as attractive to us as more anguished reckoning. . . . It is a voice that forbids itself the requisite tones of despair or contrition or bewilderment—literary tones, as most people understand them—although Serge's own situation was increasingly grim" (*AST*, 64):

> In short, there was nothing, ever, triumphant about his life, as much that of the eternal poor student as the militant on the run—unless one excepts the triumph of being immensely gifted and industrious as a writer; the triumph of being principled and also astute and therefore incapable of keeping company with the faithful and the cravenly gullible and the merely hopeful; the triumph of being incorruptible as well as brave and therefore on a different, lonely path from the liars and the toadies and careerists; the triumph of being, after the early 1920s, right.
>
> (*AST*, 64)

Sontag sought to be right, in this fashion. If I have left the impression of a deep conservatism in the premises of her critical standards, I do so because those are the guideposts of a deeply political person who holds out hope and writes to those values. Her remarks on Gide and Sartre in this essay echo many she had made before on the problems of betraying one's greater insights for common causes and expedient interpretations of what is a useful position to hold in the present "stage of development." Perusal of most if not nearly all her political comments (with a few unfortunate quips aside) will reveal a consistent search for the higher grounds, a search to understand the world as it lies before her without worrying if she is keeping company with the faithful, without being distracted by the microphone that will likely be set before her. Consistently she has asked that we face down totalitarianism, face down cynicism, face down ignorance, face down moralizing that cannot grasp the ethics of freedom in the aesthetic, and do something about a world leveling its sensibilities into "insolence."

David Rieff, in his foreword to Sontag's posthumous collection, also sees the correspondence in his mother's political commitments (from "Vietnam to Iraq") from which she could not "wall herself off" in this evocation of Victor Serge's era, with which he believes she strongly identified. He then quotes her on that era's admirable qualities: "'its introspective energies and passionate intellectual quests and code of self-sacrifice and immense hope'" (*AST*, xvi). They are hers.

Notes

1. In a preface to a Spanish translation of *Against Interpretation*, entitled "Thirty Years Later," Sontag remarks that "the freedoms I espoused, the ardors I was advocating, seemed to me—still seem to be—quite traditional. I saw myself as a newly minted warrior in a very old battle against philistinism, against ethical and aesthetic shallowness and indifference. . . . The dedication and daring and absence of venality of the artists whose works mattered to me seemed, well, the way it was supposed to be. I thought it was normal that there be new masterpieces every month" (*WSF*, 269).

2. Sontag defends her choice of *Waiting for Godot*: "this is a great European play and they [the people of Sarajevo] are members of European culture. For all their attachment to American popular culture, it is the high culture of Europe that represents for them their ideal, their passport to European identity . . . [they stand] for European values—secularism, religious tolerance, and multi-ethnicity" (*WSF*, 303–4).

chaptertwelve

Susan Sontag, Cosmophage

WAYNE KOESTENBAUM

Susan Sontag, my prose's prime mover, ate the world. In 1963, on the subject of Sartre's *Saint Genet* (her finest ideas occasionally hinged on gay men), she wrote, "Corresponding to the primitive rite of anthropophagy, the eating of human beings, is the philosophical rite of cosmophagy, the eating of the world" (*AI*, 98). Cosmophagic, Sontag gobbled up sensations, genres, concepts. She swallowed political and aesthetic movements. She devoured roles: diplomat, filmmaker, scourge, novelist, gadfly, essayist, night owl, bibliophile, cineaste. . . . She tried to prove how much a human life—a writer's life—could include. Like Walter Benjamin, she was entranced by multiplicity, and, like him, she was an aphorist at heart, honing pluralities down to terse sentences not without Jamesian evasions and excesses. Again, Sontag on Sartre's *Genet*: "Jerking off the universe is perhaps what all philosophy, all abstract thought is about: an intense, and not very sociable pleasure, which has to be repeated again and again" (*AI*, 99). Thus in her Yeatsian tower she wrote, wrote, wrote; reiterating, she made writing's asocial motion pornographic—a subject on which she dilated in her essay "The Pornographic Imagination." Remember, she was no stranger to Mapplethorpe's milieu.

Transference: in the early 1990s, the night before I gave a lecture on Sontag's *Illness as Metaphor*, I dreamed that she reclined, wearing a pink miniskirt, on her living-room couch. I've had dozens of Sontag dreams, in which she represents intellectuality's phantasmagoria, prose's succulence, quality's fearsomeness, and aphorism's bite.

The first time I saw Sontag in person, she was speaking at a Samuel Beckett homage in the 1980s. Listening to her eloquent presentation, I whispered to my boyfriend, "Susan Sontag's got a crush on me." I meant the reverse: "I have a crush on Susan Sontag." Instinctive, preposterous substitution: for an instant, Sontag-besotted, I ate the world.

My essays would not be mine without the influence of her prose's Mercurochrome aesthetic, her stern, self-conscious, tense sentences.

The ends of her novels are the best parts. Closure sharpened Sontag's scalpel. The last three sentences of *The Volcano Lover*: "They thought they were civilized. They were despicable. Damn them all." The last two sentences of *Death Kit*: "Diddy has made his final chart; drawn up his last map. Diddy has perceived the inventory of the world." The last sentence of *The Benefactor*: "You may imagine me in a bare room, my feet near the stove, bundled up in many sweaters, my black hair turned grey, enjoying the waning tribulations of subjectivity and the repose of a privacy that is genuine." And here are the concluding lines of her 2001 essay "Where the Stress Falls": "Nothing new except language, the ever found. Cauterizing the torment of personal relations with hot lexical choices, jumpy punctuation, mercurial sentence rhythms. Devising more subtle, more engorged ways of knowing, of sympathizing, of keeping at bay. It's a matter of adjectives. It's where the stress falls." Dig the word *engorged*. Like Jean Rhys, Sontag kept rules and torments at bay by generating stressed prose—magnifying, through emphasis and engorgement, the opportunities for attentiveness.

In her first novel, *The Benefactor*, published in 1963, a year before "Notes on Camp," she wrote the following sentence: "I am a homosexual and a writer, both of whom are professionally self-regarding and self-esteeming creatures." Admittedly, this line occurs in the voice of her character, Jean-Jacques. But Susan wrote the sentence, not Jean-Jacques. *I am a homosexual and a writer*. Each of her books and essays contains a similar coded declaration. Sontag "came out" in her own way, forcibly, repeatedly. Her seeming refusal of queer identity may have enraged others (e.g., Adrienne Rich's 1975 quarrel with Sontag—supposedly on the subject of Leni Riefenstahl but covertly on the subject of feminist and lesbian identification—on the letters page of the *New York Review of Books*), but in retrospect Sontag's reticence seems picturesque, contrarian, and human. And it did not preclude admiration for Gay Lib, even if her theory of sexuality emphasized the saturnine, not the cheerful. Listen to her admiration (in a 1972 essay) of poet and social critic Paul Goodman's erotic forthrightness: "I admired his courage, which showed itself in so many ways—one of the most admirable being his honesty about his homosexuality in *Five Years*, for which he was much criticized by his straight friends in the New York intellectual world; that was six years ago, before the advent of Gay Liberation made coming out of the closet chic. I liked it when he talked about himself and when he mingled his own sad sexual desires with his desire for the polity" (*USS*, 9–10). *Sad* sexual desires? Allow Sontag that adjective's aptness.

Sontag spoke up on hot-spot issues (Bosnia, 9/11, racism, Vietnam) and was indiscriminately pilloried by Right and Left for her quirky, vatic pronouncements. Like her idol Antonin Artaud, she wanted to be a creature of passion, not reason: her positions, even when logically worded, subtly dismantled sensibleness. Responsible intellectual statements weren't her forte; her temperament demanded rash, provisional utterances. In a 1975 interview, first published in *Salmagundi*, she defended the intellectual's right to be partial: "people who reason in public have—and ought to exercise—options about how many and how complex are the points they want to make. And where, in what form, and to what audience they make them" (*CSS*, 62). After her death, only a few obituaries referred to her as a feminist. In the *Salmagundi* interview, she defended her sexual politics: "I'd like to see a few platoons of intellectuals who are also feminists doing their bit in the war against misogyny in their own way, letting the feminist implications be residual or implicit in their work, without risking being charged by their sisters with desertion. I don't like party lines. They make for intellectual monotony and bad prose" (*CSS*, 62). Though Sontag and Rich argued in print, they had much in common; as essayists, they knew how to be intimately magisterial, definitively tentative. And Sontag, like certain other sisters, among them Joan Didion and Avital Ronell, threw away security and pusillanimousness for the sake of daredevil phrases.

Sontag's credo: *move on*. The phrase comes from her grief-ennobled, expansive essay on her friend Roland Barthes: "The aesthete's radicalism: to be multiple, to make multiple identifications; to assume fully the privilege of the personal. . . . The writer's freedom that Barthes describes is, in part, flight. The writer is the deputy of his own ego—of that self in perpetual flight before what is fixed before writing, as the mind is in perpetual flight from doctrine. 'Who *speaks* is not who *writes*, and who *writes* is not who *is*.' Barthes wants to move on—that is one of the imperatives of the aesthete's sensibility" (*WSF*, 84). Move on, Sontag urged. Leave the field untilled. Switch projects. Change hemispheres. Make a film. Direct a play. Write a novel. Fly to Hanoi. Nonspecialist, she refused restriction, scorned the limiting identity of expert. She would rather have been considered a collector, connoisseur, sad pervert—anything but an academic.

Sontag achieved her customary tone of passionate detachment by refusing academic thoroughness. As writer she was solely self-commanded, not taking editorial orders, obeying only her own momentary or abiding enthusiasms: Fassbinder, Robert Walser, Marina Tsvetaeva, *bunraku*, Alice James . . . So what if she stopped endorsing a certain strain of countercultural American art and experience (Jack Smith, Happenings, drugs, science fiction) and turned toward sober European and Asian pleasures? She loved fragments; her finest fictions and essays use the fragment as heuristic device and as musical measurement. In this predilection, she was influenced by Benjamin and Barthes, though I imagine that these writers merely confirmed her native inclinations. And, like Benjamin and Barthes, she respected philosophy and social criticism as forms of *writing*; though she never (to my knowledge) referred to Derrida, they shared a genealogy, a set of assumptions—above all, a respect for any text's unruly, tricky self-contradictions. Sontag is usually cited for her content rather than her form or style, and yet her paragraphs and sentences bear close and admiring scrutiny as exemplars of experimental writing: avatar of *move on*, she sought prose forms that would permit maximum drift and detour.

Fiction was one escape ramp; she used it to flee the punitive confines of the essay. And she used essays to flee the connect-the-dots dreariness of fiction. Her essays behave like fictions (disguised, arch, upholstered with attitudes), while her fictions behave like essays (pontificating, pedagogic, discursive).

At no other writer's name can I stare entranced for hours on end—only Susan Sontag's. She lived up to that fabulous appellation. No wonder Joseph Cornell loved her. He made a collage (*The Ellipsian*, 1966) incorporating a photograph of her (see fig. 9) and courted her, in his fashion. Attuned to synchronicity, he believed that Henriette Sontag, nineteenth-century opera diva, led to the modern Susan. The second Sontag must have savored her own iconicity, a notoriety ensured by her severe good looks and by a style of intelligence (intelligence as style) that seemed a mode of locomotion (how to get through Western Thought without stopping for traffic lights) as much as a *project*—one of her favorite words. Stardom was one project she pursued. See her 1963 essay on Resnais's *Muriel*, especially this footnote: "In this film (but not in *Marienbad*), Seyrig has the nourishing irrelevant panoply of mannerisms of a star, in the peculiarly cinematic sense of that word. That is to say, she doesn't simply play (or even perfectly fill) a role. She becomes an independent aesthetic object in herself. Each detail of her appearance—her graying hair, her tilted loping walk, her wide-brimmed hats and smartly dowdy suits, her gauche manner in enthusiasm and regret—is unnecessary and indelible" (*AI*, 240n). Here is Sontag's brief theory of stardom: *unnecessary and indelible*. Those antithetical adjectives recall the concluding lines of Elizabeth Bishop's poem "The Bight": "All the untidy activity continues, / awful but cheerful." Another Bishop poem about placelessness gave placeless Sontag—Hollywood? Hanoi? Sarajevo? Manhattan?—the epigraph for her last collection, *Where the Stress Falls*. Sontag belongs with Bishop in that constellation of brilliant aesthetes, mostly women, whose public positions on sexual eccentricity were, shall we say, complex.

Adventurous as Tarzan, Sontag consecrated her life to the task of being exemplary; consciousness, for her, was a grand experiment, a spiritual vocation, like Simone Weil's. Such lives leave always a sense of the unfinished. Naturally, Benjamin's incomplete *Arcades Project* ghosts Sontag's work, not least her autobiographical short story "Project for a Trip to China," the only thing she wrote about her longing for her dead father.

"Authority, idiosyncrasy, velvetiness—these are what make a star": from Sontag's *In America* (352–53). I wonder what Sontag means by "velvetiness." Velvety complexion? Velvety aura? Velvety effect on beholders? Is *velvet* the zone the spectator steps into when watching a film? Is velvet the trance state of the reader who experiences identification?

Figure 9 Joseph Cornell, *The Ellipsian* (1966). *Source*: Courtesy the estate of Joseph Cornell, VAGA Rights.

Does velvet—as an emotion—precede initiation into the echo chamber of *I, Etcetera*, the replication booth of Sontag-admiration?

So far I've failed to mention cancer, AIDS, photography, atrocity—four of her major subjects. She was comfortable staring at apocalypse. She cut her critical teeth on the Six Million and the Atom Bomb. From horrors, she learned what mattered.

In 1968 she described Jean-Luc Godard's art as "a cinema that eats cinema." Cosmophagic, cinematophagic, bibliophagic, Sontag's literature ate literature—and ate itself. No wonder she enjoyed Bataille, Leiris, Sade, and other savants of the mind consuming itself, and no wonder she had a nose for intertextuality. She alluded to it when defending herself against silly charges of plagiarism: "There's a larger argument to be made that all of literature is a series of references and allusions."

Sontag was a shameless apologist for aesthetic pleasure. Accordingly, I revere her essays not only for what they say but for how they say it. The *essay*, in Sontag's hands, became perilously interesting, governed by caprice masquerading as commentary. Her capriciousness, like foppish fiction maverick Ronald Firbank's, turned on the dime of the sentence, that unit of fidelity to the "now," to contemporaneous duration. Sentence maven, she enmeshes me still: in her prose's hands I'm a prisoner of desire, yearning for a literary art that knows no distinction between captive and captor. Such art can be sadomasochistic in its charm, its coldness, and its vulnerability.

She died on December 28, 2004. A few days later, I began rereading André Breton in private tribute to Sontag, who loved French seriousness, even when it was surreal. On January 1, 2005, imitating Sontag, I saw a new print of Antonioni's *L'Avventura* screened at MOMA. Daily, Sontag's spirit exhorts me: *Move on! Eat the world!* In 2005, everything I do, say, read, and write will be an oblique elegy to her attainments and postures. My Susan Sontag Commemoration Project begins here.

Bibliography

Acocella, Joan. "The Hunger Artist." *New Yorker*, March 6, 2000, 68–77.

Allen, Woody. *Zelig*. Feature film. Orion Pictures, 1983. DVD: MGM, 2001.

Angell, Callie. *Andy Warhol Screen Tests: The Films of Andy Warhol: Catalogue Raisonné*. Vol. 1. New York: Abrams, 2006.

Barthes, Roland. *Camera Lucida*. Trans. Richard Howard. New York: Hill and Wang, 1981.

——. *S/Z*. Trans. Richard Howard. New York: Hill and Wang, 1970.

——. *Writing Degree Zero*. Trans. Richard Howard. New York: Hill and Wang, 1968.

Bawer, Bruce. "That Sontag Woman." *New Criterion* 10, no. 9 (May 1992): 10–17.

Bergman, David, ed. *Camp Grounds: Style and Homosexuality*. Amherst: University of Massachusetts Press, 1993.

Berman, Paul. "On Susan Sontag." *Dissent* (Spring 2005): 109–12.

Bockris, Victor. "Susan Sontag: The Dark Lady of Pop Philosophy." *High Times*, March 28, 1973, 20–37.

Brackman, Jacob. *The Put-On: Modern Fooling and Modern Mistrust*. Chicago: Henry Regnery, 1971.

Brockes, Emma. "My Time With Susan." Interview with Annie Leibovitz. *The Guardian*, October 7, 2006, 18–35.

Brooke-Rose, Christine. "Eximplosions." *Genre* 14 (1981): 9–21.

Brooks, Peter. "Death of/as Metaphor." *Partisan Review* 46 (1979): 438–44.

Bruss, Elizabeth. *Beautiful Theories: The Spectacle of Discourse in Contemporary Criticism.* Baltimore, Md.: Johns Hopkins University Press, 1982.

Caraval, Doreen. "So Whose Words Are They: Susan Sontag Creates a Stir." *New York Times*, May 27, 2000.

Cathcart, Michael. "Interview with Susan Sontag." Radio National, February 6, 2000. www.abc.net.au/rn/atoday/stories/s133826.htm.

Chan, Evans. "Against Postmodernism, Etcetera—a Conversation with Susan Sontag." http://www.iath.virginia.edu/pmc/text-only/issue.901/12.1chan.txt.

Chapier, Henri. Review of *Les Gémeaux. Combat* (Paris), January 24, 1973.

The Charlie Rose Show. "A Remembrance of Intellectual Susan Sontag." PBS. Broadcast January 7, 2005. Archived at http://www.charlierose.com/view/interview/1098.

Chatwin, Bruce. "Howard Hodgkin: Indian Leaves." In *Writers on Howard Hodgkin*, ed. Enrique Juncosa, 57–67. Dublin: Irish Museum of Modern Art, 2006.

Ching, Barbara. "High Regard: Words and Pictures in Tribute to Susan Sontag." *American Quarterly* 59, no. 1 (2007): 157–64.

Cleto, Fabio. Introduction to *Camp: Queer Aesthetics and the Performing Subject*, ed. Cleto, 1–42. Ann Arbor: University of Michigan Press, 1999.

Creed, Gerald W., and Barbara Ching. "Recognizing Rusticity: Identity and the Power of Place." In *Knowing Your Place: Rural Identity and Cultural Hierarchy*, ed. Barbara Ching and Gerald W. Creed, 1–38. New York: Routledge, 1997.

Cruse, Harold. *The Crisis of the Negro Intellectual.* New York: William Morrow, 1967.

Danto, Arthur Coleman. "The Abuse of Beauty." *Daedalus* 131, no. 4 (2002): 35–57.

Deleuze, Gilles. *Proust and Signs.* 1964. Trans. Richard Howard. New York: George Braziller, 1972.

Denby, David. "The Moviegoer: Susan Sontag's Life in Film." *New Yorker*, September 12, 2005. http://www.newyorker.com/archive/2005/09/12/050912crat_atlarge.

Denning, Michael. *The Cultural Front: The Laboring of American Culture in the Twentieth Century.* London: Verso, 1996.

Derrida, Jacques. "The Theatre of Cruelty and the Closure of Representation." In *Writing and Difference*, trans. Alan Bass, 232–50. Chicago: University of Chicago Press, 1978.

Dolan, Jill. Introduction to the special issue "Utopian Performatives." *Modern Drama* 47 (2004): 165–76.

———. "Performance, Utopia, and the 'Utopian Performative.'" *Theatre Journal* 53 (2001): 455–79.

——. *Presence and Desire: Essays on Gender, Sexuality, Performance*. Ann Arbor: University of Michigan Press, 1993.

Dosse, François. *A History of Structuralism*. Trans. Deborah Glassman. 2 vols. Minneapolis: University of Minnesota Press, 1997.

Douin, Jean-Luc. "Les Gémeaux." *Télérama*, February 3, 1973.

Du Bois, W. E. B. *The Souls of Black Folk: Essays and Sketches*. Chicago: A. C. McGlurg & Co., 1903.

Dyer, Richard. *Only Entertainment*. New York: Routledge, 1992.

Elderfield, John, and Howard Hodgkin. "An Exchange." In *Howard Hodgkin Paintings*, by Michael Auping, Johen Elderfield, and Susan Sontag, 65–80. New York: Harry N. Abrams, 1995.

Farnsworth, Elizabeth. "Conversation: Susan Sontag." Interview, *News-Hour with Jim Lehrer*, February 2, 2001. http://www.pbs.org/newshour/conversation/jan-june01/sontag_02-02.html.

Feingold, Michael. "Pity the Poor Theater, Sick and Bedridden—Except When It Gets Up to Dance." *Village Voice*, November 21, 2000, 79.

Fiske, John. *Media Matters: Everyday Culture and Political Change*. Minneapolis: University of Minnesota Press, 1994.

Galvin, Cathy. "Archive: The Intimate Secrets of Susan Sontag." *Times* (London), May 25, 2008.

Garis, Leslie. "Susan Sontag Finds Romance." *New York Times*, August 2, 1992.

Gorman, Paul. *Left Intellectuals and Popular Culture in Twentieth-Century America*. Chapel Hill: University of North Carolina Press, 1996.

Hayes, Julie C. "Fictions of Enlightenment: Sontag, Süskind, Norfolk, Kurz-weil." *Bucknell Review: A Scholarly Journal of Letters, Arts and Sciences* 41 (1998): 21–36.

Hofstadter, Richard. *Anti-Intellectualism in American Life* . New York: Knopf, 1963.

Hollander, Paul. *Political Pilgrims: Travels of Western Intellectuals to the Soviet Union, China, and Cuba, 1928–1978*. New York: Oxford University Press, 1981.

Howard, Gerald. Introduction to *The Sixties: The Art, Politics, and Media of Our Most Explosive Decade*, ed. Howard, 1–55. 1982. New York: Marlow, 1995.

Hughes, Robert. "Gliding Over a Dying Reef—the Venice Biennale." *Time*, July 2, 1984, 76–77.

Iannone, Carol. "At Play with Susan Sontag." *Commentary* 111 (February 2001): 55–58.

Ibsen, Henrik. *The Lady from the Sea*. In *A Doll's House, The Wild Duck, The Lady from the Sea*, trans. R. Farquharson Sharp and Eleanor Marx-Aveling; rev. Torgrim and Linda Hannas. 1910. London: J. M. Dent, 1985.

James, C. L. R. *American Civilization*. Ed. Anna Grimshaw and Keith Hart. Cambridge, Mass.: Blackwell, 1993.

Jameson, Fredric. *Archaeologies of the Future: The Desire Called Utopia and Other Science Fictions*. New York: Verso, 2005.

Kakatuni, Michiko. "'In America': Love a Distraction That Gets in the Way of Art." Review. *New York Times*, February 29, 2000. www.nytimes.com/library/books/-022900sontag-book-review.html.

Kaplan, E. Ann. *Trauma Culture: The Politics of Terror and Loss in Media and Literature*. New Brunswick, N.J.: Rutgers University Press, 2005.

——. "Women, Trauma, and Late Modernity: Sontag and Duras, 1960–1980." Paper presented at the Society for Cinema and Media Conference, Philadelphia, March 8, 2008.

Kennedy, Liam. "Precocious Archaeology: Susan Sontag and the Criticism of Culture." *Journal of American Studies* 24 (1990): 23–39.

——. *Susan Sontag: Mind as Passion*. New York: Palgrave Macmillan, 1997.

Kerr, Sarah. Review of *In America*. March 12, 2000. www.nytimes.com/books/00/-03/12/reviews000312.12kerrlt/html.

Kramer, Larry. *Reports from the Holocaust: The Story of an AIDS Activist*. New York: St. Martin Press, 1989.

Kroll, Jack. Interview with Susan Sontag and Agnés Varda. *Camera Three*, host Jim McAndrew, prod./dir. Merrill Brockway, writer Stephan Chodorov, CBS-TV, October 12, 1969. Videocassette, Creative Arts Television Archive, Kent, Conn., 1977.

Kruger, Steven F. *AIDS Narratives: Gender, Sexuality, Fiction, and Science*. London: Garland, 1996.

Langer, Susanne K. *Feeling and Form*. New York: Scribner's, 1953.

Leibovitz, Annie. *A Photographer's Life, 1990–2005*. New York: Random House, 2006.

——. *Women*. Photographs. Essay by Susan Sontag. New York: Random House, 1999.

Luketic, Robert. *Legally Blonde*. Feature film. Metro-Goldwyn-Mayer, 2001. DVD: MGM, 2001.

Marcuse, Herbert. *One-Dimensional Man: Studies in the Ideology of Advanced Industrial Society*. Boston: Beacon, 1964.

——. "Repressive Tolerance." In *A Critique of Pure Tolerance*, by Herbert Marcuse, Barrington Moore Jr., and Robert Paul Wolff, 95–137. Boston: Basic Books, 1969.

Marin, Louis. "Frontiers of Utopia: Past and Present." *Critical Inquiry* 19 (1993): 397–420.

Marranca, Bonnie, and Gautam Dasgupta. "Art and Consciousness." *Performing Arts Journal* 80 (2005): 1–9.

Marx, Leo. *The Pilot and the Passenger: Essays on Literature, Technology, and Culture in the United States*. New York: Oxford, 1988.

Massumi, Brian. "The Autonomy of Affect." *Cultural Critique* 31 (1995): 83–109.

Mauriac, Claude. "Les blessures de l'amour." Review of *Brother Carl*, *Express* (Paris), January 29, 1973.

Mazars, Pierre. "Les Gémeaux." *Figaro* (Paris), February 12, 1973.

McGuigan, Cathleen. "An Exclusive Look at Annie Leibovitz's Compelling—and Surprisingly Personal—New Book." *Newsweek*, October 2, 2006, 44–62.

McRobbie, Angela. "The Modernist Style of Susan Sontag." *Feminist Review* 38 (1991): 1–19.

———. "Susan Sontag: Modernist Style." In *Postmodernism and Popular Culture*, 77–95. New York: Routledge, 1994.

Merkin, Daphne. "The Dark Lady of the Intellectuals." *New York Times Book Review*, October 29, 2000.

Meyer, Moe, ed. *The Politics and Poetics of Camp*. New York: Routledge, 1997.

Meyer, Sara. "Susan Sontag's 'Archeology of Longings.'" *Texas Studies in Literature and Language* 49, no. 1 (Spring 2007): 45–63.

Miller, Nancy K. "Theories and Methodologies: Regarding Susan Sontag." *PMLA* 120, no. 3 (May 2005): 828–33.

Mills, C. Wright. *Power, Politics, and People: The Collected Essays*. New York: Oxford University Press, 1963.

Monette, Paul. *Borrowed Time: An AIDS Memoir*. San Diego: Harcourt Brace Jovanovich, 1988.

Morris, David. "Postmodern Pain." In *Heterotopia: Postmodern Utopia and the Body Politic*, ed. Tobin Siebers, 150–73. Ann Arbor: University of Michigan Press.

Morris, William. *News from Nowhere; Or, an Epoch of Rest: Being Some Chapters from a Utopian Romance*. 1890. Ed. Krishan Kumar. Cambridge: Cambridge University Press, 1995.

Munk, Erika. "Only the Possible: An Interview with Susan Sontag." *Theater* 24 (1993): 31–36.

Myers, Kevin. "I Wish I Had Kicked Susan Sontag." Telegraph.co.uk, January 2, 2005, http://www.telegraph.co.uk/comment/3613939/I-wish-I-had-kicked-Susan-Sontag.html.

Nelson, Cary. "Reading Criticism." *PMLA* 91, no. 5 (October 1976): 801–15.

———. "Soliciting Self-Knowledge: The Rhetoric of Susan Sontag's Criticism." *Critical Inquiry* 6, no. 4 (Summer 1980): 707–26.

Nunez, Sigrid. "Sontag Laughs." *Salmagundi*, no. 152 (2006): 11–19.

O'Brien, Charles. "Sontag's Erotics of Film Style: Between Meaning and Presence." *Post Script* 26, no. 2 (Winter–Spring 2007): 41–52.

Oppenheim, Louis. "Playing with Beckett's Plays: On Sontag in Sarajevo and Other Directorial Infidelities." *Journal of Beckett Studies* 4, no. 2 (1995): 35–46.

Paulson, Steve. "Sontag's Final Wish." Interview with David Rieff. *Salon*, February 13, 2008. http://www.salon.com/books/feature/2008/02/13/david_rieff/index1.html.

Peucker, Brigitte. "Looking and Touching: Spectacle and Collection in Sontag's *Volcano Lover*." *Yale Journal of Criticism* 11, no. 1 (1998): 159–65.

Pirandello, Luigi. *As You Desire Me*. Trans. Samuel Putnam. New York: Dutton, 1931.

Poague, Leland, ed. *Conversations with Susan Sontag*. Jackson: University Press of Mississippi, 1995.

Poague, Leland, and Kathy A. Parsons. *Susan Sontag: An Annotated Bibliography 1948–1992*. New York: Garland, 2000.

Rabkin, Gerald. "Milan and His Master." *Performing Arts Journal* 9, no. 1 (1985): 17–24.

Ricouer, Paul. *The Rule of Metaphor: Multi-disciplinary Studies of the Creation of Meaning in Language*. 1977. London: Routledge, 1978.

Rieff, David. *Swimming in a Sea of Death: A Son's Memoir*. New York: Simon and Shuster, 2008.

Rieff, Philip. *Freud: The Mind of a Moralist*. New York: Viking, 1959.

Robertson, Pamela. *Guilty Pleasures: Feminist Camp from Mae West to Madonna*. Durham, N.C.: Duke University Press, 1996.

Roemer, Kenneth. "Defining America as Utopia." In *America as Utopia*, ed. Kenneth Roemer, 1–15. New York: Burt Franklin, 1981.

Rollyson, Carl. *Reading Susan Sontag: A Critical Introduction to Her Work*. Chicago: Ivan R. Dee, 2001.

Rollyson, Carl, and Lisa Paddock. *Susan Sontag: The Making of an Icon*. New York: Norton, 2000.

Ross, Andrew. *No Respect: Intellectuals and Popular Culture*. New York: Routledge, 1989.

———. "Uses of Camp." In *No Respect: Intellectuals and Popular Culture*, 135–170. New York: Routledge, 1989.

Ruas, Charles. *Conversations with American Writers*. New York: Knopf, 1985.

Sayres, Sohnya. "For Susan Sontag, 1933–2004." *PMLA* 120, no. 3 (May 2005): 834–38.

———. *Susan Sontag: The Elegiac Modernist*. New York: Routledge, 1990.

Sennett, Richard, and Jonathan Cobb. *The Hidden Injuries of Class*. New York: Knopf, 1972.

Shelton, Ron. *Bull Durham*. Feature film. Orion Pictures, 1988. DVD: MGM, 2002.

Showalter, Elaine. *Inventing Herself: Claiming a Feminist Intellectual Heritage*. New York: Scribner's, 2001.

Siebers, Tobin, ed. *Heterotopia: Postmodern Utopia and the Body Politic*. Ann Arbor: University of Michigan Press, 1995.

———. "Introduction." In *Heterotopia: Postmodern Utopia and the Body Politic*, ed. Siebers, 1–38. Ann Arbor: University of Michigan Press, 1995.

Silverblatt, Michael. "For You O Democracy." *Los Angeles Times Book Review*, February 27, 2000, 1–2.

Sklar, Judith. "What Is the Use of Utopia?" In *Heterotopia: Postmodern Utopia and the Body Politic*, ed. Tobin Siebers, 40–57. Ann Arbor: University of Michigan Press, 1995.

Soloski, Alexis. "A Parsifal." *Village Voice* 51, no. 9 (March 1–7, 2006): C59.

Solotaroff, Ted. "Interpreting Susan Sontag." In *The Red Hot Vacuum and Other Pieces of Writing of the Sixties*, 261–68. New York: Atheneum, 1970.

Sontag, Susan. "Afterword: Thirty Years After. . . ." 1996. In *Against Interpretation and Other Essays*, 305–12. New York: Macmillan, 2001.

———. *Against Interpretation*. New York: Farrar, Straus and Giroux, 1966.

———. *Alice in Bed: A Play in Eight Scenes*. New York: Farrar, Straus and Giroux, 1993.

———. *At the Same Time: Essays and Speeches*. Ed. Paolo Dilonardo and Anne Jump. New York: Farrar, Straus and Giroux, 2007.

———. "Beauty: How Will It Change Next?" *Vogue* (May 1975): 116–17, 174.

———. *The Benefactor: A Novel*. 1963. New York: Picador USA, 2002.

———. *Brother Carl*. Feature film. 97 minutes. Göran Lindgren for Sandrew Film and Teatre (AB), Sweden, 1971. In Swedish with English soundtrack.

———. *Brother Carl: A Filmscript*. New York: Farrar, Straus and Giroux, 1974.

———. "The Double Standard of Aging." *Saturday Review*, September 23, 1972, 29–38.

———. *Duet for Cannibals*. Feature Film. 105 minutes. Writer/director Susan Sontag. Producer Göran Lindgren for Sandrew Film and Teater (AB) Sweden, 1969. In Swedish, subtitles by Sontag.

———. *I, Etcetera*. New York: Farrar Straus Giroux, 1978.

———. *Illness as Metaphor and Aids and Its Metaphors*. New York: Anchor Books, 1989.

———. *In America: A Novel*. New York: Farrar Straus Giroux, 2000.

———. Interview. "Susan Sontag: The Art of Fiction CLXIII." *Paris Review* (Winter 1995): 177–209.

———. Introduction to *Antonin Artaud: Selected Writings*, trans. Helen Weaver, xvii–lix. New York: Farrar, Straus and Giroux, 1976.

———. Introduction to *A Barthes Reader*, ed. Susan Sontag, vii–xxxviii. New York: Hill and Wang, 1982.

———. *Lady from the Sea*. *Theater* 29, no. 1 (1999): 93–115.

———. Liner notes to *Land*, by Patti Smith (1975). Arista 07822-14708-2 (2002).

———. "Literature Is Freedom." Speech upon receipt of the Friedenspreis des Deutschen Buchhandels (Peace Prize of the German Book Trade). October 28, 2003.

——. *On Photography*. New York, Farrar, Straus and Giroux, 1977.

——. "On Self: From the Notebooks and Diaries of Susan Sontag, 1958–67." *New York Times Magazine*, September 10, 2006, 52–58.

——. *A Parsifal. Antaeus* 67, no. 3 (1991): 180–85.

——. "Pilgrimage." *New Yorker*, December 21, 1987, 38–54.

——. Preface to *Plays: Maria Irene Fornes*. New York: PAJ, 1986.

——. *Promised Lands*. Documentary film. 87 minutes. Assistant director David Rieff. Prod. Nicole Stéphane. Distributed by New Yorker Films, New York, 1974.

——. "Réflèxions sur la Liberation des Femmes." *Les Temps Modernes* (1972): 907–44.

——. *Regarding the Pain of Others*. New York: Farrar, Straus and Giroux, 2003.

——. "Regarding the Torture of Others." *New York Times Magazine*, May 23, 2004.

——. "Rewriting *The Lady from the Sea*." *Theater* 29, no. 1 (1999): 89–91.

——. [Koff, Calvin.] "Some Notes on Antonioni and Others." Reprint, intro. Colin Burnett. *Post Script* 26, no. 2 (Winter–Spring 2007): 137–142.

——. "Some Thoughts on the Right Way (for Us) to Love the Cuban Revolution." In *Divided We Stand*, ed. the Editors of *Ramparts* with Richard H. Dodge, 164–70. San Francisco: Canfield Press, 1970.

——. *Styles of Radical Will*. New York: Farrar, Straus and Giroux, 1966.

——. *A Susan Sontag Reader*. Intro. Elizabeth Hardwick. 1963. New York: Vintage Books, 1982.

——. "The Third World of Women." *Partisan Review* (Spring 1973): 180–206.

——. *Under the Sign of Saturn*. New York: Farrar, Straus and Giroux, 1980.

——. *Unguided Tour*. Feature film. 72 minutes. Writer/director Sontag. Prod. Giovannella Zannoni. Produced by Lunga Cittata Cooperative, RAI channel 3, Italy, 1983.

——. *The Volcano Lover: A Romance*. 1992. New York: Anchor Books, 2003.

——. "*Waiting for Godot* in Sarajevo." *Performing Arts Journal* 47 (May 1994): 87–106.

——. "The Way We Live Now." *New Yorker*, November 24, 1986, 42–51.

——. *The Way We Live Now*. Illus. Howard Hodgkin. London: Jonathan Cape, 1991.

——. *The Way We Live Now*. Illus. Howard Hodgkin. Lim. ed. London: Karsten Schubert, 1991.

——. *Where the Stress Falls: Essays*. New York: Picador USA, 2001.

——. "A Woman's Beauty: Put-Down or Power Source?" *Vogue* (April 1975): 118–19.

Sontag, Susan, and David Rieff, "Notes on Optimism." *Vogue* (January 1975): 100, 148, 154.

Stacey, Jackie. *Teratologies: A Cultural Study of Cancer*. London: Routledge, 1997.

Suleiman, Susan Rubin. "Culture, Aestheticism, and Ethics: Sontag and the 'Idea of Europe.'" *PMLA* 120, no. 3 (May 2005): 839–42.

Sylvester, David. "Interview with Howard Hodgkin." In *Howard Hodgkin: Forty Paintings 1973–1984*, ed. John McEwen and David Sylvester, 97–106. London: Whitechapel Art Gallery, 1984.

Wagner-Lawlor, Jennifer. "The Play of Irony: Theatricality and Utopian Transformation in Contemporary Women's Speculative Fiction." *Utopian Studies* 13 (2002): 114–34.

Wang, Jennifer Hyland. "A Struggle of Contending Stories: Race, Gender, and Political Memory in *Forrest Gump*." *Cinema Journal* 39, no. 3 (2000): 92–115.

Watney, Simon. "Sense and Less Than Sense about AIDS." *Guardian Weekly*, March 26, 1989.

Warhol, Andy, and Pat Hackett. *POPism: The Warhol '60s*. New York: Harcourt Brace Jovanovich, 1980.

Wells, Sandy. "Susan Sontag." Youtube.com. Posted March 24, 2007. http://www.youtube.com/watch?v=81cgYC5056Y.

Willis, Ellen. "Three Elegies for Susan Sontag." *New Politics* 10, no. 3 (2005), http://www.wpunj.edu/~newpol/issue39/Willis39.htm.

Wiseman, Susan. "'Femininity' and the Intellectual in Sontag and Cixous." In *The Body and the Text: Hélène Cixous, Reading and Teaching*, ed. Helen Wilcox et al., 98–113. New York: Harvester/Wheatsheaf, 1990.

Wolin, Richard. "September 11 and the Self-Castigating Left." *South Central Review* 19, no. 2/3 (2002): 39–49.

Wood, James. "The Palpable Past-Intimate." *New Republic*, March 27, 2000. www.powells.com/review/2001_07_26.html.

Wood, Michael. "Susan Sontag and the American Will." *Raritan* 21, no. 1 (Summer 2001): 141–47.

Zanker, Paul. *The Mask of Socrates: The Image of the Intellectual in Antiquity*. Trans. Alan Shapiro. Berkeley: University of California Press, 1995.

Contributors

TERRY CASTLE is the Walter A. Haas Professor in the Humanities at Stanford University. A cultural critic and scholar, Castle was once described by Susan Sontag as "the most expressive, most enlightening literary critic at large today." She specializes in the history of the novel, especially the works of Defoe, Richardson, and Fielding, and in the study of eighteenth-century popular culture, and has taught courses on Gothic fiction, women in eighteenth-century literature, psychoanalytic theory, opera, the literature of the First World War, and lesbian writing. The most recent of her many books are *Boss Ladies, Watch Out! Essays on Women, Sex, and Writing* (2002) and *Courage, Mon Amie* (2002). She is editor of *The Literature of Lesbianism: A Historical Anthology from Ariosto to Stonewall* (2003); she also writes regularly for the *London Review of Books*, the *New Republic*, and other magazines and journals.

BARBARA CHING is associate professor of English and cultural studies at the University of Memphis, and until recently director of the Marcus W. Orr Center for the Humanities. Her work on the distinction between high and low culture appears in publications on American literature and, particularly, on country music. Her books include *Knowing Your Place: Rural Identity and Cultural Hierarchy* (coedited with Gerald W. Creed; 1997); *Wrong's What I Do Best: Hard Country Music and Contemporary Culture* (2001); and an essay collection on "Alt. Country" coedited with Pamela Fox.

DANA HELLER is professor of English and director of the Humanities Institute and Graduate Program at Old Dominion University. Her books include *The Selling of 9/11: How a National Tragedy Became a Commodity* (2005); *The Great American Makeover: Television, History, and Nation* (2006); and *Reading Makeover Television: Realities Remodeled* (2007).

E. ANN KAPLAN is distinguished professor of English and comparative literary and cultural studies at Stony Brook University, where she also founded and directs the Humanities Institute. She is past president of the Society for Cinema and Media Studies. Kaplan has written many books and articles on topics in cultural studies, media, and women's studies, from diverse theoretical perspectives including psychoanalysis, feminism, postmodernism, and postcolonialism. The most recent of her many books include *Feminism and Film* (2000); *Trauma and Cinema: Cross-Cultural Explorations* (coedited with Ban Wang, 2004); and *Trauma Culture: The Politics of Terror and Loss in Media and Literature* (2005). She is working on two further book projects, *UI*, and *Screening Older Women: Desire, Shame, and the Body.*

WAYNE KOESTENBAUM has published five books of poetry: *Best-Selling Jewish Porn Films, Model Homes, The Milk of Inquiry, Rhapsodies of a Repeat Offender,* and *Ode to Anna Moffo and Other Poems.* He has also published a novel, *Moira Orfei in Aigues-Mortes,* and five books of nonfiction: *Andy Warhol, Cleavage, Jackie Under My Skin, The Queen's Throat* (a National Book Critics Circle Award finalist), and *Double Talk.* His newest book, *Hotel Theory,* a hybrid of fiction and nonfiction, was published by Soft Skull Press in the summer of 2007. He is a distinguished professor of English at the CUNY Graduate Center and currently also a visiting professor in the painting department of the Yale School of Art.

LESLIE LUEBBERS has been director of the Art Museum of the University of Memphis since 1990. In that capacity she has organized as many as 250 exhibitions, greatly increased university and community involvement in museum planning and programming, and helped develop and administer a graduate program in museum studies. Before coming to the University of Memphis, she was an independent curator and critic in New York and San Francisco. She holds a doctorate in twentieth-century art from New York University's Institute of Fine Arts.

NANCY K. MILLER, distinguished professor of Comparative Literature, English, and French at the CUNY Graduate Center, is author of many articles and books. Among the most recent are *But Enough About Me: Why We Read Other People's Lives* (2002); *Bequest and Betrayal: Memoirs of a Parent's Death* (1996); *French Dressing: Women, Men, and Ancien Regime Fiction* (1995); *Get-*

ting Personal: Feminist Occasions and Other Autographical Acts (1991). She is also "Gender and Culture" series editor for Columbia University Press.

CRAIG J. PEARISO is Andrew W. Mellon Postdoctoral Teaching Fellow in the Department of Art History and Archaeology at Columbia University. His work has appeared in the journal *Third Text* and in the *Dictionnaire mondial des images* (Gallimard, 2007). He is currently at work on a book dealing with protest and performance entitled *Re/Citing: Radical Activism in Late-1960s America.*

JAY PROSSER is senior lecturer in American literature and culture at the University of Leeds. He is author of books on photography and autobiography, including *Second Skins: The Body Narratives of Transsexuality* (1998); *Palatable Poison: Critical Perspectives on The Well of Loneliness* (2002; coedited with Laura Doan); and *Light in the Dark Room: Photography and Loss* (2004). He is currently coediting a collection of essays, *American Fiction of the 1990s* (forthcoming, 2008), and is coordinator of a collaborative international project on photography and atrocity.

SOHNYA SAYRES is associate professor of humanities at the Cooper Union. She writes and lectures on contemporary cultural issues, ecology, technology, and the environment. She also writes fiction and poetry. She is a founding editor of the journal *Social Text.* Her books include *Susan Sontag: The Elegiac Modernist* and, as coeditor, the anthology *The 60's Without Apologies.* Current projects include a study of the cultural history of the 1970s.

JENNIFER A. WAGNER-LAWLOR is associate professor of women's studies and English at Penn State University. She also serves there as director of Study Abroad Programs in the College of the Liberal Arts. She is author of *A Moment's Monument: Revisionary Poetics and the Nineteenth-Century Sonnet* (1995) and editor of *The Victorian Comic Spirit: New Perspectives* (2000), and she has published many articles on nineteenth- and twentieth-century literature, as well as on utopian literature. She is working on a book on the forms of irony in women's utopian and speculative literature.

JULIA A. WALKER is associate professor in the Department of English at Washington University. A specialist in modern drama and performance theory, she is the author of *Expressionism and Modernism on the American Stage* (2005) and is currently working on a manuscript entitled *Modernity and Performance.*

Index

GENDER AND CULTURE
A Series of Columbia University Press
Nancy K. Miller and Victoria Rosner, Series Editors